Outsiders

Outsiders
A Study in Life and Letters

Hans Mayer
Translated by Denis M. Sweet

The MIT Press
Cambridge, Massachusetts
London, England

Originally published in the Federal Republic of Germany under the title *Aussenseiter*.
© 1975 by Suhrkamp Verlag, Frankfurt am Main.

English translation copyright © 1982 by Massachusetts Institute of Technology

This book was set in VIP Baskerville
by DEKR Corporation
and printed and bound by the Murray Printing Co.,
in the United States of America.

Library of Congress Cataloging in Publication Data
Mayer, Hans, 1907 Mar. 19–
   Outsiders: a study in life and letters.
   Translation of: Aussenseiter.
   Includes bibliographical references and index.
   1. Outsiders in literature. 2. Women in literature.
3. Homosexuals in literature. 3. Jews in literature.
I. Title.
PN56.5.095M3713   809'.93353   82-7219
ISBN 0-262-13175-7   AACR2

Contents

Foreword

Hans Mayer incarnates the history of our future: he embodies those rare and perdurable qualities which permit humanity to claim for itself a past, a place, and a prospect on this earth. Such qualities, salient enough in *Outsiders*, may be all we have to redeem time from its terrible blankness.

No doubt, readers of this book will construe their own versions of its excellences. Myself, I discern here immense learning, intelligence, a style answerable to its various occasions. I discern also that high and stubborn seriousness without which no moral life can take root. But I discern, too, solitude, vulnerability, a suppressed vein of uneasiness: some mute accusation that can turn against itself before turning outward again to become a deeper, wiser accusation. Let us call it knowledge of the dark. How else could Mayer write of outsiders, our doubles all?

The subject is not new for him. Mayer has been inward with outsiders from the start, commencing with his leading book on *Georg Büchner und seine Zeit* (1946)—shockingly untranslated into English still—through his selection of essays, *Steppenwolf and Everyman* (1971), to the present work. Himself an illustrious outsider, he has remained at the very center of European cultural life for half a century, having served as jurist, journalist, translator, radio speaker, television panelist, literary critic, music and opera commentator, lecturer (nearly everywhere), professor (at Leipzig, Hannover, Tübingen), and perhaps, above all, as cultural historian. His honors are legion; his students, scattered across several continents, now include many distinguished literary and public figures. In German, his books currently number forty, in English, three.

Why, then, is Mayer's name not as current in America as that of Barthes, Foucault, Derrida? Has our hieratic moment become indifferent to writings of wide intellectual appeal (the names of Edmund Wilson and Lionel Trilling come to mind)? Do German departments in universities command less cultural power than other departments of literature? Or is it rather, in our current rage for delegitimation, that we have become wholly intent on expropriating Gallic theory in order to "demystify" our institutions, our discourses? Mayer, in any case, has undertaken here another project: to realize in the same gesture of generous understanding both the concreteness of human suffering and the historical conditions which mediate suffering as well as that very understanding. Not "traditional," not "experimental," perhaps simply classic, his work initiates a debate between irony, history, and ideology without acquiescence to dogma—or even to theory.

Yet some have called him a Marxist critic, or at least para-Marxist. True, dialectical materialism has qualified his view—as it did Brecht's or Benjamin's—from the start; and it qualifies still *Outsiders,* signaled by such words as "bourgeois," "contradiction," "provocation," signaled by an unflinchingly "progressive" stance. But as Mayer would be first to ask: what does it mean to be a practicing Marxist after Hungary, Czechoslovakia, Poland, Afghanistan, after all those Siberian utopias we call Gulag? Unillusioned as ever, without a trace of feeble complaisance in the conduct of politics, he has little to recant; he has even less comfort to offer mendacity and oppression under *any* guise. "Marxism" in him, I think, is a personal history, an intellectual experience, a commitment to social justice, a feeling for the complicities of culture and power, above all, an aversion, almost tactile, toward that middle class whose amenities he sometimes enjoys, whose art, literature, music he so profoundly esteems.

This ambiguity, this creative "contradiction" which, as a German Jew, he shares with so many "bourgeois" writers (preeminently German, whether Gentile or Jew), this "provocation" behind which stand other silent provocations, this historical tergiversation which the West has inherited from its Enlightenment—all these, together, constitute the driving center of his *oeuvre.* It makes for irony, irony wavering between outrage and sadness, irony recovering lucidity from both hope and loss. Mayer's irony is immaculate of the cynicism of our day.

Nowhere is this more evident than in his insistence on particularity in the knowledge of pain. Thus, despite the vast synoptic schemes of *Outsiders,* Mayer notes in his introduction that Plato, Rousseau, Hegel, and Bloch—he could have easily added Marx—ignore the alienated subjectivity of the victim. This is indeed the burden of Mayer's book, and our burden too. Again, as he remarks in "Open Ending," no path leads from one outsider to another: "there is no community of outsiders."

Foreword

Liberal, fascist, or socialist systems wreck themselves on this fact. "A species of thought that disdains every so-called personalization and recognizes only collectivities, quantitatively contrastible normed phenomena, instead of the individual case, promotes fetishized thought and with it an inhuman practice."

All this is to say that Hans Mayer has intuited the crux of our postmodernity. I mean that fierce dialectic of centers and margins, assimilation and rupture, master codes and idiolects, totalitarianism and terrorism—in short, the One and the Many, as Parmenides used to say—which the earth reveals to us every day. Planetized by immanent technology, the world retribalizes itself by indeterminate desire. The outsider finds himself as both Steppenwolf and Everywoman. This is what an older dialectic, that of the Enlightenment, has bequeathed.

But Mayer ends his book by recalling Goethe—"One does not do well to remain too long in the abstract"—and so warns us against imposing schemes upon schemes. For the true "conclusion" of *Outsiders* is its very story. As a narrative of live and sustained human interest, affective no less than conceptual, the work engages the reader's informed desires, disciplined freedoms. In doing so, it transforms narration—that is, human choice and voice under the aspect of destiny—into value. To say, then, that one may read *Outsiders* as a novel is to admit into its spectacle of human bondage the element of imaginative freedom. Whose freedom? Three freedoms, three *desires*, become in this narrative compact: of author and reader who "return" to the victim a measure of freedom.

I stress desire because love is the secret grievance of *Outsiders*, the nexus of Woman, Sodomite, and Jew. Mayer enmeshes them all continually, subtly, in threads of history and filaments of desire. Eroticism intertwines sexism and racism, crosses melancholy and death. It even runs through "the deep spiritual, almost erotic ensnarement of the anti-Semite with his Jewish victim." Read Mayer on *The Merchant of Venice*, which weaves all his themes into a tapestry rich and strange, its hues sometimes so dark as to be invisible—till the author illumines the whole.

Mayer, of course, has not been the first to cast a light on this tenebrous domain, nor will he be the last, for our labor here is unending. He himself cites Leslie Fiedler's *The Stranger in Shakespeare* (1972), and would have cited *Freaks* (1978) had it not postdated the publication in Germany of this book (*Aussenseiter*, 1975). Fiedler's apprehension is finally more mythic than historical; yet both might agree with Foucault when he says in *The Order of Things*: "Knowledge of man . . . is always linked, even in its vaguest form, to ethics or politics; more fundamentally, modern thought is advancing towards that region where man's Other must become the Same as himself." This, too, is the end toward which Mayer's alien vision moves.

American readers of *Outsiders* may experience here a particular "shock of recognition." For ours is the alien strain of Wieland, Leatherstocking, Arthur Gordon Pym, Hester Prynne, Ishmael, Ahab, Huck Finn, Joe Christmas, Nick Adams, the Great Gatsby, Miss Lonelyhearts—not to mention their authors—isolatoes all. I wonder what book Mayer might have written about our literature to stand beside all those others since D. H. Lawrence's *Studies in Classic American Literature.* The Outsider in America: woman, homosexual, Jew; red, black, yellow, and olive; Puritan dissenter and Jehovah's Witness; trapper, tracker, pioneer, cowboy, wetback, hustler, intellectual, freak. . . . The list is nearly endless, its meaning somehow locked in Pudd'nhead Wilson's teasing statement: "It was wonderful to find America, but it would have been more wonderful to miss it."

America is an alembic of time wherein the mysteries of modernization take effective shape. Here the dialectics of Self and Other, the One and the Many, point to an uncertain future. And as the world presses upon each of its parts, South upon North, and East upon West, the dialectics of human differences may take still stranger shape. Yet Mayer's history— his implicit prophecy—of outsiders situates itself foremost in a European context, indeed a postwar *German* milieu. Like other German intellectuals in reaction to the Third Reich, Mayer often returns to the Enlightenment, especially the French Enlightenment, to recover that reasoned decency of universal thought, which also failed. But unlike many of those intellectuals, he understands German Romanticism intimately; nor does he place poetry, music, and myth, because they are "irrational," under permanent suspicion. This gives him peculiar access to deviance, aberration, all the intricacies of history and the human heart: it gives him, above all, access to the nature of our contemporaneity. The Outsider, as it is easy to say and desperately hard to realize, is us.

But forewords should be mercifully brief, especially to works both long and rewarding. *Outsiders* makes perfectly its own case with a density of historical allusion and psychological perception extraordinary in our epoch. It makes its case also with patience, that quality akin to Keats's "negative capability" which marks the "Man of Achievement, especially in Literature." Traces of polemic passion remain in this work, as when

Mayer makes the outrageously plausible claim that fascism extends, not merely perverts, bourgeois normality itself. But Mayer also reveals how victims victimize other victims as well as themselves suffer victimization; confronting the malice of history, he knows what he does not know. He links, patterns, compares; he traces all the subtle metamorphoses of a type into its versions of affliction; but in the end, he can only point to the ineluctable provocation.

Does this book really "redeem" the outsider by its labor of vast recall? Hans Mayer would not answer glibly. He may not answer at all, except by another such labor, which he continues to perform with an imaginative endurance that rivals the outsider's pain. They both share that thing we call conscience, subject of our eternal ontological amazement.

Ihab Hassan

What Are Outsiders? A Note for the American Edition

It is customary for authors of books that appear in translation in a foreign country simply to make a few cordial remarks; that one is happy with the translation, that the translator is to be thanked, and that one hopes (or is sure) that the book will engage readers in a far-off place.

All of this scarcely seems possible in a book about outsiders. I mean that even in translating the title, a concept that is well enough understood in Germany comes to have different interpretations in France and Italy, or seems to make no sense at all. When my book appeared in Italy, a Catholic country, where the discussions it unleashed were just as vehement as those in Spain, critics could not accept my characterization of Jews as outsiders. In interviews with Italian newspapers I was obliged to point out that under Mussolini Italian Jews had been deported and murdered.

The notion of the outsider entails particular difficulties for the American reader. What *are* outsiders? Nowhere that I know of has this concept been exactly and decidedly defined: not by my predecessors, by Colin Wilson, say; not even in the original German version of *Outsiders*, which appeared in 1975. My experiences with this book and its translators have shown that in divergent cultural and linguistic communities thoroughly divergent conceptions of outsiderdom are apparent. The German title, *Aussenseiter,* conveyed the subject fairly accurately. With the American translation it was clear from the start that the idea embodied in the English word *outsiders,* which undoubtedly shaped the notion expressed by *Aussenseiter,* had long since become unusable in characterizing the themes of my book. So vague and imprecise had it grown that without a clarifying subtitle the word and concept "outsider" could not be employed. What had become of it through undiscriminating use is more or less what had happened to "philosophy." It amused the philosopher Ernst xiv

What Are Outsiders? A Note for the American Edition

Bloch to relate an encounter in a Cambridge, Mass., supermarket with a man who wanted to know what this German emigré with the striking physiognomy did. He was a philosopher, he said. To which the man immediately rejoined, "You know, I have my own philosophy."

The Spanish translation entirely avoided such quibbles. The book appeared in this Catholic country shortly after Franco's death as *Historia maldita de la Literatura,* a cursed or infamous history of literature. The Italians likewise stayed clear of terminological difficulties by means of a term from everyday life. My outsiders appeared there as *I Diversi.* The French translator and publisher continue to rack their brains because the French language obstinately perceives only so-called marginal figures as outsiders: those *en marge,* the *marginaux.* But are not the outsiders of whom I have spoken nothing more in fact than marginal figures in an otherwise thoroughly homogeneous society dominated by insiders?

Perhaps this private excursus on title and terminologies demonstrates only that we can in no way speak of a unitary conceptualization of conforming or nonconforming behavior, of affirmation or affirmation withheld on the part of the outsiders.

What manifests itself at first glance in western societies, the contingency of the concept of outsider, is only confirmed in historical survey. One may even venture the thesis that in our history there has hardly been a human group that in certain social configurations has not been edged into outsiderdom and treated accordingly—which has often amounted to annihilation.

Yet another assertion can result from historical review: that the outsider who in the modern societies of the West (not to mention those in the East) is always eveloped in an aura of negativity was in certain social orders valued highly, a fact that could be a positive force in the biographies of the outsiders of those times.

Here, as in my book, I should like to proceed from the thesis that the social problem of outsiders in the modern period in Europe, since the disintegration of the medieval *corpus christianum,* must be understood as a process of secularization. Christian monotheism was acquainted with outsiders only in the realm of the unity of faith. There, outsiders through deed and conviction were sinners. The postulate that outsiders are possible beyond myth and dogma developed as part and parcel of a process of secularization. It broadened during the Renaissance, becoming an integral part of early bourgeois thought.

What Are Outsiders? A Note for the American Edition

At that time appeared the great outsider figures in literature, who again and again, to this day, disturb and fascinate: Doctor Faustus, Prince Hamlet, Don Quixote de la Mancha. The figuration of these three outsider types, oversteppers of boundaries all, was the work of outsiders, as is evidenced by the works themselves beyond any historical and biographical acquaintance with Marlowe, Shakespeare, and Cervantes. All three types are melancholics. The significance of melancholy and its practice in the disintegrating world of feudalism can scarcely be overrated. There are undercurrents of the melancholic Montaigne in Shakespeare's later works. The melancholy outsider Prospero in *The Tempest* could find no place in the banal world of political intrigue at court, and he remained equally out of place in Caliban's mythic world. On which account Caliban, in planning his murder, recommends first and foremost the destruction of this outsider's books.

The melancholy outsider was thought of as a noble gentleman in every sense of those words. He was well regarded among his own kind, just as artists, born under Saturn, and erotic outsiders were treated with regard—by their own kind.

The bourgeois reaction against the noble outsiders, with their stylized sadness, denounced such elitist behavior as arrogant, undisciplined, and licentious. Who in the seventeenth century had been respected as an aristocratic misanthrope was attacked in the enlightened eighteenth for being a libertine—whereby the words *libertine* and *libertinage,* and their German equivalents of *Freigeist* and *Freigeisterei,* came to express a decided disapproval of insolent and cheeky living and thinking. The aristocracy had been able to afford a noble melancholy: the bourgeois critic regarded such behavior simply as spleen.

Nonetheless the elitist concept of the noble outsider echoed on for a time, continues to echo today, even in the midst of a bourgeois society. A book like Robert Burton's *Anatomy of Melancholy* of 1621 helped whole generations of real and pretended outsiders find themselves. It seems no accident that Burton's work was one of Karl Marx's favorite books, as can be read in his letters.

The French Revolution, seen from today's vantage point, is shadowed by the paradox that the most radical theory of bourgeois democracy, comprised in Jean-Jacques Rousseau's "social contract" and theory of education, was produced by a thinker and social theoretician who in almost monstrous fashion lived and worked as outsider and was so regarded, even up to his (still inexplicable) death by accident or by force.

With the example of Rousseau a new paradox becomes recognizable in the relationship between minorities with aberrant lives and thoughts and the majority of a bourgeois society. Both Rousseau and Hegel, two philosophers of social optimism, de-emphasize the concretely suffering individual in favor of a suffering humanity. It appears to me that the same can be said of Ernst Bloch and his "principle of hope." In all these cases, not to mention Plato and his *Republic,* there is a disregard of outsiders' subjectivities, an almost impatient embarrassment in the face of such aloneness, shared by no collectivity.

The modern, contemptuous concept of outsiderdom belongs to the bourgeois society of the nineteenth and twentieth centuries. Within the confines of the dominant bourgeois world the cry "Woe to the outsiders!" held and holds. All of its institutions abet the removal of an offending foreign body, the elimination of offense, the constraint of normal existence. The bourgeois who is a churchgoer, or at least member of a recognized religious body; the bourgeois who is the model of civil law; the bourgeois who is the healthy and normal citizen: all this represents the supposed classical harmony and ideal of the maxim *mens sana in corpore sano.*

Despite this, the eighteenth-century debates on genius have relevance to our topic insofar as the bourgeois rebels against feudal and clerical society hoped to arrive at historical and mythic legitimation with the help of the cult of the genius. What was needed and made use of were exemplary rebels who revolted against God, gods, princes, and fathers. The young Goethe characterized his Götz von Berlichingen as a "self-helper in an anarchistic time." Prometheus, too, and Doctor Faust, who signed his pact with hell in blood, were such self-helpers, who rose up against authority. Lucifer as well, the devil as fallen angel, belonged to this negative mythology, to this cursed and infamous history of literature, and not only in Germany. Only in Germany the idea of self-help remained literary. Scarcely anything was changed in reality.

Among the most astonishing results of the dialectic of the bourgeois Enlightenment is the fact that the underlying principles of liberty and equality, not even taking fraternity into account, inordinately encouraged combatting all forms of outsiderdom in favor of a bourgeois normal existence. One characterized in France, say, by the derisory expression *les bien-pensants,* used to describe those who think rightly, or normally, which is to say according to a precept that one should not attract attention. It is a precept of equality.

From this I mean to draw the conclusion that our modern concept of outsiders necessarily presupposes a fully developed bourgeois society. Only in a society dominated by the bourgeoisie could there come to be what I attempt to define in my book in the antithesis between intentional and existential outsiders. Up to now consideration has been only of conscious and volitional outsiders, figures who consciously transgress boundaries. Whoever crosses over a boundary stands on the outside. With or without success: Faust knew what he was doing, as did the Titan Prometheus, the brigand Moor, the naysayer Prince Hamlet who refuses to participate and is thus a source of disturbance at festivities. There was as well (and still is) an intentional outsiderdom that was aware of transgressing boundaries but had little acquaintance with the geography of the place on the far side. The foolish Rousseau, whom Diderot could not take seriously and personally held to be a charlatan, made more happen than all the Voltaires and Diderots together, brought about a paroxysm of equality. There is no question in my mind that Jean-Jacques, had he lived longer, would have come under the guillotine as did his pupil, Maximilien Robespierre.

In bourgeois society there came to be two new positions in outsiderdom: the existential outsider and the clear verdict of negativity and contempt against any form of outsiderdom at all, intentional or existential.

Existential outsiders, it must be clear, are those who were, literally in their cradles, sung to of what they would one day be. They are those whose move into the margins and the outside was enjoined at birth through sex, origins, or psychic and corporeal makeup. A further characteristic of existential outsiderdom is that it is no longer a single individual who is envisaged, a rebel, one marked man or woman. Existential outsiders are "people who. . . ." They have become a genus. They can be lumped together as a minority with specific characteristics. The negative judgment stands.

Not much has changed in all this in our own time. By which I mean to say that as much as ever we have to live in and with a bourgeois society, its history, its traditions and prejudices, its confrontations and wicked laughter. Anyone who tries to behave well and play by what seem for the moment to be the rules of the game passes judgment on others who are xviii

What Are Outsiders? A Note for the American Edition

outside the mainstream because they break the rules or do not even bother to acknowledge them. They have first thought silently, then truly thought back, with the help of history, in order suddenly to think out loud. It is simply that their laughter can very soon freeze over.

In this book I analyze three types of existential outsiders: women who are exceptional because they ignore the rules; men who are outsiders on account of sexual inclination; the Jewish outsider within bourgeois society. In all these cases outsiderdom, once again in the form of a dialectic of Enlightenment, was initially codified through bourgeois emancipation. That became especially clear in the example of Jews. As German citizens they were naturally equal under the law. That was what the Centralverein deutscher Staatsbürger jüdischen Glaubens (Union of German Citizens of the Jewish Faith) made appeal to. Yet equality before the law did not hinder Auschwitz.

It seems to me time for the phenomenon of the Third Reich to be thought through and reinterpreted. Hitherto theories about fascism have explained nothing. They have all spoken, starting with an analysis from Moscow that saw in fascism a perversion of bourgeois society, a perversion that Leon Trotsky rightly warned against when he called the Third Reich a degenerative process in the bourgeois order. That is of course correct insofar as it refers to the abrogation of civil rights, formal democracy, the sphere of liberty. Yet it does not seem to me far from the mark to interpret the Third Reich, which Eugen Kogon analyzed as the sociological model of the "SS State," *as a logically consequential expression of bourgeois thought.* The Third Reich put into practice the concept of the desirability of normality and the undesirability of deviation in any form. That was demonstrable not only in the degradation of women, with those forced to wear a pink triangle, and with the Jews, but in all areas. Here, to be sure, arose a new and grotesque paradox. Bourgeois normality came to be ordained by an outsider of monstrous dimensions. Simultaneously, the mandated German normality was coupled with an outsider program of the master race and its special prerogatives everywhere in the world.

When the war was over, Jean-Paul Sartre wrote his *Réflexions sur la Question Juive* (translated as *Anti-Semite and Jew*). He had planned his study in the final phases of the war while the gas chambers were still in operation. The text appeared in Paris in 1946. The analysis concludes: "It has to be made clear to everyone that the fate of the Jews is also *one's own* fate. No one in France will be free as long as the Jews do not enjoy xix

What Are Outsiders? A Note for the American Edition

their full rights. No Frenchman will be secure as long as a Jew in France *or the whole world* has to fear for his life."

Sartre naturally took his examples from French reality. His anti-Semites were Frenchmen: it was their arguments he took to task. The foundations of French provincial life in the peasantry played a part and had to be discussed. The Dreyfus affair was not forgotten. Nonetheless the analysis, as in the quotation, reached far beyond a specifically French world. Sartre closed his reflections of 1946 with the postulate that as long as one Jew in the world had to feel himself persecuted as a Jew, then no Frenchman would be sure of his life because he too as Frenchman or white or whatever could be degraded to the object of a global scheme of annihilation. Put in other words: could be made into an outsider whose life could be declared valueless.

All of this has remained true, or, actually, has become true. The outsiders have almost always recognized this earlier than the famous silent majority everywhere in the world. When William Faulkner delivered his acceptance speech in Stockholm for the 1949 Nobel Prize, this outsider from the American South said things much quoted—but only as the literary impressions of William Faulkner. Yet he himself had understood things differently when he said that our tragedy today is a general and universal fear so long sustained by now that we can bear it; that there are no longer problems of the spirit, only the question: When will I be blown up?

Thirty years ago that may have been an interesting thesis open to discussion. Today it has become actuality for all of us. It becomes more and more difficult, as I see my experiences since the completion of this book in 1975, to distinguish at all any more between outsiders and majorities. Everything can be turned around, so that the historical process that I attempted to sketch must perhaps be understood as the path from the intentional to the existential outsider that then ends with a virtual outsiderdom for everyone, of whatever origin, skin color, language, or tradition.

In all of this there becomes manifest in contradictory fashion both the recantation of the bourgeois Enlightenment and its frightening fulfillment. Again and again in the nineteenth century significant critics of the bourgeoisie yearned for a return to prebourgeois conditions. The consequences of an egalitarian Enlightenment became recognizable in peoples' turning to precisely that which appeared to them *not* as equal and xx

What Are Outsiders? A Note for the American Edition

similar but as incomparable: their town and their landscape, their linguistic usage and their origins. It was a process with which we are acquainted today to a far greater extent. It is a strange condition in the face of which all modish formulas of progress or regression fail. What is progressive and what regressive? The ambivalence to my mind corresponds almost exactly to the ambivalence in the relationship today between the outsiders of the moment and those who hold them to be such and treat them accordingly.

Thus I would characterize the lines along which my book has developed, the part it has played in my own development. My thinking has changed with the experiences that have overtaken us in all parts of the world between 1968 and now. Jean-Paul Sartre explained to his countrymen after the Second World War why under certain circumstances everyone can become a "Jew" to others. Today we have to recognize that anyone can become an outsider in the eyes of the others, with all the frightful consequences it entails. One need only glance at Ireland, the Near East, Teheran. Perhaps we Europeans as a group are in the process of becoming outsiders for the rest of the world: a little part of the earth to the immense continents. Perhaps it is possible even that white people will be pushed into the role of outsiders on this planet. There are indications for this as well. One need only follow attentively the debates in the United Nations.

My book, I repeat, was originally planned as a treatise on problems of literature. More and more people, however, are beginning to recognize that to the question, "What are outsiders?," there is no possible answer, or that there is an answer, which comes down to: Everyone, under certain circumstances.

Hans Mayer
Tübingen
December 1981

Acknowledgments

A book that oscillates between the disciplines, that desires to join past and present, that means to be at once narrative work and scholarly analysis, has need of many who advise and warn. For advice and warning, then, those whose names follow are cordially thanked: Elisabeth Borchers, Elisabeth Freundlich, Inge Jens, Elfriede Zimmermann and Jean Améry, Pierre Bertaux, Elmar Buck, Christian Gneuss, Reinhold Grimm, Ihab Hassan, Jost Hermand, Walter Jens, Robert A. Jones, Leo Kreutzer, Robert Minder, Jürgen Peters, Wolfgang Promies, Gert Ueding, Hans-Dieter Zimmermann, and Jack D. Zipes.

Many difficulties in obtaining material were overcome thanks to the help of Ronald Aeschlimann, Patricia Counsell, Erika Greifelt, Andreas Huyssen, Amadou B. Sadjii, Gerd Schienstock, Gottfried Wagner, Gerhard Wilke, Larry Williams.

Heartfelt thanks are due to the University of Wisconsin/Milwaukee, especially to the dean of the College of Arts and Sciences, William Halloran, and the Center for Twentieth Century Studies.

H. M.

Outsiders

Premises: Outsiders and Enlightenment

The Monster as a Serious Issue for Humanity

This book proceeds from the contention that the bourgeois Enlightenment has failed. This contention can scarcely be contradicted if one takes into account the Enlightenment's postulates of equality. Formal equality before the law must not be confounded with an actual, materially present equality of opportunity to make one's way in life; as the history of bourgeois society can demonstrate, such formal, legal equality is well suited as an impediment and a constraint. The dialectic of the Enlightenment is ubiquitous: in the contrast between the notion of Freedom and actual freedoms, between de facto and de jure equality, and in the attempt to concretize politically and legally the high-minded emotions of "fraternity." The heirs to Gracchus Babeuf in the nineteenth century began finally to avoid the generous term *fraternité,* replacing it with the more logically precise expression *justice.*

Such actualities do not disprove the substance of the bourgeois Enlightenment but, rather, confirm it. One can improve on the imperfect, demand solutions that have been withheld; one can take over postulates from the bourgeoisie and bring them to realization by means of new social agents who struggle against the erstwhile, bourgeois protagonists. This Enlightenment, severed from its bourgeois and historical origins, becomes synonymous with permanent revolution.

From the failure of the bourgeois Enlightenment does not necessarily follow the bankruptcy of enlightened-humanistic thought. The contradictions in the nature of society necessitate a permanent enlightenment. In his work *Naturrecht und menschliche Würde* (Natural Law and Human Dignity) Ernst Bloch attempts to clarify the inner connection between the bourgeois natural law of the eighteenth century and the contrabourgeois social utopianism of the nineteenth. He hesitates to disengage completely "these two kinds of dreams for a better life in society," because "they take hold of each other, intertwine; hopes and teachings for happiness do not have a zoo for tame pets in mind, doctrines of human dignity do not presuppose asceticism and the hard surface of a column." He accentuates the necessary permanency of the two visions of society: "It is a surety that there is no human dignity without an end to misery and want, just as there is no happiness for men without an end to ancient and new subservience."[1]

Ernst Bloch's philosophy of hope, with its fundamental postulates of a human, erect stride and a way for man to a new home where no one has yet been, has proclaimed the permanency of the Enlightenment outside the bounds of the bourgeoisie, has proclaimed it more in earnest and more uncompromisingly than has ever been the case before. Alongside the principle of hope there has always belonged the "program of the *citoyen*." By *citoyen* was to be understood the bourgeois citizen who had remained true to the dreams of his youth, that is, true to the bourgeois revolution as a permanent Jacobin.

Yet the "principle of hope" has in common with all the philosophies of social optimism, and not simply with Rousseau, the disregard of the individual suffering human being in favor of a suffering humanity. Bloch speaks forcefully of the oppressed and wronged but has in mind only the communality of their fate, not the oppressed and wronged individuals themselves whose actions and sufferings cannot be subsumed under universal laws of nature. Amid the numerous references to Plato, Rousseau, and Hegel (thinkers who withdraw their sympathies from the singularly strange and estranged individual), the three minute references in *Das Prinzip Hoffnung* (The Principle of Hope) to Montaigne seem almost disdainful. A single quote from the *Essays* is to be met precisely at the spot where Bloch approaches the isolated and untypical individual.[2] He has in mind setting up "signs along the way of loneliness" next to those of friendship, the individual, and the community. Nonetheless this irreducible and wayward subjectivity so important to Montaigne is soon shoved aside by Bloch: the light of hope shines for many in the darkness, but scarcely for the one who consciously seeks out the dark. Bloch's philosophy knows the idealized "high couple" but not the Strindbergian battle of the sexes. As in all bourgeois Enlightenment thought, nature is equated here with so-called normal behavior; the Jew Ernst Bloch never finds his Jewishness of significance or cause for reflection. He sees in it at most, as did Karl Marx and Leon Trotsky, an accident of birth. *The Principle of Hope* falls into a reverie of reflection on the music of the spheres from the scene at Belmont in the last act of *The Merchant of Venice,* ignoring Shylock, not to mention his monstrous adversary, the merchant Antonio.

All this is part of the principle: ignoring the subjectivity of the outsider; impatience, being at a loss in the face of a loneliness that cannot be collectivized; and last this philosopher's lack of affinity for the philosophy of Michel de Montaigne. Here, in a word, Bloch's philosophy of humanity seeking a home for men bares its unresolvable contradictions. The trumpet call from *Fidelio,* the music of Belmont: they necessarily ring out as well for those who are oppressed but unable to rise up as an oppressed mankind. Florestan is a daring Everyman who corroborates the philosophy of freedom. But whether a permanent enlightenment still has prospects under present conditions and in the future has to be demonstrated through those outsiders who were born as monsters. The light of the categorical imperative does not shine for them, for their actions cannot be made into a principle of universal natural law. It is for just that reason that the Enlightenment must prove itself by them.

A compendium of outsider types is to be found in Elizabethan drama: in astonishing completeness and exactitude in Christopher Marlowe; in all their shadows and monstrous depths in Shakespeare. That Shakespeare as a playwright was strongly influenced by Montaigne's *Essays,* which appeared in Flory's translation in 1603, has been established by modern scholarship. Montaigne's essays, the first two important volumes of which first appeared in 1580, eight years before Marlowe's *Doctor Faustus,* ignore humanity as a whole, together with utopias, sun states, and visions of a New Atlantis. They have only the actual, singular human being in view: he is not encircled in pity; rather, an attempt is made to grasp him as he is. Much ado has been made of Montaigne's skepticism and his seeming lack of a fixed viewpoint. In his famous 1938 essay against such an interpretation, "Montaigne and the Function of Skepticism," Max Horkheimer put forward the view that "in Montaigne crucial aspects of bourgeois mentality are brought to expression. The positive content of his skepticism is the individual."[3] In contrast with this, the movers of the Reformation must seem inhumane, the utopians vague. Among other things, it undeniably reflects aspects of a bourgeois quietism in Montaigne, but it should not be equated, as Horkheimer did in 1938, with the philosophy of liberal egoism. One does not have to go far to discover Montaigne's motivations: wanting to defend the truth of individual experience in the face of the struggles between the Catholic league and the Huguenot purists. The religious war allowed but one ideological abstraction: friend or foe. Montaigne chose the concrete and unique individual—even in the case of a monster.

In the second book of the *Essays,* chapter 30 has the heading "D'un enfant monstrueux."[4] Montaigne chooses, as is his custom, an everyday event. What he reports took place "not so long ago" among the peasants in Gascogne: a family has a child fourteen months old who rejects all nourishment but his nurse's milk; he drags the body of his headless twin around with him. After a precise description of the situation, the essayist comes to speak of the case of a shepherd in Médoc about thirty years old who does not have any sex organs: "He has a beard, is sensuous, seeks contact with women."

Montaigne makes an attempt at interpreting the phenomenon. His undecided manner of analysis, incessantly oscillating between religion and philosophy, appropriately takes first recourse in the divine plan of creation. "What we call monsters are not monstrous in the eyes of God, who encompasses an infinity of forms in the surpassing work of his own hands." We, however, do not know His plan for life and are astounded. There then follows the no less obligatory recourse to ancient sources; Cicero is quoted, who had interpreted whatever causes wonder simply as that which is unfamiliar. Montaigne seems to agree with him, then proffers his own conclusion: "We call that contrary to nature which is contrary to law. Nothing is without law. May this universal and natural reasoning drive out of us error and the astonishment that comes over us with novel phenomena." [Que cette raison universelle et naturelle chasse de nous l'erreur et l'estonnement que la nouvelleté nous apporte.][5]

That is at once something more than and other than tolerance. The demand for equality with the pathetic reference to everything bearing a human face will remain contradictory, if not benighted, as long as it attempts to proceed from a seeming regularity of everything human. Then equality is the norm and feudal and hierarchical inequality whatever transgresses against it. From this must be concluded that the barriers of "fashion" (Schiller's term) have to be torn down in order to set enlightenment free.

Ernst Bloch's "program of the *citoyen*" was meant to be understood in precisely this way, yet it ignored the inequality in the human makeup, not simply in social conditions. Did humanity truly consist only of equal men and women, races, intellectual, bodily, and spiritual complexions?

Outsiders and Enlightenment

More precisely: Did the monsters of every provenance belong to humanity so that the light of enlightenment would shine for them too? At this juncture, in this antinomy, the Enlightenment has miscarried to this day. It has failed in the face of the outsiders.

Intentional and Existential Outsiders

Literature is the province of the individual. It belongs to the category of the specific, the unique, the contingent. This is true for the creative subjectivity of the writer as well as for the particularity of form and content in his work. Literature forever deals with exceptional cases. All cultural and political appeals that have demanded of it the representation of fully mended everyday lives have been thwarted by this scheme of things.

One has only to look at Greek tragedy, the effect of which transcends temporal limitations. Almost as if disconcerted and astonished, Karl Marx, in his outline for an introduction to the *Critique of Political Economy*, had to recognize that the demise of an economic and social order of things did not in fact render obsolete the works of art and literature produced under that order. Marx made this clear with the example of Greek art and epic poetry: "But the difficulty is not to be found in understanding that Greek art and epos are knotted together with certain stages and forms of social development. The difficulty is that they even yet grant us enjoyment, and in a certain sense have the value of a norm and unattainable standard."[6]

That ancient tragedy must also be meant here seems certain; Marx, by the way, repeatedly called Aeschylus his favorite poet. The intellectual answer to such difficulties that Marx attempted here (he never published the introduction) does not quite satisfy: the enjoyment of ancient Greek art and poetry is not sufficiently explained by saying that we are moved by humanity's happy youthful age. "Why should not the societal childhood of mankind, where mankind unfolds and develops most beautifully, hold out an everlasting charm as a stage that will never return again? There are misbehaved children and children wise beyond their years. The Greeks were normal children." This is self-contradictory, for it tries to interpret the works of the Greeks as the work of childhood and as perfection at one and the same time. Besides, such an interpretation stands in contradiction with the facts of Greek drama, and not simply of tragedy. The Greek stage, at a far cry from reflecting the normal life of happy and normal children, dealt exclusively with abnormal outsiders. The division into comedy and tragedy can also be understood as the contrasting realms of the intentional and the existential outsider.

The comic heroes of Aristophanes are volitional lone wolves and misfits, either because like Trygaios and Lysistrata they do what is reasonable amid universal nonreason or because, like the distorted and caricatured Euripides and Socrates, they are shown up as dreamy buffoons by their comic poet, speaker for the healthy and normal Greek children. The protagonists of tragedy, on the other hand, are prototypical existential outsiders insofar as most of them are cursed by the gods and have not actually desired the tragic (and therefore unresolvable) constellation of which they partake. Consider the curse over the House of Atreus at Argos and the curse over the royal house in Thebes, Ajax struck mad by the gods, the Bacchae inspired to frenzy by Dionysus, and Philoctetes with his stinking, fetid wound. Then there are hybrid forms of volitional isolation conjoined with that inflicted by hubris or ordained by divine curse: Prometheus or the deluded Xerxes in Aeschylus; Sophocles' Antigone; Hercules and Medea in Euripides. When Marx noted that "Egyptian mythology could never be the basis and fertile origin of Greek art," he saw that Greek art and poetry were bound to the Greek myths and therefore to the religiosity of the Greek peoples. In the fifth century B.C. this religiosity was still intact in Aeschylus and Sophocles and their public; even in Aristophanes when he sacrifices Euripides, who is obviously atheistic or at least skeptical, to Aeschylus. The role of the gods in Euripides has been characterized by Jean-Paul Sartre in the introduction to his adaptation of *The Trojan Women* (1965) as follows: "On the one hand they rule the cosmos: the Trojan War was their handiwork. At closer inspection, however, one sees that they act no differently than human men. . . . Euripides, making use of religious clichés only to smash them to bits, takes up the legends and myths to play out the one against the other, and so to represent all the difficulties of a polytheism in which his public has already lost belief." [7]

This process is continued in the tragedies of the Roman Seneca. Stoic philosophy and the religious pluralism of the Roman Imperial era forced a formalization and aestheticization of tragic drama. Seneca's Medea or Phaedra, his Hercules, his members of the House of Atreus thereby became educational literature for Roman citizens. The tragic outsiders of the Greeks degenerated to the level of literary edification. They had lost their cathartic function.

Outsiders and Enlightenment

Christian monotheism knows the outsider only in relation to the unity of the faith. There is exoteric and esoteric. Unbelieving pagans, Jews of the synagogue with a blindfold over their eyes, Catholics, schismatics, heretics: everything is reduced to an inside or outside relative to the *corpus christianum*. Within its community solely an intentional outsiderdom is conceivable. Monsters by deed and opinion are sinners. There is but a single existential monster populating the entire world of the Evangelists, the traitorous apostle Judas Iscariot. A traitor for the ridiculous sum of thirty pieces of silver; the man, perhaps, to whom it was appointed to execute the prophesied treachery; or even the true apostle who had taken the task upon himself so that what was written would be fulfilled.[8] His condition as an outsider appears in all accounts and interpretations scarcely as a miserable voluntary decision to betray, more nearly as the fulfilling of a providential role. Judas thereby becomes the incarnation of the Jewish people irretrievably tainted by the murder of the Christ. The Jew becomes Judas. His identity is that of existential outsider.

The realization that outsiders are not limited solely to the confines of myth and dogma dawns as part of the process of secularization. It gains ground during the Renaissance and is an aspect of modern bourgeois thought: as a common, everyday experience of the men in the Italian city-states; as part of the experience of a bourgeois magistracy in France that remains loyal to the centralist monarchy as it is hard-pressed by feudal nobles and the warring religious leagues; and also that of English townsmen and seafarers who have to watch the self-destruction of the feudal regime of the white or red rose.

It is in this epoch that those romantic figures come into being who have been the only counterparts to the mythical figures of Greek tragedy to pass the test of time, in that they can still grant us enjoyment: Faust and Hamlet, Shylock and Till Eulenspiegel, Don Juan and Don Quixote, Joan of Arc and the women seductresses. What they all have in common is their strangeness in the existing order. They are condemned not by an order structurally and ideologically opposed to them but by their own kind. Faust is a scandal of the bourgeoisie as Don Juan is an objectionable member of the aristocracy, objectionable to the aristocrats, that is. Hamlet practices bourgeois thought in the morbid courtly society of Denmark; Don Quixote lives in an isolated and imagined feudal world in the midst of its universal demise. In *The Principle of Hope*, Ernst Bloch subsumes Faust and Don Juan, Hamlet, and even Prospero under the rubric of "guide figures in the surpassing of boundaries."[9] He places the knight of the woeful form, modifying the rubric, under "guide mark in the abstract and mediated surpassing of boundaries." The mediation in the case of Don Quixote is seen in the amalgam of anachronism and utopia. The beatings that a knight errant receives in the commonplace world of the bourgeoisie cannot educate him. "Therefore Don Quixote cannot be cured by experience," Ernst Bloch says, because "this pitiful person is not once a match for the coalescence and encrustation of dreams that alone give him vision, that lie in wait for him all covered over." Cervantes has his knight say to Sancho Panza, as Bloch quotes, "For know well, my friend Sancho, that heaven gave leave for me to be born so that in this iron age I might awaken once more a golden one" (*Don Quixote,* I, chapter 20).

All of these figures who have passed over boundaries, with or without mediation, have the peculiarity that, like Oedipus and Orestes, Antigone or Phaedra, they have broken free of the context of a single drama and its author. There are more than forty versions of Amphitryon; there is the Electra of Aeschylus and that of Euripides, of Hofmannsthal and of Giraudoux. There are Don Juans far beyond Tirso de Molina and Mozart, contradictory interpretations of the Faust legend in between Marlowe and Goethe, Paul Valéry and Thomas Mann.

The phenomenon is not to be got at by research into the history of literary motifs. Neither is the creative and defining energy of a great writer sufficient to explain the transformation of a singular character into a lasting type. Hamlet and Don Quixote prove to be incompletely exploited, even by a Shakespeare and a Cervantes. Tirso de Molina merely called up an image in his *Burlador de Sevilla* of 1630 but was unable to root it firmly; Marlowe's "tragical history" of Doctor Faustus does not have the dimensions of the great Shakespearean dramas.

Such figures who break bounds, surpass boundaries, can provoke the historical surpassing of boundaries in a two-fold fashion: either by forming a model anew, as in the case of the maid of Orléans, Don Juan, or Faust, or by causing a permanent reinterpretation that in time delineates the corresponding intellectual transformation, as can be demonstrated in Hamlet, Shylock, and Don Quixote.

One must differentiate here between the intentional and the existential oversteppers and transgressors of boundaries. Whoever goes beyond boundaries stands on the outside. The term *titanism* could be used for what one undertakes of one's own free will in Promethean rebellion. Signed in blood like Faust's pact with the devil. Dutiful to one's voices like Joan of Arc. But what is it then if the precipitating step outside, into the margins, is a condition of birth, a result of one's sex, parentage, physical and spiritual makeup? Then one's existence itself becomes a breaking of boundaries. This discovery belongs, it seems, to Elizabethan England. Christopher Marlowe and William Shakespeare have provided the materials and, with them, a manner of grasping the phenomenon.

Marlowe and Shakespeare

Harry Levin gave his study of the life and work of Christopher Marlowe the title *The Overreacher* (1952).[10] With that this Elizabethan dramatist was characterized essentially as a man who had crossed boundaries. In a most singular fashion Marlowe, in his short life, which was most likely brought to an end by a prearranged murder, practiced being an outsider to society. Not only did he practice it, but he also understood his dramatic work to represent the tragedies of outsiders. To what extent specific facts of his own life are reflected in these works—which appear fascinated by agnosticism, acts of violence, homoerotic love, treason—remains insignificant compared to the astonishing precision that Marlowe brings to his task. He portrays magnificently the Machiavellian overreachers who misuse power, as in *Tamburlaine,* and those who misuse knowledge, as in *Doctor Faustus,* tale of the born outsider and overreacher. In the case of the Jew, Barabas of Malta, and of King Edward of England, entangled by love for his favorite, Gaveston, the free-willed breaking of bounds is displaced by an inescapable outsiderdom.

This appears to be but is not the tragic ground of the ancient dramatists, from whom Hegel drew the conclusion: "It is the true strength of great characters that they do not choose but simply and quite thoroughly are that which they desire and do. . . . It is the honor of the great character to be guilty."[11] The ancient protagonists stood under a divine curse: their necessity had been imposed upon them. Consequently, as the public in the Dionysos theater at Athens well knew, it could be averted by a subsequent change of the divine will.

The heroes of a secularized world beyond the curse of the gods or Christian sinfulness are encased in their immediate and solitary corporality, lineage, and sexual drive. Christopher Marlowe uncovered this circumstance for himself and literature but did not drive it forward to its necessary, logical conclusion. His Jew Barabas is not really Jew and outsider but much more nearly, as I shall show, the representative of a third religion among the Christians and Moslems in Malta. Even his King Edward is represented as a vagarizing freely willed pederast rather than as someone on the margin of things who has inescapably succumbed to the love of his own sex.

William Shakespeare, Marlowe's contemporary and admirer, was aware of this, which is why the case in his two plays that would be unthinkable without Marlowe, the royal history of *Richard II* and *The Merchant of Venice,* has been put differently. In the first, the tragedy of the ambivalent king vacillating in the face of power is separated from the case of the sexual outsider inescapably branded because he is contrary to the norm. Antonio, the merchant of Venice, is the title-figure of a "comedy," as is Shylock, the Jew of the Rialto. In the dramatic confrontation of these two existential outsiders (for in Shakespeare Shylock really is a Jew), Shakespeare uncovers the specifically bourgeois elements of tragedy in a secularized world: a heterogeneity that seems to resist every single proposition of equality. That this conflict can be resolved by Shakespeare in the form of a comedy is to be explained by a feudal scheme of things. It is a scheme that cultivates individualization within its own firm hierarchy and therefore can at once grasp and laugh at a wide spectrum of outsiders as members of a separate, unequal realm: fools and melancholics, the puritan Malvolio and the Jew Shylock, homosexuals as well as promiscuous erotics in higher and lower social spheres.

Only woman as outsider is not a theme for comedy in Shakespeare. Leslie Fiedler's study, *The Stranger in Shakespeare,* makes clear how strongly in Elizabethan drama the portrayal of the varieties of man, the normal and the abnormal, is connected to the understanding of individuality.[12] To the extent, however, that as with Puritanism the process of bourgeois hegemony in society and economy gained ground, the uncovering of outsiders was transformed into a repressive toeing the line.

Fiedler offers an interpretation of four outsider types in Shakespeare's works. First, "the woman as stranger," that is, woman as outsider. Then the Jew. Then the Moor. Finally, "the New World savage as stranger," that is, Caliban from *The Tempest* as incarnation of the colonial slave. But the scope of Fiedler's analysis goes far beyond the individual instances of Lady Macbeth, Shylock, Othello, and Caliban. It is not only in these monsters that Shakespeare's dramatic cosmos is revealed as an alienated world and a world of aliens. This becomes evident in the case of Shakespearean women, who again and again are shown overstepping bounds. The thesis Fiedler puts forward may be shocking, but it comes as the conclusion to long analysis: "Hard enough, Shakespeare apparently felt, for two unique individuals of the same kind, two males, to achieve unity in love; impossible for male and female (i.e., alien beings), each the other's other, to attain such communion."[13]

Fiedler is far from favoring such a proposition; yet, as a specialist in English and American letters, the permanence of a literature wherein woman is interpreted as an outsider who brings ruin to man inclines him to be somewhat reflective on this point. The instances run the gamut from Shakespeare through Melville's *Moby Dick* to Henry Miller's *Tropic of Cancer*. Certainly Posthumus Leonatus' soliloquy in a late Shakespearean work like *Cymbeline* can be explained as an outbreak of wrath and jealousy over supposed female treachery. Yet it begins with a universal attack in the verses: "Is there no way for men to be, but women / Must be half-workers? We are all bastards; . . ." (II,5) It is not at all astonishing that such an outcry by a man that men cannot come into the world but by the help of women was taken by nineteenth century editors as reason for doubting Shakespeare's authorship.

The personal psychology of the man Shakespeare is of no use to us here. He was quite likely formulating perceptions common to his age and society, that is to say, perceptions of the aristocracy under a virgin queen, then under a homoerotic king, James I, who never succeeded in untangling himself from memories of his mother, Mary Stuart. These perceptions are certainly expressed when woman is interpreted as nature's outsider, and all Shakespeare's comedies that seem to end so happily in marriage must be seen as soirées at the theater where men play as men with men in women's roles. Fiedler emphasizes that in these comedies the women (played by men) constantly disguise themselves as men, but in only one case does a man disguise himself as a woman: the miserable Falstaff.

Within a society that views women in general as outsiders, the real women outsiders will not be far off. I mean Judith and Delilah, the woman with the weapon and the erotic murderess. In Marlowe the characters of women are represented as having only a political function or they are put to work as instruments of power, as by the Jew of Malta. In Shakespeare there is the treacherous murderess, Lady Macbeth, and the erotic destroyer of heroes, Antony's Cleopatra.

It is curious that the newly revealed existential outsiders come again and again to be bound to each other. Each stands alone against the regular world of the nonoverreachers, and they also stand in alliance with one another. W. H. Auden, in a most significant analysis of *The Merchant of Venice,* summed up the relationship between the two outsiders, Shylock and Antonio, in the following reference to Dante: "There is no reason to suppose that Shakespeare had read Dante, but he must have been familiar with the association of usury with sodomy of which Dante speaks in the Ninth Canto of the Inferno."[14] The subsequent history of European society will counterpose these two qualities again and again, either in actual confrontation, as with Heine and Platen, Maximilian Harden and Prince Eulenburg, in a personal union in Marcel Proust, or in the figures of literature.

Melancholia and Misanthropy

In his book dealing with the history of persons who fall out of the norm, with misfits who appear in German literature, *Der Sonderling in der deutschen Dichtung* (The Misfit in German Literature), Herman Meyer mentions a definition of the phenomenon provided by Caspar Stieler at the end of the seventeenth century. In Stieler's reference work, *Der deutschen Sprache Stammbaum und Fortwachs* (The Growth and Development of the German Language) (Nuremberg, 1691), he who disengages himself from society is characterized as a "homo singularis et peculiaris opinionis, alienus a consortio hominum, solitarius."[15] That noteworthy term *alienus,* which surfaces here is used today in English and French to signify strangeness, stranger, alienation.

The isolation of the person who falls outside the norm is not simply confined to linguistic terminology. There are two processes. It is one thing to retreat from society oneself, another for society to reject, distance, and isolate from itself an individual or special group. The path of the existential outsider takes an entirely different turn from that of the intentional, abnormal odd fellow—whether melancholic or misanthrope. It is strange that those who have thought to stand apart from the general goings-on have never been the object of a systematic isolation. Quite the contrary, he who isolates himself has been esteemed and admired by those on whose society he has turned his back.

Fools were never cut off and isolated. Under feudalism and absolutism they had a strictly integrated function. Wolf Lepenies, in his study *Melancholie und Gesellschaft* (Melancholy and Society), discusses them and is somewhat caustic toward those who find Shakespeare's fools pitiful. (It is a pity that comes to have its place later, vis-à-vis the fools and prostitutes, say, in Wedekind's art nouveau dramas.) "The court fools' function was relief, their task to drive out the ruler's melancholy and thus to support and endorse him. At court, the fool has the privilege of melancholy. At the same time, the fool acts as a substitute; he takes upon himself—through the distracting emotions of his foolery—that which might impede the ruler in his ruling." Lepenies goes on to say that "the fool is finally put out of work by the rise of a bourgeois melancholy. When it is no longer the ruler alone who may be melancholic, there falls away the necessity of an institution that had driven out the general melancholy and had at the same time possessed its privilege."[16]

The melancholic as well as the fool has his place in society, and he is in no position to make the claim of being its adversary and its outsider, all common notions to the contrary. Shakespeare always showed fools and melancholics in their exact function. And Shakespeare made a clear differentiation between noble and pretended or ignoble melancholy. Jaques's melancholy while attending the banished duke in the Forest of Arden in *As You Like It* is noble and aristocratic, whereas the illegitimate and comical melancholic Don John in *Much Ado about Nothing* has simply usurped the pose. Yet these melancholics belong without exception to the world of comedy. They are not tragic.

Ever since Plato the melancholic has been thought to be gifted, particularly in the realm of the arts and sciences. Aristotle saw a relation between melancholy and artistic genius; the Italian Renaissance philosopher Marsilio Ficino equated the melancholy of genius with what Plato had called the divine gift of "mania," that is, inspired madness, possession by the god.[17]

Starting with the Renaissance melancholy had come to mean two things: being born under Saturn and isolation from the common people by birth and genius. Hamlet incorporates both; he is prince and genius melancholic.

Even where melancholy is carried to the extreme of misanthropy, the total isolation desired by the misanthrope is attained in appearance only. Shakespeare, once again, with his great reservoir of social types can provide a pertinent example: the misanthropic Timon of Athens. The play of that name is weak as tragedy because Timon's disposition is altogether too much inclined to social intercourse. He leads the life of a bon vivant, is reputed rich beyond measure, and seeks to purchase friendship and affection by the favors he bestows. The abrupt loss of his possessions brought about by accident, mismanagement, and extravagance does not drive him—as in similar circumstances it had driven the melancholy merchant of Venice—into regrettable dealings with a Shylock; no, it sends him into paroxysms of hatred for the human race. As if to relativize the superficial misanthropy motivated simply by ill fate and thanklessness in the case of Timon, Shakespeare juxtaposes him to a thoroughly cynical misanthrope of philosophical persuasion, Apemantus, who is the more organic misanthrope, so to speak.

Apemantus says,
This is in thee a nature but infected,
a poor unmanly melancholy sprung
from change of future. Why this spade? This place?
This slavelike habit, and these looks of care?
Thy flatterers yet wear silk, drink wine, lie soft,
Hug their diseas'd perfumes, and have forgot
that ever Timon was. Shame not these woods
by putting on the cunning of a carper. (IV, 3)

Alceste in Molière's *The Misanthrope* would like to remain a man of society, true to its norms, and simultaneously by a freely chosen isolation enjoy the fruits and pleasures of homegrown decency. His misanthropy is simply dissatisfaction with the forms of behavior and propriety of the French aristocracy, fixed and determined almost to the state of being a mincing ballet. It is for this reason that society laughs (as Molière wished) at the good joke of the halfhearted and thus botched misanthrope. Shakespeare, on the other hand, had no inclination to place Timon's tragic situation in jeopardy.

Alceste is nothing but the figure of comedy. Society demands compromise, and Alceste, instead of refusing, compromises halfway, which is to say not at all. He wriggles in *politesses* in the face of Oronte's ludicrous verses, is a man at court without wishing to be polite, strives for authenticity and falls in love with a *mondaine*, despises his judges and places himself at the mercy of their court. In all of this the power of the social setup can be recognized through him—who despises it. There is no solution, neither tragic nor comic. The play of the misanthrope ends "en queue de poisson." He can retire to his estates in the country like the nobility of the Fronde or the Duc de la Rochefoucauld. Nothing whatsoever is decided by that—it is all one if he returns to society or not. A century later Rousseau was to be more steadfast and unrelenting; he fully rejected the demicompromise and lived in protest to the end. He may appear strange, bizarre, but one thing is certain: he was not comical. Yet

Outsiders and Enlightenment

it was precisely this Rousseau who became Alceste's advocate against Molière. His "Letter to D'Alembert" was to be the salvation of the misanthrope's honor in the face of all the ridiculers.

To the same extent, however, that the melancholia of the Renaissance artists and absolutist princelings is displaced by a bourgeois form (Lepenies discusses the process under the rubric "flight into nature and inwardness"), Alceste's behavior grows simply incomprehensible to the new, bourgeois Everyman of the age of the Enlightenment. Cromwell's Puritans in the English revolution of the seventeenth century had overthrown—albeit but for a short time—the world of the aristocracy and its fools, melancholics, and misanthropes. Jean-Jacques Rousseau once again, who was a misanthrope, fool, and melancholic all in one, simultaneously provided two ingredients toward bourgeois emancipation: the theoretical construction of a hegemony by bourgeois Everymen who aspire to the honor of a *citoyen*, and the melancholy solitude of one who has fallen out of the norm, living as the "promeneur solitaire" on the Île St. Pierre in the lake of Bienne.

All of this seems paradoxical but is not. That Rousseau wanted to act the fool after his own fashion—he who was a melancholy genius, literary prevaricator, and propagandist, a hermit addicted to an active place in public view—only reflects certain personal aspects of the man that were outweighed by far more important social consequences.

The contradictory drives toward solitude on the one hand and an egalitarian, bourgeois fight to the death against the *ancien* hierarchically structured society on the other, cannot be explained away as Rousseau's own personal eccentricity. They are together, rather, a pure incarnation of the bourgeois Enlightenment. When the Everymen stormed the Bastille, the bastion of the feudal regime, they did so with the aim of establishing equality. As members of the bourgeoisie, they aimed at the same time for full self-realization as individuals. Equality and individuality loomed, the one against the other, in contradiction. Bourgeois individuality—motivated by the class situation—won out. The *citoyen* was to become a bourgeois.

But as a bourgeois he once again wanted the irreconcilable: the stabilization of the now established bourgeois hegemony *and* an unencumbered realization of his own individuality. This contradiction was not to be solved by jest, ridicule, and laughter as in Molière—which is why his *Misanthrope* immediately came to be viewed with a jaundiced eye by the new *citoyen*/bourgeois.

Goethe was disquieted by this process and came back to it again and again; *The Misanthrope* was one of his favorite plays. As late in his life as July 1828, he wrote to his musician friend in Berlin, Zelter, how happy he was that Zelter had discovered Molière and had not been led astray by Schlegel's denunciations of Alceste. Goethe continued:

The French themselves are not quite clear what to make of "Le Misanthrope." They say Molière took his model from a known gentleman at court with somewhat coarse manners; they just as often say he used himself as the model. I am convinced it poured forth from his own heart; it could come no other way. He had to depict his own relations to the world. But what sorts of relations these are! They are the most universal that exist. I'd like to wager you caught yourself in the act more than once. Don't you play the same role vis-à-vis those you come to deal with day to day? I have grown old enough all right, but I have yet to come to sit down at the side of the epicurean gods.

Goethe decidedly separates the so-called universally human aspects, aspects common to all men, of the misanthrope from his accidental integration into a certain form of society. He approves of both things at once in Alceste: being a man at court and being a misanthrope. With that the abrupt isolation from society practiced by Rousseau, albeit theatrically, is transformed into a mere inner attitude. Bourgeois misanthropy presents itself, as does bourgeois melancholy, as an inward reservation, a holding in abeyance of heart and mind.

The Principle of Equality as Challenge

It has every appearance of being a Chinese puzzle for logic, yet it is actual historical fact that the natural rights and dignity of the existential outsiders were best respected and secured in that period under the *ancien régime* when aristocratic supporters of the Enlightenment represented the demands of the bourgeoisie. This was so not merely in Germany, where the proliferation of ministates had hindered the development of a strong and autonomous middle class; in Russia, Hungary, and Italy as well, the bourgeois Enlightenment with its call for the dismantling of privilege was represented by spokesmen from the nobility in league with members of the middle class: officials of the magistracy and those with banking and commercial interests. The Enlightenment heroes in Lenz and in the young Schiller were aristocrats, as were Montesquieu, Condillac, and Holbach in France.

Outsiders and Enlightenment

The nostalgic saying of former anti-Bonapartists after 1871 that the Third French Republic had been at its best when Napoleon III was still ruling might equally be applied to the last days of the *ancien régime* toward the end of the eighteenth century. The bourgeois Enlightenment was harmonious and practically without conflict as long as the bourgeoisie had not yet come to the point of seizing power for itself. While the czarinas prevailed in St. Petersburg and Maria Theresa fought her vendetta with the "bad man" of Sanssouci, in which she did not hesitate forming an alliance with the Marquise de Pompadour, equality of the sexes was secure—within a feudal realm. Sodom's vice was viewed as being so widespread among the ruling monarchs, the officers' corps, and the members of court in Rococo society that only *médisance* was thinkable, as with Voltaire's barbs against Frederick the Great, but not outright repression. The institution of court Jews counted as part of the game: the banker Ephraim in Berlin (with whom Voltaire entered into financial speculations of various sorts) owned a magnificent palace in town. The trial of the Jew Süss-Oppenheimer was an exceptional occurrence that did not repeat itself. A strange communality embraced all of them: the Czarina Catherine and Denis Diderot, Frederick the Great of Prussia and his erstwhile subject Winckelmann, Lessing and Moses Mendelssohn, the freemasons Emperor Joseph, Wieland, and Mozart, the Englishmen Fielding and Hogarth.

Literature enjoyed an immense respect: it was thought that it was within its means to found a new human community beyond all feudal privilege. Literature was given the purpose of making extinct the emotional prejudices against men of other races and religions, mores and morals, by means of rational argumentation. There is scarcely a work that pursued this program more comprehensively than Adolph Freiherr von Knigge's tractate *Über den Umgang mit Menschen* (Concerning Intercourse with Mankind), which first appeared in 1788.[18] In later times this Hannoverian baron was misunderstood as an inculcator of well-bred manners for the members of his class and those of the privileged haute bourgeoisie. Quite the contrary, Knigge strove for a universal and uniform human kindliness that would level social distinction and differences in the service of universal rationality. He did not hesitate to apply this postulate of universal equality even to man's relations with animals. The chapter entitled "Concerning the manner of dealing with animals" demands complete respect for every being's sphere of freedom: "I have never been able to understand what sort of joy one could possibly have in locking up animals in cages and boxes. The sight of a living being deprived of using and developing its natural powers cannot provide a rational man with happiness."

This comprehensive conception of Enlightenment did not propose to make strangeness in society into a special case; it was not going to except it from the general demands for equality. Shakespeare's Caliban is in the eighteenth century at least no longer the stranger but an educator for and toward universal humanity—a challenge. The noble savages in Montesquieu's *Persian Letters,* in Voltaire, or in J. M. R. Lenz's *New Menoza* are meant as exercises toward equality, and not simply toward a "tolerance" that puts up with the outsider and other but does not lead toward integration.

Bourgeois society in the nineteenth and twentieth centuries has regressed; it has rescinded all of this effort. This has been due not simply to the principles of economic competition, which presuppose inequality rather than equality. Neither has it been due to a high bourgeois morality that set out to stem the tide of aristocratic perversions. More decisive has been the fact that the now destroyed feudal hierarchy had to be replaced by a new bourgeois order that could be founded only on economic inequality, albeit within the framework of a universal equality so far as the letter of the law is concerned. This order transformed women into parasitic slaves since they did not earn money and were not supposed to. It fought Jewish emancipation via education and property. It was xenophobic from the start and became increasingly nationalistic. Count Gobineau's *Essai sur l'inégalité des races humaines* (Essay on the Inequality of the Human Races) (1853–1855) is actually and precisely a manifesto of the counter-Enlightenment. From now on there would be the normal and the degenerate, worthwhile and worthless human life. Each and every outsider became a provocation. Was then anyone inconceivable as an outsider?

Judith and Delilah

1 The Second Sex and Its Outsiders

The European Romantic writers were greatly enamored of the undines, bastard beings somewhere between human and animal, femininity and an insensate ghostliness. They could never have enough of them. The Romantics attempted a certain humanization of the undines in the form of an earthly male. This attempt miscarried, as all their stories and operas demonstrate. A certain sense of relief is to be found in these works, relief that the undines could not be incorporated into humanity. Their monstrously feminine nature was not to be domesticated. Hofmannsthal, to be sure, let his sprite princess participate in human happiness and mortality through the act of love. She was able in the end to cast a shadow. She became pregnant while Galathea, the creation of the sculptor Pygmalion, remained barren—a point Büchner makes approvingly in the art discussions in *Danton's Death*. Giraudoux's *Ondine* ends in the usual fashion, on account of the female's nonhumanity, in the death of the man and an eerie, inhuman loss of memory on the part of the water sprite. Giraudoux seemed possessed by the notion that a man's every intimate relation to a woman is merely an act of self-deception.

The undines of the *belle époque* at the turn of the century possessed a name good for the whole genus: *femme fatale*. It made little difference in each specific case whether these childlike and unfeeling creatures who destroyed men (and whom Gerhart Hauptmann tried again and again to overcome) were undines exactly, such as Rautendelein in the *Sunken Bell*, or were barbaric monsters like Gersuind in *Emperor Charles's Hostage*, or Jewish intellectual tormentors like Hanna Elias in the artists' drama, *Gabriel Schilling's Flight*. They all correspond to the same type. They are all of them not amenable to language and (man's) reason. Hauptmann nervously, anxiously created dramatic figures whose type he resisted, while Wedekind celebrated a demonic and unrestrained middle class "nature" in his figures of Lulu and Franziska. But both accept a radical differentness, an otherness, as evident. They are all unreachable and inexplicable—all one whether the dramatic action is determined by classical or biblical myth, fairytale or the interior of a bourgeois salon. And here it should be noted that such *femmes fatales* are essentially artificial figures meant for the stage. They all resemble one another in this: Lulu and Wilde's Salome, Maeterlinck's Melisande, and Hofmannsthal's Electra. What appears to be merely a superficial contiguity, namely that Strauss, Debussy, and Berg were all inspired as composers precisely by this phenomenon of very distant nearness in such undines, is part of the matter at hand. Unreachable femininity did not belong in the end to the discursive sphere of the drama, where through discussion and rational discourse a matter can be commented upon. The fateful woman who brings ruin with her—as that literature posits collectively—is not about to be overmanned by the word. Wedekind's dialogues are set up as topsy-turvy conversations, conversations stood on their heads, where everyone talks past everyone else. One can only comment upon the *femme fatale* in the way that one comments upon voodoo.

The world of the bourgeoisie was from its beginnings in the age of Humanism, Renaissance, and Reformation almost addicted to evoking woman's status as outsider. The plastic arts far surpassed the productions of writers, who vacillated between pedantry and vulgarity in the era between Shakespeare and Erasmus, in the representation of women as outsiders. It was not simply the well-known inclination of the late Middle Ages to depict the martyrdoms of the saints in a fashion at once enjoyable and horrible (St. Lawrence's agony on the gridiron or the Massacre of the Innocents were favorites, for example) that led artists to render the three marked women's scandals reported by the Bible: Salome, Delilah, Judith. The childlike Jewish princess swinging the head of John the Baptist, swinging it in dance as her booty: the incident is to be seen in red and gold Byzantine mosaics in St. Mark's in Venice. Judith as well becomes a stock theme for artists, though the first part of the story, Judith at the banquet with the general Holofernes, is rarely depicted. It is the story's consummation that is meant to be feared and enjoyed: the woman with the sword and the captured head of the man and enemy in her hands.

Delilah from the land of the Philistines does not seem to fit immediately into this ambivalent and evocative art of cruelty. But she too seduces and brings ruin, calling up all men's fears of castration as she does. The elder

Lucas Cranach painted her as a goodly German woman from the ranks of the bourgeoisie in rich Renaissance robes. He has given her an expression that looks more like a feeling for duty than lasciviousness or a lust for destruction as she cuts off the blond locks of the slumbering Samson. Thus is he rendered powerless and delivered into the hands of his enemies, who will blind him.

Cranach was a painter who allowed himself no unbounded wealth of motifs but seemed keen on repeating and embellishing certain basic themes—themes that corresponded for the most part to the degree of his relative popularity with his contemporaries. I mean here the Reformers and princely patrons of Reformation history who were stylized by him into legend. One sees again and again in his work the conjunction of male and female nudity as Adam and Eve. Again and again as well, assuming the proportions of his contemporaries' favorite story, a story fixed fast and objectified in these figures, the Salomes, the Delilahs, the Judiths.

Precisely in the schematism of these themes in Cranach's work, in the work of contemporary artists, and in the world of their public, a certain perspective becomes recognizable. It is a suprapersonal, exceedingly sinister, and threatening perspective in which Salome, Judith, and Delilah have been placed since the beginning of the bourgeois, secularized, modern age.

They signify the world as hell. They are thus the antipode to the Madonna. The figure of Venus as a woman had dried to an abstract, somewhat colorless and flat allegory. And as it was not practicable to paint the Mount of Venus as a pleasure dome without admonition, without the character of warning, the three women seductresses and destroyers known from biblical report came into service. Salome destroys a man of God just as Delilah does. Judith, on the other hand, acts in the name of the Lord to save the chosen people. Nevertheless, all representations of Judith by painters from Cranach to Corinth evoke no admiration for this heroine but a shuddering as if before a monster. They are decidedly antifeminine pictures, painted, depending on circumstance and chronology, as warning; as repulsive contrast of femininity with its negation; finally as coquettish juxtaposition of passion and death, the sensuousness of the female body and the murder performed by its hands.

Simone de Beauvoir in her book *The Second Sex,* analyzing the "facts and myths" of feminine existence, comes to speak of fundamental polarities. "It is always difficult," she writes, "to describe a myth; it never lets itself be grasped or encompassed; it distresses consciousness because it never appears to it as a gelled object. This myth is so free-flowing and self-contradictory that one at first does not discover its unity: Delilah and Judith, Aspasia and Lucretia, Pandora and Athena—woman is simultaneously the Virgin Mary and Eve. She is an idol, a servant, the source of life, a power of darkness. She is booty to man; she is his ruin. . . ." [1]

In the interpretation of this proposition one must keep in mind that the antagonistic qualities arrayed one next to the other are not at all of equal substance. They do not even complement one another as mythic parts to a whole but in such an addition rather mask the phenomenon of woman's state as outsider. Of course there has always been a distinction between heavenly and earthly love, understood in Titian's famous painting in the antithesis between the nude and the woman clothed in the prim and proper robes of the bourgeoisie. The hetaera Aspasia, who at Athens as Pericles' paramour was admitted to council along with the men and ephebes, and Lucretia, the legendary incarnation of feminine modesty: they too were both favorite themes of Cranach and his contemporaries. Pallas Athena and Pandora are not understood antagonistically in Greek mythology. They do not even have the same theological and mythological order of significance. It is Minerva and Venus who can be brought into contrast to one another far more decisively and clearly. Pandora brings ruin to the Titan Prometheus as a divine instrument punishing his hubris. It was the speculative thinking of the eighteenth century, however, that conceived Pandora as the antithesis to Minerva in a conflict between primal instinct and reason, between uncontrollable libido and discursive enlightenment. Goethe's fascination with Pandora is to be explained from this, a fascination that lasted well past the writing of his Prometheus fragment and the demise of the *Sturm und Drang* movement. [2]

There remains from de Beauvoir's list of examples what can only be accounted as the incredible ranking together of Judith and Delilah, the Philistine and the pious woman Jew who fights in the name of God. The unity in seeming opposition is evident. But it is based on the fact that both have to be seen as the minority of a minority! Those other opposite partners: the chaste Lucretia and the impure Aspasia, the hetaera and the saint, Eve and Mary, were all part of a view of female existence, a general view seen from men's eyes, seen pejoratively as an existence of outsiders. This is exactly what Simone de Beauvoir understood in using the ironic title, *The Second Sex,* wherein woman, corresponding to men's hidden conviction, is interpreted as second-rate. Her book pursues this seeming axiom in its mythological, historical, and biological moments. In a wealth of examples from the past women, blacks, and Jews are all placed together as outsiders.[3] Leslie Fiedler in *The Stranger in Shakespeare* pursues a similar historical inquiry into the depiction of characters in literary works. He precedes the chapters on Jews, Moors, and Negroes (on Shylock, Othello, Caliban) with a fundamental exposition regarding "woman as stranger."[4] De Beauvoir refuses to accept the treatment that women experience in bourgeois society more than anywhere else, refuses to accept her minority status next to Jews, Negroes, and sexual outsiders, with the simple statement of fact: Women are not a minority in any sense!

One must proceed from this point if one means to interpret the correlation and even unity of Judith and Delilah. Both represent a minority within a minority that never really was one, but was and is treated as such. Delilah has come down to us as the incarnation of a liar and ruinous bed-partner to a guileless, pious, and strong man. Oddly enough, even Frank Wedekind in his 1913 play *Samson, or Shame and Jealousy* (which he calls a dramatic poem)[5] rigs out Delilah with all the conventional perquisites of the treacherous hetaera. All this very much in contrast to his figures of Lulu, Franziska, or of Effi in *Wetterstein Castle*. The righteous punishment of a man deceived falls on her. (The king slits her throat with the words: "here you have your death. / She deserved this punishment a thousandfold."[6]) Samson, a pious man, is heard by the Lord in his prayer for vengeance. In no sense did the composer Saint-Saëns modify these roles. Indeed his opera *Samson and Delilah* of 1877 pursues them down into the voice characteristics: against the unsuspecting heroic tenor of Samson is placed the deep and sensuous voice of Delilah in the famous seduction aria.

Delilah brings ruin and is a foreigner. In Cranach she is of the same race as the slumbering German Samson, but the biblical story is told from the point of view of a Jewish legend of heroes and their God. Delilah is there the foreigner, the heathen, the Philistine. It is just as essential to Carmen's role as seductress that she is a gypsy. In the world of men, Delilah signifies a minority of a minority of a minority. She is a minority as treacherous companion, as foreigner, and as woman.

It seems the distance separating Delilah from Judith could scarcely be greater. That contiguity, that position taken by Simone de Beauvoir that they belong together (and rightly so), appears to lack the minutest credibility. Judith is modesty personified, and modesty in a sense that far surpasses the Roman Lucretia. She is the virgin widow chosen by God. For the playwright Friedrich Hebbel this was to be a central motif in the whole monstrous tragedy. Judith is a folk heroine of the Jewish people; more than that, she is God's heroine, someone to be associated with Samson far more than with the treacherous foreigner Delilah.

But on the very account of Judith's pious heroism, she becomes deeply susceptible to mistrust; she becomes altogether questionable in men's world and literature. The biblical history of the Old Testament, to be sure, treats of other pious heroines. There is the story of Jephthah's daughter. But the fact of the matter is there are as few prophetesses as priestesses, not to mention a high priestess; that is to say, none at all. The Jewish code of purity opposed it. Salome with the head of Jochanaan suffers divine condemnation: a seductress, like Delilah, in whose wake ruin flows. Salome, however, becomes an instrument of divine providence by thus provoking the martyrdom of John the Baptist. And she too is— now following the New Testament—a foreigner. Sentence is passed on her by the God of the New Testament acting through the Tetrarch. The tradition of painting this Jewish princess proceeds from the supposition that the decapitated, bloody head of the Baptist is the head of the predecessor of the Savior.

Holofernes, by contrast, is the enemy and oppressor, the adversary of the Jewish people and their God. Judith simply carries out the judgment of God. Yet there is neither a pictorial representation nor a literary example of the Judith story, so far as I can see, which simply and unreservedly glorifies the heroine for her actions. There is a thoroughly similar structure between the two biblical stories of Judith and Holofernes and of David and Goliath—the pious weaker side against the powerful enemy of the people, not to say enemy of God. Yet all the representations of David with the head of Goliath exude a measure of admiration and joy; there is nothing of the sort in the portrayal of Judith with the head of Holofernes.

Put simply, Judith acts, even if inspired by God, in a manner unbecoming her position and her sex. Her deed is "unfeminine." Hebbel was not the first who found here the makings of a tragedy conceived in complete contradistinction to, indeed as the inversion of, Schiller's *Maid of Orléans*. It is Judith much more strongly than even Shakespeare's Joan of Arc who should be understood, using Fiedler's terminology, as the "woman as stranger." Consider in this context Friedrich Nietzsche's famous diatribe against the emancipation of women in the seventh chapter of his book *Beyond Good and Evil*: "Indeed, there are enough dim-witted woman-lovers and chasers-of-skirts amongst the learned asses of the male sex who propose to women to exceedingly defeminize themselves and imitate all the stupidities in which 'men' in Europe, European 'manliness' are sick—who wish to bring down women, fancy that, to reading the newspaper and to politics."[7] Seen in this fashion, Judith for Nietzsche, as before him for Hebbel, must be an extreme example, grown monstrous, of defeminization. The same can be said of Ortrud in Wagner's *Lohengrin*—one of the Wagner productions admired by Nietzsche. Such diatribes of the bourgeois and "manly" nineteenth century become systematized in Schopenhauer's tractate "Concerning the Female Race." They echo on at the beginning of the twentieth century in Otto Weininger's premise: "The undine, this creature without a soul, is the Platonic Idea of woman."[8] These attacks from the opposition make one realize that at the beginning of the modern era in Europe a great emancipatory process had set in, even if the archetypes Delilah and Judith continued to be viewed with aversion and dread. But the inclination was to see exceptions in them, not exceptions to exceptions.

This emancipatory process reached its general high point in the eighteenth century, which was the high point, too, for women's equality. De Beauvoir notes: "not the courtly Middle Ages or the 19th century was most favorable for women, but the 18th century when men regarded women as having equal rights."[9]

This becomes the century of Enlightenment when *égalité* was practiced at the courts, such as at those of the Electoral Princess Sophie of Hannover and her advisor Leibniz, of the Margravine of Bayreuth, of the Marquise de Pompadour, and in Russia at the court of Catherine the Great who came from the Wettins of Anhalt-Zerbst. There developed in Germany a literary and serious feminist literature. At the end of the century Therese Heyne and Caroline Schlegel, Günerode and Dorothea Mendelssohn came forward to put equality into practice and to reject any minority status. Schiller's attempt at the beginning of the new century belongs here, to oppose Voltaire's *La Pucelle* with the new and recently assessed image of Judith in his play *The Maid of Orléans*. Yet he achieved this only by jettisoning Judith's actual and concrete historical context.

This Enlightenment of the bourgeoisie, sustained by aristocrats, concubines, women writers, and Jewesses, soon met its doom. It was abandoned to the selfsame extent that the bourgeoisie established itself as the ruling class. The path from Schiller to Hebbel, from Kant to Schopenhauer, from the successes of Germaine de Staël to the failures of George Eliot and George Sand is a path that delineates the development of a bourgeois counter-Enlightenment. Increasingly the image of woman in European literature, philosophy, and art is purged of all impetus toward *égalité*. It is ridded of "defeminization," to use Nietzsche's terminology. From this follows that the image of a woman with equal rights, not to say a happy woman, is abandoned in favor of representions of women who do not wish to live as a minority and who meet their ruin through their minority status: Mme. Bovary, Anna Karenina, Effi Briest. It is a literature of lost illusions. Tolstoy in his "Kreutzer Sonata" even surpasses the age's general recantation on the Enlightenment by his thoroughly idiosyncratic renunciation of sexuality, which he—supposedly practicing ancient Christian beliefs—finds incarnate in woman, the eternal Pandora. Zeus' punishment of Epimetheus by means of Pandora's box corresponds in Hesiod to the myth of Eve and the serpent in Paradise. Leo Tolstoy did not hesitate to understand the recantation of the Enlightenment in exactly these terms.

The breakup of the Enlightenment, as far as the transformation of women into outsiders is concerned, in the remainder of the nineteenth and in the early twentieth century, is consummated on three fronts: as a permanent reevaluation of the scandal of Joan of Arc; as a transformation of Judith into a middle class heroine; as the metamorphosis of Delilah into a vamp, a *femme fatale,* the archetype of the seductress. At the end there comes the chemically pure synthesis of Judith and Delilah in American civilization. Literature and art are again at their handiwork. Comics hold up the synthesis for universal consumption. Richard Lindner, observer and painter, portrays it.

2   The Scandal of Joan of Arc: Schiller, Shaw, Brecht, Vishnevskii

She was probably nothing more than a marvelous and colorful byway in history, for even without Joan of Arc the English would have been driven out of France. The French monarchy would never have been endangered, even if someone other than the dauphin who had been elevated by Joan had been anointed and crowned monarch. George Bernard Shaw characterized Joan the Delinquent's embarrassing and unforthright rehabilitation in 1456, a quarter century after her burning at the stake, as an event that had nothing directly to do with her. The legality of Charles VII's coronation and the legitimacy of his reign could only be assured when it was beyond question that the girl from Domrémy who had accompanied him into the cathedral for the coronation was neither witch nor heretic.

Joan remained for centuries a historical supernumerary who was made ridiculous in invented stories, pamphlets, even in serious literary works (depending on the writer and the era): represented as obscenity personified or taken as an example of that which in the age of the Enlightenment was wont to be termed "the spirit of the dark Middle Ages." Even for Voltaire, who had written at length of the supposed virgin and her doings, the adjective *gothic* retained the universal significance 'confused, superstitious, abstruse.' Joan of Arc was for the European Enlightenment no more than a "gothic" episode.

The Renaissance and the Enlightenment were intellectually unable to come to terms with the deeds of this village maid from Lorraine. Joan was no demonic politician and far removed from a Renaissance type, not a Lucrezia Borgia or a Vittoria Colonna. Two things remained against her during the bourgeois Enlightenment of the eighteenth century: her origin as a child of farm folk and her deep, unquestioning religiosity. In the course of the centuries her undoing again and again was that she,

Judith and Delilah

trusting in "voices," spoke so unreservedly of her visions of faith. That was unpardonable. Even Shaw, in the preface to his *Saint Joan,* endeavors a rationalistic interpretation of the visions and hallucinations. As weird as the girl's visions of faith appeared to her own and subsequent ages, even more so now, a half-century later, do Shaw's pacifying interpretations appear laughable when he argues in a scientific manner:

The most sceptical scientific reader may therefore accept as a flat fact, carrying no implication of unsoundness of mind, that Joan was what Francis Galton and other modern investigators of human faculty call a visualizer. She saw imaginary saints just as some other people see imaginary diagrams and landscapes with numbers dotted about them, and are thereby able to perform feats of memory and arithmetic impossible to non-visualizers. Visualizers will understand this at once. Non-visualizers who have never read Galton will be puzzled and incredulous.[1]

Joan had offended against all of the taboos of her time: as a farm maid, as woman in arms, as virgin who forgoes marriage and motherhood, as faithful Christian. During the waning of the Middle Ages, as Johan Huizinga has called Joan of Arc's century,[2] people did not think much of prophets and those who claimed to be inspired by the Holy Ghost. The last saint whom that age was ready both to place historically and to venerate as a saint (who was, in consequence, something more than a page out of the book of golden legends) was Francis of Assisi. And he, the *poverello,* soon after his death in 1226 was transformed into a formidable entity in the art world. As early as the end of the thirteenth century Francis was, so to speak, aestheticized in Giotto's frescoes in Assisi and then later in Florence. This last saint of the Middle Ages thereafter (from Giotto and Ghirlandaio to Dürer and Rubens, on to later literary mutations in Tolstoy and Rilke) was edged out of the immediate context of burning faith and relegated to a realm of aesthetic edification.

Constricted between the age of Francis of Assisi and the striving of the counter-Reformation in the sway of Loyola, which quite consciously erected new saints by means of religious propaganda, the age of Joan of Arc runs its way as the epoch of something that is no longer and not yet. There is no longer a trust in those who are beatified through the spirit; not yet the cool *raison d'état* and *raison de foi* that created saints as later great generals and good kings would be raised on high.

When Joan appeared on the scene and began to consummate her deeds, her unremitting faith was to become the most egregious source of vexation. The inevitable collision between an inspired founder of faith and the apparatus of orthodoxy can be seen here too in the reactions of Joan's contemporaries. Her faith endangered the official faith, especially since she had won over the masses. Her inspired actions upset military conceptions and dynastic interests on both the French and English sides. Those who had been enemies for the duration of a hundred years' war finally allied themselves against her. This scheme of things surrounding Joan of Arc and her fall can be taken as a historical preview of the situation of the Parisian Commune in 1871 when Bismarck and the French bourgeoisie allied themselves against the Communards in Paris. Shaw has marvelously reconstructed this turn of events in the fourth scene of his *Saint Joan,* in the famous French–English dialogue in the tent on points of diplomacy and ecclesiastical prerogative. It is only through these machinations that Joan comes to be delivered into the hands of the English—not through wily capture or military defeat. She is played into their hands. She has offended against all manner of taboo; there can be no room for clemency. Everyone bands together against this female soldier, this militant prophet, this incarnation of rustic piety: the English and French courts, the feudal lords, the high ecclesiastics. The result is the well-known trial in Rouen. Joan was burned alive at the stake in the market square on May 30, 1431.

In Shakespeare's trilogy of plays concerning Henry VI, she is simply an unpolished and obscene wench. The Irishman Shaw has allowed himself a nice anti-English barb when he asserts that Shakespeare very likely first wanted to portray Joan as pure and earnest, but was kept from it by the audience and the members of his troupe: "[He] was told by his scandalized company that English patriotism would never stand a sympathetic representation of a French conqueror of English troops, and that unless he at once introduced all the old charges against Joan of being a sorceress and a harlot, and assumed her to be guilty of all of them, his play could not be produced."[3]

At the height of the French Enlightenment, *La Pucelle* was for Voltaire the happy excuse for a parody of older heroic epics in the form of a buffo-obscene heroic poem. Joan of Arc as well as the king's mistress, Agnes Sorel, here serve as butt for *picanteries* set to verse. Voltaire had only ridicule for Joan and so much gothic superstition. The maid of Orléans and the European Enlightenment seemed to exclude each other. Even the last of the Voltaireans in the twentieth century, Anatole France, believed he was compelled as rationalist and disciple of the eighteenth century to direct polemics against the supposed romanticization of this strange rustic and hallucinating French woman patriot.

What path led from Joan's execution at Rouen to her beatification in the year 1908 and to her canonization as St. Joan in 1920? To some extent an answer can be found within church history itself, in the metamorphoses of the Catholic Church on its way from the fifteenth to the twentieth century. But another question remains: how did Schiller come to elevate a figure who was the butt of Shakespeare's and Voltaire's derision to the heights of a tragic heroine? For Schiller too all those taboos against which Joan offended retained their full validity. His conception of women, a bourgeois one, with all its philistine aspects, is known from the poem "Würde der Frauen," and from the edifying parts of the *Song of the Bell*. Joan did not in the least correspond to the bourgeois ideal of a woman in the age of Goethe. On the other hand, Schiller himself, however he valued this ideal, was formed from youth onward by the Enlightenment. One can expect no understanding from him for Joan's visions and voices. He used these elements in his material like so many romantic stage props. The actual tragedy of the virgin of Orléans played, as it seemed to him, outside of any religious realm.

But, then, in what realm? Schiller simply brought to sharp focus the viewpoint of a certain intellectual tradition—as much as the creative impulse was his own to take seriously and to interpret a figure of ridicule from the gothic era. The fruits of this were not gathered until, in his romantic tragedy *The Maid of Orléans*, for the first time he began to clarify those contradictions in modern man, contradictions that several years after the premier performance in Leipzig were to become the central theme of a dramatist who was a thoroughgoing opponent to Schiller, Heinrich von Kleist, who formulated the theme as *confusion of feelings*. The maid of Orléans became the heroine of an emotional conflict, precisely like Kleist's Penthesilea, Alcmene, or Friedrich von Homburg.

Thus appeared for the first time in Germany in the public consciousness a social phenomenon that had been noticed and interpreted in socially progressive France, with its centuries old and well-coalesced bourgeoisie, as early as the seventeenth century. I mean the conflict between two kinds of reason, rational thought in the narrower sense and that which Blaise Pascal had defined as "raison du coeur."[4]

Pascal had felt this duality (which he likely was the first to describe) as a tear, a rip, a gash in his being, in his daily life. He lived as a man of the world and had a prominent position as a mathematician; then came a moment of religious awakening that was to change his life. That was not new in the world, but it led in this instance to a new outcome. It did not lead, as in the comparable case of St. Augustine, to a renunciation of his previous life but to this genius's attempt at establishing, with all the means of his earlier thought, a scientific basis for the new religious realm. Pascal began to apply the full power of his mind to the defense of Christian dogma. He did so by a kind of differentiation of reason, by splitting it in two. He distinguishes—always within the rational realm—between a "spirit of geometry" and an *esprit de finesse*,[5] which one can perhaps translate 'spirit of sensibility.' This corresponds to Pascal's other famous antithesis in which he counterposes actual rational thought to the *raison du coeur*, the reason of the heart. His much quoted and much misunderstood sentence about the heart possessing its own reasons, which can often come to contradict the usual ratiocinations of daily life, has nothing whatsoever to do with sentimental illogic.[6] Pascal's thoughts rather, as a kind of rationalism for faith, proceed from the consideration that Christianity cannot be scientifically deduced by means of rational reflection. This is so since everything that Christian teaching demands of the Christian man and woman is only capable of bringing forth unpleasurable sensations. Everything preached in the Sermon on the Mount is actually "unrational" and "unnatural." One sees that with this Pascal belongs to the immediate predecessors of Kierkegaard and modern dialectical theology.

With this antithesis of rational, everyday reason to the heart's reason he had named something extending far beyond the realm of Christian theology, namely the opposition between reality and possibility in the bourgeois society that was coming into being at that time. Utopia, this transmutation toward a human/humane future supported by no social reality, became thereby a legitimate realm of inquiry.

All of this is simply going over once again the circumstance that led Schiller to take up the case of the maid of Orléans and to interpret it anew. For Schiller suffered as well from the contrast between the bourgeois reality of his age and the possibilities of man—of which he as a promulgator of the Enlightenment never tired speaking. After he had read Kant he did not attempt to reconcile—otherwise than did Pascal—the schism between human actuality and human possibility but, on the contrary, sought to tear it apart in sharp, dualistic fashion. From this come Schiller's abrupt antitheses of the joy of the senses and the peace of the soul, happiness and dignity, utility and human greatness. The tragedy of the maid of Orléans lies for him in Joan's daring to break through this dualism. In one fateful moment she attempts to change over from vision to the realm of daily life, desirous, in a word, of fulfillment instead of waiting in the realm of impersonal, historical greatness.[7]

The dramatist Schiller, in poignant contrast to Voltaire, decides to fashion a tragic heroine. But since he is incapable of taking seriously or empathizing with the real religious belief of the actual, historical Joan of Arc, he is obliged to lead his dramatic heroine into a conflict between human reality and inhuman virtuousness. Joan becomes a figure of reflection on possibility. Schiller himself imagined her as a prophet and wrote about it to Goethe on April 3, 1801: "Because my prophetess . . . stands by herself and is deserted by the gods in her misery, so is her autonomy and the title of her character to a prophet's role all the more cogent. The end of the next to last act is most theatric, and the thundering *deus ex machina* will not fall short of its effect."

This quotation from his correspondence documents the intimate alliance into which the dramatist Schiller enters at every moment of his production—an alliance between philosophical speculation and the genius of pandering to the public. The prophet Joan, but the whole apparatus of the theater as well, are all in the service of heavenly voices and dark riders from hell that are no longer believed in.

But this did not seem to suffice. The abrupt dualism between the joy of the senses and the peace of the soul, that is to say, between Joan's femininity and her prophetic mission, remained, as Schiller himself recognized, more or less purely speculative. It had to leave cold any member of the audience who had not read Kant. This is the reason Schiller, likely not even aware of it, returned to Pascal's formula of the reason of the heart. His famous poem "On Voltaire's 'Pucelle' and the Maid of Orléans," published in the *Ladies' Pocketbook* in 1802, explicitly claims this reason of the heart for Joan.

Das edle Bild der Menschheit zu verhöhnen,
Im tiefsten Staube wälzte dich der Spott,
Krieg führt der Witz auf ewig mit dem Schönen,
Er glaubt nicht an den Engel und den Gott,
Dem Herzen will er seine Schätze rauben,
Den Wahn bekriegt er und verletzt den Glauben.

Doch, wie du selbst, aus kindlichem Geschlechte,
Selbst eine fromme Schäferin wie du,

Reicht dir die Dichtkunst ihre Götterrechte,
Schwingt sich mit dir den ewgen Sternen zu,
Mit einer Glorie hat sie dich umgeben,
Dich schuf das Herz, du wirst unsterblich leben.

Es liebt die Welt das Strahlende zu schwärzen,
Und das Erhabne in den Staub zu ziehn,
Doch fürchte nicht! Es gibt noch schöne Herzen,
Die für das Hohe, Herrliche entglühn.
Den lauten Markt mag Momus unterhalten,
Ein edler Sinn liebt edlere Gestalten.*

The author of the "romantic tragedy" was perfectly serious with such
theses. He wrote his publisher, Göschen, on February 10, 1802, in quite
similar terms: "This work flowed out of the heart, and it is meant to do
nothing other than to speak to the heart. But for that it is necessary that
one have a heart, and that, unfortunately, is not universally the case."

"From the heart—may it proceed to the heart": Beethoven chose precisely this motto almost a quarter century after Schiller to characterize
his *Missa Solemnis*. In both cases, however, Beethoven's connection to
Schiller in the Ninth Symphony makes it apparent, the appeal to the
heart is not to be understood sentimentally. It is a positing of a humanity
of spirit, heart, and will; or, to put it differently, of reality and possibility,
of social actuality and hope for transformation.

Schiller's version of the maid of Orléans functions unsatisfactorily and
is often comic in spite of itself since it conceives as mere static antinomy
unsatisfactory reality and its better possibility. Between Arcadia and the
world of the philistines there were no communicating paths. For Schiller,
Joan of Arc's fault occurs—grotesquely so—at the moment when she
renounces her prophet's role. Her expiation can only consist in making
her way as swiftly as possible back to the heroic sphere. Friedrich Schiller,
a man of bourgeois affiliations, thereby identifies heroic steadfastness
with success, humanity with failure. It is an identification at best ques-

---

* Scorning the noble image of humanity, / Mockery ground your face in the dirt, / Forever
the railing mind wages war upon beauty, / And believes neither in angels nor in God, /
And means to rob the heart of its treasures. / It opposes idolatry and injures faith. // Yet,
as you yourself, from a childish race, / Even a pious shepherd lass like you, / Is given divine
rights by poetry, / Which climbing up with you to the eternal orbs, / Encompasses you with
glory. / The heart made you, you will be immortal. // The world loves to darken brightness,
/ And pull down nobility into the dust, / Yet fear not! There are still lovely hearts, / Which
burst aflame for the sublime. / Momus entertains the market square, / A noble mind loves
nobler forms.

tionable. Stalwart, Joan as heroine rapidly proceeds from victory to victory until her attack of woman's feelings, after which she tumbles into misery. Misery understood as her own fault, as guilt.

Posterity has sentimentalized and ridiculed no other work of Schiller's to such an extent as *The Maid of Orléans*. The reason lay in Schiller's exorbitant equating of innocence with victory in battle, of guilt with human frailty. I am going to relate a well-worn anecdote here because it shows in its own self-contained way how maliciously language is capable of doing away with heroes. Essay topic in a girls' school of yore: "Guilt and expiation in *The Maid of Orléans*." For which one of the budding ladies wrote: "The maid of Orléans' guilt consists in having provided a young Englishman on the battlefield with his life."* It is perfectly legitimate to laugh here because our schoolgirl has indeed transposed (and not parodistically, either) Schiller's tragic content into everyday life, with a linguistically quite funny connotation as well.

At the heart of it Schiller's drama is wrecked by the abrupt Kantian dualism that allows only an either/or. The reason of the heart is provided a form but simultaneously deprived of its rights. Schiller's Joan transforms herself, to make use of Schiller's terminology for certain philosophical conceptions, from a naive into a sentimental protagonist. And she does this not in any psychological development but in a point-for-point about-face as if on cue. It can come as no surprise therefore that precisely the most important critics were obliged to find the misuse of a stage figure to demonstrate philosophical antitheses as a grave shortcoming. Goethe protested heartfeltly against his friend's dramatic construction in the name of Joan's original naiveté. Hebbel, on the other hand, criticized from the viewpoint of pure reflection the girl's oddly eroticized self-knowledge in front of Lionel, her enemy. In both Goethe as well as Hebbel there was no dearth of perspicacity. Both critics hit the weak points of this play that had been so ambitiously conceived.

Schiller's depiction of the story of the maid of Orléans seems to have lost in the running to Shaw's *Saint Joan*. Nowadays it is scarcely possible for anyone to put out of mind for the entire length of the production that Joan did not receive a mortal wound on the battlefield—as in Schiller's drama—then deliver after the battle several prophetic and gripping verses while dying, whereupon the banners of her king are dipped,

---

* The German idiom can also mean 'in having given birth to.'

in her honor, as a last military farewell. The actual Joan of Arc was publicly burned to death as a heretic on the market square of Rouen. The dramatic problem connected with this singular human life and destiny does not develop—as in Schiller—out of love and war, freedom and necessity. Instead, it has to do with the historical occurrence completely omitted by Schiller, namely with Joan's trial. It was no accident that this exciting historical event remained entirely irrelevant for Schiller whereas Shaw guided his play precisely toward it. Not only Shaw did that: following him has been the French dramatist Jean Anouilh in his play *The Lark* and Brecht in his stage adaptation of a radio drama by Anna Seghers entitled *The Trial of Joan of Arc at Rouen, 1431*.

What captured Shaw's attention is not difficult to guess. In the Joan of Arc story he found material that in his eyes demonstrated an English political crime. Reason enough for an Irish patriot and Fabian socialist once again to lay bare on the stage the obtuseness and brutality of the English ruling classes, as he had done in *Widowers' Houses, Major Barbara, Heartbreak House,* and many other of his "unpleasant plays." In *Saint Joan*[8] this theme is represented in the deeds and opinions of the Earl of Warwick and, additionally, by the Chaplain de Stogumber, an aristocratic and dyed-in-the-wool Englishman.

It seems most important for Shaw to have found in Joan of Arc one more figure who allowed the development of another of the themes he loved so well. I mean the superiority of female reason in contrast to all the economic, political, military (and, I might add, scientific) undertakings of the male world. In Joan, Shaw reached the apex of his earlier heroines Cleopatra, Candida, and Eliza Dolittle, who were so impressive for their rationality and for their *raison du coeur.* Joan combined in herself the political instinct of Cleopatra with the plebeian vigor of the flower girl Eliza. And thus did Shaw compose his figure: a subject matter hostile to the English; superiority of feminine reason; and then adding two elements that were consciously anachronistic, but which for Shaw (as he explains in the preface) were decisive for an understanding of his Joan figure: Protestantism and patriotism. The anti-English Irish patriot Shaw has Joan appear as an anti-English French patriot. For her English counterparts in the play, this is the central crime. Warwick, in the tent scene, sees expressly therein "the Maid's secular heresy," and accuses the French cardinal, Cauchon, of certain sympathies with this heresy of a political nature. Cauchon protests, defining the matter at hand with the word *nationalism,* since "I can find you no better name for it." But even this French cardinal characterizes such French patriotism as "essentially anti-Catholic and anti-Christian."

Warwick had just ingratiated himself to the Church by offering the following explanation of Joan's central spiritual sin. "It is the protest of the individual soul against the interference of priest or peer between the private man and his God. I should call it Protestantism if I had to find a name for it." In Shaw's dramatization Joan is presented as a patriot *before* the existence of a French fatherland or any other fatherland. The bourgeois nation of the nineteenth and the early twentieth centuries is projected back into the first half of the fifteenth. Joan is furthermore a protestant *before* Luther. With this, a dramatic constellation is provided parallel to the intellectual one. Joan is superior to her mortal enemies and the plotters against her in three ways: as woman, as farm maid, as precocious model for humanity's later historical development. She is filled with Pascal's reason of the heart. Blaise Pascal had himself aspired to a synthesis of the spirit of geometry and the spirit of the heart; Schiller had postulated a radical antinomy incapable of synthesis of a heroic world versus the pragmatism of daily life; it was Shaw who represented the reason of the heart incarnated by Joan as a superior attitude toward life that is perfectly capable of realization. All of Joan's adversaries are pragmatists in their actions and consequently are hemmed in. Joan's reason of the heart guides her to the correct actions—from the viewpoint of the future, to be sure. She simply came too early and therefore had to die. Joan's death in Shaw is anything but a tragic event, however.

It is for this reason that in the trial scene in Shaw there is only a fleeting moment of something like a confusion of feelings. Joan recants when for an abrupt interlude she no longer gives heed to the reasoning of the heart—her voices—but goes over to the side of "commonsense" pragmatism: "I have dared and dared; but only a fool will walk into a fire: God, who gave me my commonsense, cannot will me to do that." But the ensuing complementary pragmatism of her adversaries, who intend to imprison her for life, forces her heart's logic to triumph. Joan recants the recantation, recants her confession: "My voices were right." With that she has triumphed as an individual, or, to use Shaw's words, she has triumphed as a "Protestant," but is, at the same time, condemned to death. She had come too early, this Joan of Arc, an impotent possibility amid a reality that appeared to know nothing of utopia as a reasoning of the heart.

Through her death, so Shaw intimates, Joan becomes a historical personage of continuing significance, "Saint Joan" to be exact. More is meant to be expressed in this than the mere fact of canonization. The skeptical English earl has the last word in the trial scene. The executioner assures him, "You have heard the last of her." To which Warwick answers, "The last of her? Hm! I wonder."

Shaw appended an epilogue to the history of Saint Joan. The idea is a master stroke: his intent was to loosen the case of Joan of Arc from its historical foundation and to view it from the perspective of posterity. But Shaw refrains from taking the simple way and having contemporaries from the year 1920 discuss the case of the maid from Domrémy. His Irish love of contrarity once again produces the exact opposite of the expected, and this is well and good. The epilogue is situated in the period immediately succeeding Joan, in the year 1456, after her rehabilitation at the behest of the French king, whose interests, of course, lay in that direction. Instead of having figures from the fifteenth century appear in the Europe of 1920, Shaw has a Vatican spokesman from 1920 appear amid the figures of 1456, causing them, by his dress and mentality, a good deal of hilarity.

This Shavian epilogue ends in Dostoevsky's sense in the talk between Christ and the Grand Inquisitor. Everyone is more than willing to venerate the incinerated farm girl as martyr and saint, under the condition that she does not return. Her reason of the heart must not disturb everyday pragmatism. Joan and her reason of the heart—that is for Shaw the spirit of contrarity. One could also call it the spirit of progress, skepticism, or resistance. Shaw chose the expression "Protestantism" and did not mean Luther or Calvin with it, but the spirit of protest. Reason of the heart and the spirit of protest: these are, to a great extent, identical for him. It is on this account that in the year 1920 Joan must be made a saint: so that her spirit of contradiction can be socially integrated and, with that, rendered innocuous. Wherefore such an epilogue. How could it be otherwise but that it concludes with a question addressed to God and the world that can have no answer?

Bertolt Brecht, a younger contemporary of Shaw, thought much of him. An appreciative review like the "Ovation for Shaw," which was written for Shaw's seventieth birthday, is certainly a rarity in the works of the young Brecht.[9] He applauds above all what he calls Shaw's "terrorism." "The Shavian terror is unusual, and it makes use of an unusual weapon, namely humor." Brecht does not offer an analysis of individual works; yet one senses an easy familiarity with them, especially with the Salvation Army piece, *Major Barbara*. Certain reflexes and reactions to and from it can be ascertained in the Black Straw Hats in Brecht's *Saint Joan of the Stockyards*.

At the conclusion of his "ovation," Brecht distances himself from Shaw's biological, evolutionary credo; but on the other hand he subscribes to what he at least holds to be a Shavian "evolutionary theory": "At any event, his belief that humanity is infinitely capable of improvement plays a decisive role in his works. One should bear in mind that it comes to the same thing as a sincere ovation for Bernard Shaw when I admit without reservation that I . . . blindly and without qualification subscribe to this Shavian theory."[10]

Perhaps Brecht took this nearness to Shaw—but scarcely to Shaw's Fabian socialism—as a certain stimulus to demonstrate in a treatment of the Joan of Arc story both his distance from Schiller and his criticism of social reformism. It was something that, by the very nature of the themes chosen, had to bring him into opposition with German classicism and the so-called culinary theater of the late bourgeois period. In opposition at once to Schiller and to Shaw. His *Saint Joan of the Stockyards* was meant to provide a synthesis of his critical occupations with Marxism. It was on this account that Brecht conceived for it a material rather than a formal dramatic technique. The action is not built up around the elements of the story—for it is not its concern to relate a story at all. The events are "quoted" from the very first and, through the reference to Saint Joan, stripped of all the usual and traditional elements of tension. One knows at the start how a story about a Saint Joan has to end: badly. Therefore there is no dramatic action that might be inspired by the behavior of the characters or by a rising and falling turn of events, but only representation of an economic state of affairs. The dramatic course of events is to be guided by the economic cycle of crisis and prosperity. It is a well-known fact, expressly mentioned by Brecht himself, that he endeavored to represent the process of the circulation of capital in the play.[11] This was the dramatic event of each scene, and it followed Karl Marx's analysis as found in the second volume of *Capital*. When "classical" writers are mentioned in Brecht's plays and poems, the classical writers of Marxism are the ones always meant. Only their ideas had for Brecht the authenticity of classical texts. And now in *Saint Joan of the Stockyards* the classical ideas of Karl Marx and Friedrich Engels are juxtaposed in a thoroughly malicious manner with texts that were viewed in the German bourgeois world as classical: Schiller, Goethe, and in one place even Hölderlin. Let me start by citing the last-mentioned episode. In the tenth scene Graham, with all the flourishes of classical rhetoric, provides one of those accounts of battle so familiar from *The Maid of Orléans*. But in this case the account is of a battle at the stock exchange. The corpses littering the ground are not those of actual people but of artificial people, namely corporations. Graham reporting on the repercussions in the price of beef: "To the prices namely / it was given from quotation to quotation to fall / as water thrown from crag to crag / deep down into infinity." That is Hyperion's song of fate mutated, simultaneously quoted and parodied, to represent an occurrence at the Chicago stock exchange.

A further example: In Schiller's final scene, Joan's banner is extended to her at the king's bidding as she lies dying on the battlefield. The final verses of the romantic tragedy are spoken, after which Schiller adds the following stage directions, meant to exploit advantageously the theatric effect: "The banner falls from her grasp; she sinks down dead upon it. Everyone stands for a long time in speechless emotion. At the king's faint gesture, all the banners are gently touched down to her so that she is completely covered over with them." Whoever reads Brecht's *Saint Joan of the Stockyards* finds a thoroughly familiar line in the last scene: "Give her the flag." This is what the king had commanded in Schiller. In Brecht the line is spoken by Pierpont Mauler, the meat-packing king of Chicago. The flag is passed to her and falls out of her grasp as she dies. Mauler's parodistic, Goethe-like aria ensues, whereupon we come across more lines familiar from Schiller: "Everyone stands for a long time in speechless emotion. At Snyder's gesture all the flags are gently touched down to her so that she is completely covered over with them. The scene is lit with a rosy glow." [12] This time it is not the king but the major of the Salvation Army who commands that the flags be lowered—the Salvation Army flags, namely those of the Black Straw Hats. The rosy glow at this juncture is Bertolt Brecht's imaginative contribution.

It is evident what is going on. Brecht is confronting in the body of his work the classicism of the bourgeoisie with the classicism of socialism. The material events roll along according to Marxist analysis. The events taking place in the characters' consciousness, however, are represented— at least seemingly so—through the means of idealist drama. All characters of the ruling order, starting with Mauler, declaim in classical intonation. Mauler's first few sentences at the very beginning are intended as con- scious parody of a classical exposition, namely the hero's dialogue with the one who has his trust. For Brecht it does not suffice to have the crudest deals declaimed in a high pomp verse; he at the same time situates this pomp verse as bourgeois ideology, that is to say as false consciousness. Mauler and his broker Slift not only speak in blank verse, they also ostentatiously pluck here and there the most famous and best loved expressions from Goethe and particularly from Schiller:

Ach der Mensch in seinem Drange
Hält das Irdische nicht aus
Und in seinem stolzen Gange
Aus dem Alltäglichen
Ganz Unerträglichen
In das Unkenntliche
Hohe Unendliche
Stösst er übers Ziel hinaus.*

Joan Dark's monopoly-minded antagonist is presented at the end—after the demise of Saint Joan of the stockyards who now in rosy light is made out to be a saint—as a Faust from Chicago with the famous two souls passage:

Denn es zieht mich zu dem Grossen
Selbst- und Nutz- und Vorteilslosen
Und es zieht mich zum Geschäft
Unbewusst!†

Quotation and parody are used here not merely as dramatic techniques but as the elements of an ideological critique that is grounded in the substance of the work. To put it bluntly, one would have to say that Brecht interprets German classicism, in particular Friedrich Schiller, as the ideological superstructure of bourgeois business dealings. In doing this he allows no distinction between the superstructure of a society with an ascending bourgeoisie and a later, bourgeois-monopolistic form. As later in *The Good Woman of Szechuan,* in his adaptation of Lenz's *The Tutor,* and finally in the comedy about intellectuals dealing with Turandot and the Congress of Whitewashers, Brecht takes up battle with Immanuel Kant's bourgeois philosophy, particularly with the categorical imperative,

---

* Woe, that man cannot abide / in his stress the earthly bond / and that in his haughty stride / from the daily grind / that breaks his mind / toward an unknown / infinite throne / he hurtles far, above, beyond!

† I'm drawn to what is truly great / free from self and the profit rate / and yet impelled to business life / all unawares!

The Scandal of Joan of Arc

and with Friedrich Schiller's Kantian drama. *Saint Joan of the Stockyards* is explicitly set up as a counterversion to *The Maid of Orléans*. And with that the title figure comes to be interpreted in a decisively different fashion. Brecht has conceived his Joan Dark at once against Schiller and Shaw. For the first time in one of his main works a title-figure is presented who will serve as a demonstration of false behavior. Brecht has written his play against Joan, just as he later undertook to demonstrate the false behavior of Mother Courage, of Shen-Te, of Galileo, and probably even of Schweyk.

The fundamental error of this Joan Dark, in the eyes of the author of the piece, is precisely that attribute of character that provided her in Schiller with the dignity of a tragic heroine, in Shaw with the superiority over all her adversaries; I mean of course the *raison du coeur*. In Brecht as well as in Schiller and Shaw, Joan trusts in her inner voice and seeks to help, to mediate, to relieve material distress. The voice can do no wrong. She is taken in by everything that is presented convincingly. If she reads in the newspapers that the stockyards are going to be reopened, that the lockout is over, she believes it and asks: "Why shouldn't it be true if these gentlemen say it is so? You can't joke around about such a thing." To which the wife of the fallen worker, Luckerniddle, responds: "Don't talk so stupidly. You have absolutely no idea. You haven't sat here long enough in the cold." Joan Dark comes from a middle class family and is unfamiliar with the life of the poor. Therefore she trusts the newspapers and assurances of the bourgeoisie. She wants to decide with her heart and resists both "cold" ideological criticism and the use of force. She objects to the workers' decision to offer resistance:

Halt, lernt nicht weiter!
Nicht in so kalter Weise!
Nicht durch Gewalt
Bekämpft Unordnung und die Verwirrung!*

But the turn of events has produced a confusion of feelings in her as well. She no longer trusts her own "warm" humanity because she has begun to feel the inconsequentiality of such virtue. In a monologue she postulates: "I'm going to leave. What's done by force can't be good. I don't belong to these people. If hunger and the tread of misery had

---

* Stop! no more lessons / so coldly learned! / Do not use force / to fight disorder and confusion.

taught me force as a child, I'd belong to them and ask no questions. As it is, I've got to leave."

Here the contrarity between Brecht and Schiller is driven to its limit. Kant had postulated that there is nothing in man that unreservedly could be called good but goodwill. Karl Marx poked fun at that and said it was but an expression of immature German social conditions that Kant had appraised mere goodwill so highly. Brecht here too follows Marx. And so he wrote his play against Joan's goodwill and against her reasoning of the heart. Such goodwill was simple immediacy. It reflected real conditions, but it did not reflect *on* them, which is to say grasp them by intellect in their social context. Schiller led his Joan from a naïve frame of mind and frame of acting to a sentimental one. Brecht too, composing a counterversion to idealistic tragedy, has his Joan Dark go through a "change of character" in the sense of classical drama.

The main character of a later play, Mother Courage, goes along pulling her canteen cart, remaining unchanged in her complete lack of insight. Brecht's Joan Dark, however, dies transformed. Transformed to be sure from idealism to materialism. Her last lines therefore are not at all sad, but are an angry renunciation of the *raison du coeur* and the simple, unreflected will to be good. She says,

I've learned one thing and I know it on your
behalf, dying myself:
how can it be that there is something in you
that won't come out! WHAT do you know in your knowing
that has no results?
I, for example, have done nothing.
Let nothing be counted good, although, as always, it may seem
really helpful, and nothing henceforth be considered honorable
except what changes this world once for all: it needs it.
Like an answer to their prayers I came to the oppressors!
Oh, goodness without results! Unnoticed attitude!
I have altered nothing.
Swiftly, fruitlessly vanishing from this world
I say unto you:
Take care that when you leave the world
you were not only good but are leaving
a good world!

Here in Brecht's interpretation of Joan there is added a third Marxist element. To the drama's layout, constructed according to the rules of Marxist political economy, to the ideological criticism of philosophical idealism and its classical representatives in German literature, comes the criticism of that school of politics that would like to act in the whole social order much as Joan Dark, that is, inspired by *raison du coeur,* harmonizing, mediating. Joan had joined the Black Straw Hats, but the play does not have to do with the Salvation Army as does Shaw's *Major Barbara.* Brecht is not at all concerned with the badness of monopoly owners and the heroism of the proletariat. Both are of little consideration in the play. Mauler possesses—at least this is my personal impression—a character one can warm up to. There is just under the surface a partiality for each other between Joan and Mauler. The workers, as so often in Brecht, are presented as poor miserable wretches so that Joan is forced to say that Mauler did not demonstrate the badness of the poor to her, but only their impoverishment.

If the play demonstrates anything at all, it has to do with the function of those who desire to mediate and smooth over matters between classes in the name of universal humanitarianism. Where that leads is the subject of some of Joan's final words: "How handy I was for the oppressors!" In so far as she gave heed to her reason of the heart and joined the Black Straw Hats, whose function of political pacification is shown quite maliciously by Brecht, Joan herself became an instrument of repression.

It is common knowledge that Brecht was expressing a criticism of reformism within the German workers' movement of 1930 in the manner in which he has Joan Dark act. This play, like many a poem and so many of Brecht's tracts of the same time, deals with the Marxist opposition between social reformism and revolution. To reduce this Joan Dark to a logical formula: Goodness without effect equals wishfulness for harmony, equals idealistic apologetic, equals contribution to repression.

As so often in Brecht's writings of his first Marxist period, there is here—and this is a fact that must not be lost sight of—a radical reaction into a kind of mediated inhumanity. Brecht places the blame on Joan Dark for her lack of dialectical thinking, yet he himself offends here by a black and white, undialectical breaking apart of ends and means, struggle for reform and struggle for absolute and complete change. In the poems from the period of exile much of what here is still undialectical antinomism is taken back. There is ineffectual social reform, and there is just as surely ineffectual revolution. The relationship between the author Brecht and his figure of Joan Dark is a commentary on both.

In *Saint Joan of the Stockyards* he had chastened his lead figure and forced her to a metamorphosis in the Aristotelian sense with which he had broken. But that does not suffice for the dramatic figure of Joan. At the end of Brecht's career it became clear that he had occupied himself with this figure from a mere historical episode to an extraordinary extent—more so than with any other historical personality. Even Julius Caesar had not provided him so many ideas and so much difficulty to work out as had this girl from Lorraine. One has today in Bertolt Brecht's collected dramatic works three attempts at sorting out the phenomenon of Joan of Arc. In addition to *Saint Joan of the Stockyards,* there is the play *The Visions of Simone Machard,*[13] written in the period of exile and inspired by his friend Lion Feuchtwanger's report about certain events connected with the French military collapse in June 1940. And there is finally, as adaptation for the Berlin Ensemble in East Berlin, the stage version of Anna Segher's radio play about the trial of Joan of Arc.

Simone Machard is a child. Brecht specifically calls for the stage role to be filled by a little girl. Simone experiences first-hand the behavior of the French bourgeoisie and civil service when the German troops of occupation march in: treason, collaboration, compromise, at best impotent rage. In her favorite storybook she had read the history of Joan of Arc, how she rose up and drove out the enemy, crowned the king, and was in the end convicted by an ecclesiastical court and bound over to the civil arm for execution. And so too do dreams and visions come to Simone Machard. As in Gerhart Hauptmann's *Hannele's Ascension,* the girl clothes her dream figures in the features, clothes, and characteristics of the persons familiar to her. That includes the angel who gives her her orders:

Daughter of France, Joan: something must be done
Or our great France will perish before two weeks have run.
The Lord our God has looked around for aid
And now His eyes have fallen on His little Maid.

It is the very familiar angel in the very familiar church, left of the altar, his robe at the sleeve having, as Simone says later, "peeled off the tiniest bit." To put it bluntly, an angel of the poor. With that everything is said and decided. Simone Machard was the France of the people; in her dreams she saw the rising up of the poor and felt their power to drive out the enemy. The rich, however, behave in June 1940, in actual fact and in Brecht's play, just as the nobles and ecclesiastics did in Shaw's tent scene. They league together to make common cause against the masses and against Joan, the little Simone Machard who has become a threat. She is bound over to the nuns of a cloister to be kept in custody. Before she is taken away her angel speaks once more to this little saintly Joan of June 1940, alone:

Daughter of France, don't be afraid.
None will endure who fight the Maid.
The Lord will blast the arm
That does you harm.
Where they take you it matters not
France is wherever you set foot.
The day will soon be coming when
Glorious France will rise again.

This is a different tone and a different interpretation of the Joan of Arc story. In *The Visions of Simone Machard,* which likely never was put into its final form as a theater piece, Brecht discovered something of the original scandal surrounding the historical person of Joan of Arc. For so long before that he had simply drawn Joan in opposition to Schiller and Shaw. Now there was a Joan who offended against taboos, unpardonably against two above all: that she wanted to make history though she came from the lower classes and that she possessed visions and utopias that reached far beyond the dogmas dictated by the officials of State and Church.

In Brecht's adaptation of *The Trial of Joan of Arc at Rouen, 1431,*[14] Joan is likewise understood as a representative of the masses. She dies, but the girls of France burst into song, a song with the refrain: "Fight on, Frenchmen, for French soil, you who till it." The concluding words of the peasant Jacques Legrain (who has a name reminiscent of the peasants' rebellions, the Jacqueries, and in which the word *grain/corn/seed* occurs) are a comment on this song: "they are singing it now in both Frances, here and over there." What Brecht must have meant with that when he produced the play for the "Theater on Schiffbauerdamm" at the beginning of the fifties is manifest. He had found his way back to Joan, to the adversary of religious and state authoritarianism, to the breaker of taboos.

The *Optimistic Tragedy* of Vsevolod Vishnevskii was written in 1932, two years after Brecht's *Saint Joan of the Stockyards.*[15] Vishnevskii was born in 1901, had served as a machinegunner in the Red Army as a nineteen-year-old, and had experienced at first hand the establishment of the Red Navy. It was this experience that provided the historical context of the *Optimistic Tragedy.* Since the writing of his first drama, the *First Cavalry Corps* in 1929, he had been essentially a playwright. It has been ascertained that in 1932 he did not know of *Saint Joan of the Stockyards.* Neither had he read *The Maid of Orléans,* either before then or in the years

Judith and Delilah

thereafter, as he has observed to me in conversation.[16] The *Optimistic Tragedy* thereby becomes an all the more singular continuation of Western European dramatic *and* social constellations. What otherwise would have been simply an interesting example in literary history of the continuity of a particular theme suddenly takes on an altogether different quality. It is a new, namely postbourgeois coming to terms with the scandal of Joan of Arc.

In Vishnevskii too the lead figure is the woman with a weapon. She kills in the manner of Joan or Judith. At the first confrontation on the ship commandeered by anarchists between the woman commissar, a member of the Bolsheviks who had been sent by the government in Moscow, and the anarchist delegates from the sailors, one of these libertarian potentates, despising Bolshevism, commissars, and women in uniform, starts a shoving match. She shoots him on the spot. Judith defends her honor; Joan kills her class enemy.

The commissar has no name: she incorporates an idea, a party, a mission. The lonely outsiderdom of the maid of Orléans, even that of the transformed Joan Dark in Brecht, finds its logical conclusion here. The female member of the party feels herself the equal of, and on an equal footing with, any other member, male or female. Schiller's heroine lived in the antinomy of her own feminine individuality and her historical mission. The one had to give way to the other, but it was the task of the "romantic tragedy" to demonstrate both sides of the alternative. Vishnevskii's commissar writes home to relatives. Curiously enough, our Bolshevik dramatist has given her only relatives, no husband or children. "Nicht Männerliebe darf dein Herz berühren / Mit sündgen Flammen eitler Erdenlust . . ."* So spoke Joan's voices in Schiller's *Maid of Orléans*. We see that the taboo in the antinomy of feminine existence and action as woman with a weapon is carried over into a tragedy no longer bourgeois (and therefore "optimistic").

This tragedy's optimism, which in the final scene—precisely as in Schiller—is laid out in state with the commissar dying on the battlefield, is derived from two premises. They are premises based upon a certain hope and philosophical understanding of the processes of history. To wit: socialism brings to a close a protohistorical epoch of man; the life of the fallen commissar was a part of socialism, therefore her death served

---

* "The love of men must not move your heart / With the sinful flames of vain earthly pleasure . . ."

the realization of historical necessity. Vishnevskii's artificial dramatic figure was herself of this same understanding. To a fainthearted comrade she once explained: "Don't you know that even death can be a task for the good of the party?" That could just as well be a line in Brecht—in *The Measure Adopted.*

The second premise of this tragic optimism means to provide a cure for isolated individuality's suffering and mortality. The cure is collectivity, which integrates and transcends all individual suffering—and which itself outlives its parts. Within the framework of a thoroughly similar optimism, one of the most famous and most widely propagated works of Soviet literature was conceived; I mean the frankly autobiographical novel *How the Steel Was Tempered* by Nikolai Ostrovskii. Vishnevskii, of course, knew the work. His conception of tragic optimism coincides with the philosophy of life and survival of the suffering Pavel Korchagin in Ostrovskii. The final scene of the *Optimistic Tragedy* shows the dying commissar. Vishnevskii's stage directions are far more than mere guidelines for a director when he writes: "The sailors stand frozen a moment, out of breath, bewildered; the old sailor, the boatswain, the commander stand at attention and salute; one after another the sailors salute their dead commissar, even the wounded, finally Alexei. They surround the dead commissar in a mighty living ring."

Here the individual representative and activist of an idea died. But the idea and the organization carry on. The apotheosis is not consummated in any "speechless emotion" as in Schiller, but it takes place as preview, as anticipation of a future order of men.

Brecht had parodied *The Maid of Orléans* and the Kantian system of ethics that Schiller had adopted. In *The Tutor* he made the Kantian Paetus the butt of derision. Vishnevskii's *Optimistic Tragedy,* on the other hand, he produced in his Schiffbauerdamm theater, even arranging the staging himself. The piece's dialectical relationship both to Schiller and to his own *Saint Joan* had not escaped him. In a Brecht text dating from 1954, one finds the following lines concerning the drama of social realism, in which Brecht, though probably not in full agreement with such a realism, makes use of the sanctioned terminology: "The social-realist work of art shows characters and events to be historical and changeable . . . and to be contradictory. This signifies a great about-face." [17]

Brecht died in 1956, exactly 500 years after the first opportunistic and disconcerted rehabilitation of Joan of Arc. He never quite came free of the story of the girl from Lorraine despite his threefold attempt. As little as did the Catholic dramatist Paul Claudel or the commercial playwright Jean Anouilh. This phenomenon of never quite coming free of Joan touches on the reasons that led Schiller to ignore Joan's trial whereas Shaw, Claudel, Anouilh, and Seghers/Brecht took great pains to make the trial and execution come alive. Schiller's demurral, however, can only be seen as a complement to the other writers' insistence. He wrote at the high tide in Germany of the bourgeoisie's Enlightenment optimism. Joan is the Idea incarnate, at the price of surrendering not only her femininity but also her individuality. Only forty years later Friedrich Hebbel set up against Schiller a newly individualized and newly "feminized" counter-version in his *Judith* and in his plans for his own version of the story of Joan of Arc.

Shaw and Brecht grasp Joan as an exception who gives the lie to all the trivial rules of political, ecclesiastical, and familial routine. And so they are obliged to bring to a clear focus her state of existence as outsider, and the trial with its turning point of recantation, and recantation of the recantation, is extraordinarily well suited to that. In this way Joan becomes an actualizer of utopia. She practices Pascal's *raison du coeur*; she incorporates Protestantism in herself before Luther; without books and in the stockyards of Chicago she imbibes the lessons of class struggle: Joan of Arc as permanent scandal—consequently as permanent actual, concrete moment of utopia.

This development from Schiller to Vishnevskii is comparable to a Hegelian triad. In *The Maid of Orléans* is postulated an idea that through abstraction is removed from the actual, concrete reality of its carrier. In Shaw and Brecht the idea and all idealistic confidence and conviction are negated through confrontation with a nonideal reality. This is brought home in the actual figure meant to incorporate the idea. In Vishnevskii the transcendence is postulated of all opposition between idea and negation of the idea in a new reality. The idea is made concrete in the Bolshevik party. The antagonism between society and individual dissolves in the dialectical energy field of the collective. The commissar has been delegated. There is consequently no longer an autonomous Joan of Arc.

This synthesis by Vishnevskii in 1932, however, marks the beginning of a new dialectical process. The days of the collective and party from the heroic age of war and civil war at the beginning of Soviet history are long gone. The situation has changed. The political premises of "optimism" have been consigned to the ash heap, and so too have the aesthetic premises of an optimistic tragedy. A Joan of Arc has become thinkable who is a negation of that collective. History and literary history know the names: that of the poet Anna Akhmatova, that of Nadezhda Mandelshtam. The scandal will not end.

3 Judith as Bourgeois Heroine

Women with Weapons

Judith's ire can come as no surprise
That she to Holofernes' sabre crept,
And severed head from trunk as prize:
The fool was alone with her and—slept.

J. W. L. Gleim in the Göttingen
Muses' Almanack of 1776

Martin Luther provided the story of Judith and Holofernes from the apocrypha of the Old Testament with an earnestly thought-out interpretation: "Judith signifies Judea, which is the Jewish people, and is a chaste, pious widow. That is to say, God's people are always a widow left alone, but chaste and pious. Holofernes means *prophanus dux vel gubernator*: heathen, godless or un-Christian lord or prince. Bethulia means a virgin." The age-old story disappears behind the "What is this?" of theological interpretation and meaning-hunting.[1]

What is fascinating in this story of a woman who commits murder, and not simply in defending herself, has little to do with the study of divinity down through the ages. What is fascinating is this woman's all at once incorporating everything that had been solely a male privilege: prophecy, acting as agent of the Divine, victory in subduing the enemy, deliverance of all the unheroic others. Judith was a favorite motif of painters and sculptors, who were attracted by the contrast of feminine beauty to the dreadful crime represented in the severed head of Holofernes. In this, Judith in the art of the Middle Ages and Renaissance surpassed in popularity even the Princess Salome. Salome's dance on the wall of mosaics in St. Mark's in Venice, and Judith armed with sword and holding her bloody trophy: what is produced and consumed here is the pleasure in monstrosity. A sacred text has been interpreted—to show both holiness and infamy, the dual character of *sacré*.

The theme's popularity is to be found throughout religious, social, and national traditions. The history of German literature reveals adaptations as early as in the transitional period between old high and middle high German. We find it in troubadour poems of Frankish origin; in the universal chronicle of Rudolf of Ems in the thirteenth century; in both an epigrammatic poem, "De Judit mit Holoferne ob der belegerung der stat Bethulia," and a stage piece by Hans Sachs;[2] in meistersinger dramas played by traveling artisans; and as a favorite theme of Jesuit theater, of which a text still to be found in the Düsseldorf state archives announces, "Judith victorious over Holofernes, presented by the scholars of the fifth form. At the fathers of the Society of Jesus in Düsseldorf, the 25th and 26th of September 1754." It provided favorite material as well for the baroque theater and the development of the opera. Martin Opitz wrote the libretto to a Judith opera in Alexandrines, iambs, and trochees: it is at once a love drama of the unhappy Holofernes, a story of liberation aimed at boosting German spirits during the Thirty Years' War, and not least, since Opitz was writing for the Silesian nobility, an event at court in which Judith appears not as a princess to be sure, but as an aristocratic representative of the people.[3]

A discrepancy between Judith's position as outsider and that of other monsters such as Faust or Don Juan is unmistakable. Faust has remained a theme of emancipation in bourgeois literature; Don Juan Tenorio represents aristocratic libertinage. Judith appears to belong neither to the aristocratic nor to the bourgeois nor the plebeian sphere; she is dissected in the theological exegesis of the Jesuits and Martin Luther; the ruling nobility share with their subjects viewing a stylized Judith opera tragic amusement in Judith's horrible deed—where the audience can laugh on the market square, in Styria say, where such a manuscript has been preserved, when a merry-andrew appears in the role of an Assyrian messenger.[4]

The scandal of Judith, which like all scandals expressly causes the viewer pleasure, has nothing to do with religion. It has nothing to do with any kind of national identity (for which reason *any* particular identity might be read into it). It is not a social characteristic that is monstrous here, rather it is a traditional sexual characteristic encrusted with taboos. Herein lies at once the affinity to and divergence from the other woman in arms, namely Joan of Arc. The figure of La Pucelle, from the patriotic popular tradition of France up through Brecht, has always been associated with the masses, has always been their representative. Joan of Arc was meant to be the people; she was meant to act for and as Everyman. On this account individual close combat with a particular male adversary had to be strenuously avoided on the stage. Even Schiller took pains to reduce Lionel to a mere episode, as rapid as possible. Judith on the other hand is the perpetrator of a solitary deed on a singular adversary and victim. Through this she becomes a monster. Her deed may lead to edification and it may be worthwhile in a didactic sense, but she herself remains strange, incomprehensible, an inhuman paradox, widow and virgin, woman and assassin. Luther well knew why he allegorized her, which is to say blotted out her individual existence.

It is quite logical that the discrepancy between Joan of Arc and Judith did not diminish but widened in the course of the Enlightenment. The emancipation of women according to the postulates of reason and natural law remained as abstract as the emancipation of the Jews. The debates at the Paulskirche in Frankfurt during the revolution of 1848–49 devote a great deal of argumentation and goodwill to both themes without ever bridging the gap between the demands of reason and popular emotional contraversion.

Thus the reactions in the process of bourgeois emancipation to what Joan and Judith had done fell out at opposite extremes: emotional involvement and identification with Joan and her *raison du coeur*; denunciation of the "unnatural" act and the transgression against her proper role in the case of the heroine of Bethulia. In the course of the development of the modern nation-state, the monster Joan becomes the French national symbol, the monster Faust the German. Judith, however, in the bourgeois modern world becomes for the first time a total outsider.

The virulence of the Judith theme starts off at the exact same spot historically and socially where Don Juan, Faust, and Joan slip away into the vaguely aesthetic. Behind the discontent of the bourgeois nineteenth century with Judith's life and action, one senses discontent with the earnestness for women's equality of rights. The literary monument to, and document of, a regressing Enlightenment vis-à-vis the demands of feminism is to be found in Friedrich Hebbel's *Judith* of 1841. This work, which had so many consequences not only for its author but also for the development of modern drama, even well into the twentieth century (from the Expressionists to Giraudoux and Sartre), represents first and foremost a new ideological position in the Enlightenment. More precisely, it is to be understood as the mutual agreement of bourgeois society in Germany that women's equality of rights, not to mention women's politicization and activation, is neither possible nor desirable. The recantation of the Enlightenment can be demonstrated in the case of Judith as bourgeois heroine.

It was part of the aggressive and doubtless progressive character of the bourgeois Enlightenment as against the old feudal order that it held all human relationships to be classifiable and conformable to norms. This included the relationships between the individual and the state, between states, between parents and children, between husband and wife. Feudalism individualizes: it lives by the nuance, that considerable and significant differentiation within seemingly intransigent hierarchies. The bourgeois Enlightenment, as in Schiller's *Love and Intrigue,* replaces with a singular humanity all the customs of the feudal social pyramid. *Humanity* understood as *equality.* The accident of birth as prince or pauper, black or white, man or woman, is insignificant—as least in doctrine—compared to the universal postulates of equality. That had become a commonly held position, a commonplace even, by the end of the eighteenth century. In *The Magic Flute* Sarastro, countering the objections of his priests to the fact that Tamino is a prince, declaims: "He is more than that—he is a human being!" As a doctrinaire representative of the counter-Enlightenment in the early part of the twentieth century, Raoul Überbein, tutor to Prince Klaus Heinrich in Thomas Mann's *Royal Highness,* pokes a great deal of fun at this high-minded and so unreal catchword in the Mozart opera.[5] Even husband and wife are, according to the doctrine of equality, strictly complementary phenomena that must be kept free from any preferential treatment or subjugation. Kant postulated marriage as a contract that includes the reciprocal use of the sex organs—something at which Brecht in his turn would later poke fun. Kant saw the complete realization of a human being only in the cooperation of man and woman. The one sex complements and completes the other.

During the French Revolution, which supposedly and on the face of it institutionalized the bourgeois Enlightenment, Rousseauism in particular, there began in all areas, though at first barely perceptibly, new differentiations and movements toward antiequality. The bourgeois's true self came to be glimpsed from behind the Enlightenment mask and role of the *citoyen.* Take the many stipulations establishing inequality in the (bourgeois) Napoleonic Code, for example that a child born out of wedlock is not related to its father and that no investigation into its paternity is lawful. Far more conspicuous were the transformations in the feminine role that accompanied the successive stages of the Revolution from the storming of the Bastille to the Directorate. At the start were the revolutionary women with equal rights after the model of Théroigne de Méricourt, who led the march of Parisian women to Versailles; later the Rousseauist or Girondist intellectual Mme. Roland; after Thermidor the elegant and corrupt Mme. Tallien, wife of one of the opportunist "directors" who made his fortune by the revolution, *dame de salon,* mistress and businesswoman. Finally Joséphine Beauharnais, the Creole, first empress of the French, *maîtresse de l'ancien régime* and simultaneously the bourgeois, if imperial, "first lady," who has no part in the men's work of war and peace. Joséphine's Imperial master in the year 1807, answering the Prussian Queen Louise, who after having lost the war had asked her gallant adversary for the fortress of Magdeburg, simply and gruffly replied that fortresses where not the playthings of pretty women. In such a manner he, Napoleon Bonaparte, came to hate with an abiding hatred of all his enemies one most of all, the wealthy banker's daughter, Germaine Necker, Baroness de Staël, a writer and politicizing female. By the beginning of the nineteenth century the postulate of equality for the sexes had withered. The Empire took back the abstract postulate in favor of the bourgeois double standard that sees woman on the one hand as a virtuous and domesticated spouse, on the other as hetaera. The Kantian Friedrich Schiller published his poem *Song of the Bell* in the *Muses' Almanack* of 1800; it sings of the modest housewife who holds sway "wisely in the domestic circle" and who is responsible for doing the wash. "Und sammelt in reinlich geglätteten Schrein / Die schimmernde Wolle, den schneeigten Lein, / Und füget zum Guten den Glanz und den Schimmer, / Und ruhet nimmer."* A self-confessed Jacobin like Caroline Schlegel laughed herself almost to death when she read that. She was wrong. Precisely at the turn of the nineteenth century all the signs were gathering, not only in life but also in literature, that the bourgeois family was to go on being constituted on the basis of inequality. The process of discrimination against political (and therefore "unfeminine") women had begun, in the wake of which the century would come to be filled with endless debates about women's suffrage, higher education for women,

---

* "And the neat burnished chests, she gathers them full / Of linen snow-white, and of glistening wool, / The gloss and the shine to the good she adds ever, / And resteth never."

and free love. The unmarried woman had become a figure of caricature: as a randy old maid or as a "bluestocking."

In his *Maid of Orléans* Schiller, in contrast to his *Song of the Bell,* had presented the figure of a woman with a right to a political and military mission—as a departure, to be sure, from her own femininity. Schiller's successful women figures on the stage are experts in political strategy and conspiracy and intrigue: Eboli, Terzky, the queens Maria and Elizabeth, the princess Isabella in *The Bride from Messina,* even the tankard-maker in *William Tell.* Only in this, the consequential application of the principles of the Enlightenment, did the playwright of Joan of Arc stand at the end of a period of emancipation, not at its beginning. The path from *The Maid of Orléans* to Hebbel's *Judith* went the way of contradicting and resisting progressive thought. The bourgeois counter-Enlightenment that was already well under way was inspired by the postulate of women's inequality and the depiction of that inequality in literature. Schiller is controverted by Hebbel who is absolutely clear about what he is doing.

This controversion, this revocation so to speak, of previous progressive thought, had been prepared by Heinrich von Kleist's disillusioned Rousseauism. Few years indeed lie between Schiller's dramatization (1801) of the story of the farm maid from Domrémy and Kleist's *Penthesilea* (1808). In that interval, Beethoven had been struggling with the allegorical meaning of his Leonore/Fidelio. All these figures of women and dramatic heroines are women in arms, women with weapons: women like Joan in men's clothes, such as Leonore who hires herself out as a manhelper to the jailer Rocco; women with their virgin's sword that cuts down men on the battlefield, and Leonore's pistol before which Pizarro is made to back off. There are the sword and dogs and rites of defeminization of the Amazon queen in Kleist, and Hebbel's immaculate widowed Jewess who takes up Holofernes' sword against him.

Helmut Kreuzer in his essay "The Virgin in Arms"[6] has interpreted the succession of Schiller–Kleist–Hebbel, and its continuation into modern drama, not as the history of a literary motif, but as a process mirroring developments in society at large. He quotes Kleist's famous letter of May 1800 to Wilhelmine von Zenge: "A man is not only husband to his wife but is also a citizen to his nation; a woman on the other hand has no other duties than those to her husband." The nation of the Amazons is, in Kleist, a consummate perversion of nature, an anti-Rousseauan utopia. What is in accord with "nature" seems to be for Kleist the thoughtless servility of Käthchen of Heilbronn in the service of her "high lord."[7]

In Schiller and in Beethoven an emancipatory equality, which is also to be understood to entail women's political activism, is seriously taken up and given credence. In Kleist and later in Hebbel, not only is equality denied, and new inequalities between the sexes established, but in the decidedly monstrous exceptions of Penthesilea and Judith the exception is made the rule. In the actions of women with weapons, women's unfitness to do battle in general is proclaimed—and that includes by generalization the battle with intellectual weapons. The deeds of their representatives—Joan, Judith, Penthesilea—are used politically to disenfranchise the female majority.

Friedrich Hebbel is far more a chronicler of the signs of the times than their initiator and promoter. It is incontestable that his concern was with the dramatization of extreme situations, between rising and declining social groupings. In almost identical form to the argumentation in Kleist's letter of 1800, there is an entry in Hebbel's diary of 1836, when he was twenty-three. He notes: "Man has to tend to the affairs of society, woman has to tend to the affairs of man." At the end of Hebbel's tragedy, Judith is immobilized, petrified, longing for death because she has made an (unsuccessful) attempt to overstep her bounds. Hebbel time and again considered a reinterpretation of the story of the maid of Orléans as well. It would have paralleled his *Judith*, which was itself a counterversion to Schiller's romantic tragedy. That would not have been just one more motif among others; and it cannot simply be explained away in formal and stylistic terms as postclassical epigonism. Between *The Maid of Orléans* of 1801 and *Judith* of 1841 there stand four decades of bourgeois disillusionment. Hebbel had labored doggedly and embitteredly for the continuation of tragedy and the German-bourgeois *Trauerspiel* at a time when defeudalization and de-Christianization were reducing all of the fundamental concepts of tragedy to nothing, namely: honor, guilt, character, freedom of decision. It was Hegel who had still spoken of possible decisions in life, and not simply in those of the great literary examples, when he noted in his *Lectures on Aesthetics* that "it is the true strength of great characters that they do not choose but simply and quite thoroughly are that which they desire and do. . . . It is the honor of the great character to be guilty."[8]

The spread of the bourgeois economy and form of society had welded the concept of honor to economic solidity, equated guilt with debt, reduced character to an interiorized private sphere, delimited freedom to freedom of speech. Hebbel's female dramatic figures after Judith become more and more anachronistic. Judith's overstepping her bounds was an exercise as disastrous as the extreme social conformism of Klara in *Mary Magdalene*.[9]

With Hebbel there ends for the whole of European literature the fierce attempt, an attempt no longer in step with the times, to legitimate the dissolution of women's equality in the wake of the bourgeois counter-Enlightenment as the tragic failure of an individual's overstepping her bounds. The bourgeois literature of the nineteenth century, however, relinquished tragedy in favor of the novel. Flaubert and George Eliot, Hawthorne and Tolstoy, Fontane and Henry James are fascinated by a seemingly ever-changing situation that is nevertheless structurally uniform—of a woman who presses for freedom and equality in the male world and who is broken for her trouble. The transition from tragedy to the novel is a formal indication that the presentation of "unfeminine" women with weapons had been replaced by the narration of the downfall of "feminine" women.

The Individual and Her Property: The Countess Faustine

The tractate written by a petit-bourgeois of Bayreuth, Max Stirner, entitled *Der Einzige und sein Eigentum* (The Individual and His Property; 1845), has no apparent connection with a novel that had appeared four years earlier, *Gräfin Faustine*, by Ida Countess Hahn-Hahn, an aristocrat who had come into the world in 1805 on the estate of Tressow in Mecklenburg.[10] One can assert in complete confidence of Johann Caspar Schmidt, who went by the name of Max Stirner, that "the ideology of the middle class found its earliest formulation in Max Stirner's work, *The Individual and His Property*, . . . Stirner did not forge the ideology of the middle class: the development of ideology is a consequence of social and economic conditions. *The Individual and His Property* is simply their consequential formulation."[11] Ida Hahn-Hahn for her part always remained countess and the offspring of aristocrats, even if she fell passionately in love with the lawyer and democrat and Jew, Heinrich Simon, the later parliamentarian of the Paulskirche in the revolution of 1848 (something for which she afterward could never quite forgive herself.) Her outpourings before and during the revolution of 1848 are more or less as follows: "Oh, this Mme. Roland, how I despise her! This representative of the Third Estate in their jealousy, in their cheap phrases, in their haughty and miserably inept desire to take the place of their betters, in

Judith as Bourgeois Heroine

their comedy with high-sounding words and no deeds, in their vain overestimation of themselves! And I am supposed to admire her? Oh, this Robespierre, how I despise him!'" (diary entry of October 10, 1847).[12]

That and more of the same was her reaction to Lamartine's then much read *History of the Girondins*. The countess was putting her credo to paper four months before the outbreak of the February revolution in Paris, which would catapult said Lamartine into the provisional revolutionary government—along with the socialist Louis Blanc and the half-anonymous, almost "symbolic" worker Alexandre Albert.

In Dresden, where the beginning of her novel *Gräfin Faustine* had been situated, she experienced first-hand the May revolution, with the players Bakunin, Gottfried Semper, and Richard Wagner. She remained true to herself and her furious principles of intellectual superiority. This was for her the end of culture in the world, at least for Germany. "The mortification of being a German I shall never outlive." Personal matters are involved here: Heinrich Simon was one of the speakers of that very same democratic popular movement. Her biographer Arthur Schurig has transmitted a later reminiscence: "I lived like a salamander in fire, in inextinguishable hatred and incontrovertible contempt for the democratic principle and its representatives, supporters, and hangers-on."[13]

One could simply throw out this exalted Junker blather, and add that the Countess Hahn-Hahn soon thereafter, on New Year's Eve 1849–50, made the decision to convert to Catholicism, which she accomplished under the spiritual guidance of the bishop of Berlin, Freiherr von Ketteler. The rest of her life was all edification: novice in the order of the Good Shepherd in Angers, founder of a convent in Mainz, author of proselytizing literature and of an autobiography with the grotesque title *From Babylon to Jerusalem*. Even Schurig speaks of the "rapidly sinking standard" of her later little tractates. But there is more here than a bizarre life of gadding about, traveling, opining, even of blindness, of erotic and social mortification. What seems to be a talented, socially indifferent subjectivity actually proves to be a typical, socially formed attitude. Over the portals of time, Stirner had reflected, there no longer stands written the Delphic "Know thyself!" but a utilitarian "Market yourself!"

In this sense Ida Hahn-Hahn is a sociologically noteworthy, totally artificial figure from the heart of society prior to the revolution of 1848. Life and writing fuse together in her to a complete stylization of individual uniqueness. Just as she in reading a book about the French Revolution valued only her own sympathies and aversions without for a moment reflecting on the historical process, and brought everything down to the personal characteristics of the political protagonists, so was there for her the neat division between the usurping hoi poloi with their bombast and their "betters" who are the natural aristoi. Betters, by the way, in art too.

The story in *Gräfin Faustine* is narrated in this same vein. It is the report studded with autobiographical details of a female Faust from the ranks of the true believers in social and artistic aristocracy. Love without marriage, because that would be comparable to bourgeois ties; ecstasies of free love and feelings of motherhood; the haughtiness of the nobility and the elitist humility of a spectacular flight into a convent. Not the least of the curiosities is that Ida Hahn-Hahn in her later life sought to act out the novel she had written. The narrator concludes the novel with a moralism: "Such a sensitive vampire nature burns and uses itself up, first the veins, then the rest. Beware of the Faustines! It is no good to try to live as they do."[14] Faustine the vampire and Faustine the female Faust. Dracula and the serpent and a female Don Juan adapted from Lord Byron, whom the countess von Hahn had come to admire in her youth.

Yet Faustine is no metaphysical phenomenon; she is not even sensationally unique. What is important is that she brought a certain *type* to its purest delineation. The elitist notions behind that are all one.

This despiser of the plebs, this cultural aristocrat, Ida Countess Hahn-Hahn was above all else a thoroughly best-selling writer. The provocations in her novel *Gräfin Faustine,* seemingly so ensconced in aristocratic and intellectual haughtiness, were avidly devoured. Here it becomes apparent that the novel's seeming outsiderdom follows social norms, is even postulated by those norms.

In her foreword of October 5, 1844, to a new edition of *Faustine,* our author is concerned with certain criticisms of the novel and quotes approvingly someone who found her heroine to be a sublime egotist. The countess is delighted with so much understanding and adds: "And if I had to sit down today and ask myself how a splendidly talented, richly organized woman would act who seeks, wants, and desires nothing but her own satisfaction without regard to others, so would I have to write my Faustine a second time over."

Something similar, this time said by a man about men, could just as well stand in Max Stirner's *The Individual and His Property.* The hereditary and openly declared elitism of the novel-writing countess had no quality of the outsider about it. The success with bourgeois readers makes it evident: even Faustine's egotism is bourgeois egotism; the countess has outlined the dreams of the bourgeois middle class. It is elitism for Everyman.

In those days, at all events, it was not for Everywoman. Since the beginning of the nineteenth century there have been over and again in all of the European countries ideal, typical cases of women's emancipation both in actual life and in literature: the wives of the German Romantics, Dorothea Mendelssohn-Schlegel and Caroline Schlegel-Schelling, the once scorned and hated Jacobin of Mainz; Mme. de Staël and George Sand in France and George Eliot in England. There was no lack of derision and social proscription. It stretched from Schiller's hatred of Caroline Schlegel, "Madame Lucifer," to Napoleon's police actions against Mme. de Staël, to the anti-Semitism that reviled Moses Mendelssohn's daughter, who had converted to Catholicism; from the erotic scandal provoked by George Sand to the ecclesiastical one provoked by George Eliot's translation of David Friedrich Strauss's *Das Leben Jesu* (The Life of Jesus). In all cases, however, these women were not offending against the established dogmas of the Enlightenment but were putting them into practice. Tolerance was much in need to come to the aid of these hard-pressed women who had not offended against the norms of reason, but only against those of an intellectual disenfranchisement. Moreover, they one and all put bourgeois literature to the task of bedeviling corrupt Bonapartism, the restoration of monarchy, and Anglican orthodoxy.

The scandal around Faustine and Ida Hahn-Hahn is of another sort. Curiously, a woman's emancipation here, in life as well as in a form of literature that was understood as providing values for life, is *not* united to the bourgeois notion of universal, humanistic liberation. Quite the contrary, it is united to its malevolent opposite. Faustine and her author want their own unlimited pleasure or bursting of taboos *and,* at one and the same time, the continuing frustration of everyone else. This from the right of their own elect, chosen state which is naively identified with aristocratic lineage.

The second paradox is even more confusing: in the novel *Gräfin Faustine,* equality of rights for women is not postulated, including the right to some kind of sexual say-so, as it was in Karl Gutzkow's novel, *Wally the Doubter,* which had appeared in 1835, five years before *Faustine.* Gutzkow's novel immediately met with massive suppression. Wally and her lover Caesar are not far removed from Hahn-Hahn's aristocratic circles, but the intellectual as well as the erotic division of roles remains in traditional boundaries. That is to say, Caesar is the corporeal-intellectual-spiritual seducer. He calls up Wally's social, and above all, religious questionings through the postulation of a moderate deism. This was unnerving enough for Wally to take refuge in death.

Faustine, on the other hand, is not an emancipated woman but a "sensitive vampire nature." In the novel's last sentence she is described as a "demon." Hence she carries out a switch of gender roles. Faustine is a female Faust who—with aim and control, as I would not fail to admit—while sated with pleasure pines for the fulfillment of each passing desire. So gorged with herself, she is the seductress who picks out, grabs up, and deserts, who goes through all the standard recipes of seduction like so many tirades of doom in the *Weltschmerz* literature of those days. Childe Harold, Manfred, Pechorin (Lermontov), Rolla (de Musset) have one more name to be added to their company: the Countess Faustine. What could be the stuff of serious satire becomes a literary success greedily consumed by countless readers. This is an indication that the inversion of the process of emancipation, an inversion that would seem to be disgraceful and paradoxical, called forth no social outcry, but rather social and literary blessings.

This must be seen in connection with the extreme and openly proclaimed egotism of both Faustine and her author. In their *Dialectic of Enlightenment,* Horkheimer and Adorno emphasize that "the Enlightenment had fully committed itself to Liberalism. If all emotional drives are posited as being equal, then the drive toward self-preservation (which, in any case, dominates all of the aspects of this system) appears to provide the most probable basis and justification for all actions. Such a drive toward self-preservation should be unfettered in the free market economy. The somber writers at the beginning of the bourgeois era, Machiavelli, Hobbes, Mandeville, who took the side of the self's egotism, recognized society thereby as the destructive principle, denounced harmony."[15] Ida Hahn-Hahn's aristocratic arrogance should not mask the fact that *Gräfin Faustine* was written as an apologia for middle class egotism. All the more so since there is an anticipation here of that equality of rights for women in the capitalist economy in the sense of universal productive capability: from factory worker to telephone operator, department store salesgirl to waitress. With this the feudal world with its idle "high dames" is really over. Faustine, once the delicate aestheticizing blather is peeled off, is a far less romantic heroine than the energetic female imperialists in Shaw of whom she is a precursor.

When Stirner at the end of his argumentation characterizes "the individual," he does so precisely in the sense of the bourgeois middle estate: "He does not recognize himself as an instrument of ideas or as a vessel of God; he recognizes no vocation; he does not believe he is there for the development of mankind and that he has to contribute his little bit; he only lives out his desires, uncaring how well or how poorly humankind gets along."[16] The Countess Faustine, that demon who merely described the human condition of her time or presaged that of the future, could have spoken so, though not so soberly.

Hebbel's *Judith*, which appeared in 1841, the same year as *Gräfin Faustine*, had been conceived as a literature of warning. The conservative Hebbel pronounced Judith's confusion of feelings as evidence of woman's inability to carry out "manly' action. Judith, doubting her own autonomy, delivers herself up to God's judgment. Faustine already acts as Stirner had required of his Individual: with unconcern for God and humanity, for ideas as well as utopia. Seven years after Judith and Faustine, only three after Stirner's work, in the year of the revolution of 1848, Richard Wagner, who was familiar with Stirner, completed his romantic opera *Lohengrin*. It was to present a new incarnation of the woman with a weapon in the figure of Ortrud: the political woman come to replace the fairytale witch. Ortrud no longer believes, as Hebbel's Judith still did, in judgments of God.

The Political Woman: Ortrud and Lohengrin

Ortrud is to all appearances, as she ceremoniously presents her consort Telramund to the German king Heinrich as "Rabods, sired by the prince of the Frisians,"[17] a typical fairytale witch. She is the scary opposite to oppressed girlish virtue, the evil queen from *Snow White*. The antithesis of the innocent girl, the guilty woman has been a recurrent theme in all cultures. The theme was pagan and then Christian (taken up in the lives of the saints) and is to be met in the North and in the South; even the struggle of the guilty Clytemnestra and the dangerously pure Electra may be viewed as one of the variations. The bourgeois Enlightenment delighted, in Richardson and Lessing and Laclos, in contrasting the (bourgeois) propriety of a girl to the (aristocratic) libertinage of a woman. Then there is in Lessing Mrs. Marwood against the officiously pious Miss Sara Sampson.

German Romanticism made use of all kinds of female figures: the devil

Judith and Delilah

and the saint; the "natural" girl and the artificial, guilt-laden wanton. Heinrich von Kleist worked quite consciously, almost cynically, with the tried and true recipes to produce *Käthchen von Heilbronn*. There could be no one who takes things as they come more innocently, more unawares, than Käthchen; no one meaner, more contrived, than the wicked Kunigunde.

All this was destined to be an opera before a score was ever composed. Carl Maria von Weber, filled with ambition despite his illness, thought much of and hoped for much from Helmine von Chézy's libretto, which had already defied Franz Schubert's attempts at dramatic vivification. His opera *Euryanthe* was first performed at the Vienna opera house in 1823. It is put together as an amalgam of the romantic and antithetical cliché of knightly fidelity and courtly treachery, purity and defamation, heathen magic and Christian trust in God. Of course innocence and fidelity are victorious. The color and the timbre of the music are bright for the pure Adolar and Euryanthe, dark for their adversaries Lysiart and Eglantine. Whoever sits through one of the rare performances of Weber's *Euryanthe* supposes himself transposed into the world of Lohengrin: one hears lovely but unfamiliar music. Richard Wagner admittedly made use of the opera's dramatic scheme in his *Lohengrin*. Here too is a symbolism in the music's timbre, which Wagner reinforced by a tonal symbolism: the A major of the world of the grail opposed to its minor equivalent in Ortrud's and Telramund's F sharp minor.

More than twenty years lie between *Euryanthe* and Wagner's commencing to work on *Lohengrin*. He began to lay out the basic concepts of this new romantic opera in Marienbad in 1845, and at the same time to conceive the scheme for the future *Meistersinger. Euryanthe* is unmistakably part and parcel of a romanticism become cliché, a romanticism of restoration. *Lohengrin,* on the other hand, is the political poesy of the *Vormärz,* which is to say, the product of an epoch lying between the two European revolutions of 1830 and 1848. The knight's declamations in Helmine von Chézy's libretto are at once pithy and colorless. The king's admonition to his vassals on the bank of the Schelde in Wagner, however, breathes the spirit of German unification:

Für deutsches Land das deutsche Schwert!
So sei des Reiches Kraft bewährt! *

---

*A German sword for German land / In this way our Reich will stand!

Even the Holy Grail seems something of German consideration. Lohengrin in leaving prophesies:

Doch, grosser König, lass' mich dir weissagen:
dir Reinem ist ein grosser Sieg verlieh'n.
Nach Deutschland sollen noch in fernsten Tagen
des Ostens Horden siegreich niemals zieh'n!*

It is nothing more than a dramatic prediction made after the event where everyone already knows what is going to happen. The reference is to Heinrich's victory over the Hungarians at the Unstrut. But what is signified, what Wagner intends here, what an audience of his contemporaries makes of it, is a cry for German unity and resistance against czarism as the main pillar of the restorative European princes' alliance.

The politicization of an old romantic fairytale model, its identification with contemporary political events, is manifested most forcibly in Wagner's figure of Ortrud. She too is a woman with a weapon. As a practitioner of magic, or as someone privy to the secret powers in nature, she resembles so many other Wagnerian heroines: Venus, Isolde, Brünnhilde, Kundry. Ortrud transforms—she kills—by magic. What did she do to Gottfried, the heir apparent of Brabant and brother of Elsa? She too is a superwoman like the Countess Faustine; she disposes of the noble count Telramund in her altercation with him "with fearsome derision." What was represented in Ida Hahn-Hahn four years before the start of Wagner's labors on *Lohengrin* as a female titanism, a titanism she quite approved, comes to receive in Wagner a thoroughly negative accentuation. It is strange then that both the Countess Faustine and Ortrud are reactionaries. There is a divergence, of course, namely that Ida Hahn-Hahn, incapable of drafting the Countess Faustine other than as her own mirror image, transfigures as progressive the elitist consciousness of her aristocratic egotist Faustine. Wagner on the other hand in a progressive work (historically speaking) such as *Lohengrin* denounces Ortrud's position as reactionary. It is precisely in doing so that he himself becomes reactionary. In the dramatic figure of Ortrud Wagner condemns the phenotype of a political and politicizable woman.

Wagner himself understood the matter in these terms. In a letter to Franz Liszt of January 30, 1852, scarcely two years after the premiere

---

*O great king, let me tell you what will come; / You, so pure, will be great and victorious. / Even in the farthest days will never come / To Germany hordes from out the East victorious.

performance, which Wagner, the exile of 1849, was unable to attend and which Liszt directed, he expounded on this subject at length. Princess Caroline von Sayn-Wittgenstein, who had been living with Liszt in Weimar since his separation from Marie d'Agoult, was a remarkable connoisseur of drama, and, moreover, had written an interpretation of *Faust*, had communicated with Wagner concerning a new casting of *Lohengrin.* On that occasion she had tendered an analysis of Ortrud's character and of the singers who had played her. Wagner made an answer in his letter to Liszt. He praised the "ingenious remarks on the role of Ortrud" and continued with a veritable epistolary eruption against this figure and against the world that she represented for him. Ortrud was for him a woman who "knows no love. With that everything—even the most terrible—is said. Her being is politics. A political man is repulsive; a political *female* ghastly. It was this ghastliness I had to represent."[18]

Even in Richard Wagner's rank correspondence there is scarcely a document that steeps itself in contradictory absurdity as much as here. Political man is repulsive; political woman ghastly. Loathing on the one hand; fear on the other. It does not especially have to be mentioned that this is an exiled revolutionary and companion of Mikhail Bakunin writing, the author as well of works on "Art and Revolution" and "The Art Work of the Future," which even in the formulation of its title embraces Ludwig Feuerbach's philosophy of the future.

Wagner sees his ideas confirmed by historical example: "We know in history of no more ruthless figures than political women." Whom does he have in mind? The English Elizabeth, the Russian Catherine? He sticks to generalities but specifies the supposed peculiarity of female politics: it is in essence always directed backwards. Ortrud, he says, loves the past, its vanished races. It is "the shockingly insane love of ancestor worship." Man as a reactionary simply becomes laughable; in woman, however, reactionary politics is coupled with a "murderous fanaticism." That can be ascertained in Ortrud. "She is a reactionary, and I mean this in the most fervid sense of the word: one who is concerned only with what has been and is consequently the enemy of anything new. She would purge and exterminate nature and the world if only she could bring her moldy gods back to life again." The deep emotionalism of this letter is striking. It is not the eternally didactic Wagner, the Wagner attempting to win one over to his cause, who is writing here but the emotionally involved and fearful Wagner. He is afraid of Ortrud and he marvels at her. She is "frightfully grandiose." This too is an ambivalence of feeling bound in an impure mixture with strangely ambivalent thinking. For Ortrud's reaction is directed against Christianity and its embodiment in Lohengrin, a knight of the Grail, whom she holds to be a weakling and a cheat. She has the same estimation for the Christians' god. On the other hand, the Wagner who is the student of Feuerbach is at a far remove in *Lohengrin* from any belief in the suprahistorical value of Christianity. Prayer, judgment of God, the enchantment of the Grail are all simply romantic stage props. Lohengrin is actually no Christian knight but a highly gifted and lonely artist in the modern (bourgeois) world, just as were his predecessors, Ahasver of the ocean and the artist Tannhäuser, free-ranging between the Wartburg and the Mount of Venus.

The rejection of Ortrud as a politicized woman is in itself reactionary. It is furthermore strange that Ortrud's call to the pagan gods is interpreted negatively, although Wagner only a few years later will start interpreting the world of the Germanic gods envisioned by Ortrud as a kind of secret code for bourgeois society. And he will find his own place in that world as a "wanderer." The contradiction lies in the fact that for Wagner Lohengrin is really not a Christian knight and Ortrud not a conjuror of the pagan gods. Lohengrin is the epitome of the solitary artist in a rationalized and skeptical world hostile to art. Ortrud personifies all of the opposition in this aristocratic and at the same time bourgeois, calculating world.

What connects and what separates Wagner and Hebbel becomes visible. Both hold the actions of "political females" (where *political* is broadly defined) to be contradictory to their feminine natures. For both, a political woman is the woman with a weapon. Hebbel believes himself to be more modern than the dramatist of *The Maid of Orléans*; Wagner is, in his own estimation, more modern than the Beethoven of *Fidelio*.

Hebbel well knows what political reaction is; he is its contemporary. Nevertheless his sympathies, in contradistinction to Wagner, sympathies scarcely still secret, sympathies almost openly declared, belong to the social order and to ideas that are in decline. This is the case even with his carpenter, Anton; without any doubt with Queen Rhodope, who in *Gyges and His Ring* monomaniacally holds fast to the old ways, just as Ortrud does, killing and dying. King Kandaules comes to feel the dialectic of the Enlightenment since he has dared disturb "the sleep of the world."

Wagner is at one with Lohengrin and Elsa. This heiress of Brabant has an existence of her own only in so far as she can partake of Lohengrin's missionary ego. As Wagner explains later in a "communication for my friends," she is "the opposite quite contained in his own nature, and necessarily a complement of his male, individual nature which he calls forth in desire." For that reason Elsa was unable to go on living when Lohengrin returned to the Grail. Ortrud, on the other hand, does continue.

Hedda Gabler's Beautiful Death

It was George Bernard Shaw who toward the end of the last century first and most tenaciously asserted that the tendencies of bourgeois society in the second half of the nineteenth century had found their purest delineation in Wagner's operas and in Henrik Ibsen's plays. He attempted to demonstrate the complementary character of Wagner–Ibsen drama in his books on the quintessence of Ibsenism and the art of Wagner.[19]

A half-century after Shaw, Thomas Mann in American exile put forward the thesis that no German was the equal, particularly in terms of international significance, of the great French, Russian, English, even American writers. "The name that Germany has to counterpose to that proud list, or to add to it, is Richard Wagner."[20]

Hebbel, Wagner, and Ibsen made their debuts with dramatic meditations on declining cultures and the fates of their representatives. Ibsen's "world-historical play," subtitled *Emperor and Galilean* (1873), calls up the figure of the emperor Julian the Apostate who tries to set a religion of Neoplatonism against the all-victorious Christianity and who meets his doom in so trying. A work in Hebbel's spirit and with positions typical to Hebbel, it was written in the same period that Wagner completed his tetralogy and was attempting to stage it in Bayreuth. A "negative dialectic" is common to both of them. In this sense Hebbel's and Wagner's *Nibelungen* are like each other. In Ibsen, the emperor Julian, Pastor Brand, and Peer Gynt all fail. They fail in two attempts: the first to have everything all at once indiscriminately, the second to have everything or nothing at all.

Hebbel, Wagner, and Ibsen all know the woman with a weapon. Hebbel seeks to expose the basis of her thwarted and perverted life, as does Ibsen. Wagner here, as in so many themes, is concerned with the one thing as well as with the other; I mean the figure of Ortrud, the "ghastly" reactionary, as well as the Valkyrie, the incarnation of a utopia that is blown to oblivion.

Ibsen in *Hedda Gabler* attempted a bourgeois and contemporary synthesis of Judith, Ortrud, and Brünnhilde. This is not to be understood as a confusion of motifs but as an interpretation of women outsiders in the modern world. Naturally it is done in the form of a stereotype, as the battle of a romantic individual with the ugliness of bourgeois society. The poetic works of European Romanticism posited the possibility of individual freedom and self-realization as being within reach. But as early as E. T. A. Hoffmann the discrepancy between creative life in Atlantis and the realities of bourgeois life in the capitals of the German petty principalities became clearly drawn. Nevertheless poetry and reality had not yet become antinomies for the artist. In German Romanticism, even in its worn-out and corrupt later phase, there was to be found an integral part of the continuity of the Enlightenment.

As life progressively came under the sway of the bourgeoisie, such self-realization according to one's own capabilities and sensibilities appeared more and more as an illusion, as a heady step in the wrong direction, if not simply as spleen. From now on the novel is the dominant literary form instead of tragic drama, which had held fast to the possibility of great (free) characters. Works are written that in substance can only be called texts of disillusion, having at bottom a single theme: the foundering of romantic individual development in the face of the stupefaction of bourgeois life. It is the representative theme in Flaubert's *Madame Bovary*. More and more decidedly the later Ibsen as well places this single theme at the center of works such as *Rosmersholm*, *The Lady from the Sea*, *The Master Builder*. The most consummately delineated example is to be found in *Hedda Gabler*.

General Gabler's daughter quite consciously and with all exactitude places her life at the intersection between an impossible romanticism of conduct and the seemingly possible ideal beauty of death. This archromantic concept winds its way from Novalis up through Thomas Mann's autobiographical *Reflections of a Non-Political Man* and, formulated as a renunciation of the theme, on to Mann's *Magic Mountain*.

Georg Lukács in his early collection of essays, *Soul and Form* (1911), writes: "It was the tragedy of German Romanticism that only Novalis's life could become poetry; his victory was a death sentence for the whole school. Everything with which they sought to conquer life merely sufficed for one beautiful death. Their philosophy of life was only one of death, their art for the living of life one for dying."[21]

Nowadays one has to proceed from the assumption that this does not adequately reflect Novalis, that the legend of his sympathetic death fol-

Judith and Delilah

lowing the demise of Sophie von Kühn is a questionable mixture of reality and romantic aesthetic. Lukács had need of the legend not simply as argumentation against the Romantic school (in those days in the name of neoclassicism) but above all for his interpretation of the doctrine of "beautiful dying." And here he has less the Romanticism of the early nineteenth century in mind than the neo-Romanticism of the early twentieth. In this fashion the legendary configuration of Friedrich von Hardenberg and Sophie von Kühn became for him a prefiguration of the stage figures of Hedda Gabler and Eilert Lövborg.

Lukács had come under the influence of Ibsen rather early. His first writings as an aesthetician and literary historian show him fascinated by drama and the theater. In 1911, the year that his first collection of essays appeared in German (he was then twenty-six), he published a two-volume history of modern drama in Hungarian.[22] In later times Lukács came back to Ibsen time and time again despite the fact that after his *Theory of the Novel* (1920) he was little inclined to return to questions of the theater and dramatic theory. In what appears to be a confession of his own heart—on the occasion of Thomas Mann's seventieth birthday—he quotes Ibsen, who says that writing literature means "holding judgment over one's own ego."[23]

Lukács interprets the crisis and beautiful death of Hedda Tesman née Gabler as did the majority of his contemporaries, who were themselves younger contemporaries of Ibsen, as the conflict between aesthetic nostalgia and an insufferable bourgeois life. So that General Gabler's daughter immediately comes to be placed near Madame Bovary. The Norwegian and the Norman bourgeois constriction; the mediocre husbands Charles Bovary and George Tesman; death by arsenic or a shot in the temple. In his essay "Erzählen oder Beschreiben?" written in the thirties, Lukács interpreted in detail Flaubert's "Madame Bovary, c'est moi!" He noted that all of Gustave Flaubert's later poetic, his cult of form and language, his alternately writing books about bourgeois stupidity and historical novels in a Mediterranean setting, means nothing more than that the beauty of art must be pressed into service when everyday life has become unutterably small and ugly. Whether Sartre was familiar with Lukács's line of reasoning or not, his monumental study of Flaubert, *L'Idiot de la famille,* comes to similar conclusions.[24]

Hedda Gabler is no slightly cheap Norwegian imitation of Madame Bovary, however. The last sentence in the play is sufficient to demonstrate that. Ibsen composed his plays with great precision and craft, and he

Judith as Bourgeois Heroine

held to the dramatist's rule—as did Schiller before him and Brecht after—that lines easily learned and quoted can help the audience from time to time to grasp a play's meaning. Schiller found the beginning and especially the concluding lines best suited to such an intention. Ibsen liked to make use of metaphorical formulas: Peer Gynt's "person"; the "lie of a lifetime" in *The Wild Duck*; Oswald Alving's "sun" in *Ghosts*; Hedda Gabler's beautiful death. And the concluding lines of a play were for the later Ibsen by far the most important.[25]

Judge Brack, who dallies in provincial intrigue, a man of moral order who threatens others with scandal, has the last word in *Hedda Gabler*. The woman whom he thinks he has won over has just killed herself in the next room with a pistol shot to the temple. "Fancy that!" says her now widowed husband George Tesman, who has no stronger language at his command. Brack lies "half-fainting in the armchair." Then from his lips issues forth the quintessential phrase: "Good God!—People don't do such things."

What don't people do? Commit suicide? No, naturally not, for that is for a Christian—and *Hedda Gabler* takes place among Lutherans in the west side of the Norwegian capital—a mortal sin. A pastor must deny Christian burial to a suicide. At the same time it was not completely unheard-of for a woman to die by her own hand. For there were the stereotypical and the unusual manners of death: Ophelia's death by drowning (and Klara's in Hebbel's *Mary Magdelene*); arsenic for Madame Bovary; the adder for Cleopatra; and even Anna Karenina's ghastly end under the wheels of a locomotive.

But a pistol shot to the temple? That was, in the bourgeois nineteenth century, the privilege of the dishonored officer—of a Colonel Redl in Vienna, say, who had been a spy; or of a banker gone bankrupt; or of a successful physician suddenly under investigation by a grand jury—a manly form of death. Consequently, almost a reconciling settlement.

The general's daughter Hedda Gabler, on the contrary, becomes scandalous in death. Or to put it more correctly, she creates scandal by her death. Such extravagances as a love of shooting pistols, horseback riding, intercourse with Bohemia in the person of Lövborg never led to doors being closed in the face of Dr. Tesman's wife, to use Brack's words. The scandal lies in the manner of Hedda Gabler's death. With that Ibsen, retrospectively from the drama's final words, delineates the real tragedy of this woman.

Hedda is only on the surface of things a successor to and imitator of

Judith and Delilah

Madame Bovary, Anna Karenina, Effi Briest—all of them vigorous women with strong personalities and unloved husbands (a Russian councillor of state, a provincial French bourgeois, or a Prussian district magistrate). All of these women offended more or less scandalously against the rites of an aristocratic or bourgeois world, but by doing so merely lived up to general norms of female behavior—behavior that had itself been defined and categorized by men. That is to say, they were all mistresses outside the bounds of marriage, mistresses who valued real love—or in the case of Madame Bovary, imagined love—more than their position as married women, thereby proving their "true womanhood."

Hedda is once again the woman with a weapon. When in their first confidential talk in the second act Hedda's and Lövborg's common past is recalled, again and again fall the words *comradeship, daring, cowardice*:

HEDDA: . . . Shame on you Eilert Lövborg! How could you think of wronging your—your frank comrade?
LÖVBORG (*clenching his hands*): Oh, why did you not carry out your threat? Why did you not shoot me down?
HEDDA: Because I have such a dread of scandal.
LÖVBORG: Yes, Hedda, you are a coward at heart.
HEDDA: A terrible coward . . .[26]

Quite irresistably Hedda Tesman's words and deeds slip off into the male world. When Brack, speaking of her feelings for her husband, uses the word love, Hedda answers: "Faugh—don't use that sickening word!"[27] Comradeship, daring, cowardice, not love. Man's world. There is no sexual inversion here; Hedda Gabler is not an inhabitant of Gomorrah. She proves that quite clearly in her behavior toward all other women, especially toward the stupid little Mrs. Elvsted, Lövborg's mistress. Hedda is a woman who as woman wants to speak, feel, and act as a man; I mean live a fashion of life that in her day was reserved for men only.

The culmination of these desires is that she succeeds at the last, in the manner of her death. The romantic dreams of before—to die with garlands of vineleaves in her hair—have long been rejected as nostalgia for the South, both by Hedda and by Lövborg, who has written a book on the culture of the future. But the futurologist Eilert Lövborg, whom one must imagine according to the indications that Ibsen provides as a man of true genius and not a dissimulating *poseur,* just as pronouncedly slips off into an "unmanly" world. Lövborg does not die "beautifully" as Hedda had desired for him as well as for herself. He does not die out of free will, consciously, and in an impeccable, aesthetic fashion, but by ineptitude or drunkenness in Mademoiselle Diane's bordello, by a bullet in the bowels—as Hedda later learns from Brack, "looking up at him with an expression of loathing." That vision is destroyed that caused her to cry out that "I only know that Eilert Lövborg has had the courage to live his life after his own fashion. And then—the last great act, with its beauty! Ah! That he should have the will and the strength to turn away from the banquet of life—so early."

To turn away from the banquet of life in order to put on another banquet, that of death. But since nothing of the sort transpired, Hedda must now, as it seems to her, take his place and bring to pass what he has failed to do for himself and for her. She herself dies, as she imagines, in beauty: as a man, by means of one of the pistols of her parental superego, General Gabler.

Is Henrik Ibsen on her side? It is difficult to decide. Looking at this playwright's last works such as *John Gabriel Borkman,* one does not come to the conclusion that he might have wanted to demonstrate the absurdity of such a question. That is not the case. For Ibsen, Hedda is neither a "megaera," that is, a shrew, as Otto Weininger might have diagnosed, nor an androgynous exception to the rule. Hedda Gabler does not meet her ruin in society's order of things as do Bovary and Karenina. Or only in so far as this social realm is unwilling to make any place for women with weapons. Unwilling to make a place even after death, for there too one says, "Good God!—People don't do such things."

4 The Bourgeois Way of Life as an Alternative

Victorian Morals

Matthew Arnold's book *Culture and Anarchy*, which first appeared in 1869, contains a stinging and nasty, yet earnestly meant typology of the moral predilections of English society and its class stratification.[1] Arnold distinguishes the aristocracy, the bourgeois middle class, and last the mass of the people. To the aristocrats he appends the title "Barbarians," to the middle class "Philistines," to the people "Populace," which I take to mean something more like rabble. Arnold is a bourgeois cultural and literary critic; he espouses Goethe and Goethe's concept of world literature as much as Sainte-Beuve's moralistic-psychologizing interpretations of literary works. His book is meant to do battle against English self-satisfaction and complacency in matters of morals and art, a complacency that has its roots in capitalist business practices carried over into the private, domestic sphere.

His typology looks like this: "The graver self of the Barbarian likes honours and consideration; his more relaxed self, field-sports and pleasure. The graver self of one kind of Philistine likes fanaticism, business, and money-making; his more relaxed self, comfort and tea-meetings. Of another kind of Philistine, the graver self likes rattening; the relaxed, deputations, or hearing Mr. Odger speak. The sterner self of the Populace likes bawling, hustling, and smashing; the lighter self, beer."[2] This characterization, whether justified or not, is a part of the sociology of the middle period of Victorian England. Queen Victoria, who ascended to the throne at eighteen, wed her cousin Albert von Coburg at twenty-one, was widowed at forty-two, was proclaimed Empress of India in 1876 by the Jewish Tory Prime Minister Benjamin Disraeli, and was celebrated as a universal institution at her Diamond Jubilee in 1897, did not provide a name to the Victorian Age simply by longevity. The "Georgian" style of the eighteenth century is merely an art historical technical term; the kings of the House of Hanover with the name George provided nothing more than easy points of reference. Victoria Regina, as she signed her name, the Queen as she was called everywhere in her later years, gave her stamp to Victorianism, as she herself was formed by it—not without pain. If Victorian morality is equated with prudery and hypocrisy, especially in all the realms of sexuality, with zealous churchgoing and unctuous oratory, with the fanatical striving to pluck out the eye that offends, then the widow Victoria lived out this morality as an exemplary in everything she sanctioned, and particularly in everything she disapproved. She took pleasure in reading George Eliot's novels but put off any thought of ever receiving their author, who lived in common-law marriage because her lover could not obtain a divorce. When the jubilee of 1897 was celebrated as a kind of culmination of Victorianism, Oscar Wilde had been released from Reading Gaol, yet Victorian morality continued to find in him and to make use of him as a permanent source of annoyance. Laborers and middle class passersby recognized the prisoner in a transport and felt called upon to revile him. Wilde was obliged to live the rest of his days under an assumed name in French exile. His two sons themselves took another name: Holland. When Lord Alfred Douglas and Wilde rented a room at a hotel in Capri, English tourists threatened the owner with a boycott. Victorian morals were conceived as an either/or. Either total moral and social conformity or permanent irritation running to scandal. Edward Bond's play *Early Morning* targets this still present moral residue of Victorianism when he places the queen and her offspring in a museum of pathology and when he goes so far as to associate the widowed queen with the stigma of the city of Gomorrah, using for this purpose the figure of Florence Nightingale. It was and is meant to be a provocative, even blasphemous play, by a present-day author; it reminds one of an exorcism, driving Victorianism out of English life in the latter part of the twentieth century.[3]

This presupposes pressing the woman and her epoch into the realm of the demonic. But the peculiarity of this princess and queen of ancient lineage is her middle class quality. Victoria and Albert lived a thoroughly bourgeois married life. In a photograph of man and wife dating from 1854, one senses a strangeness between them; Victoria is wearing the strange expression and clothes of an odalisque by Ingres. Artists and literary people were welcome at court; Felix Mendelssohn-Bartholdy

The Bourgeois Way of Life as an Alternative

prized discussing art affairs with Victoria and Albert. He composed his piano trio in C minor for her. The prince consort, Albert of Saxe-Coburg-Gotha, was a liberal, respectable family man with a love of progress and science. His speech in Mansion House a few weeks before the opening of the Great Exhibition of 1851 is filled with the naive trust of enlightened Manchester liberalism. "We are living," he said, "at a period of most wonderful transition, which tends rapidly to accomplish that great end to which all history points—the realization of the unity of mankind."[4]

This unified mankind, however, is at once conceived as a homogenized humanity. Woe to outsiders! At the height of the Victorian era, the Bible is once again, as in Cromwell's time, and in contradistinction to the aristocratic and libertine veneer of the Restoration and Regency, the solid spiritual and social foundation of everyday life for the English bourgeoisie. Declaration is made in the Bible of what is proper for woman and what is not. The Bible depicts that which God punished in Sodom. St. Paul only confirmed the curse. And the British Parliament is a Christian institution. Jews, however, are not equal. Lionel Rothschild in his unceasing and stubborn struggle to take a seat in Parliament could always count on a majority of votes from the electorate, but as a new member of Parliament he had to take a Christian oath, something this proud Jew from Frankfurt declined to do.

The biblical Christianity emphasized so much in middle class life, which mattered as much to the bourgeois pair Victoria and Albert as to the skilled working class, colored even the agnosticism of the natural scientists and the manner of life of working class leaders.[5] The heart of that Christianity was largely made up of evangelicalism. It proceeded from the conviction that a good Christian is recognized by his moral behavior. The English historian David Thomson explains: "In this sense it [evangelicalism] transcended all barriers of religious sect, and marked the religious outlook of a Quaker like Bright and of a High Churchman like Gladstone, a Low-Church Tory like Shaftesbury and a Presbyterian like Livingstone. It even colored the outlook of an agnostic like T. H. Huxley and a man like Disraeli, who although Jewish by race was a practising Christian. Its basis was biblical."[6]

Woe to the outsiders. They were declared in the Bible to be a scourge. There was to be no legitimation of women with weapons derived from the book of Judith. Just how mercilessly the bourgeois and biblical overriding principle toward conformity had already come to outlaw, then to expunge, those who broke out of society can be seen in the literature of the time. When Victoria ascended to the throne in 1837, the poetry of the exorbitant rebels (the partly Promethean, partly *Weltschmerz* figures of Byron and Shelley) had already grown out of keeping with the times. The English novel of the nineteenth century, I mean the Victorian novel here, knows neither the monsters of Balzac and Hugo nor the Julien Sorels. What it narrates is meant as a world within walls. Marian Evans failed at integrating herself into society; as the novelist George Eliot, however, she always remained within the walls of social convention. Only the hero of her last novel, *Daniel Deronda,* breaks with society and quits home and country—and he is a Jew.

Judith never becomes a theme of great Victorian literature. Neither does the sensuous seductress Delilah. German literature was long familiar with amoral seductresses, beginning with Goethe's Philine, Schlegel's Lucinde, Peregrina in Mörike, even Gutzkow's *Wally the Doubter.* Wedekind's Lulu—something he did not care to recognize—is a cliché in German literature: the message of the free and clear-sighted women of the *Sturm und Drang* and the early Romantic period had not been forgotten, not even by the Philistines who feared it.

The example of George Sand's life in France shows both the necessity and the possibility of proclaiming the Enlightenment as an earnest proposition, namely proclaiming integral equality for women as well as for men. Yet clearly George Sand's later life and writings demonstrate that scandal is in the end unable to simulate equality. Baudelaire learned that lesson early. And he himself proved in turn the incommensurability of an exorbitant *bohème* with bourgeois existence. He was well aware of why he took to E. T. A. Hoffmann and Edgar Allan Poe.

William Makepeace Thackeray depicted for English society the extremes of female outsiderdom in his novel *Vanity Fair* (1848). Becky Sharp is to English readers quite possibly the most odious figure from a novel in all of English literature. She too is marked with the double stigma of the stranger: she is half French and has her origins in the circles of Bohemia. Thackeray himself was an exponent of the Enlightenment and hated snobs, clodhopping squires, philistines, and pious hypocrites. His thoughts on aristocratic barbarians, the philistines of the middle class, and the coarseness of the mass of the people restrained and unenlightened very closely paralleled those of Matthew Arnold. And therefore it is a symptom of deep contradictions in the notion of equality that he conceived woman's longing for emancipation of her own individuality as the sorry intrigue of Becky Sharp.

The Bourgeois Way of Life as an Alternative

The lives of representative people can be interpreted as phenotypes. The courses of their lives then become (possible) social alternatives. The Victorian era, which is not understood here as peculiar to England, but as a manifestation of a European crisis within the bourgeois Enlightenment, provides a wealth of examples of this kind. George Eliot and George Sand demonstrate a double failure: that of famous conformity and that of famous scandal. Cosima Wagner attained that to which no other had succeeded: the integration, indeed even apotheosis, of a bastard and adultress. That is to say, she went over to the side of the counter-Enlightenment when its time had come.

George Eliot, or the Elimination of Offense

George Eliot's life reads like a novel by George Eliot.[7] The matters at hand are marriage and respectability; there is a woman caught between two men; there are the traditional beliefs transmitted by school and church and a ticklish, socially disadvantageous spirit of free thought, aristocratic hauteur, and the meekness of the little folk who allow their own customs to be decided by all of the above.

It is a path from provincial constriction, from some place called Arbury Farm in Warwickshire where her father, Robert Evans, worked on the estate of a member of the Newdigate family. Ever thereafter it was denied by Marian Evans (George Eliot) that her father had been a simple farmer. Perhaps he had indeed been a kind of steward. Mary Ann, who later adopted the spelling Marian, was raised in all the hierarchies and spiritual orthodoxies of a social order apparently still credible as a worldly and spiritual power. Interior asceticism was both duty and joy. The story of Dorothea Brooke's youth in *Middlemarch,* the most significant of George Eliot's novels, depicts this state of affairs; to all appearances as the author's remembrance of her own girlhood. When the sisters Celia and Dorothea go to divide up the jewelry they have inherited from their mother, "worldly" Celia wants to know whether Dorothea ever intends actually to wear her jewelry, to which she receives the proud answer: "Perhaps . . . I don't know how far I shall sink."

In those days this author of the later excessively philo-Semitic novel *Daniel Deronda* still held that all Jews were ugly and beneath the dignity of social intercourse. Her path would lead her from the provinces to Coventry, later to London, finally repeatedly to the continent: Geneva, Weimar, Berlin, Florence, Rome, Paris, Spain. She could speak, read, and write German, French, and Italian and read Greek and finally Hebrew. She grew to be a respected literary figure in London, known for her book reviews and editorial activities but above all for her translations of David Friedrich Strauss's *Das Leben Jesu* (Life of Jesus) and Ludwig Feuerbach's *Wesen des Christentums* (Essence of Christianity), the latter bearing her name, Evans, as translator. She also translated the Latin text of Spinoza's *Ethics,* but it remained unpublished in manuscript.

She was thirty-eight years old when her first book, a collection of three stories, was published under the title *Scenes of Clerical Life.* When this collection appeared in 1858 Marian Evans chose for herself the masculine nom de plume that was to become famous. In 1846 Miss Evans had received an honorarium of £20 for her translation of the three-volume Strauss work; the translator's name was not indicated. When she died in 1880, the novelist George Eliot left behind an estate of £43,000. A new publisher, inducing her to leave her own faithful Blackwood, who had published her works up to then, offered her an advance of £10,000 for one of her novels. It was a sum unheard of in those days for any English author. The book, by the way, a tedious Renaissance affair with the title *Romola,* was not a success, whereupon Eliot returned to Blackwood.

It is a career that shoots to the top. From the provinces to London, from naive bigotry to the ironic, literary craftsmanship of *Middlemarch,* the mastery which prompted Virginia Woolf to declare in 1919 that this "splendid novel" was one of the "few English novels written for adult readers." A career with a lavishly furnished literary salon not far from Regent's Park. Among its visitors were the biologist T. H. Huxley, the violinist Joseph Joachim, the poet Robert Browning, and of course her close friend, Herbert Spencer.

Eliza Lynn Linton, Marian Evans's erstwhile rival for the favors of the publisher John Chapman, provides a not altogether favorable picture, not only of the provincial and "unkempt" Marian of the first London years, but also of the later empedestaled George Eliot: "She was a made woman . . . but made by self-manipulation, as one makes a statue or a vase. I have never known any one who seemed to me so purely artificial as George Eliot. . . . But never for one instant did she forget her self-created Self. . . . She was so consciously 'George Eliot'—so interpenetrated head and heel, inside and out, with the sense of her own importance as the great novelist and profound thinker of her generation, as to make her society a little overwhelming."[8]

This self-constructed monument may have been artificial, but so too was the social position that was meant to be demonstrated. It was a position that had less to do with glamour than with scandal painstakingly kept at one step remove. Marian Evans had twice been driven from the homes of respectable citizens, allegedly for seducing the men of the house. The first time was from the flat of an elderly English pedant with whom she discussed positivism and theology so long that the man's wife felt called upon to show the visitor to the door. Mr. Casaubon in *Middlemarch,* who marries young Dorothea Brooke, is supposed to bear some of the characteristics of that Mr. Brabant. But Miss Brooke in the novel is comely and radiant; Marian Evans was plump, had a large nose and a protruding chin. A photograph has remained from those days from which George Eliot would later come to disassociate herself.

In January 1851 she moved into the London residence of the publisher John Chapman, who had published her translation of Strauss. Ten weeks later she was driven out, the result of Mrs. Chapman's alliance with Chapman's official mistress. Marian returned in tears to Coventry. She was then brought back to London by Chapman, who had meanwhile bought the *Westminster Review* and needed her as a literary collaborator.

But the real scandal in Victorian England began as a paradox, namely when Marian Evans decided to live with a man without the blessing of the church and without marriage certificate because he, for legal reasons, was prevented from marrying her. That must have been a year or so after she was driven out of the Chapman house, at the end of 1851 or the beginning of 1852. From then until his death in 1878, she lived with George Henry Lewes, adopted his Christian name in her pseudonym, and demanded of the world to be treated as Mrs. Lewes. It was something in which she met with no success. Lewes thought of himself as something of a free spirit and had lived for a time with his wife Agnes, and his friend Thornton Hunt and his wife, all together in a kind of commune that soon broke apart. Lewes had three sons; a fourth boy borne by his wife Agnes was Hunt's natural child. Lewes recognized this child as his own, thereby legally sanctioning the adultery. When yet another child from Mrs. Lewes's affair with Hunt needed legitimation, Lewes resolved to separate. Agnes went with Hunt, who later deserted her; Lewes was obliged to provide for all of the children. In this condition he met Marian Evans; the two set up a new household that lasted until his death.

It was a "free marriage," and consequently in Victorian England an impudent scandal. Lewes was unable to consider a divorce from Agnes; he had "forgiven" the sometime adultery and could therefore not make use of it in evidence. Even a reform of the civil statutes governing the divorce law did nothing to alter this state of affairs. And so Marian Evans lived in actuality as Mrs. Lewes without ever being it de jure. The consequences were appalling. Isaac Evans, her brother in Warwickshire, ordained for the entire family to have nothing whatsoever to do with her. She was to be an outcast. Only after Lewes died and Marian (who had in the meantime uncovered documents alluding to the deceased's occasional infidelities) had married John Walter Cross, her financial advisor some twenty years her junior, and was on her honeymoon in Venice with him, did a communication come from her brother. It was a note of congratulation to the now properly married Mrs. Cross.

Her brother's repudiation of her did more than simply hurt her feelings. In the lyrical cycle *Brother and Sister,* and especially in the relations of the Jewish brother and sister in her novel *Daniel Deronda,* this rejection has found a literary form. The Evans family simply reflected general attitudes. For decades George Eliot, despite her fame, lived the life of a woman whom one does not invite to one's house. Her letters never fail to mention the topic. Lewes is invited; she is not. On a single occasion a book dealer of some influence invites Mr. as well as Mrs. Lewes to a reception. But it is already too late. George Eliot declines the invitation.

Lewes was an intellectual of some merit, an essayist, popular science writer, and positivist critic of society, art, and mores. His book on Goethe is a classic in the ranks of nineteenth-century English books. Nevertheless the bond between these two remarkable people did not have the least effect toward altering public opinion. On the contrary, the unsanctioned liaison of a talented and successful man with a famous woman of genius only heightened their being outsiders. Everyday life was permeated with some manifestation of the scandal: the celebrities of the day, the male ones, were keen on visiting this salon, though as a rule unaccompanied by their wives. It had the aura of conversations with a hetaera. Marian Evans had decamped, arriving as a middle class Judith with pen in hand. A legal circumstance compelled her to play the role of the seductress with no legal ties, which despite her self-proclaimed lack of prejudice, was not of a piece with her emotions. Besides, it was not a matter of George Eliot's prejudice, but of that of the society around her.

The Scots writer Robert Louis Stevenson was one of George Eliot's younger contemporaries. He died in 1894 shortly before the outbreak of the scandal around Oscar Wilde. His story of the strange life of Dr. Jekyll and Mr. Hyde can be taken for a most penetrating parable of that social condition which in the name of bourgeois respectability allows only one alternative; either one renounces natural desire or one leads a compulsory double life. George Henry Lewes resisted this rule of the game when he neglected immediately to sue his adulterous wife for divorce. He did not wish to play the game of the respectable Dr. Jekyll because of his concern for the fate of a divorced woman and the then illegitimate child. Consequently he saw himself transformed against his will into a Mr. Hyde. The lawful husband of an unfaithful wife becomes the lover of a woman who acts scandalously in a twofold fashion: as concubine and as adulteress in a marriage that continues to be formally valid.

The woman's fame as a writer had only a damaging effect in all of this. Marian Evans was clear in her mind why she took a masculine nom de plume and did everything to preserve her anonymity as the author of George Eliot's books. As anonymity grew untenable in time, her apprehension of how the critics would react who dictated the moral code in the name of queen, church, and ruling class proved correct. If from then on one of George Eliot's novels seemed morally not up to snuff, the hue and cry was "No wonder! That can only be expected." If an exemplary moral subject matter was treated, the critic could then vent his indignation at the schism between real life and literature. One critic, pleased with one of her books, nonetheless spoke of her as a "polluted source."

The matter is not solved by thinking of the conflict in George Eliot's life as a mere historical reminiscence or by scoffing at the morality of old Queen Victoria and her age. Edward Bond took Victorian England to be still a very real and present influence when in his play *Early Morning* he interpreted the queen and her court as the quintessence of the most shocking scandals and named Florence Nightingale as the widowed queen's lesbian partner. Neither the scandal in George Eliot's life nor that in Oscar Wilde's at the era's end has become simply historical. A look at women authors of our own century (such as Virginia Woolf or Simone de Beauvoir) is sufficient to corroborate this thesis instead of disproving it. Simone de Beauvoir lived with Sartre in a relationship that might seem reminiscent of the Leweses'. Nonetheless she openly declared the insufficiency of feminine emancipation.

George Sand and Scandal

She reminded Count Alfred de Vigny at their first meeting of a museum painting of Judith.[9] They had met at a supper that his actress friend,

Judith and Delilah

Marie Dorval, had arranged for five people: her husband, the actor Merle; her lover, Vigny; the Baroness Dudevant, whose nom de plume was George Sand; and the latter's lover and literary partner, Jules Sandeau. George appeared in riding breeches and boots, to the displeasure not only of Monsieur de Vigny. "A woman of about twenty-five years of age," he noted in his diary. George Sand was then twenty-seven. "She looks like the famous Judith in the museum. Her hair is black and curly and falls down to her collar as in Raphael's angels. Her eyes are large and black, with a form the mystics have, and as in the loveliest Italian faces. Her serious face is rigid. The lower part of her face is less pleasant, her mouth a failure. Ungracious in posture, rude in demeanor. A man in her motions, in speech, in the tone of her voice, and in the boldness of her expressions."

She in turn, from the first moment on, did not particularly care for Alfred de Vigny. The writer she found remarkable; the man she rejected. She kept herself to the women, that is, Marie Dorval. Either this was all clear to de Vigny or he suspected it. In two of his letters to Marie he demands that she break off with this "damned lesbian." George Sand at twenty had caused a furor in the provinces, at thirty she was the admired *femme scandaleuse* of the Parisian salons; she was snubbed by the aristocracy and the bourgeois royal court; caricatured in men's clothes, in frock coat, trousers, and top hat, and was mistress to Prosper Mérimée, Alfred de Musset, and several others.[10] She was a thoroughly successful storyteller whose works were avidly read even by those who contumaciously avoided even the mention of her name. To this extent her life previews George Eliot's later fate in Victorian England. The difference was that she was living on the other side of the Channel, in Paris, in that memorable epoch between 1830 and 1848, a period between two revolutions. It was a period whose contributions to the spirit can be felt down into our own times. Among George Sand's friends were Balzac, Heine, Delacroix, and the socialist Leroux, whose ideas she stubbornly continued to support after the failure of the revolution and on into the Second Empire and the beginning of the Third Republic of 1870. Her son, Maurice Sand, became the mayor of their hometown of Nohant after the February revolution of 1848. Before her windows angry farmers assembled and cried, "A bas les communisques!"

Gossip and legends have distorted the real dimensions of this woman's life.[11] Various successful pieces for the theater, fictionalized biographies, and polemical writings were the fruit of George Sand's adventure with

The Bourgeois Way of Life as an Alternative

Alfred de Musset in Venice, where she cheated her bedridden lover with the man's physician. She is reputed to have destroyed Chopin's health, which is nonsense, since she, who was six years his senior, had lived with him in a common law marriage for nine years and the whole time had carefully taken heed of Chopin's great fear of scandal and of his Roman Catholic scruples. The break between George Sand and Frédéric Chopin had nothing to do with the passions of the heart as before in de Musset's case. It was the result of acrimonious differences in an adder's nest of familial relations: a mother of some stature and a daughter who hated and slandered her; a daughter who was successful for a time in winning Chopin over to her side. When her ally retreated, George Sand penned a farewell note that concludes quite nobly: "Adieu, my friend. May you recover soon from all your sufferings; I hope for that now, and I have reason to, and I thank God for this bizarre ending to an exclusive friendship of nine years. Send news of yourself now and then. It is unnecessary to ever mention the rest again."

Her friends and lovers had made names for themselves, de Musset, Chopin, Mérimée, Liszt, Balzac, Delacroix, the men of 1848, later Flaubert and the younger Dumas: the notoriety of her friendships with famous artists has tended to shift the focus away from this exceptional woman herself. It is not her talent as a writer that differentiates her from the many talented women of the European bourgeoisie who attempted to make a go of it in the masculine world and lead their lives beyond the supposedly fixed norms of "womanhood." Nor is George Sand of the order of enthusiasts like Rahel Levin-Varnhagen in her salon in Berlin, where the double scandal of Jewishness and feminine emancipation had to be forever counterbalanced. Her outsiderdom is more austere, more impersonal, than that of her friend Marie d'Agoult, the aristocratic countess, who traveled around the world with the famed Franz Liszt (who had no less fame as a lover), who raised four children by him only to lose him, and who finally came to revile him in the form of a novel written under the pseudonym Daniel Stern. Neither does the writer George Sand desire a revolutionary transformation in erotic affairs or in the makeup of the family as does the German Ida Countess Hahn-Hahn, who imagines herself to be a female Faust.

It is striking that these various attempts at emancipation by women in the so-called Romantic era in Europe between 1815 and 1848, whether detailed in their books or carried out in actual life, intersect with real, actual, everyday bourgeois life only as the exception. Jewish outsiderdom and aristocratic disdain of the bourgeoisie: both are to be found again and again in these lives of scandal undertaken by courageous women. Henriette Herz, Fanny Lewald, Rahel Levin, the Countess Hahn-Hahn and the Countess d'Agoult, Jewess students and Russian women aristocrats in the conspiracy of the social revolutionaries against the czar: in all of this the dialectical linking of *bohème* to revolution corresponds to that other dialectical pair of Jewishness and aristocracy in the process of women's emancipation. As late as the beginning of the twentieth century, the lives of a Lou Andreas-Salomé, a Rosa Luxemburg, or a Franziska Countess Reventlow corroborate this particular nexus or linkage of those outside the confines of the bourgeoisie. George Eliot's tragedy is connected to the fact that she was unable to transcend the ideology of the bourgeoisie, either through familial descent or through personal resolve.

George Sand too belonged to the aristocracy, even if to an aristocracy itself somewhat on the margin. George Sand, née Aurore Dupin, could just as well go by Du Pin de Franceuil. She came to marry a Baron Dudevant. In her death notice she is referred to as Madame George Sand, Baroness Dudevant.

There is no account of the celebrated woman's life that neglects to mention her curiously contradictory extraction. She comes from a mixture of European high nobility and Parisian plebs on the skirts of the underworld. George Sand's great-grandfather was Marshal Moritz of Saxony, a famous general and ladies' man, and an illegitimate son of August II, Elector of Saxony and King of Poland, by Aurore Countess of Königsmarck. Aurore Dupin, our George Sand, bore the Christian name of this ancestress. Moritz of Saxony had a daughter by a pretty Parisian girl; he refused recognition, but through the intervention of a Saxon princess the child was registered by the parliament in Paris, the supreme adjudicator in matters of marriage law, as the "natural daughter of the Marshal of Saxony." The French aristocracy acted in accord with this decision.

Moritz of Saxony was an illegitimate child as was his daughter; nonetheless both belonged to the aristocracy. The daughter of the marshal could, in consequence, be educated at Saint-Cyr, could marry a Count Horn, who died early, after him a Monsieur Dupin de Franceuil, who was sixty-one when he took Count Horn's twenty-nine-year-old widow as his wife. They had a happy marriage; a son survived, one Maurice Dupin, who was given the Christian name of his grandfather the marshal. He was the father of Amandine Lucile Aurore Dupin, the later George Sand.

The Bourgeois Way of Life as an Alternative

This was the paternal side. Illegitimacy but an aristocratic illegitimacy that enjoyed full recognition. To that came considerable wealth from grandfather Dupin. The country estate at Nohant derived from that inheritance.

Her maternal origins are to be found in a depraved Parisian twilight world at the end of the *ancien régime*. George Sand described this world in attempting to come to terms with it. Her grandfather had been a dealer in birds and flowers. "My mother was a poor girl from the streets of Paris." She and her sister were soldiers' sweethearts; under Robespierre, George Sand's mother was imprisoned. Maurice Dupin made her acquaintance during one of Napoleon's Italian campaigns; she was living at the time with an officer in Milan.

Maurice Dupin took the Marshal of Saxony as his model. He became an officer of the Revolution; Napoleon promoted him to the rank of lieutenant on the battlefield at Marengo. The portraits depict a handsome cavalry officer. His looks are reminiscent of the painter Théodore Géricault; both of them lost their lives early on account of a horse. He had married Sophie Delaborde on June 15, 1804, without the knowledge and against the will of his mother. George Sand came into the world in Paris on July 1.

After her father's death, the child was raised by her grandmother in an aristocratic ambience. Her mother appeared from time to time in her life from then on merely as a kind of shadow. An arrangement seems to have been struck with her. The girl's first lovers belonged to the landed nobility in Berry. At eighteen Aurore Dupin married Baron Casimir Dudevant, the natural but legitimized son by a serving wench of a Napoleonic colonel and baron. He is a lawyer. The marriage rapidly goes downhill; Dudevant drinks and chases skirts after the manner of country squires; he has no interest whatsoever in literature and art. There is a son, Maurice, afterwards a painter who takes the name Sand; a daughter Solange, who apparently is not Dudevant's child. As of 1828 husband and wife separate. Dudevant, later on, however, tries time and again to gain custody of the children, but fails.

A mass of illegitimacy in all of this but without the middle class scandal. What would have ruined a life in the case of Mary Ann Evans/George Eliot appears at first glance in the life of Aurore Dupin to be no more than a not unusual *piquanterie*. The *ancien régime* with its mistresses who were raised to nobility and somehow married off, placed more value on noble origins than on the blessings of the Church. That was the case for

Moritz of Saxony and for his daughter, George Sand's grandmother. Revolution and Empire had made the barriers between the aristocracy and the people, even between the upper classes and the underworld, permeable. Thus the marriage between Aurore Dupin's parents was not at all a scandalous occurrence according to the norms and mores of the erstwhile Bourbon aristocracy, much less according to those of the new Napoleonic one. The Baroness Dudevant was socially quite acceptable, both by origin and by marriage.

In *Lélia ou la vie de George Sand,* André Maurois's two-volume biography of George Sand, the first chapter, entitled "Aurore Dupin," is followed by the chapter "Madame Dudevant," succeeded by a third under the heading "George Sand."[12] Three names that stand for a process of development in her relations to society at large; her individual development, we see, corresponds closely to the larger historical developments about her. The writer George Sand, preexisting until then only in the Baroness Dudevant's little writings for her own amusement, first attained her own proper identity through the July revolution of 1830. The Bourbon restoration at an end, a precarious kingdom of and for the bourgeoisie under the aegis of the Orléans dynasty managed to set itself up for a while. All manner of social contradictions were now established, clearly visible to everyone, as the result of a revolution unable to consummate itself. Aurore Dudevant belonged to the aristocracy and to the common people, not to the bourgeoisie. It is this class, however, that is to rule from now on; King Louis-Philippe fiddles about being the perfect husband and daddy. James Rothschild rules the court and country. Ludwig Börne mockingly suggests that Rothschild should arrange a coronation for himself—in the Cathedral of Notre-Dame-de-la-Bourse (Our Lady of the Stock Exchange).

Aurore Dudevant respects the aura of bourgeois respectability to the extent it suits her. She regularly returns from Paris to her children and to Monsieur Dudevant in Nohant. She summarizes the situation in a letter to her mother dated May 31, 1831: "My husband may do as he likes; he should have mistresses or not according to his appetites; he should drink muscatel or water as he likes; he should save or spend money as it takes him; . . . it doesn't concern me; at the same time it is only right that this freedom that he enjoys should be reciprocal. If that were not so he would be despicable and loathsome to me—something he does not wish. I am, therefore, quite independent; I get up when he goes to bed; I travel to Le Châtre or to Rome; I come home at midnight or six in the morning; all of this is solely my concern."[13]

She had met a nineteen-year-old young man by the name of Jules Sandeau. He too was to become a well-known writer. She lived with him in Paris, and they wrote together. Writings common to the two of them were signed with the pseudonym Jules Sand. Then Aurore, without Jules's collaboration, wrote her first and immediately successful novel, *Indiana*. Marian Evans became George Eliot by coupling the Christian name, George, of her lover, George Henry Lewes, together with the common English surname Eliot: in the anxious attempt at feigning to be a male writer. Aurore Dudevant became George Sand by combining a part of her lover's name, Sandeau, with a common first name. From now on it is important to her to be known as *the writer* George Sand. This writer is a he. In contradistinction to George Eliot, the new novelist George Sand does not make the slightest attempt to cover up the fact of Mme. Dudevant's authorship. This is something that is directly connected with the content and purpose of her first novel, *Indiana* (1832).

"Indiana . . . is a type: she is woman, a weak creature who had the task of incorporating passions which are hedged in by laws, or, to tell the truth, are quite suppressed. She is volition in battle with necessity. She is love who blindly butts her head against all of civilization's barriers." So it stands in the novel's foreword. Samuel Edwards, an American biographer of Sand, has characterized her as "the first modern, liberated woman."[14] That is a subject to which I shall return. It is, however, correct that the novel *Indiana* for the first time makes the matter of women's equality the theme of a book that has a woman as its author. Moreover, Sand speaks in it of her own direct experience, of a woman's life between passion and law, love and marriage. Indiana is the name of a Creole woman. "She did not love her husband because loving him was required of her as a duty, and because inner resistance to any form of moral coercion had become second nature to her, a principle of life, a law of her conscience."

This Creole woman who finally is only able to decide on the rejection of both husband and lover, is, at the novel's end, returned by a noble Englishman—in the Enlightenment tradition of the eighteenth century—to a Rousseauan paradise in the West Indies. George Sand made use of accounts of the Ile Bourbon for that. It is the departure from the usual male scheme of a novel of a woman caught between marriage and free love that is remarkable. With the exception of the aforementioned Sir

Ralph Brown, the *deus ex machina,* men and their world, including their aspects as husband and lover, are spurned. Indiana desires absolute and untrammeled feeling and merely hits upon erotic opportunism. She is already a Madame Bovary but, at least for the moment, without the final victory of the Norman bourgeoisie.

The success of the book was sensational. Balzac wrote that "the book is a reaction of truth against the spread of phantasms, the present against the middle ages, intimate drama against the tyranny of the historical genre." Nonetheless the public took its theses to be nothing more than the stuff of a novel. When its author attempted to lead her life according to its premises, the scandal began that even in our own times flares up at nearly every mention of George Sand's name.

It is and was a reaction not simply limited to the bourgeois philistines of the "correct" salons and houses, especially of the French provinces. Alfred de Vigny was revolted, a friend like Heinrich Heine visibly irritated, the Prussian representative, von Bismarck, read Mme. Dudevant's books as so many obscenities despite the fact that what happens in them is usually quite virtuous, what with dissolute types from the nobility and gallant souls from the common people, particularly country folk.

What is really quite remarkable is the corresponding antipathy directed against George Sand from among a certain class of artist that grows more and more pronounced the more the disillusionment after 1848 deepens. In the romantic-democratic and protosocialist era before 1848, George Sand's doctrines of immorality, her attempt to break through taboos, her appearing in men's clothes freely following her erotic impulses come what may, not simply proclaiming emancipation but living it, all this was simultaneously a scandal for the bourgeoisie and a *succès de scandale* for the bohemians. Liszt and Delacroix and Balzac were all in a position to take a stand against the salons and respectable houses where Mme. Dudevant was unwelcome.

Yesterday's scandal, however, rapidly becomes today's mediocre conventionality. To the new aestheticism that no longer put its trust in Leroux or Proudhon but constructed aesthetic counterworlds instead, Sand appeared more and more to be merely an exceptionally doubtful variant of bourgeois moralism. Charles Baudelaire in his book, *Mon Coeur mis à nu,* provides one of the sharpest and nastiest attacks. The tone is artifically vulgar. "La femme Sand est le Proudhomme de l'immoralité. Elle a toujours été moraliste. Seulement, elle faisait autrefois de la contre-morale." One could not put it more cruelly. Sand is the close-minded philistine of immorality. She has always been a moralist. Only in the past she used to work at countermorality. "She was never an artist. She has the famous, fluid style beloved of the herd. She is stupid; she is cumbersome; she is garrulous; in matters of morals she has the same depth of judgment as a concièrge."[15]

Then there are her enthusiasms for the working population! For Baudelaire her success as a writer is only to be interpreted as a symptom of general intellectual decline. What he, the architect of "artificial paradises," discovered with his mean, antipodal eye, was the dialectic of scandal and bourgeois co-optation of opposition in the life of George Sand. It had begun as a physiological peculiarity, was transposed into erotic reality and the reality of literature, in the end to lead inevitably to disappointment, both George Sand's and her admirers'.

Baudelaire had sensed it. The scandal of this woman apparently so free, who disdained all constraints of bourgeois morals, who publicly cultivated adultery, who changed lovers, who was unfaithful because she desired to be true only to herself: this provocation had its source in a deficiency. It was a scandal that had not been entered into voluntarily; more than that: a scandal with limited liability. Her novel *Lélia* (1833) is probably this writer's most forthright work. She later came to hate its honesty, revised the novel extensively, in her old age spoke only grudgingly even of the revised version. She had uncovered too much of herself in it. Lélia is a woman who in all her *amours* seeks the gratification of her body without ever attaining it. She makes a pretense of being passionate in order to arouse her partner and thus to be aroused in turn. And so her life and not simply its erotic realm is broken in two in the all too familiar traditional duality of body and mind. "My dreams were too sublime. I could no longer lower myself to the gross, inordinate desires of matter. Without my knowledge there had come to be a complete break between body and mind."[16]

Our writer, in this a great deal ahead of her time, had followed in grandiose fashion this personality split down to the moment of copulation. "Instinct was in me a passion of my soul that lamed all power of the senses even before it was fully awakened . . . it was a wild flailing that captured my brain and was to be found there only. My blood turned to ice, wretched and faint under my enormous application of will."[17] In the face of this description medical terms such as frigidity or dual sexuality become inconsequential. The totality of failed emancipation was rife with consequence, however, because it reached far beyond the instance of one

George Sand. Where her contemporaries and even present-day biographers see and interpret the exemplary free decision of a woman who wanted to be both at once, Delilah and Judith with a pen, there was compulsive behavior—which says nothing against George Sand's courage and determination of attending to her compulsion relentlessly and at all cost. Yet as an unfree and compulsive scandal it could neither have a liberating effect nor provide an example. It was this that Baudelaire had in mind when he spoke of immorality issuing out of a sense of morality.

Sand's return then to the rich preserves of bourgeois-aristocratic archrespectability was predictable from the very start. Maurois, as a Jewish man of letters who has succeeded in being admitted to the Académie Française and is familiar with such processes, heaps praise on the later George Sand since she in her novel *Consuelo* has, as it were, retracted *Lélia*.[18] That is no more than a division into before and after, scandal and conformity, which contradicts the paradigmatic aspects of her life. Flaubert, who admired the later Sand, wrote a curious note to Turgenev after her death: "One would have to know her as I knew her to know how much femininity there was in this great man, how much tenderness in this genius."[19]

What remains is the drama of a woman's failure at emancipation. The rupture between provocation and assimilation familiar to George Sand in the social and erotic spheres and in her own writings, did not lead, as Maurois and other biographers have asserted, from scandal to the holding of court at Nohant. Everything was from the start a superficiality and a half-measure.

A Sand admirer like Simone de Beauvoir holds the whole business to have been a sham. Through her connection with Sartre, and through him to his work on the phenomenon of Flaubert, she came to reread the volumes of Sand's correspondence, at least to the year 1848.

I find the mask of virtue odious that she loves to put on. To take on lovers, to be unfaithful to them, to lie to them—why not? But one should not then make much of one's love of veracity. . . . At thirty she is already playing the woman broken and crippled by life, who sacrifices herself without reservation, while she in reality dominates her entire surroundings. What I forgive her least of all is the systematic falsification of her inner voice, by which she succeeds in prettying up whatever she happens to be doing into an example for the purposes of edification. There is such a fundamental untruthfulness evident here that I even come to doubt the stand that she takes in 1848.[20]

The Bourgeois Way of Life as an Alternative

It is precisely her behavior during the revolution of 1848 that displays all the moments of superficiality, of halfheartedness, a dilettantism, that takes up with the actors Ledru-Rollin or Barbès, but at the heart of it is uncommited, is simply voyeurism. A letter to Barbès imprisoned in Vincennes after the suppression in June 1848 of the workers' rebellion speaks clearly enough: "It is said that I have been the 'accomplice' of something or other. I don't know what. I have neither the honor for having done something in the matter, nor can I take credit for having done anything. I knew nothing, I understood nothing of what was happening; I was there simply as one curious, one astonished, one disquieted. It had not yet been forbidden by the laws of the Republic to belong to a group of onlookers."[21] Doubtless the letter is stylized; it was meant to be read by the authorities. And yet its contents describe the facts.

During the Parisian Commune in the spring of 1871 she is once again an onlooker but full of hatred for the communards. Her journal entry for March 23 is a mass of catcalls; it rejects as well the reactionary stupidity of the Versailles regime. When everything is over, Sand notes: "It is all over in Paris. The barricades are being removed, the corpses buried; simultaneously new corpses are being produced, for many are being shot and great numbers arrested. Many innocents, or half-innocents, are being made to pay for the guiltier ones who escaped."[22] What is guilt here and innocence? And still her inordinate desire to hand out advice, to revise proclamations wherein reading the Gospel according to St. John is recommended as practice for the new social order yet to be created.

Sand's daughter Solange despised her mother, who seemed to be conversant with motherliness only in men's company. There is a deep ambivalence everywhere in her life and writings. In the end her life seems typified by, modeled on, ambivalence.

The Countess d'Agoult and the Baroness Dudevant, who had so audaciously scorned tradition, were in the end so at odds with each other that the feminist Juliette Adam who had wanted to visit both was obliged to choose one over the other. Common to both of them, however, was an old age of complete recantation. A brilliant attempt at women's emancipation within an especially auspicious historical constellation proved itself a failure. George Sand's children became respectable citizens. There was no message to be transmitted further: neither that of Indiana, nor of Lélia, nor of Consuelo. The child produced by the adulterous liaison

Judith and Delilah

between Liszt and the Countess d'Agoult, the child who came into the world in ambiguous circumstances and who afterwards in her own marriage was forced into ambiguous circumstances, saw to the reerection of the tablets of the bourgeois commandments with a growing alacrity and rigor: Cosima von Bülow, the later Cosima Wagner.

5 Excursus: Otto Weininger, *Sex and Character*

The lowliest man, therefore, still stands *immeasurably* above the highest woman, so high indeed that comparison or a ranking of the two scarcely seems feasible.

The greatest, the single opponent to the emancipation of woman, is woman herself.

Otto Weininger, *Sex and Character*

Max Nordau used the phrase "a shot in the dark" when he first publicized Otto Weininger's work in an article in the Berlin newspaper, the *Vossische Zeitung*. That was shortly after Weininger, on October 4, 1903, had killed himself with a pistol shot in the Beethoven House in Vienna. He was twenty-three, and his book *Sex and Character* had appeared only a few months before. The sudden, posthumous fame of the young psychologist and cultural critic could only become tainted. The private aspects of his life were disagreeable: particularly the importunate accumulation of book, pistol, Beethoven. The debate, as if directed post mortem by Weininger himself, immediately headed off in the wrong direction. The question now was if *this* suicide could be used as confirmation or refutation of *these* scientific propositions. It came down to either a logical outcome or a self-contradiction.

In the preoccupation with his character and the workings of that character, any larger frame of reference, any notion of what was common to the times was overlooked. Weininger was no great solitary genius, isolated in his age, as he had supposed. "But the scientific, psychological, philosophical, logical and ethical foundations I had to construct to a very large extent myself," he explained in the introduction. The clumsy poking about in heterogeneous fields, psychology and philosophy, logic and ethics, appears somewhat dilettantish in a work that demonstrates anything but a dilettantism after the fashion of Houston Steward Chamberlain or some of the ambitious cultural résumés in Ludwig Klages. The

Judith and Delilah

association with such names allows situating Weininger and his propositions at a far remove from the popular debates so well loved at the
beginning of the century, debates on genius and madness in the tradition
of Cesare Lombroso, the Turin psychiatrist. (One still finds traces of
them almost a half-century later in the intellectual world of Gottfried
Benn.)

Otto Weininger, however, is far less the post-Nietzschean genius who
kills himself à la Kleist than perhaps indeed a genius in his own right
who brings to fruition the "demands of the times." His loneliness was
expected of him and certainly sought. The shock supplied by his writings
was greedily lapped up. If the reader's interest was first provoked by the
nexus of book and suicide, the formulation of its verdicts and the arrogant, in Nietzsche's sense, "fateful" *form* of the book fairly guaranteed
success. A summary by the publishing firm of Wilhelm Braumüller,
Vienna and Leipzig, in the "people's edition" of 1926 provides a list of
the various printings that *Sex and Character* went through.[1] The first
edition appeared in May 1903; the second in November, immediately
after Weininger's death. In January 1904, the third; by the end of that
same year, the sixth. A pause between 1911 and 1914; a further pause
after the outbreak of the war, but as of February 1916, the continuation
of the rhythmical success story. Two new printings (the eighteenth and
the nineteenth) in the first year after the war and revolution; the same
for 1920; in the year of inflation, 1922, two right after each other: the
twenty-third and twenty-fourth editions.

War, revolution, devaluation of currency, the demise of a middle class
in central Europe that had lived on annuities and had pursued literary
and philosophical interests, in all of this Weininger's book had remained
a sought after item. An additional feature of its success was Weininger's
incorporating in the book's finale the perspective of a renewed mankind—and that as early as 1903, several years before the Expressionists'
"crepuscule of mankind." Strangely disharmonious indeed Expressionism's theses of patricide and an essential maternal tie. In Weininger, quite
on the contrary, the conclusion is "The education of women must be
taken out of the hands of women; the education of the whole of mankind
must be taken out of the hands of mothers."[2] Did Weininger know that
he had almost literally paraphrased Sarastro in *The Magic Flute*, who had
put it to Pamina that "a man must guide your hearts, for without him
every woman is wont to proceed out of her own sphere of action."

What is passed on in *Sex and Character* is in the tradition of the Viennese

Enlightenment: an educational dictatorship in the hands of the bourgeois male. The final question, "Will woman let herself be governed by the moral idea, by the idea of humanity?" seemingly posed in trepidation and skepticism, was actually rhetorical. The male world as well as that of emancipated women in that prewar, then postwar epoch would not have it any other way. They were long since used to the barbiturates that Weininger promptly supplied: Culture is higher than civilization. Genius is qualitatively different from talent. The works of genius and intelligence are two different things. Jews are without genius. German humor surpasses Jewish irony. The Jews are "a ferment of decomposition" (something which Theodor Mommsen, whom we have to thank for this formulation, weighed quite positively—in contradistinction to its later usage). Soul means more than mind.

All of this was to be found assembled in Weininger as well. One could read there that woman is "alogical and amoral." The bourgeois male had always understood things thus, smiling at female nonlogic, filled with dread before Nana and Lulu. Weininger's work, with its vague and enormous title, *Sex and Character,* and its subtitle promising "an investigation according to principles," is at once a continuation and an anticipation. The assonance is apparent to titles like *The Foundations of the Twentieth Century, The Mind as Opponent of the Soul, The Fall of the Earth in the Spirit*: the works of Chamberlain, Klages, Theodor Lessing. *The Coming Things* of Walter Rathenau is prefigured, and Spengler's reflections on the Apollonian, Faustian, magic soul in *The Decline of the West*: "What is undertaken nowadays in the name of art is paralysis and prevarication; I mean post-Wagnerian music as well as painting after Cézanne, Manet, Leibl, and Menzel."[3] Spengler wrote those lines during the First World War, a decade after Weininger; he wrote them as a contemporary of Stravinsky, Bartók, Berg, Klee, Picasso, and Kandinsky. Tristan and Parsifal ornamented for Spengler "the end of Faustian music." Weininger, too, saw in Parsifal an extreme—and at the same time an end. Since modern civilization was thought by him to be growing increasingly "Jewish," therefore in a stage of decay and decadence, his conclusion was only logical, for Weininger had decreed that the Parsifal music would remain "a closed book for all eternity to the true Jew, as nearly unapproachable as the Parsifal saga itself."[4]

For all eternity. The latent, from time to time patent homosexuality of the book perhaps has to do with the man Otto Weininger's own personal impulses. It is of little import; of far greater import, however, are the analogous efforts of the "men's pacts" (*Männerbünde*) of the same time. Weininger wrote as a contemporary of the "circle" around Stefan George, as well as of the German *Wandervogel* movement, which was dominated from the start, following the studies of Gustav Wyneken and Hans Blüher, by homoeroticism and antifeminism.

If the book *Sex and Character* is to be taken in its propositions and in its reception as the expression of a particular social situation, then that situation must first be delineated in its own right. Weininger expressed a good deal of truth for a particular social stratum. His work was far from being simply the pointless ratiocinations of an unhappy genius it has been asserted to be by various feminist critics. On the contrary, his propositions disclose, and this is proven by the book's reception, the traumatic states of consciousness of the bourgeois orders in central Europe. For this to become evident, one has only to subject to a closer analysis Weininger's thoughts on the English and the working classes. The Englishman in *Sex and Character* fares scarcely better than the Jew. Strangely enough, Weininger does not include the whole population of the British isles but expressly contrasts (and in a positive fashion) the Scots and Irish to the English. The English were neither great architects nor outstanding philosophers, he says, not to mention their vacuity in the field of music. Since in *Sex and Character* the founders of religions—whatever is to be understood by that—are brought to stand at the very apex of superior humanity, the English are admonished for having produced nothing in that category. "Shakespeare and Shelley, the two greatest Englishmen, do not represent the pinnacle of humanity; they do not even begin to approach Michelangelo and Beethoven."[5]

The cadence of the Nietzsche epigone is manifest. The abrupt decrees offered without supporting evidence, which are to be found in such profusion here, anticipate Spengler's later judgments of sweeping damnation and seem to parody Nietzsche's weakest passages—that passage, say, where the revaluator of all values sets up a figure from the mass press like "Madame Gyp" as the most outstanding psychologist of her age.

Nietzsche played psychology against the psychologists; Weininger only displayed superciliousness toward them. "Let us never forget," he wrote, "that the soulless branch of science known as psychology proceeded from England. The English have always impressed the Germans as being productive empiricists, as being political realists as well as theoreticians, but with that their importance for philosophy is exhausted. There has never been a profound thinker who has remained at the stage of empiricism; and there has never been an Englishman who has proceeded beyond that stage of his own power."[6]

Psychology as an empirical science is for him a subaltern science. Jews are psychologists for Weininger, not philosophers; even Spinoza is not a philosopher. Psychology is a matter for women. It is a subaltern matter for them, too, namely "uncreative." Once again it would be missing the mark simply to reject such obviously unfounded theses as oddities. Weininger is a social phenomenon who is by no means an oddity but representative of and typical to his time. He stands between Nietzsche and Spengler as an intellectual power, and in the historical flux he is centered precisely there. Traces of his battle with empiricism, fought in the name of speculative social philosophy, echo late into the century: in Adorno's battle with positivism, or in the bitterly ironic reports of his experiences among the Anglo-Saxons and their always asking for scientifically verifiable evidence. Otto Weininger provided the principles of a philosophy of bourgeois culture at the beginning of the twentieth century that is romantic in its longing for lost creativity and regressive as the later German Romantic school was, not as that movement was at the start. What anxiety in him vis-à-vis the utilitarianism of a capitalism that replaces ostensibly incalculable genius by quantitatively measurable particular abilities and reduces talent to memory! In his nostalgia this author is the contemporary of Hermann Hesse's *Peter Camenzind*. Various aspects of an antibourgeois restoration of the feudal past to be found in Adorno's cultural critiques are presaged in Weininger, whereby strangely enough baroque Vienna assumes for Adorno the positive aspect as opposed to America as the negative, while for the Viennese Otto Weininger, the German-Jewish Vienna of the *Neue Freie Presse* is seen with the eyes of Jewish self-hate as an anticipation of cultural destruction. How much the partner of Karl Kraus he was in that!

Weininger possessed a fine mind, and it certainly did not escape him who had learned so much from hated psychology that his book *Sex and Character* had to be ascribed to Jewish self-hate. "One does not hate something totally alien from oneself. The fact of the matter is, it is the other person [we hate] who reminds us of what ugly and hateful characteristics we have in ourselves. And so too is to be explained why the most rabid anti-Semites are to be found among Jews."[7] To which I must add that there has been for some time a parallelism between German and Jew, noted by Heinrich Heine for one, which manifests itself in a German

Judith and Delilah

self-hate as a kind of vis-à-vis to the Jewish one. It is that "sorrowful suffering of men on Germany's account" (Thomas Mann's expression) that is exemplified by Hölderlin and Nietzsche and not only by them.

That this romantic-regressive anticapitalism of Weininger's was proclaimed to the world from Vienna is one more aspect of Weininger's representative significance. His book is eminently "cacanic"* in that it attempts to establish the worried minority of a minority as high judge in the court trial of civilization. The Germans of the Austrian motherland were the minority in the imperial conflux of nationalities under the Hapsburgs. As bourgeois elements they were the minority of a minority, for Austria was largely agricultural and composed of a farming population. Metternich had designed to keep out the institutions of capitalism, and it had not proved possible to counteract that condition of things with rapidity. The bourgeois Jews of Vienna in this picture, the conscious assimilators of an aesthetic mass culture, were quite the minority of a minority of a minority.

All of this is to be found shored up in Weininger, whose work is a document of preservation, of hate-filled self-disavowal, of a metaphysical plan for a "humanity" delivered from Jews and feminine decline of culture. Like Nietzsche, Weininger ventures a blend of cultural criticism and ahistorical utopia. To oppose the romantic regression, a manly and Aryan utopia is summoned up, which, however, in the name of Immanuel Kant, propagates none other than the bourgeois Enlightenment. That is to say, it wishes to reestablish the body of thought and teaching that lay at the foundations of Jewish enlightenment and emancipation.

Otto Weininger, born in 1880, was six years younger than Karl Kraus. There is in both of them sorrow over lost "origins" and common to both a marked Jewish self-hatred. The intonations of their concrete criticism of contemporary civilization are quite similar. Both are Kantian moralists. The difference is that Krausian metaphysics are one of decline and fall, whereas Weininger very much paints the picture of an emancipated humanity in the sense of the eighteenth century, where man, following Sarastro, guides the hearts of women.

It is at this point that the communality of Kraus and Weininger stops. The young man Weininger, quite apparently tortured by the anxieties of pubescence and filled with inhibitions, thought he had uncovered a

---

* Robert Musil's scatological neologism made up from the "k. u. k." (*kaiserlich und königlich*) epithet of the Austro-Hungarian government (translator's note).

parallel between Jewish existence and women's pandering and amorality, or, as he put it, between women's and Jews' "soullessness." Karl Kraus, on the other hand, and this is part of his greatness, in all his battles over morality and criminality again and again defends and mourns for the women victims of a dissolute man's world, even those "whores" whom Weininger so hatefully and disdainfully denounces.

Weininger time and again refers to Schopenhauer's and Wagner's metaphysics of compassion, yet he himself is no compassionate thinker. He merely ignores, though it belongs at the heart of the thematic of *Sex and Character,* or summarily discharges in the most trivial sense of an enlightenment not even entered upon, that trinity of "barbaric ways of life for women" that Frank Wedekind would come to denounce a few years after Weininger's suicide in his play *Hidalla*: harlotry, old maid-hood, virginity anxiously guarded for the purpose of landing a better marriage contract.

Karl Kraus quite clearly took Wedekind's position. A year after Weininger's death there was a private performance in Vienna organized by Kraus of Wedekind's *Pandora's Box.* Otto Weininger had understood Wedekind's "amoral" Lulu in much the same fashion as Dr. Schön, a character in *Earth Spirit,* understood a lesbian character he had wanted to force to do away with herself but by whom he is done in instead. Wedekind perceived Lulu's beauty and seeming soullessness, as did Weininger, as animality. Something that Weininger, however, reckons as her fault: "An animal has just as little metaphysical reality as an actual woman; the animal cannot speak, however, and consequently does not lie."[8]

This too is the *apologia* of a ruling men's and bourgeois code of morality. The topsy-turvy of Enlightenment and counter-Enlightenment is far more manifest in Weininger than, about a decade later, in Walter Rathenau, who, as far as the composition of their characters goes, is his close relation. Their conclusions were identical to those of the middle class youth movements of their day: friendship instead of sexuality; men's pacts (*Männerbünde*) instead of the eroticized, feminine forms of culture like theater or ballet; folk dance instead of the sex substitutes of can-can and waltz; loden costumes and not silk or velvet, which at one and the same time conceal and display; manly philosophy instead of feminine/effeminate psychology; Germans, not Jews.

One thing is evident in all this: the bourgeois Enlightenment proceeding over Ibsen came to plumb the limits of bourgeois blocks to consciousness all the more clearly and broadly the more decidedly the question of

Judith and Delilah

women's emancipation was made part of its own, men's, cause. I mean Karl Kraus, Wedekind, Heinrich Mann, G. B. Shaw, Brecht, Wilhelm Reich: it is a demonstration of the permanence of the Enlightenment and a rejection of a regressive and men's-pact antifeminism.

The opposing ranks are not unfamiliar to us: Strindberg, Weininger, D. H. Lawrence, Henry de Montherlant, Jean Genet, up to that phalanx of American dramatists and filmscript writers who glorify male potency and sexual dominance, ranging from Tennessee Williams up through the popular films of war and sports and violent criminality in the womanless world of the buddy. The connection to an antirational set of beliefs is everywhere visible, as is the connection to an elitist master's ideology. The class struggle is meant to be replaced by the battle of the sexes. That phenomenon had already made its appearance in Weininger, who, growing displeased after the fact with Richard Wagner's ephemeral attraction to the philosophy of Ludwig Feuerbach, had decreed: "Socialism is Aryan (Owen, Carlyle, Ruskin, Fichte)—Communism is Jewish (Marx)."[9]

That does not display much knowledge of the matter at hand. And Weininger would be embarrassed if he admitted, as he would have to, that his examples of "woman" are taken exclusively from an urban, bourgeois milieu where, in fact, his antithesis of "maid" and "megaera" might be apt on occasion. This exponent of the prebourgeois era grandiosely dismisses the matter of the particular characteristics of the farm woman, not to mention the women of the working class. They would not fit into his analysis. Otto Weininger is a reactionary thinker. The antithesis in which women are meant to be permanently constituted as outsiders once again ends up as Judith and Delilah, the vamp on the one hand and the woman with the weapon on the other.

6   Delilah as Bourgeois Vamp

Lulu and Other Female Demons

As the nineteenth century moved to its close, the great bourgeois heroines fell away into the past. In the boom years after the founding of the German Empire in 1871, they came to enjoy one last flourish: as figures on the stage, as the subjects of excessive and grandiose oil paintings, in common bourgeois life, which was wont to imitate somewhat the sublimity of the art before it. It was all conceived larger than life. So many women who love and hate in superhuman dimensions, who die and bring death to others: Medeas, Sophonisbes, Fredegundas, Brunhildas. No Joans of Arc.

Artistically and even intellectually they are imitative productions at one remove from a creative pulse. Nevertheless, no matter in what absurd appearance, an authentic bourgeois enlightenment once more goes through its paces. All these heroines, in a word, stand with equal rights against the hero. Behind so many theatrical demises there shines with an undiminished clarity the image of a duality of man and woman: I mean the human synthesis out of complementary difference. It is the hour of the Brunhildas. Paul Ernst, so much admired by the young Georg Lukács, here once again the ideological straggler from an earlier time, in his verse tragedy of *Brunhilda* (1909)[1] poses Siegfried's liaison with the unheroic Kriemhild and his desertion of Brunhilda as an offense worthy of death. Brunhilda causes Siegfried's death and thereby helps him back to his heroic identity. In dying he thanks her: "My thanks to you, Brunhilda, that you have slain me." She follows him in death.

That is an amalgam of Hebbel and Wagner. Nevertheless, surrounded by the then popular Lulus, Melisandas, and Rautendeleins—by the un-conscious, almost vegetative female figures of the neo-Romantics that ceaselessly propagate the isolation of the sexes—it has preserved the image, larger than life to be sure, of a sharing between man and woman, yet a sharing that reaches its consummation only in death. One may be inclined to smirk at all these Brunhildas, yet they are for one last time the conscious continuation of the wives of an earlier bourgeois period, Pamina with her Tamino, Leonore with her Florestan, Brünnhilde and her Siegfried in Wagner's tetralogy, who remained, for their part, true to this Enlightenment postulate.

That which even the acutest critics of bourgeois life were unable to provide themselves, a heroic overtone to love and wedlock, is evoked toward the end of the nineteenth century, on the operatic stage. Ibsen did not provide his Hedda Gabler a beautiful death in common with her lover, neither did Flaubert deem such fit for Emma Bovary. But Isolde, Brünnhilde, and Aïda die a *Liebestod,* which, to be sure, does not end a communality and sharing in life with dignity and love, yet at least provides a unification of hero and heroine in death.

For one last time, that vision of a better humanity, the vision of the elevated or idealized couple made its appearance in a bourgeois world in which all relations between the sexes and the generations had become increasingly reified. That such couples could only come to the fore on the opera stage, surmounted by music, consequently dematerialized, was a consequence of the matter. In the chapter "Fullness of Harmony," the author of *The Magic Mountain* analyzes the death scene of Radames and Aïda as both reality and unreality.

When Ernst Bloch interprets the communality of the "high couple" as a utopian appearance and wonders why Bachofen in his studies of matriarchy passed over precisely this duality or communality, and as Bloch puts it, "always sets up either man or woman alone on the seat of the matriarchal/patriarchal principle,"[2] the utopian nature of the high couple concept becomes all the more evident. Bachofen resembles his colleague Nietzsche despite all divergence in that he proceeded from the material fact of a falling apart of the male and female principles in the bourgeois world of his day. He then assumed this to be a permanent structural antinomy and attempted to discover it in the historical and prehistorical past. In a reverse fashion Ernst Bloch's anticipatory thought, his continuation of the bourgeois Enlightenment tradition, is manifested precisely in his utopian evocations of the heroic community of man and woman. "In this the high couple has developed a most characteristic desired image of marriage . . . man and wife are imagined here as a concentric

Delilah as Bourgeois Vamp

image, the one graceful and providing, the other vigorous and ruling; but it is only their bond together that becomes beneficial."[13] Yet one has to admit that even this is a patriarchal formulation: duality or community is not postulated as equal opportunity but as complementarity through the social division of labor.

Frank Wedekind's double drama having Lulu as central figure was composed during the years 1892–94.[4] It came into the world at the same time as the beginnings of imperialism, the philosophy of inequality and of the great individuals, political aesthetics and aesthetic politics, at the same time as the nationalistic decisionism of the European superpowers, the excesses of prudery in private life, at the same time as an anti-Semitism for the first time institutionalized and politically organized; one needs only recall here the Adolf Stöckens and Karl Luegers in Berlin and Vienna.

It can be supposed that Wedekind was scarcely aware of these developments. What was essential to him was the negation of bourgeois morality and its replacement by new kinds of relations between the sexes. The new vision, which Wedekind later characterized in *Hidalla* as the overcoming of "the barbarous forms of life" for women in bourgeois society, is based on three fundamental theses: on the fundamental antagonism of the sexes, which does not allow for an independent equality of each; on the failure of the institution of bourgeois marriage in the face of this phenomenon; on women's right to erotic "magnanimity."

By calling his double drama *Earth Spirit* and *Pandora's Box* a tragedy, Wedekind explicitly places himself, despite all "unclassical" stylistic devices, in the heroic-classical literary tradition. This dramatist negates all of Naturalism's recipes. There is in his dramas, particularly in the two dealing with Lulu, neither a palpable psychology nor discursive conversation that could provide any kind of explanation or commentary to events. Neither is there any kind of intelligible machination in the manner of traditional conspiracy or intrigue. Wedekind's dialogues are confused; everyone talks past everyone else. The characters are driven; they do not plan what they do. Where one does in fact plan, as does Dr. Schön, all cabals fall undone before Lulu's primordial corporality and end up no less disastrously than Lulu's earlier so-called marriages.

The famous scene of exposition (*Earth Spirit*, I, 7) where the painter Schwarz, who will later slit his own throat, asks the woman about belief and the soul and love only to have her respond "I don't know" is une-

Judith and Delilah

quivocal. As much as Lulu otherwise lies, here she is speaking the truth. The subjective evidence of nonknowledge.

The nonrationality that has severed thought and action from each other, severed body from soul, so that Lulu's identity can come to realization only by offending against norms of social life that remain meaningless for her since she knows nothing of them, brings in its wake the dehumanization of this woman. That was in fact how Wedekind conceived it. The animal trainer's prologue done after the fashion of a street minstrel must be taken in complete seriousness.

Lulu is the serpent in this paradise. The animal trainer, whom Frank Wedekind loved to portray on the stage himself, explains to the audience: "She was made to be ruinous, to egg on, seduce, poison—to murder with no one sensing it."[5] These are concepts of the bourgeois (and male) order that must be quite foreign to a serpent, the true wild and beautiful animal so praised by the animal trainer. But with that Wedekind, if with the opposite accentuation, anticipates all of the theses Otto Weininger was to bring to expression a decade later. A profound differentness is expressed in the facing off of the two sexes. Weininger, as little as his model Nietzsche, could not free himself from Immanuel Kant; his vision of a future humanity is to be sure an exclusive male world, yet a humane one. Woman, like Wagner's Kundry, is reduced there to "serving." Frank Wedekind is no Kantian; his brand of enlightenment, it cannot be denied, separates the processes of individual emancipation, particularly of women, from all questions of social emancipation.

In Martin Kessel's long essay, "Frank Wedekind's Romantic Inheritance,"[6] Friedrich Schlegel's *Lucinde* of 1799 is compared with Wedekind's *Lulu,* which was first performed on February 25, 1898, in Leipzig. But Lulu is no Romantic creature; she is neither discursive nor emancipated like Friedrich Schlegel's eponymous heroine, that heroine so despised by Schlegel's contemporaries as being obscene (a consequence of which was Schlegel's banning the heroine and the novel from his collected works after his conversion to Catholicism.) Kessel must admit that "while Lucinde's consciousness is ingenious through and through . . . that is to say, while she aestheticizes, something lost on Lulu, Lulu's consciousness is completely instinctual, tacitly expansive."[7] Between Lucinde and Lulu there stretches a century of failed Enlightenment. Schlegel's heroine is no Delilah; she is neither traitorous nor unconscious. She was conceived in the human spirit of equality, and in that was not only chronologically a close neighbor to the ethos of *The Maid of Orléans* of 1801, something about which the Romantics in Jena might jest. Lucinde was modeled on the actual life of Dorothea Mendelssohn. She has to do with that short-lived moment between the end of the *ancien régime* and an as yet untried, yet nonetheless earnestly meant bourgeois citizenship of complete equality. The woman with intellectual weapons is still recognized by man's world here; indeed, even the woman who practices a free selection of partners and a no less free changing of them.

This is soon taken back. Lulu too is such a retraction. She is no longer a partner but someone totally alien who withdraws from all communality. Not heady with consciousness like Lucinde but dumb, without words. Not part of a human couple, whether high or low, whether Pamina or Papagena, but nonhuman, a wild, beautiful animal.

Beyond that, Lulu is a trauma to men. She is once again the treacherous woman who brings ruin. No longer in her incarnation as dame of courtly intrigue, as in the novels and theatrical pieces of the eighteenth century; not even as a bourgeois Judith, the woman with a weapon. Merteuil in Laclos, Marwood in Lessing, Judith, and Ortrud were all women who destroyed with plan and reason. Unconsciousness was their least fault. The female demons in Lulu's retinue are existentially unconscious.

The great anticipation in this development was Carmen: the gypsy woman, that is, the woman without rights and morality who belongs nowhere. It is a strange path from Prosper Mérimée's Carmen novella of 1846 to Bizet's opera of 1875. Mérimée was still fascinated by the exoticism of the gypsies; Carmen is described indirectly by the report of the condemned Don José Lizzarrabengoa as he awaits execution. Bizet's opera, with its sensational success, has its chronological place precisely between *Aïda* of 1871 and Camille Saint-Saëns's opera *Samson and Delilah* of 1877.

As at the beginning of the nineteenth century when the conceptions of women of Schiller and Beethoven were rapidly displaced by Kleist's or Hebbel's long-suffering females and seductresses, so too now, in a similar manner in a period gradually announcing the last days of the bourgeois era as a time close at hand, the concepts of a more and more disavowed high couple with a common *Liebestod* are confronted by operatic worlds in which men and their female seducers are completely alienated from one another. On the one hand Aïda and Brünnhilde, on the other Carmen and Delilah.

One can still follow the reasoning behind Carmen's actions. She always seeks out the stronger and more successful man: the better man, in a

Judith and Delilah

word. And the Delilah of the operatic world is the traditional seductress, a Philistine, a tool of the priests enjoying seduction and treachery. Lulu, however, evades any such explanation. She is neither foreign Philistine nor gypsy. Her femaleness itself is the cause of her strangeness. A writer in the Enlightenment tradition by the name of Frank Wedekind came to create the new female phenotype for the counter-Enlightenment: the bourgeois Delilah.

Another writer in the Enlightenment tradition and admirer of Immanuel Kant, as well as of women, supported him. I mean Karl Kraus. As Nietzsche in his time was fascinated in a completely ambivalent way by the gypsy Carmen, far beyond any enthusiasm connected with the music, so Karl Kraus looked to Lulu and was captivated. There must have been corresponding inner attitudes to the famous photograph showing Nietzsche together with Paul Rée as draught horses behind whom sits the seductress with whip in hand: Lou von Salomé. Kraus's introductory speech to the first performance of *Pandora's Box,* put on by himself in Vienna on May 29, 1905, is a strangely ambivalent document of emancipation and counteremancipation.[8]

The speech was delivered before an audience that Kraus had himself selected and invited. He was in a position to speak more openly there, better protected against ignorant misunderstandings than in one of his usual evening lectures. And so he allowed glimpses into his own intimate relation to the dramatic character Lulu, glimpses that penetrate all stylizations and provide a presentiment of that Karl Kraus who would only be discovered decades later in the letters to a woman he loved. It is the speech of one who suffers on the account of love and who is capable of enjoying this suffering. Proceeding from Alwa Schön's and the Countess Geschwitz's alliance to protect Lulu, who is indifferent to both, proceeding from this "alliance of a heterogeneous sexuality," as Kraus puts it, he invokes the world of the Shakespearean sonnets. "O, what a mansion have those vices got / Which for their habitation chose out thee." This is Shakespeare's "dark lady," but it is at the same time Pandora, in this case Lulu. Then follow two astonishing sentences. "One can call it masochism, to use that silly medical term found in novels. Yet it is perhaps the fundament of the artistic sensibility."[9]

The inequality of the sexes is postulated here, not to say longed for. To men's notions of domination and ownership, at which Kraus ceaselessly aimed his sarcasm, the attitude of submission is found preferable.

Delilah as Bourgeois Vamp

Let woman reign: lovelessly, treacherously, thanklessly. It is all right with Kraus as it had been with Alwa and the Countess Geschwitz.

Toward the end of this speech delivered to an audience of theatergoers, one finds stated, at first as if assuagingly, that Lulu's wretched and horrible end might simply be taken as her creator's moral condemnation of her. Whether Wedekind might actually have tended toward such is left unasked. Whoever might find no favor with the material in a play like *Pandora's Box* had then at least the author's moral intentions to identify with. "It is unfortunate. For *I* hold such intentions for bad enough. I see in the figure of a woman whom men think they 'have,' when in truth they are had by her . . . the complete vindication of immorality."[10] Kraus meant it as high praise. His notions of emancipation oppose the ideas of male property ownership or patriarchal inequality. Nonetheless, it is not equality that is aspired to here, but inequality stood on its head. Wedekind apparently, despite the horsewhip and the business of the animal trainer, wanted it no other way—as Kraus informs us.

That Kraus in his apotheosis of Lulu was also formulating his own thoughts and speaking for himself is something early discovered and commented upon by Walter Benjamin.[11] Taking as his start one of the *Fackel* editor's aphorisms, "Hunger can make any man into a journalist, but not every woman into a prostitute," Benjamin lays bare the underlying corresponding assumption, that the man refuses journalism by becoming a literary writer, and he thereby establishes the woman who lives only for sex and is the incarnation of it and who then abstains from harlotry. This is the correspondence between Lulu and Karl Kraus. "For night is the mechanism of contact and change," Benjamin interprets the matter, "where intellectuality turns into sexuality, sexuality into intellectuality, and both these contrary abstractions, recognizing each other, come to rest."[12] Benjamin's sharp, perhaps even malicious eye, caught one other thing: Kraus understood himself as being Jack the Ripper, Lulu's murderer. He was the last of a line, just as Karl Kraus, displacing and negating all journalists, in language, in woman, wanted to be the last, the epigone. "How he keeps his step to the rear," says Benjamin, "and seeks the farther path of the epigone in order finally to end the pleasure of the line with the last thrust—which Jack has at the ready for Lulu."[13] Masochism and sadism are complementary phenomena. One has a notion why Karl Kraus kept a respectful distance after reading Benjamin's analysis and claimed not to have understood everything exactly.

Since the beginning of the twentieth century Lulu dramas have been more and more successful. The reason is not to be found in a relaxation of bourgeois morality. On the contrary, Lulu was victorious at the very same time in Germany that the sex lives of Krupp, Eulenburg, and Moltke were being publicly dissected, when a new era of suicides and scandals came to be celebrated. In the assorted texts authored by Karl Kraus on the theme of morality and criminality, the social context is carefully preserved. Lulu was not victorious despite the prudery but on account of it. She is its triumph.

Wedekind's Lulu was to become a central figure in the literature of warning, precisely like the popular tale of Doctor Faustus at the end of the sixteenth century. The literature of warning, however, is always ambivalent. One reads it filled with both fright and delight. It demonstrates where one ends up if one does not have oneself under control (in which a more universal control is glimpsed). Faustus is taken away by the devil; Lulu meets her end as the victim of someone who murders for kicks. Christopher Marlowe recognized very well, since he had gone over to the side of the outsiders, what had drawn him to the tragic history of Faustus. Wedekind, no matter what he may have intended, presented the picture of a system of domination turned upside down, in which a woman first as seductress subjugates men (and lesbians as well), only to be progressively overtaken by an unabiding revenge as if in irresistible slow motion. The carrier of that revenge is not the world of men but time itself. It had established the old, men's, system of domination and ownership. It is there as if confronting Lulu in the London harlot's apartment in the lovely portrait of her done by the painter Schwarz, a counterpart to the London picture of Dorian Gray.

Lulu had lived without belief, without love, without hope; that understanding of the drama was there from the start. She had wanted to replace an existing inequality with a new, inverted one, if it is even permissible to speak of something like an act of volition in her. She too was doomed to end like Doctor Faust. God the Father did not show her mercy; neither did any principle of femininity.

The outsider Judith, even in her bourgeois guise, came to realize herself by means of rational, planning inner reflection followed by a consequential act. She was a mistress of discourse. The outsider Delilah, even appearing in the world of the bourgeoisie, is wordless and without intellect. She realizes herself in dance. Carmen's and Salome's dance of seduction; Lulu dancing on the stage seduces Dr. Schön in his box so that he signs his "warrant of execution." Dance and death are enmeshed.

Delilah as Bourgeois Vamp

Indeed, even Hofmannsthal's Electra, who is discursive and a woman with a weapon, having both the buried ax and the goading remark, ends in dance. The seductive and intentionally murderous dance in the instance of Karl Schönherr's drama, *The Female Demon*,[14] drew catastrophe in its wake as well. "This impoverished season, buffeted by the events of world history, has in the end had the privilege of seeing a dramatic masterpiece," was the way the *Berliner Tageblatt* put it in April 1915, after Max Reinhardt, simultaneously with the Burgtheater, had produced the premiere of this play by the Tyrolean Schönherr.[15] It was the time of the First World War. For Kraus *The Last Days of Mankind* had begun, yet a bourgeois audience "buffeted by the events of world history" found delight as much then as ever in she-devils. This new dramatic masterpiece, which had originated in the war year 1914, simply translocated the Carmen story to a Tyrolean farmer's ambience: smugglers, customs officers, and the female devil. Unity of space, time, and action. This time, however, the diabolical world of women is simply interpreted as an inferior outsiderdom. The formula being, woman equals she-devil. Carmen was a gypsy; Princess Salome could be understood from the viewpoint of childish morbidity; Lulu came from Schigolch's underworld and returned there. Schönherr, however, as would later become popular among the Expressionists, deindividualized his three characters. The man, his wife, a young customs officer—those are the parts. A farm woman who at first seems shy but who is strong, sensual, and married to a man who is not up to her. The seductress in the everyday farm world. It is meant to be understood as a *Cosi fan tutte*. The woman devil wishes the destruction of the two men. The customs officer knifes the husband and collapses. The woman "throws off her apron and runs off through the front door, slamming it shut with a bang." But this is no Nora who has learned to see. No, the she-devil will be up to more devil's work. One supposes that she will dance once more. "Hey, look how I dance. Especially for you. Hopstrallala, hopstrallala! (During the dance she holds the customs officer captive with her eyes.)"[16]

Delilah is the archetype. Neither Carmen nor Salome nor Lulu were that. They had been meant as warning and were denounced as outsiders, yet taken up with enthusiasm. The she-devil, on the other hand, denounces the entire species. This farmer woman has the devil in her body, and she knows it. The young customs officer provides the appropriate vocalization: "Woman, you have seven devils in your body."

The Last Days of Mankind have dawned. They are men's work, as Karl

Kraus gives us to understand. The unutterable, high-falutin Schalek, a young woman journalist of the *Neue Freie Presse,* who arrives at the front and puts on the airs of a Reinhardt premiere, and who wants to "pop off a shot too," is displayed as a virago. It seems to be perfectly all right then to bring the female devil under control: at least to get her out of the works. Otherwise she might gum up the consummation of men's work. There is no bourgeois Aristophanes, you see, who conjures up the counterpart to a Lysistrata.

Friedrich Dürrenmatt's Old and Young Dames

Establishing connections and relationships between Schönherr's marriage tragedy of Tyrolean peasants from the first war year of World War I and the play *Sodom and Gomorrah* by Jean Giraudoux, which was first produced in occupied Paris on October 11, 1943, scarcely three months before Giraudoux's death, is not quite the arbitrary matter one might think. Giraudoux had failed as a politician at the beginning of the war in 1939. His drama deals with the decline and fall of Sodom and Gomorrah, the two cities destroyed by heavenly fire. An end of the world, in a word, as in *The Last Days of Mankind.* The archangel cannot prevent the destruction. The world meets its end, for Sodom and Gomorrah are not for Giraudoux, as they are for Proust, synonyms for partial aspects of the world: they are the world as such, and it must meet with utter destruction.

Why is that? Because no single happy couple composed of man and woman is to be met there . . . neither as high couple or low. Everything has disintegrated into two separate worlds, one for women, one for men. That has meant sterility and barrenness, for which reason God decides on destruction. The angel secures a delay. If a single happy couple can be found, the world may continue.

Those are the terms. Two lovers, Lia and Jean, the man with the same first name as the author, are meant to save the world. They even discover what is supposed to happen and are on guard. The experiment proves a failure. No happy couple can be found. The world of Sodom and Gomorrah perishes in fire and brimstone.

The person who bears the guilt for that—and this remains perfectly clear despite a certain varnishing over in the play—is the woman. Giraudoux always had wanted to demonstrate the profound inhumanity of women in his dramatic works. Helen (in *The Trojan War*) and Isabelle and Ondine are in no case partners of a man whom they assert they love.

Delilah as Bourgeois Vamp

They are always completely alien women who reject and recoil from any bond. Helen is the cause of Troy's destruction, as Ondine is the cause of the knight Hans's death and Lia the destruction of the world. This playwright's dramatic figures are no female devils and Lulus. They are not evil; they do not even know what that is. The German Romantic tradition may echo throughout—and not simply in *Ondine*; nonetheless the substance of these dramas is not historical, but concerned with the present day. The man and author Jean Giraudoux has at bottom one sole theme: the profound otherness of man and woman, a divergence of the human and the not-quite-human. It is here that the concept of the happy couple meets its doom and with it the concept of a happy world.

"La scène continue" was the way the play about the destruction of Sodom and Gomorrah ended—which is to say this was an artificial end of a world; the one for the real world grows apace. In either case, destruction comes at last. The dramatist Friedrich Dürrenmatt, after the end of the Second World War, did not differ any from Giraudoux in this. His comedy *The Marriage of Mr. Mississippi* had its premiere in Munich on March 26, 1952, and was subsequently performed throughout the world.[17] The end of the world as comedy. Gottfried Benn, a critic of the work, argued that it was, instead, an "existential tragedy."[18] Nonetheless Dürrenmatt is quite right with his appellation of genre based on the assumption that the present day is incapable of tragedy. The only thing that still reaches us is comedy.

Tragedy presupposes that the characters are capable of individuation. But in the world of Dürrenmatt they are interchangeable. What are conservatives like Mississippi or revolutionaries like Saint-Claude? Are they gentlemen or ingenious criminals? They are as inauthentic and reversible as the ideologies supposedly represented by them. Only comedy gets at that, a comedy that does not exclude murder and death. Benn mistrusted the game played here with the categories of time and place. His way of thinking continued to proceed from a genuineness of loving, thinking, dying, a genuineness that Dürrenmatt had rejected as being frivolous.

Between the two male activist figures in the play, on the one hand, and the utopian Don Quixote, Count Übelohe (who can only be described as a near-cousin to Ernst Scholz in Wedekind's *Marquis von Keith*), on the other, there stands the woman Anastasia. Lulu as Anastasia. Tilly Wedekind laid bare that character's literary antecedents and brought suit against Dürrenmatt for plagiarism. The defense, delivered as the

"Confessions of a Plagiarist,"[19] gives one to recognize that while Dürren-matt continued with the language, mise-en-scène, and artificiality of the Wedekind dramatic type, nonetheless he was never in a position of cre-ating a female existential counterpart to the three male ideologues à la Lulu. Anastasia is not Lulu. She converses as a man, kills as men do, perhaps loves Übelohe a bit, wants to have power and possessions and injustice as much as the men. Tilly Wedekind, the Lulu of the perfor-mance Karl Kraus had arranged, felt obliged to expose Anastasia as a plagiarism of Lulu, Effi, or Franziska, the seductresses in Wedekind's dramas. But Anastasia is certainly not that. She is a male artificial char-acter declared to be a woman: that is to say, is the technical way out for a dramatist who is creating models for a universal theater, but one from which women have been removed. Yet not so completely. As long as Dürrenmatt took the Lulus as his model he was only able to produce figurines up to the point beyond Judith and Delilah and Lulu where he discovered his own specific world of women.

It is the world of the old dames. They have nothing more in common with Delilah, although they are the incarnation of seduction and destruc-tion to a far greater degree. They carry a weapon as does Judith. The weapon is incalculable wealth in the case of Claire Zachanassian, who pays a visit to the liquid manure town Güllen; or in the case of the psychopathic woman psychiatrist in *The Physicists*, the weapon is a formula for universal destruction with which she manipulates at will.

Once again a social phenomenon is not to be understood here by simple psychological interpretation. The appearance of the old dames is far more than a speciality of the individual dramatist Dürrenmatt. Gi-raudoux's posthumously produced comedy of the *Madmen of Chaillot* had already arrived at the point of replacing the Helens and the Ondines with quite sexless old dames incapable of an erotic partnership and certainly not even desiring one. Under the direction of their madwoman Aurélie they had planned world salvation, and practiced it, at least in Paris. The witch of the fairytale, the wicked queen, becomes the female demiurge of a cleansing of the world of speculators and warmongers; she becomes the matchmaker of happy marriages as well, for Sodom and Gomorrah were not completely and forever destroyed after all.

Dürrenmatt took over the old dames; in *The Physicists* his character Mathilde is even provided the madness that Aurélie had had in Girau-doux. Yet the difference in his world of old dames is the complete negation of any utopia. An entire legally constituted state that is the guarantor of law (Güllen in *The Visit of the Old Dame*) can be bought as long as the payment is high enough. Even the physicist Möbius's sacrifice in attempting to save the world by sequestering the universal formula is pointless because the old dame is nonetheless unimpeded in her efforts at putting together a trust for world domination and destruction. Dürrenmatt's *Physicists* is for its part literature of admonition. In order to preserve the world, he intimates, one should mistrust the great individuals, the activists as well as the saints. "What concerns all of us can only be solved by us all," he concludes in the seventeenth thesis to his comedy.[20]

Harold Pinter, *The Homecoming*

Whoever has read *The Homecoming* or seen it performed on the stage is carried back seventy years, back to the world of Lulu.[21] The new Lulu is called Ruth in Pinter, if that is actually her name. Even in Wedekind "Lulu" was a name casually applied. The head of the Pinter family in *The Homecoming* bears the unmistakable characteristics of Wedekind's Schigolch. The artist and wrestler Rodrigo in his incarnation here becomes the boxer Joey. In *Pandora's Box* Rodrigo had boasted: "I mean to make the most pompous trapeze artist out of her, and am ready to wager everything on it. But then I'll be the master of the house and will pick out the cavaliers myself who she'll have to entertain." As far as the substance is concerned (but not the language), that could just as well be in the second act of Pinter's play when dad and the two boys, only barely tolerating their visitor, namely Ruth's husband, plan out the details of Ruth's life as a callgirl.

It is quite apparent that the actor and dramatist Pinter was well acquainted with Wedekind's works. He expressly gave the name Lulu to a young and somewhat vulgar little thing in *The Birthday Party*, first performed in 1958, seven years before *The Homecoming*. It is evident that Pinter's *Homecoming* is as much consciously in the Wedekind tradition as I have tried to show is the case for Dürrenmatt. Anastasia is now the wife of a professor of philosophy somewhere off in California, soon to become a professional on the "meat rack": so many steps in the literary history of Lulu's influence. Nonetheless, *The Homecoming* is far more a counterconcept to Wedekind's Lulu plays than their continuation. Ruth is related to Lulu as the exception to the rule.

Lulu was the wild, beautiful animal that one pursues, spoils for a while, and then finally guts. The world of men did not regard her as a member of the human race. Dr. Schön and Rodrigo took the function of animal trainers. Schigolch beat the bushes to drive out the animal; Alwa transformed Lulu and her goings-on into literature. Ironically enough, this play within the play, I mean Dr. Alwa Schön's drama, had the title *Earth Spirit*. Only the Countess Geschwitz, as inhabitant of Gomorrah, and the prep school student Hugenberg, whom Karl Kraus rightly characterizes as the only one with any soul, are exceptions. What makes up Lulu's doom is put by Kraus thus: "The great reprisal has begun, the revenge of a world of men who make bold to take revenge for their own shortcomings."

Ruth in *The Homecoming* is lashed onward by the earth spirit as Lulu was. A nymphomaniac, to make use of a "silly medical term found in novels" (to quote Karl Kraus once again). A nymphomaniac, but what is expressed by that? If *The Homecoming* again and again has a deeply disturbing effect upon its audience, it is because of the total absence of tragedy and pathos. Neither is the work, following Dürrenmatt's aesthetic, structured as a comedy filled with corpses. It is shocking because the course of events is so elegantly nonchalant. At the finish there is merely the closing of a deal, not the cry of death. When the husband, Teddy, returns alone to America, to his three sons and the department of philosophy, Ruth at his departure simply says, "Don't become a stranger." She ends, after the door shuts, sitting "relaxed" in her armchair.[22] Now she had really returned home. Had she? The answer depends upon the audience's interpretation, with which the author, Pinter, properly does not wish to interfere. Either Ruth lived in America as a professor's wife and mother in a state of self-alienation and now in London, in the milieu of Greek Street, finds her way back to her own identity; or the apparent social establishment of a former stripper runs aground of her driven sexuality. In either event it takes place quietly and without fuss.

And so too the deep-dredging interpretations of the work that find recourse to archetypes and interpret Ruth as "primordial mother" and Astarte must fall short of the play's real provocation. Ruth is no universally human courtesan, but a Delilah in a state of self-alienation. Lulu was ahuman, exterritorial, tragic. Ruth is an eroticized and eroticizing vamp in a society, that thanks to movies and television, is all too well acquainted with such matters. Vamps are integrated. One turns a profit with them. Best of all when a poor and pretty girl, to whom is appended

Delilah as Bourgeois Vamp

a movie star name like Marilyn Monroe, can be advanced to status of man-confusing idol by the dream factory. But it is also possible on Greek Street in London, provided of course that the elegance contractually promised Ruth can be delivered. The little London flat (three rooms with bath) of Ruth-to-be cannot be compared with Lulu's dark hole. Her pimp Lenny is wise in these matters: "I'm giving you a professional opinion."[23]

This is also why husband Teddy goes back to America alone and so placidly—something that always irritates *Homecoming* audiences. He is simply relieved. Martin Esslin's interpretation details that: "If Ruth was a whore before he married her, and if during the six years of their marriage the mechanism of her nymphomania surfaced again and again, . . . then one can perfectly well understand Teddy's relief at not having to take Ruth back to America with him."[24] One senses in the background the scandal on an American university campus. On the other hand, Esslin is wrong to think of this family (including Ruth) as abnormal, while at the same time admitting that the situation in the play is "not particularly rare, to say nothing of being completely impossible."

The abnormal is made the norm here, the exception becomes the rule. Lulu's unimpinged erotic life and her social exterritoriality become in Ruth's case, and this with her active participation, institutionalized, which is to say integrated. The vamp receives her proper work place in the social division of labor.

At the price of her identity. In Wedekind the process of alienation was still in its beginnings. In the case of Lulu's three husbands, their desire to possess and own something and someone unpossessable reified all relations between husband and wife, male and female. In the second part of the tragedy Lulu has been degraded to a commodity of functional value or exchange value, depending on the circumstances: in any case, a commodity. She is that even for Alwa Schön, the man of letters who goes about trying to defraud her with literature and literary success. Only the prep school student still living in the antechamber to alienation and the lesbian retain an identity for their feelings.

None of Pinter's characters does that. Society could only be distraught by the phenomenon of Lulu as Delilah incarnate. With the phenomenon of Ruth one knows what to expect. It is something that can be manipulated, and she is eager to help at it. The really shocking element in this is that Ruth's most vital element of personality, her lust for men, is commercialized via cold planning. Through that she escapes Lulu's fate, apparently, but at the price of a shipwrecked self-realization. The men

Judith and Delilah

are duped as well. They receive a commodity that has to be paid for. The longed-for mother and mistress is nowhere to be found. One has to continue to make do, as at the beginning of the piece, with dreams, tall tales, transfigured reminiscences (because riddled with lies). A real Delilah came home, but was soon shunted into alienation and her own manipulated dreams.

Dream Factory

The title "The Dream Factory" is taken from a report that Ilya Ehrenburg made on Hollywood in 1931. It has since become part of the vocabulary of those who investigate the media. The term is well chosen for grasping the complex processes that make cinematic dreams. A factory produces according to existing needs or demands; this one fulfills the demand for dream images. By subjecting favorite dream genres to analysis, the dream factory keeps itself competitively viable. A viable competitor is characterized by the ability to anticipate demands as well and not only knows tomorrow's fads but is in a position to create them. For decades it was part of the Hollywood myth that film executives had a sensitive ear to the changes going on in the dream sector.

The typology of the female film star, in all its metamorphoses since the triumph of the film and the film industry immediately after the Great War, has always made clear what was being dreamed about. In the first, still plebeian and vulgar phase of films (Sartre in writing of his childhood in *The Words* has provided an exact description of it), the dreaming man in front of the filmscreen had the pretty, average girl from around the corner before him as the (mostly unhappy) screen heroine. The dream factory owners were on the lookout for physically average types to whom a little acting could be taught. Henny Porten was the ideal of the sentimental German girl; Mary Pickford, the all American girl. More exotic dreams were also provided: the beer hall dancinggirl type was much sought after by an audience of cynical and lasciviously minded men home from the war. And she was provided a suitable name in Lia de Putti. The name was part of the business. A Polish girl with fiery eyes, Pola Negri, promised sensuality. One of the first acts of Josef Goebbels when charged with the reorganization of the German film industry was to bring back with much ado that forgotten star of the silent film era and establish her in the talking dream factory of the Third Reich. Hollywood in its beginnings could offer as an alternative to Pickford the delicate and tender

Delilah as Bourgeois Vamp

Lillian Gish, whom any number of moviegoers would want to protect and rescue.

The advent of the spoken word and the transformation of whilom flicker galleries into moving picture palaces brought successful actresses into the movies. Elisabeth Bergner set the standard in women's fashions and probably in love as well. She was the tender, not at all beautiful, yet intelligent woman with large eyes and nervous, almost boyish, movements. In the male world's adoration of Bergner and in her imitation by younger girls, an aspect of sexual ambivalence from the dream world made a place for itself in the real world. Goebbels was to fight against the influence of "this consumptive Jewess" on his German people in a particularly incensed and virulent fashion. Bergner's successes, probably those of Greta Garbo as well, were based on a process of nonidentification in the movie theater. The paths taken by Bergner and Garbo were not open to everyone. The audience was presented with queens and heroines from filmed novels to be delectated as strange and foreign material. For the audience supplied by the dream factory UFA (which toward the end of the Weimar Republic belonged to the National German Krupp manager and newspaper magnate, Alfred Hugenberg), nearness meant "that droll little blonde thing," Lilian Harvey; later Kristina Söderbaum, so well practiced in crying and suffering. It was a sign of some refinement in ideological marketing research in the propaganda ministry of the Reich that the feminine outsiders were driven out of the movies: Bergner, Garbo, especially the sinful seductress, Marlene Dietrich. No women with weapons, for the weapons are to be carried by men. No Delilah, for she represents foreignness and treachery. The motion pictures of the Third Reich return to the female type of the girl next door. The German people were supposed to dream (even erotically) within the confines of the self-sufficient folk community.

Hollywood was able to get at its business more grandiosely. The market was immense and far from self-sufficient. The movie theaters from Times Square in New York to Market Street in San Francisco, to the only picture show in town somewhere in Wyoming or New Mexico had to be serviced. That presupposed a supply of femininity for dreams of intimacy and of remote allure: Mae West's curves and husky voice, the attraction of her loose speech; Gloria Swanson, with the manners of a great lady, which were constantly at odds with her body and the way she stared at people; the crafty intrigues of the ugly and enjoyably wicked Bette Davis (but that was the art of a great actress; one could shudder and admire, but it was not the stuff one dreams about).

In the thirties, Marlene Dietrich and Gary Cooper became the American dream couple. It was the story of male American youth running away from home, wanting to start out on the great adventure somewhere with a couple of dollars in his pocket. Gary Cooper: the good hero, the foreign legionnaire or small-town boy who falls into the hands of the big-time bosses. He fights the good fight, and Marlene, despite all the fuss to the contrary, loves only him.

The French motion picture reproduces Parisian life even for viewers sitting in theaters in Nantes or Narbonne. The marked literary quality of French film, until the end of the Second World War, led successful Parisian actresses to the screen. They were somewhat older naive women or ladylike sentimental ones whose famous stage roles were done: Gaby Morlay, Edwige Feuillère, whom Giraudoux admired, Danielle Darrieux; at the end the hardened and somewhat plebeian Michèle Morgan. But this was not the stuff of which dreams are made.

No woman in the dreammaking business ever embodied (in the most literal sense of the word!) so consummately the unity of the near and the distant dream as Marilyn Monroe. Dietrich was known to be a foreigner, a German, a successful actress. Katharine Hepburn was too clever, sarcastic, not cuddly, not even soft. Vivien Leigh came from England and a theater background, which was doubly alienating. Marilyn was a Lulu by origin. Was she an illegitimate child who had a hard and joyless childhood deprived of all happiness, as she herself hinted from time to time, or was that only part of the well-packaged myth? Norman Mailer's book *Marilyn*[25] does not proceed from any intention to clarify these things; it simply adds to the construction of the legend. Her beauty was clear and bright: the photographs of her in private life are far more charming than the stills from her films. Here indeed was the stuff dreams are made of. Yet the dreams of millions were to destroy the idol. Professional actresses were able to retain bits of their feminine and human identity in the face of the gossip columns and their fans. Monroe was ground down by a process of alienation meant to extinguish her identity in order to achieve the perfect union of real life existence and film star role. When she had decided to end it all, and this is documented, she withdrew herself from this self-alienation. She no longer played her role. Now nothing was left to stand in the way of her media apotheosis.

7 Women's Liberation and Norman Mailer

The male claim that females find fulfillment through motherhood and sexuality reflects what males think they'd find fulfilling if they were females.—Women, in other words, don't have penis envy; men have pussy envy . . .

Valerie Solanis, excerpts from SCUM (Society for Cutting Up Men)

In God we trust.—She will provide.

Slogan at the American Women's Liberation Convention, 1973

The first quote derives from that representative of women's emancipation of extreme consequence who tried to assassinate Andy Warhol. The acronym SCUM proclaiming the abolition of men as if with a brand name product, has obscene connotations. The second quote was used as a slogan and sold as a lapel button and bumper sticker at a women's convention. It is not out to "get" men, the first sentence simply being the official motto of the United States found on every dollar bill, the second sentence proclaiming hope in divine providence—everything, apparently, according to the usual American political-puritanical tradition. Only God has been made into a female, a lady God, as it were. The religious superego is not to be abandoned but is to be taken into a matriarchy.

Behind these notions stands, to the great confounding of the "male" world, seeming silly even, the collectivization of female outsiders in this society. There is repeatedly the analogy to the great cry in the *Communist Manifesto* for the proletariat of all countries of the world to unite. The minority groups were being followed here. The cry of "Black Power" had been heard and was now imitated. Jews of the world, unite! That had already long since had its place, and was now called Israel.

Even the city of Sodom destroyed by fire and brimstone seemed to rise up from the ashes. At the same time militant and absurd, some of its

Judith and Delilah

inhabitants let loose with the cry "Gay Power!" No transmogrification of sexual outsiders issued from it, of course, bringing them into the circle of life of the established Everyman. Yet reforms of the law did take place. Homosexuals' legal status as criminals fell in most Western countries.

So I return once again to the new slogan of community and defense. A cry as it were, "Women of the world, unite!" The seemingly blasphemous transference of the communist formula of 1848 onto the mottoes of a women's emancipation movement—seemingly indifferent to class antagonisms—which knows no distinction between wives of millionaires and half-enslaved black women, makes not only such contradictions clear but no less so the oppositions between the bourgeois and socialist women's movements on the one hand and the quite divergent theses of women's liberation on the other.

In the United States, where women's liberation got its start, there was to be found as well, of course, the old byword subscribed to by socialist and communist labor functionaries, namely that the emancipation of women is not possible without a restructuring of social conditions; the material exploitation of women, not only in the factory but throughout society, can only be rooted out in a social order universally free of exploitation. Norman Mailer's *The Prisoner of Sex*[1] quotes from a pamphlet put out in Kansas City by Linda Phelps, in which appears a line of argumentation that must go against the propositions of women's liberation: "Since 1945 we have spent one trillion dollars on military expenditures and $25 billion of that on weapons which were obsolete as soon as they were produced. Our priorities are not day-care centers and hospitals; our priority is preserving our empire, as we have demonstrated by our activities in Viet Nam. It is useless to think that women are going to get what they want and be able to live as full human beings without facing and changing this vast system of waste and exploitation which is our present economic system."[2]

It is precisely the opposition between such conventional socialist argumentation (an argumentation not at all in contradiction with historical experience, I should note) and the line of thought of the new, radical feminists mostly abstracted from historical analysis that occupies Mailer. He would like to agree, almost against his will, with the traditional analysis of Linda Phelps, but is forced to the recognition, once he has read his way into feminist literature, that an analysis of the conditions is necessary under which such an ahistorical movement, concentrated not on class but sex-struggle, made such a successful debut. Yet he is fully unable to provide the analysis called for. Norman Mailer, example of an antagonist of women's liberation, arrived there mostly via his arguments with Kate Millet and her literary bestseller *Sexual Politics* (1970),[3] is sucked up by the opposing front. Oftentimes he argues like one of the women in women's liberation, simply turned inside out. Dear God is female.

The twentieth century had unfolded itself in manifold ways in the era between Otto Weininger and Norman Mailer. Not only are the changes and metamorphoses astonishing; so too are the constants. A Weininger risen again, catching sight of the most recent American feminists, would promptly expostulate the old antithesis: maid or megaera. On the one side is that mentality one notices in the headings of women's magazines: "Should Women Talk So Much?" or "Cooking Is Fun for Me." On the other side the broad battleranks of the women warriors against male priorities and particularities, from Kate Millet to Valerie Solanis. Women in arms once more. From the Joan of Arc type in Kate Millet, who egged Mailer on so that he came to write on her account and directed against her *The Prisoner of Sex,* to the Judith type in Valerie Solanis, who means to transform a rabid individual instance by the name of Andy Warhol or Holofernes into a representative act of liberation.

Yet these seeming constants have become more and more questionable since Weininger's day (when they would not have described "women," to be sure, but nonetheless would have been informative about the women's world of those days in the bourgeois-aristocratic Vienna of Emperor Franz Joseph and Professor Sigmund Freud). Weininger's supposedly strictly scientific (in fact, neo-Nietzschean) speculation about the factors M and F returns once again, almost seventy years later; it is here in Norman Mailer enriched with the latest results of modern biology and biochemistry. It is simply that it has nothing to do with the pronouncements of real laws.

Even the similarities that seem so astonishing between Weininger's and Mailer's subjective sides are more bewildering than telling. The Jew from Vienna and the Jew from New York: both provide an amalgamation of feminism and Semitism. Weininger even set up the equivalence of female and Jew. He characterized his era as "not only the most Jewish, but also the most female of all time."[4] With that, Otto Weininger, male and Jew, pronounced judgment on himself. He later came to carry it out.

Between Weininger's and Mailer's experience comes the hiatus of Auschwitz. With it the development of modern technology. In the light of these experiences Mailer, for his part, sets up a correspondence be-

tween Jews' and women's "homelessness." But he, the American, otherwise than Weininger, sharply dissociates femininity from feminism.
Weininger's subsurface and anxious homosexuality in argumentation has
equivalents in Mailer, who treats of it at length and not only in the
analysis of the literary examples D. H. Lawrence and Jean Genet. Nevertheless Mailer, unlike Weininger, is a praiser of women. His private
metaphysics of the problematic of the sexes (once again in complete and
astonishing accord with Weininger) projects the conflict into a curious
temporal dimension. *Sex and Character* pursued the speculation that there
was a male (and, consequently, a morally and culturally productive) historical past; that now the age of woman was beginning. The age of the
Jew on top of that. Mailer in *The Prisoner of Sex* grasps the antagonism
between the sexes as one between present and future. Maleness represents the present. Femaleness, on the other hand, as the creation of life,
has intrinsic antennae toward the future: "that somewhere in the insane
passions of all men is a huge desire to drive forward into the seat of
creation, grab some part of that creation in the hands . . . for man is
alienated from the nature which brought him forth, he is not like woman
in possession of an inner space which gives her link to the future, so he
must drive to possess it, he must if necessary come close to blowing his
head off that he may possess it."[5]

That is no longer thinking like Weininger, which is also why the linkage
between sexuality and politics in Mailer scarcely has anything more in
common with him. Mailer's metaphysics of sex is in fear of the alliance
of totalitarianism and biological technology. Women's liberation is for
him both a narcissistic and a totalitarian movement; the questionable
concept of what is and is not totalitarian is made use of on occasion in
quasi-serious provocations, to equate Hitler, Stalin, and the FBI. Kate
Millet is sarcastically given the epithet Comrade Millet, which is apparently meant to be insulting. At first she is compared to Molotov, then, as
if to correct that, with Vyshinskii, the state prosecutor in Stalin's purge
trials. Mailer has a young couple of the future carry out futuristic dialogues, written in the manner of horror films, before a court of communards. The man is a pitiful drone, as you would imagine in a vision
of the future after the taste of the feminist liberators! The woman is self-
assuredness personified. The court has been applied to for an exemption
to the compulsory abortion called for as a measure against a crushing
overpopulation. The alternative of whether the man should be shot by

way of parity is brought to mention at one point, yet Mailer offers a roguish happy end.[6]

What is most astonishing is Mailer's linkage of women's emancipation, fascism, and Jewish emancipation, indeed, enlightenment in any sense. Proceeding from the well-known theses of *Mein Kampf*—the male watches over the nation, the female the family; man and woman are fundamentally different by their very nature, the one has reason, the other emotions—Mailer does not make things easy for himself by quoting Hitler, who had come to the conclusion that "the message of woman's emancipation was thought up by the Jewish intellect." The American Jew Norman Mailer finds delight in provoking New York relatives and friends with sentences like the following (speaking of himself in the third person):

Well, he had come to the conclusion a long time ago that all thought must not cease with Adolf Hitler, that if, in the course of living with a thought, it might appear to run parallel for a time to arguments Nazis had also been near, one should not therefore slam the books, close the inquiry, and cease to think in such direction any further. That would be equivalent to letting the dead Hitler set up barriers on all the intellectual roads which could yet prove interesting and so would be a curious revenge for that Nazism.[7]

In order to pursue this line of thought, Mailer is obliged to come to terms not only with Jewish emancipation, but also with its historical origins: the beginnings of the Enlightenment, with the Renaissance. In one of those yard-long sentences that quite consciously mean to continue the tradition of the European epic, not of the novel, Henry Miller, as troubadour of the twenties, is defended against the verdicts of Kate Millet (namely that he is a despiser of women as mere sexual objects). Then Mailer, "the prisoner of sex," undertakes interpreting the 1920s, the beginnings, in a word, of a tolerant, no longer repressive sexual morality, those Roaring Twenties of American literature, that is to say Henry Miller's twenties, as the continuation of a process of enlightenment that began with the Renaissance, the sexual as the continuation of the intellectual revolution. The theoreticians of women's liberation had defined the period of 1930 to 1960, which generally had been understood as a time of irresistible loosening of taboos (in typical male misrepresentation of facts, as those women critics claimed), as an epoch of "sexual counterrevolution." Whereby one is forced to ask where and when the real revolution is supposed to have taken place. Mailer replies: "Miller is an archetype of the man of the Twenties, is indeed the true sexual revolutionary if we are willing to grant that any equivalent figure of the Renaissance would by that measure also be a revolutionary, since no revolution picks up momentum without a profound change in the established consciousness of the time." Straight upon that follows the historical comparison: "Just as the Renaissance was a period in which men dared, as perhaps never before in history, to allow themselves to pursue the line of their thought . . . so the Twenties were a species of sexual renaissance where man emerged from the long medieval night of Victorian sex with its perversions, hypocrisies, and brotherly dispensations."[8] The conclusion for Norman Mailer is that this process, which is to be equated with the dialectical progress of the bourgeois Enlightenment, is thereby something that closely binds Jewish emancipation with all the manners and forms of human self-liberation, not least with the "sexual revolution."

Once again a yard-long sentence with fine periods and cadences. The Jews unceasingly, according to Mailer, wrested themselves free from the "sensuous penury of ghetto life." All manner of taboos were beat out of them, thus putting them in a position to "acquire influence in every field of science, medicine, law, and finance." That was the logical and consequential outcome of Enlightenment in the age of capitalist society. Yet capitalism increasingly had need of a more exact and mechanized technology. Here too, Mailer postulates, the emancipated Shylocks grown bourgeois became at the same time missionaries of that technology. "And technology, like the Jews, was waiting to burst the traditional and cultural restraints which had kept it penned across the centuries. So of course the Jews would be blamed for all the insidious diseases of technology—they were the missionaries for it."[9]

At this point in a progression of thought that is in no sense amicable to the Spinozan demonstration *more geometrico,* a progression of thought that rambles, runs off at tangents, glides off into the author's personal and private sphere, encompasses both polemics and literary criticism, yet nevertheless remains astonishingly stubborn in the pursuit of its fundamental theses and aversions, Mailer's treatise against both theory and practice of women's liberation abruptly returns to the subject. He had dealt at some length with artificial insemination, using colorful and disconcerting quotes from the literary cornucopia of the new feminists, of artificial growth of the fetus outside its mother's body in the future, of hygienic and inconsequential forms of abortion; Mailer does not fail to bring up a quote from Ti-Grace Atkinson's essay, "The Institution of Sexual Intercourse": "The first step that would have to be taken before

we could see exactly what the status of sexual intercourse is as a practice
is surely to remove all its institutional aspects: We would have to eliminate
the functional aspect. Sexual intercourse would have to cease to be Society's means to population renewal."[10]

Two primordial visions are once again summoned up by modern technology: famulus Wagner's labor on the homunculus and Aristophanes'
talk in Plato's *Symposium*: "Now there were these three sexes, because the
sun, moon, and the earth are three; and the man was originally the child
of the sun, the woman of the earth, and man-woman of the moon, which
is made up of sun and earth." But the gods had changed this original
biological form of mankind, and moved the genitalia from the inside of
the body to the outside. "Therefore we shall do well to praise the god
Love . . . who is also our greatest benefactor, leading us in this life back
to our own nature, and giving us high hopes for the future, that if we
are pious, he will restore us to our original [whole, unsundered] state,
and heal us and make us happy and blessed."[11]

Aristophanes, as we know, does not have the last word in the *Symposium*.
Yet he is not derided; his myth can be used to clarify the nature (and
function) of the erotic. In Mailer's quotes, however, he is called up as the
possibility of a technological invention similar, say, to heart transplants,
and with the same publicity character. Doublesexedness as triumph of
the laboratory over nature: just as the famulus in *Faust II* had wanted it.
Norman Mailer has this in mind when he sets up the untenable equation
that the logical conclusion of women's liberation in the sense of the
modern emancipatory program could only mean total technology, which
in turn is understood as total inhumanity, for which Mailer comes up
with the somewhat slovenly conceived concept of fascism. Hitler, according to his view, in incessantly speaking of *Blut und Boden*, and of a return
from a Jewified world of Enlightenment, quite actually and unsuspect-
ingly led to the expansion of the "Jewish-liberal" world of modern capitalism. "The confusion was that they [the Nazis] had called for a return
to traditional, even primitive roots of existence and had indicated the
Jews as the whippets of the unisexual, classless future. If Hitler had done
more to accelerate such a future than any Jew ever born (since the Second
World War had been a centrifuge to drive technology into every reach
of social life), his political genius had been to do it in the name of its
opposite. Blood has more to tell us than the machine, he was forever
telling us as he built the machine."[12]

Mailer's turns of thought appear all too capricious in the form in which they are presented, a mixture of tractate, essay, short story, and maligning. Yet they are meant entirely in earnest and are astonishingly close, certainly without Mailer ever having been aware of it, to some of the fundamental positions found in Horkheimer and Adorno's *Dialectic of Enlightenment.* That in itself is not astonishing, for that work, which describes the paths from myth to Enlightenment to myth to Enlightenment, and so on, was also conceived in the United States, meant to denounce shortly after the end of the war the changeover from Fascism to positivist technology.

Mourning and nostalgia in Adorno (less evident in Horkheimer) as well as in Norman Mailer. Yet the conclusion to *The Prisoner of Sex* is a vision of the future that is more in keeping with George Orwell or with Aldous Huxley's *Brave New World.* Our writer Mailer, possessed by politics, including sexual politics, the unsuccessful candidate for the office of mayor of New York, calls up the image of a city of the future where various sexual special desires are divided according to block, neighborhood, or borough. New York, with its national ghettos of blacks, Chinese, Puerto Ricans, and of Germans, Italians, Irish, or Poles mixed in, clearly served as the model: "but he saw no major reason why one could not await a world—assuming there would be a world—where people would found their politics on the fundamental demands they would make of sex. So might there yet be towns within the city which were homosexual, and whole blocks legally organized for married couples who thought the orgy was ground for the progressive action of the day."

Mailer ferociously and mockingly paints the Sundays of masturbators in the deserted city streets, of pseudo-Victorian quarters with old-fashioned brothels, even "tracts for old-fashioned lovers where the man was the rock of the home. . . . There would be every kind of world in the city, but their laws would be founded on sex."[13]

Does Mailer really believe, as he asserts he does, that such an idea would free the relations between the sexes of aggression and violence, that is to say, pull the rug from under the women's liberation movement? It is really more nearly the last provocation of an unserious, embittered book. A sure recipe for maximalizing aggression. Mailer responds to a perverted motto taken over by Kate Millet and Valerie Solanis of the Society of All Women for the Last Battle, with no less of one—freely adapted from Marx—that it is not the social life of human beings but their sexual life that determines their consciousness.

8   The World of Images of Women

If one translates the title of a sociological study published by Pascal Lainé in 1974, *La Femme et ses images*,[1] as "Woman and Her Images," the ambiguity of the subject becomes evident. In both the English and the French titles ambiguity exists. Does the book have to do with images that women make of themselves or simply accept, without contradiction, as being socially evident? Or are images of women meant that are produced by a male-structured society and declared to be as evident for men as for women?

If the self-interpretation of women could be differentiated from all external interpretation, both the verbal and the real ambiguity might be avoided. But images that women in the present age accept as their identity and want to emulate are determined from the outside. Brecht's thesis seems to be true everywhere, that to love or respect another person one is required to conceive an outline of him and see to it that the person so outlined is brought to conform more and more closely to the image. The world of images of women means, in consequence, a male world of images assumed by women, taken up into their wills, imitated until it presents itself in fact as an image world of women.

It is not possible to restrict this reciprocal relation to the middle class and the women of the bourgeoisie or petite bourgeoisie. In the first instance, where can a clear dividing line be drawn before the world of an assimilated working class woman who also sees herself as consumer, who visits the hair stylist, reads women's magazines and carries their world of images around with her? Even nations with planned economies that have integrated women a great deal more in the material process of production and political administration do not appear to want to get by without specific women's organizations, not even without certain kinds of women's magazines.

Judith and Delilah

The passages and transitions in the world of images of women from self-determination to outside determination are in flux. Unmistakably the male element asserts itself at that point where the taboo and proscription of women outsiders is taken over without hesitation into the image world of women. The highly intellectual woman superior to men, as the woman with a weapon, has no place in this panorama. The vamp, on the other hand, appears to dominate; she has simply lost her vamplike qualities, as it turns out; she has lost too what Wedekind provided, the characteristics of a beautiful and wild beast of prey. In the women's magazines of the Western world the tamed vamp makes her appearance as the household pet, pretty and strange and existentially an outsider, but harmless. The deceased Marilyn Monroe was built up as an idol; it is simply that this idolatry was plotted out behind the scenes as a literature of warning.

Even this process of domestication displays the same ambivalence of simultaneous outside determination through male conceptual and emotional worlds and female self-representation according to said norms and rites. What could be glimpsed in the example of Ruth in Pinter's *The Homecoming*: the readiness of a Lulu for social (male) cooperation, becomes especially recognizable in the American woman and her world of images. The outsider types in Judith and Delilah continue to exist and are recognized as having marginal significance for the world of women. But a certain process of interiorization has taken place. Stranger still, a synthetic amalgam of Judith and Delilah is set up as the female norm. The exceptions are made into aspects of the norm, and thereby into a model image that can and should be imitated. The painter Richard Lindner, a specialist of outsiderdom in modern society, has captured this specific image world of woman, and not only of the American world, has captured it as one who comes from the outside and looks in.

Excursus on Paintings by Richard Lindner

"The Meeting,"[2] a picture painted in New York in 1953, brings together in a cool room done in gray and green tones, a room with a somewhat heterogeneous seating arrangement, a no less heterogeneous group of guests: five women, two men, a young boy in a German sailor suit circa 1912, and a tiger. They are standing or sitting with no relationship to one another, as if incommunicable monads. Only the German boy holds tight to his ample-breasted mother, who is dressed according to the fashion of 1912, and probably would have been characterized in those days as "an interesting, dark personality." What dominates here is the image world of women in the twentieth century. The dark lady with the starched blouse and dress of the turn of the century; the cool and slender woman with the close-cropped hair of the twenties with something of the silhouette of Lillian Gish but looking capable of self-defense; the dominating feminine American woman of the fifties, vermilion hair and red cocktail dress, hygienically regulated eroticism, unmistakably stylized along the lines of Grace Kelly; in the left back corner one of those bulging young female beings who populate the American scene and are not to be thought of sympathetically as someone having a glandular disorder but as the product of an abnormal diet. (There is no lack of corresponding male figures.) The fifth woman in the meeting party is, as opposed to the first four, shown only from the rear: a kind of Lulu who nonetheless has to fulfill simultaneously the roles of beast of prey *and* circus trainer. She is a typical figure in Lindner's repertoire: her buxomness derives from the geometrical notions of a drafting table; her garters and cords and laces can be used for torture; the rear view of the circus trainer's costume follows the contours of the tiger next to her, which seems the intended recipient of the stroking gesture.

Five women as five generations of a domineering threatfulness. The carnivore fits well into this group. Then the boy who cannot get away from his mother. To the right on a tubular chair a delicate, no longer young man with glasses and a straw hat whom no one seems to observe and who appears to see no one himself. The prototype of the American businessman with an excellent life insurance policy that his widow will one day collect. Finally, colored like a corpse and with uncovered pudgy arms, but otherwise as in the famous coronation picture: Ludwig II of Bavaria. The scepter has taken on a phallic form. He is the only one who appears to be looking at another member of the meeting; he has the circus trainer in view.

Richard Lindner was born in Hamburg in 1901 and grew up in Nuremburg. His pictures are marked, as he himself has admitted, by the deep impression left behind by the instruments of torture in the Kaiserburg, particularly by the Iron Maiden. Lindner's women are domineering. That they are modeled after his mother, "a very Wagnerian woman, I mean physically as well, with big breasts,"[3] is all too evident. Lindner's world of images of women takes on a greater significance by virtue of the fact that women are represented as the stronger sex. That is the painter's aim and corresponds to his own personal convictions.

Judith and Delilah

Lindner's American women are armed. His painting "Marilyn Was Here" (1967)[4] reproduces the familiar curvatures yet keeps her head completely in the dark. A faceless idol is meant to be shown here, not the victim but the resurrected graven image; the corsage is shown to be an instrument of torture, probably of castration. Once again the Iron Maiden. Marilyn was here; and in her train follow and multiply the outsider types, hybrids of the woman with the weapon and the bourgeois vamp. And not at all in the sense that past exceptions, Countess Faustine, Lulu, George Sand, or Lou Andreas-Salomé, were now become the rule themselves. More nearly in the sense that women's "normal existence" in bourgeois male society has been declared outsider and enemy. It is a process in which, from the male point of view (which Richard Lindner cooly registers, not in agreement with it, yet reflecting and confirming it), no longer diagnoses a Helen in every woman, but rather a Judith and Delilah. The consequence is the growing alienation between man and woman in American daily life; the homosexual pinings in American film and theater with their transfiguration of comradeship in sports, brotherhood in war, fraternity in college. Critics from the ranks of women's liberation have recognized with great acumen and have sharply criticized this dominating antifeminism, as in Tennessee Williams, William Inge, Edward Albee; in the first instance explicable by these authors' subjective viewpoints, yet which necessarily becomes more and more clearly part of the general regularity of the sexes' relations with each other. The image of woman in American letters closely corresponds to the image of woman that one meets in Richard Lindner. Martha and George in Albee's *Who's Afraid of Virginia Woolf?* play again and again, in addition to their usual repertory, the game of "Who's afraid of women?"

In Richard Lindner's picture world there is not only a synthetic, American amalgam of Judith and Delilah; even more imposing is the rendezvous set up here of all manner of outsiders. His comprehensive painting "The Meeting" provides such a rendezvous. Lindner is a Jew; his experiences in Paris and New York are those of an exile. His way of seeing he himself describes as that of someone on the outside. The American world in his paintings was seen by a non-American. Lindner's world of images issues from the Shylock experience. The conspicuous accumulation of homosexual motifs in these paintings has nothing to do with the painter's own inclinations. Lindner is not a homosexual. But obviously that same thing has struck him that struck Sartre so deeply in the example of Jean Genet: the fate of the existential outsider. Lindner had pursued this phenomenon early on in his attempt to portray Verlaine. Later, in coming to terms with Marcel Proust in his "Portrait of Proust" from around 1950, he not only simply carried out a conception for a portrait but also, as Proust's portraitist, came to realize a world of images truly his own—and that at a rather late point in his life. The individual process in this painter tends to bring the inner connection of all existential outsiders to the foreground. Werner Spies's study, "The Machinery of Dissatisfaction and Malaise,"[5] in which the Proust portrait of 1950 is confronted or, better, is brought into relation with the "Marilyn Was Here" composition of 1967, gives one to understand that Proust and King Ludwig in Lindner's paintings do not simply function as mere androgynous creatures, which they are as well, but that they are to be grasped as encodings of foreignness, strangeness. Shylock as painter paints Proust and Ludwig, ruined high couples, circus trainers and their beasts of prey, male and female consumers. All of them secretly bear weapons or are themselves weapons. A famous picture, "Telephone" (1966),[6] portrays the American myth of the telephone booth. The grinning vamp is there and the equally grinning playboy. Each is alone in a booth, back to back. Each could be talking with the partner in the booth next door as well as with an interchangeable anybody else. The telephone unites through separation. It feigns a partnership that is not at hand. The people in this painting conduct monologues. They are simply the specific expression of a more general law in which outsiders and their outsiderdom come to be manifested. Everyman is then Judith, Lulu, Proust, Ludwig, and Marilyn. He is even Shylock in a reified society that produces none of the night music of Belmont yet keeps Belmont at hand in the form of travel agency brochures for dream trips. All of this has been captured by the Shylock, Richard Lindner.

Pascal Lainé on Woman and Her Images

"The 'old maid' becomes as much a part of marginal existence as does any woman who in any fashion contradicts the rules of marriage and motherhood—the unwed mother, the prostitute, for example. A woman whose career is seen to be too brilliant likewise offends against the implicit pact with men which requires her submission."[7] Those are the conclusions of the French novelist and sociologist, Pascal Lainé, in his study *La femme et ses Images* (Woman and Her Images). He comes to the further conclusion, by interpreting the "male" position of present-day society

Judith and Delilah

from the inside in order to note the examples of female suppression contained in it, that "to be a prostitute, or an unwed mother, or an old maid, or simply a 'working woman' signifies much more than a situation which can pass in time; it becomes a socially fixed condition, approximating even a condition of nature."[8] Once again Judith and Delilah: the desirable and at the same time despised sex object and the working woman who is too brilliant. In Frank Wedekind's play *Hidalla,* the "dwarf-giant," Karl Hetmann, characterized the role of the old maid and the prostitute, and "female virginity preserved for the purpose of a better bargaining position in getting married," as the "three barbaric forms of life" for women in modern society.[9] Karl Kraus, in his introductory talk at his performance of Wedekind's *Pandora's Box* cited these theses and agreed with them.

In the case of Pascal Lainé, all of this returns once more in the year 1974. Nothing seems to have been solved by the passage of time. The sole difference is that Lainé is not a lamenting moralist, but a sociologist operating exactly with questionnaire and recording device. *Woman and Her Images* records the results of such an investigation dating from 1972. A group of researchers had put questions to 1100 French women from "all social groups, all ages, all conditions of life" concerning their self-appreciation. The group analyzed 830 of the inquiries, which thanks to the questionnaire, provided, as Lainé put it, "statistically sound, if somewhat abstract information." For the sake of concrete examples, 100 conversations with the women involved were then recorded on tape. All of the conversations centered around the question of identity of present-day French women. Did they recognize themselves in the images in women's magazines like *Elle*'or *Marie-France,* or did they side with the feminists who saw in all that merely a new domesticity thought up and put into practice by men, consequently a loss of their own identity? The results were far from reaching any unanimity. If a majority of the women questioned admitted thinking or feeling "a little feminist," then that was the manifestation of conformity with a little mental reservation.

Pascal Lainé believes that the results of his study stand in direct contradiction to Friedrich Engels's theses on the "Origin of the Family," as well as to the thoughts represented by Wilhelm Reich in his work *The Invasion of Compulsory Sex-Morality* (1932); even feminist propositions appear to him inadequate.[10] He seems even less inclined to accept the current commonplace viewpoint that the role of women in modern, permissive society must be seen as consummation of a long process of

The World of Images of Women

liberation that has meanwhile eliminated inherited inequalities. Lainé's counterthesis is cutting: "But the 'emancipation' of women does not signify liberation when it results from the tricks, or at least financial support, of an advertising mercantilism that carefully takes heed that even under the pretense of women's emancipation an essential status is maintained, namely women's status of buyer of goods: as young girl, as wife, as mother."[11]

Two aspects appear again and again in the conclusions Lainé has drawn from his investigation that illuminate the modern forms of both women's outsider status and her economic specificity: women's role as real or presumptive *consumer* of merchandise and women's loss of identity through aging and, in consequence, her loss of role as sex object. Both are very closely related in consumer society (which Lainé, by the way, docs not equate with capitalism). All advertising directed at girls and women makes them over into objects. *Marie-Claire* is quite the same as *Playboy* in that "one finds in men's magazines, for example, a sports car and a pinup girl in the same picture in intimate embrace, as it were."[12] In all cases woman has been reified, made over into an object, article of merchandise, consumer commodity. "In being reduced to a mere image, women find their real significance at the locus of their alienation." Which is to say that modern society merchandising its goods, seemingly so permissive, has in store for women of all ages merely divergent roles as purchasers of its goods. It robs these objects of every possibility for subjectivity and identity. The roles have to be played; the world of images of women manipulated by advertising becomes the role model. Self-alienation is praised and merchandised as something of value.

This becomes evident in the results of this investigation that deal with the caesurae of age in women's lives, with the ages of thirty and fifty. The questionnaires had been conceived with considerable discernment. They asked which room in the home was particularly important: living room, kitchen, bedroom, bath. What sort of hygiene, what kind of clothing, what ritual in the act of love? All the answers, independent of the differences between city and country, age groups and economic situation, displayed a conformity to the male world and the division of roles mandated by it. It came to light that young girls are unable to imagine themselves as fifty-year-olds. A young man can imagine himself as chairman of the board, people's commissar, star, government minister; something of his sense of identity is participating here, though the roles are reduced to clichés by tradition, education, advertising. The women's self-image, on the other hand, is reduced at all age levels to the role of secondary person. She makes herself then, of her own free will and at all age levels, functionally dependent on the male drive for identity, itself reduced.

Pascal Lainé made use of the results of his sociological field survey of the world of images of French women in a twofold fashion: as scientific report with logical judgments and conclusions and as the basis for a novel. Lainé was born in 1942. He published his second novel (his first was *B for Barabbas*), *L'Irrévolution* in 1971,[13] in which a young secondary school philosophy teacher in the fall of 1968 (after the events in Paris in May of that year), teaching in a technical school in the French provinces, comes to the realization that the theory familiar to him from philosophy and social inquiry must remain powerless in the face of the social realities in which his students grow up. A year after the appearance of this novel, which had been awarded the Prix Médicis, Lainé began the investigations that were to provide the basis of *Woman and Her Images*. At the same time, the novelist Lainé drew his own conclusions from the collected data. The novel that resulted, *The Laceweaver* (1974), was awarded the highest French prize for literature, the Prix Goncourt, the same prize that made Proust famous.

The laceweaver[14] is a young girl who is apparently meant to remind one of Vermeer's painting. She is called "Pomme," Little Apple, on account of her round cheeks, and is never evoked by the narrator in any other way. She works as a hairdresser's assistant in a women's beauty salon in Paris. She has not been allowed to wash or cut hair not to mention color it. She lives in a women's world made up of tradition and the constant reading of novels. A love affair with a student who has an aristocratic name shows her, a kind of Käthchen von Heilbronn, in the immediate and unflinching function of a woman who is nothing if she is not chosen. When the young man becomes irritated by so much role filling, which he mistakes for stupidity, and sends her packing, she takes her little satchel and returns to her mother. She deems herself a failure. He probably thought she was too fat, she thinks. She stops eating, and finally despite her own efforts, can actually no longer eat anything. She is destroyed by delusion. Later on in a clinic she makes every crafty attempt to intercept and do away with the pills she is required to take.

Pomme acts in perfect conformity with that world of images for/of women. It is the source of her ruination. The sociologist Lainé had come to the conclusion that "the image of woman is simply lust made visible,

The World of Images of Women

lust in itself, all one at what it is directed, for the image always provides it with enough justification. And it is all one which image, and which woman in which picture. All the pictures and women approximate themselves inwardly in the magazines, on the billboards, and in department store windows."[15] The danger is that women, and not simply those like Pomme, might take the theses of the feminists when presented in a manipulated manner by the media, as simply one more new fashion that will just as soon pass away. "In their majority," Lainé concludes his analysis, "women are 'a little' feminist. There could come a day when they have no other choice but to be it really."[16]

Sodom

9 A Chronicle of Murders and Scandal

On the battlefield of Chaeronea in the year 338 B.C. the victorius Philip of Macedon, father of Alexander the Great, is reported by Plutarch to have uttered a curious remark. The Athenians and Thebans had resisted Philip in vain. The nucleus of their fighting force had been made up of Pelopidas' "Sacred Band," which was composed of pairs of lovers. Three hundred of them had fallen. The warriors had not wished to survive without their lovers. At the sight of them lying on the battlefield, Philip is reported to have cried out, "Let him be cursed who says that these men ever conscienced or committed a base act!"

These words of the Macedonian are cited in Hans Kelsen's compendious study "Platonic Love"[1] (which, by the way, first appeared in Freud's periodical *Imago* in 1933) as proof of Kelsen's claim that pederasty was viewed in Greek antiquity more generally as a vice than as a natural phenomenon, not to mention virtue. Philip of Macedon in his view meant to say that those who fell at Chaeronea—who were quite comparable to Leonidas' band of warriors, who were similarly composed, and who also perished to the man attempting to hold the pass at Thermopylae against the Persians in 480 B.C.—were lovers. They had fought together and died together. What they did during their lives or suffered to be done cannot have been base: so much is proved by the manner of their death.

In modern times the euphemism *Greek love* has been used for homosexual relationships. The American pornography industry feeding on this market exploits this association by using "Greek" as often as possible in the titles of its productions. One of the most prolific producers of such pornography has as his pseudonym Phil Andros (*philandros*, that is to say, 'lover of men').

Ancient texts, however, as Kelsen makes apparent, oppose such an equation between Greek eroticism and the institution of *paiderasteia*. Ar-

istophanes, Xenophon, and Aristotle all seem to be at one in their negative estimation of male–male eroticism. Even the later Plato, who is
qualified as being homosexual by Kelsen, expressly turned against and
sharply criticized in *The Laws* the danger posed to the state by such an
eroticism, for pederasty "willfully contributes to the withering away of
the human race, and sows the seed on rock and stone where it cannot
take root and come to its natural fruition."[2]

Aristophanes' drastic jokes disapproving of pederasty as a form of
aristocratic libertinage are well known. Xenophon composed a counter-
dialogue to Plato's *Symposium*; in the *Nicomachean Ethics*, Aristotle views
so-called pederasty as a disease and arranges it next to cannibalism,
sadism, and fetishism, the symptoms of all of which he precisely describes.
"Pederasty too," Aristotle continues, "belongs here, which is an inclination
characteristic of some from birth, of others, for example those who have
been taken advantage of from youth, a consequence of habit."[3] There is
already here the distinction between an inherent homosexuality and one
of habit. For Aristotle's ethical system, both are manifestations of unnatural phenomena. In all of his considerations one senses a disquiet, an
unease with an erotic-social phenomenon that undeniably influenced the
modes of behavior in everyday Greek life, having the upper hand in
Sparta and probably even in Thebes.

One other distinction was worked out within the boundaries of this
conflict of norms, namely, that between an originally erotically inspired
friendship between men that forsook the physical aspects, between an
older and a younger man for the most part, and that male–male sexual
intercourse so coarsely made the butt of mockery by Aristophanes in the
name of Athenian popular opinion. Even Plato was obliged to pay proper
heed to this distinction in his political philosophy. One finds in *The
Republic,* in consequence, that "the lover may kiss his beloved and act with
him and touch him as if he were his son, for beauty's sake, if he finds
him willing."[4]

But anything beyond this is to be avoided; not even its semblance ought
to be awakened. On which account it has come historically to the curious
paradox that the deeply pederastic eroticism that Plato developed in *The
Symposium* and in the *Phaedrus* is acorporeal according to tradition. Platonic love is interpreted as an eroticism under the injunction not to touch.
Hans Kelsen is probably right in perceiving in such ambiguities the
striving of the philosopher who was an adept of Socrates not to offend
against the reigning judgments and notions of morality of his day. Just

as it seems enlightening when Kelsen traces, at least in part, the toleration, even encouragement of homosexuality among the Spartans, to the fact that "an all too marked growth in population was not in the political interests of a militarily organized aristocratic caste dependent upon control of limited territories."[5] The ambivalence found in Greek literature and philosophy has its anticipation in Greek myth. The episode of Zeus and the boy Ganymede had been inspired by an erotic exuberance (which could only expect to be met with some understanding), as a pause in Zeus' adventures with Semele, Danaë, Alcmene, and Europa. Achilles was enraptured by Patroclus and the lovely Polyxena both. Shakespeare's Thersites in *Troilus and Cressida* was the first to find that reason for reproach.

Pederasty as vice and danger to society, according to the myth, came into the world via Thebes. The curse on pederasty belonged to the realm of curse that surrounded Oedipus. King Laius of Thebes, husband to Jocasta and father of Oedipus, had made off with the beautiful boy Chrysippus. Angered by this, Hera, the guardian of marriage, loosed the sphinx upon the Thebans as punishment, for they did not prosecute the wanton love for Chrysippus. The young Oedipus, whom Laius, warned by an oracle, had left exposed as an infant, a spike having been driven through his foot, slays Laius, a man unknown to him, at a crossroads, rescues the city from the Sphinx, and weds Jocasta.[6] It is worthy of mention that Sigmund Freud, even in his later works concerning the decline of the Oedipus concept, apparently never noticed the intertwining of the pederasty theme here.

Thebes is, then, the Greek Sodom. They are both anathema: heaven's fire falls upon the one; the Egyptian mythical monster, the Sphinx, falls upon the other. The myth is simply proclaiming social reality. Eros between men was never unopposed and integrated without reservation. Where it was generally practiced and tolerated, it always violated the written law and the recognized religion of the land. Hera was against it, as were Mosaic commandment, the moral code of Augustus, the letters of St. Paul, the Koran. Pederasty in its broadest definition, which reaches from love of boys to homosexuality in the more specific sense, even where it was tolerated and left unconcealed, was seen as a practice that closely bordered on abuse. Even more commonly it was the erotic practice of an elite uppercrust. Ganymede belonged to Zeus; Chrysippus to the king of Thebes; Antinous to the Emperor Hadrian. Hafis' *ghazels* on boy love are aristocratic poetry. Gilgamesh, who loves the animal-man Enkidu and who mourns for him, as did Achilles for Patroclus and Hadrian for Antinous, is a king.

Petronius Arbiter's *Satyricon* from the early period of the Roman Empire is the only work that sketches a picture of everyday life wherein, and this in every social class, the sexual union of man with man, the older with the younger and young men with each other, is presented as a usual and not at all disturbing occurrence. The young Encolpius and his still younger pleasure-boy, Giton, tramp through Nero's Rome under the constant advances of all manner of men and women. Yet here too the wrath of the gods was risked. Through his love for Giton, Encolpius has roused the ire of the god Priaps. The consequences are ineluctable.

Yet Petronius' novel is a satire less concerned with capturing reality than with caricaturing it. The game with the ire of the god is a parody of the *Odyssey*. Encolpius as Ulysses! But by then no one believed in a moral code of divine origin; the commandments issued from the Praetorian Guard. Suetonius, in his reports of the lives of the first Roman emperors, never fails to arouse suspicions of man-boy love if his subject has displeased him. Nero's marriage ceremony/comedy with another man was meant as provocation against religion and accepted morality by one beyond the law. The rumors of Tiberius' orgies on Capri were meant to create a scandal around the unloved emperor.

The apostle Paul established a Christian sexual morality based on the Mosaic code that has lasted up to the present day. Whoever sleeps with a man as with a woman is worthy of death. Since history in the Middle Ages was equated with the wheelings and dealings of rulers, the crime of sodomy, where it could be found out, was punished by death, but not recorded in the chronicles. Scandal covered over was not allowed to become a part of history. One can only hazard a guess concerning the life of the German Emperor, Otto III, who grew up in the shadow of two mighty women, his grandmother Adelheid and his Byzantine mother Theophano, and who died at the age of twenty-two. At the end of the Hohenstaufen period, what was the bond between the friends Konradin von Hohenstaufen and Ludwig of Baden, who were decapitated one after the other in the market square in Naples? Perhaps it was a friends' compact made at puberty. Konradin was sixteen when he died.

A chronicle of murders and scandal. In history and in the body of writing reporting it, homosexuals appear without exception as criminals and victims, for the most part both in the same figure as with that Bluebeard and murderer of boys, Gilles de Rais, or the English King

A Chronicle of Murders and Scandal

Edward II. During the Renaissance a certain easing-up was striven for in these matters. In the palaces of the Italian city-states and in the artists' circles associated with them one was familiar with the pertinent Greek and Roman documents, as well as with the depictions of sexual behavior on ancient vases. Nevertheless a double standard of morality was practiced everywhere. In December of 1305, Fra Giordano in his sermon before the people of Florence made the accusation: "Oh, how many sodomites there are among you citizens! Even more than that, everyone is caught up in this vice."[7]

One of Savonarola's most famous sermons centered on this vice, especially as a debility among priests: "Give up your pomp, your banquets, your elegant meals. Give up, I implore you, your concubines and your beardless boys. Give up, I demand it, this unspeakable vice, give up the wicked sin that has brought God's wrath upon you."[8] Savonarola drew great admiration but was unable to change things. Four years after he was burned to death (1498), the laws against sodomy were made more severe, yet nothing is known of any subsequent change in peoples' manner of life. Men convicted of sodomy were castrated, the boys fined large sums of money. A building where sodomy had been practiced was razed.

In their book *Born under Saturn*,[9] Rudolf and Margot Wittkower report that it was much more lucrative in plying their trade for the Venetian courtesans to disguise themselves as men. The charges against four Florentines who were accused of having committed "godless acts" with one Jacopo Saltarelli, resulted, in the spring of 1476, in a reprimand. One of those accused was "Lionardo di Ser Piero da Vinci, living at the address of Andrea de Verrocchio." Leonardo took in the pretty ten-year-old Caprotti and kept the "little Satan," whom he painted and drew time and again, for more than twenty years.

The most astonishing case is that of the painter Giovanantonio Bazzi (1477–1549), who is known to art historians by the nickname "Il Sodoma." In 1518 Pope Leo X raised him to the rank of *cavaliere*. Giorgio Vasari makes mention of Sodoma's "perpetually irregular and disgusting life" (he reproaches him less for this than for his occasional laziness as an artist, however). Sodoma, it appears, did little to disguise his inclinations. He was, as even Vasari is forced to admit, "a cheerful and easy man, who brightened others through his unchaste life, for which reason he—always being surrounded by boys and beardless youths, whom he loved greatly—got the name Sodoma. Yet that did not particularly bother him, but seemed to make him proud." He signed his mocking refusal to declare taxes in a letter to the magistracy of his hometown, Siena, with "Sodoma Sodoma derivatum M. Sodoma." [10]

The epoch of feudal absolutism practiced a double standard of life in the form of a double standard of morality. Feudalism means hierarchical inequality. The average citizen found out as a sodomite could only expect severe punishment. The prince Condé, Marshal Turenne, Louis XIV's brother, and Prince Eugene of Savoy freely followed their proclivities, for which there was plenty of opportunity out on campaign. The slanders in the duc de Saint-Simon's memoirs make mention of a great deal of it as a common subject of court gossip. There were no scandals. One was among friends in a sense in the promiscuous escapades with soldiers and domestic servants.

These aspects of the *ancien régime* did not escape Marcel Proust, who put them to use in the world of Guermantes. In the section of his novel entitled "La Prisonnière," [11] Baron de Charlus, who has had good reason to appropriate special knowledge in this field, is carrying on a conversation with Brichot, a professor at the Sorbonne, on the subject of who was one of "those people" in the past. The professor ventures to say that "things are no longer the same with us as they were with the Greeks." Charlus is angered. It is as if one were to say that all of that had ceased going on since ancient times. "Take the age of Louis XIV," he says, "there you have, monsieur, the king's brother, the little Vermandois, Molière, prince Ludwig of Baden, Brunswick, Charolais, Boufflers, the Great Condé, the duke of Brisac." Brichot means to protest the inclusion of the Great Condé until he remembers a soldiers' lampoon of the time. Composed in vulgar kitchen Latin, it describes Condé's journey with his friend, the Marquis de la Moussaye, on the river Rhone. A storm comes up over them, and Condé is afraid they are going to drown. To that the marquis responds:

Securae sunt nostrae vitae
Sumus enim Sodomitae
Igne tantum perituri
Landeriri

Nothing is going to happen to us. As sodomites we will perish in fire rather than water. Tralala. Baron de Charlus was understandably enchanted.

The life of the Prussian King Frederick II does not even begin to reflect such cheery libertinage. The bourgeoisie from the very start,

A Chronicle of Murders and Scandal

especially in the little cities and towns north of the Alps where there could be no underworld as in Paris, London, or even Madrid, made virtue the official order of the day. One's inclinations had to be interiorized. This comes clearly to the surface in the biographies of so many: Winckelmann before he began living in Italy, the historian Johannes Müller von Schaffhausen, the Franconian count August von Platen-Hallermünde, Hans Christian Andersen, the sculptor Thorvaldsen, Walt Whitman, Tchaikovsky.

In Europe after the Middle Ages regicide was such a common phenomenon that it was not viewed as a disconcerting scandal in every instance; the assassinations of well-loved kings like Henry IV of France were, of course, another matter. Yet what scandal and rumor-mongering there was whenever monarchy, sodomy, and murder could all be evoked together! One need only look to Edward II of England or Henry III of France, who held court over a band of *mignons*. Heinrich Mann has well described the latter episode in the first volume of his Henri IV novel. In the age of Elizabethan theater, Christopher Marlowe first wrote a sympathetic dramatization of the life of Henry III, then followed it with a stage production based on the unhappy story of Edward and his sweethearts. With Marlowe, homosexual inclination and conduct of life become themes of literature.

There was widespread horror among European intellectuals and their aristocratic patrons over the manner in which Winckelmann met his end. Even Goethe's later biographical attempt to stylize this restless figure who felt driven from one place to another, who had converted to Catholicism, the simultaneously forthright and devious Winckelmann, into one of the favorites of Fortune, gives some notion of just how deep ran the disquiet in those days. Winckelmann was a bourgeois scholar. His murderer, trying to save his own neck, had asserted in the court proceedings that the deceased had propositioned him with immoral acts. That was in all likelihood a lie in this particular case, as is generally supposed today. Still, this assertion was broadcast from Trieste into the world. Naturally people must have sensed which longing the scholarly connoisseur of Greek art had in common with his beloved Greeks. But that was not a topic for conversation. Here members of the bourgeoisie spoke about an important bourgeois. There was no place for *médisance* as there was in the gossip at court.

If the bourgeois Enlightenment and moral code sought to straitjacket Greek eroticism in the modern period to being simply an aristocratic vice and consequently a privilege of the ruling class, it was Winckelmann who destroyed this fiction. Pederasty could not be reduced sociologically to any one single caste or class. Besides, when Winckelmann went to Italy where, as.was generally known to homosexuals in Europe, one could find erotic fulfillment, he gave others a signal. Throughout the nineteenth century and far into the twentieth, the exiles of Sodom sought a new home in "South Wind." That was the name of a novel by the English writer Norman Douglas that first appeared in 1917.[12] It takes place on Capri (called Nepenthe in the novel) and was the model of a new literary thematization that has come to be imitated many times over, most recently in Roger Peyrefitte's work on Count Fersen's life on Capri, *L'Exilé de Capri*. Seen historically, however, *South Wind* was a book looking back to the scandals of the times before.

Tiberius' little island was a place of exile. Scandal made no halt before it. The middle class nineteenth century characterized by the spirit of Protestant verification through the world, bourgeois family virtue, and concealed desire, forced the people of Sodom, if they could possibly manage it, to seek (and find) their identity in Italy. Only in that place did Platen, Hans Christian Andersen, Tchaikovsky, and Oscar Wilde find happiness. Ludwig II's shy attempt to follow them there can only be termed touching. But Capri too was a part of the world of the bourgeoisie. Its newspapers, gossip, and, finally, journalists appeared there. Scandal followed on his heels when Oscar Wilde, after his release from prison, traveled with Lord Alfred Douglas to Capri. The English tourists recognized him and forced their departure.

Inevitably the island's incognito was disclosed to all. Capri became the background of international scandal when first Italy's socialist newspapers, then the international press, wanted to know and report just what Friedrich Alfred Krupp was up to on his yacht and in Capri's grottoes. Norman Douglas, who knew Krupp well, has painted in his memoirs, *Looking Back* (1933),[13] a most cordial picture of the scholar, deep sea explorer, exhausted German father of a family, and friend of the little people on Capri, who had the misfortune of being Europe's richest man. Douglas has described how it all began: as a fit of jealousy between the two schoolmasters of the place. One was privileged to teach the millionaire Italian; the other was excluded. He was frustrated, knew some things, and passed them on. The bourgeoisie of the eighteenth century, struggling upwards, had prosecuted aristocratic immorality. The workers' press now repeated the ritual. Krupp's inclinations were now the manifestation of deep "bourgeois decadence." Krupp was obliged to return to Essen. Everyone deserted him. He died soon thereafter (1902) at the age of forty-eight.

Five years later (1907), the German bourgeois reading public had nothing better to peruse than reports about the past love affairs, unhappy married lives, and secret dealings of men with double lives: of Prince Philipp zu Eulenburg or of the court adjutant, Kuno Graf Moltke. The strange and in the end repulsive role that Maximilian Harden, a Jew and outsider to politics and society, played in the affair is well known. In endless litigation Harden forced Eulenburg and Moltke to perjure themselves where they were unwilling or unable to admit their actions and give account of their passions, which conformed or did not conform to bourgeois mores. In the last decade of the bourgeois nineteenth century, Oscar Wilde's life was brought to ruin—according to the rules, by the way, which obtained at the time of feudalism. I mean that Wilde was brought to trial and sentenced to two years' hard labor while the noble Lord Alfred Douglas, on the contrary, was not even once obliged to appear in the witness box.

The newspaper readers of the Second German Empire were well provendered around the beginning of the century: first Krupp, then Eulenburg and Count Moltke, the bearers of illustrious names who were uncovered as depraved outsiders. Victorian morality had succeeded in becoming the morality of the whole of the bourgeoisie. Even the German kaiser, the father of seven children, had to maintain appearances. He irritably denied the slightest knowledge of the affairs of his favorite, Eulenburg, a knight of the Black Eagle.

Maximilian Harden's position is peculiar. He had taken the side of Gerhart Hauptmann, then defended Bismarck against the young kaiser. *Die Zukunft,* of which he was editor, wanted to attract the liberal bourgeoisie to its readership. But that was not possible—excluding psychological motivations—without anachronism. Nothing, by the way, can be extrapolated from Harden's origins and character. Harden (whose real name was Max Wittkowski), the brother of a conservative entrepreneur and Germanist (Georg Wittkowski) who was never able to advance to full professorship and who later died in exile, once again exemplifies the Jewish outsider who simultaneously sides with power and goes against it—with Bismarck, but against Emperor Wilhelm. The reasoning behind his pamphlets on the political sexual morality of Eulenburg and Moltke is grotesque. He attempts to make credible the charge that Eulenburg and friends have installed "a sodomites' camarilla" around the kaiser. As a German, he, Harden, feels called upon to put an end to such machinations.

Harden and Eulenburg: once again Shylock and Antonio, Heine and Platen. Karl Kraus in his polemical piece "Maximilian Harden: A Settling of Accounts"[14] hits the nail on the head. Harden was playing a role no longer in keeping with the times: he was once again the virtuous middle class citizen waging battle against courtly vice. If one took his motives seriously, there was nothing there but a Don Quixote. But could one take his motives seriously is the question. Was it not all much more nearly an anticipation of later journalistic scandalmongering? That is the way Kraus understood the matter. He explains succinctly: "I am not a political writer, and for that reason do not feel obliged to investigate whether political figures have narrowed their sex drive to skirts or pants." His concluding sentence reads: "The case of Harden vs. Moltke is a victory of information over culture. Humanity will have to learn how to inform itself about such manner of journalism in order to survive future battles."

The diaspora of the Sodomites had to widen after it no longer seemed to go well on Italian soil. André Gide discovered the Tunisian oasis; Montherlant later the world of the toreadors; it was India for E. M. Forster, who portrayed in a novel his homoerotic experiences there as a young man.

An unreservedness or ease never appeared. Social integration did not take place even if the pertinent criminal statutes were altered slightly. Pederasty was always the subject of polemical argument—of the bourgeoisie against aristocrats, of the socialist press against representatives of the bourgeoisie, indeed, even of the liberal politicians of the Weimar Republic against the SA leader Ernst Röhm, who, by order of his *Duzfreund* and *Führer*, Adolf Hitler, was shot to death on June 30, 1934, and just as precipitously made the butt of public derision as the practitioner of moral turpitude. André Gide, who for a time sympathized with the official Communist line, was for the Soviets of that period a great writer and deeply humanistic thinker who was allowed to speak at Maxim Gorki's funeral rites in Moscow in 1936. Yet when a few months later in the same year he published his travel notes, in which there were criticisms of the Soviet Union, he was abruptly transformed back into an abominable homosexual, corruptor of youth, and agent of the bourgeoisie. Under the later Stalin (who had never wavered since he, in conjunction with Gorki, had replaced severe penalties on the homosexual activities of adult males) there was great mocking dissemination of the news from Paris that Jean-Paul Sartre, the hated author of *Dirty Hands*, was once more the cause of an antihumanistic scandal by wanting—think of it!—in all seriousness to save a thief and notorious homosexual: Jean Genet. Citizenship in Sodom was at all times and in all places a useful polemical argument.

Homosexual murderers (Fritz Haarmann or Jürgen Bartsch in Germany, John Wayne Gayce in the United States) are doubly infamous in the common mind. Murder by lesbians is seen to be an exceedingly unusual act. Again and again fire from Heaven falls down on Sodom and Gomorrah. Enlightenment has remained impotent: it postulated a rational equality of men and women, including homosexuals, yet without being able and without wanting to force the issue emotionally. As a consequence, the diaspora of Sodom lives in a condition of nonidentity: just as do the women with weapons, the vamps, the assimilated Shylocks. The self-hatred of homosexuals corresponds to the self-hatred of Jews. The Baron de Charlus, believing his secret secure, scorns pederasts as a part of his public social life in the salon. And Marcel Proust too, who provides the account of this, transforms his Albert into an Albertine. André Gide wanted nothing to do with Jean Cocteau and friends, and scarcely on account of literary reasons. The assimilated Jew in Berlin, or today in Paris or New York, despises the Eastern Jews. The sodomite caught in the constraints of a double life turns his back with disgust on the "queens." The literature that reports all this is a chronicle of murder and scandal. It reaches from Marlowe's dramatization of the life of King Edward of England to Jean Genet's figure in the novel *La Querelle de Brest*, who murders for fun and then in secret expiation surrenders himself sexually to another man.

10 Christopher Marlowe and King Edward II of England

Marlowe's history of "the troublesome reign and lamentable death of Edward the Second, King of England," is the first literary work of a new literature that deals with the eroticism between man and man not simply in passing, but as its central theme. It is a theme taken in all earnestness and led hard and fast along the line separating history and tragedy. It is sensed as a phenomenon in all ways equal to the eroticism between man and woman, equal in all its personal and social consequences as well. In Brecht's adaptation of the play, Edward's adversary, Roger Mortimer, recites the story of the Trojan War before the king, that is to say, the story of a frenzy, destructive to all for the sake of one Helen. Edward is supposed to recognize that his darling Gaveston is cut from the same cloth and could play for England and its king the role of a—this time male—Helen. "The king bursts into tears." He has grasped the point but not given way. The comparison is already to be found in Marlowe. It is made by Lancaster as Gaveston falls into the hands of his enemies and is slain, just as a soldier tricked out of his alms had predicted at the beginning of the history. Lancaster's address to the captured Gaveston is full of contempt:

Monster of men,
That, like the Greek strumpet, trained to arms
And bloody wars so many valiant knights. (II, 5)[1]

The social constellation in Elizabethan England was every bit as important to this subject and the way in which it was presented as the personal constellation of the man and author Marlowe. The Anglican split from Rome was the work of national politics, not of theology. Martin Luther's German Protestantism, by comparison, established the forms of a princely and petty aristocratic provincialism; the bourgeoisie was subject to the ruling authorities, as Luther had ordained, and left in a state of dependency in theological and scholarly matters, reduced in the end to imitating the etiquette of the courts. That forced the petty ruling princelings to be both cautious and hypocritical. Greater scandals are more readily to be found in the economically more developed area of the Electorate of Saxony, the ruling house of which, the Wettins, reverted to Catholicism toward the end of the century of Reformation for the sake of assuming the Polish crown. Catholicism had somewhat laxer practices in matters of public morality. The history of the young Crown Prince Frederick of Prussia, who was forced to view the decapitation of his favorite, Katte, in the early part of the eighteenth century reflects the Lutheran zealotry of the Prussian court, which meant to set a moral example for its citizens and to expunge the semblance of any kind of vice. Liselotte von der Pfalz, the wife of the French monarch's brother, who was little concerned with women, represents this kind of German provincialism in her letters from a court in which every kind of *plaisir* seemed perfectly acceptable as long as it was presentable and took Church, confession, and penance into account. The memoirs of the duc de Saint-Simon, not by accident one of Marcel Proust's favorite works, know of malice and gossip, but not moral outrage. The great generals in the age of French absolutism, Turenne, Condé, or Eugene of Savoy, were more involved with their officers and men than with their obligatory mistresses. The religious and moral rigorism of the Jansenists did not prevail; the Jesuits proved to be more amenable in such matters. Cases of homoeroticism were reported in memoir form or sometimes even in the Italian tradition of the novella. But it was not a theme in its own right for literature, neither in the province of aristocratic libertinism nor in the realm of Lutheran rigorism.

Theocratic Calvinism made its appearance in Geneva, the Netherlands, and later in Cromwell's England, and held indomitably to the Bible of both Old and New Testament. What had been said in it concerning Sodom and sodomy, expressly and irately reiterated by St. Paul, continued as unshaken tenet.

Elizabethan and Anglican England differed socially, and not simply theologically, from the continental Catholic and Protestant states. The original accumulation of capital was practiced by the titled great landowners themselves and not by the bourgeoisie against them. The result was that there was no sharp division between bourgeois and feudal orders of life as there was in Germany. Instead, there was fraternization and a

Christopher Marlowe and Edward II

penetrability of the aristocratic sphere. The life of the bourgeois intellectual Marlowe of Canterbury is a prime example of such behavior, not an exception to the rule.

The English aristocracy strove for humanistic education; many fine poets derived from its ranks, who drew to themselves bourgeois writers as well as various troupes of actors. Hamlet's way of dealing with the actors was not unusual. In Germany, by contrast, the comedians remained itinerant packs on the level of domestic servants. This bourgeois-aristocratic humanism, which had its Erasmus and Thomas More, which was familiar with Montaigne's *Essays,* had as a center of its discourse the possibilities of rational knowledge and via that juncture began to approach the concept central to that early (and all later) Enlightenment: the question of prejudice. Everything took place, as Marlowe and his sometime friend and roommate Thomas Kyd or later Ben Jonson would come to learn, at the very brink of scandal, torture, and condemnation. It is well known that Sir Walter Raleigh collected a court of intellectuals around himself that was suspected of being a "school of atheists"—just as well known as the fact that he diligently set out to avoid the slightest suspicion in this regard.

Out of this artificial and ambiguous world of the half-allowed and the half-repressed grew up a most astonishing breadth of themes in Elizabethan drama. John Ford, who was born about two decades after Shakespeare and Marlowe, wrote a tragedy along the lines of *Romeo and Juliet,* depicting the incestuous love of a brother and sister. After the Puritan victory the authorities well knew why they closed the theaters and forced the actors' troupes to emigrate.

Eroticism between males appears in Shakespeare's theater as a normal matter of course, yet it is a theme delimited to brief episodes. It does not appear in the histories, certainly not in the tragedies; it seems its proper realm is comedy (if we ignore the famous question of the "W. H." of the sonnets, that is). The erotic ambivalence of changes in costume and the question of who wears the pants is savored to its fullest dramatic extent. A man plays a woman who has disguised herself as a man. In *As You Like It,* the Puritan-to-be Malvolio is not accidentally contrasted with all the others, who metamorphose their sex and seem to have expunged all the boundaries to erotic attraction. The sailor Antonio loves Sebastian; it does not appear that his protestations of love are to be taken in a mere metaphysical sense.

Shakespeare's constellation is stereotypical: the weaker and suffering lover and the impatient, usurpatory beloved. Antonio loses Sebastian to the countess Olivia; Bassanio seeks the hand of the wealthy heiress Portia, whereby the man who loves her, Antonio, the merchant of Venice, falls into misfortune. Patroclus dies on the battlefield to save the honor of his beloved Achilles. Thersites alone reviles the lovers and their "lechery." The author of the comedy *Troilus and Cressida* brings to the fore all the noblesse of Patroclus as well as the erotic and military braggadocio of the beautiful Achilles.

The singularity of Marlowe's *Edward II* first becomes evident up against this literary and historical background. That he undertook to dramatize this particular story of a king who will under no circumstance abandon his love, who pays no regard to the objections of the nobles and the Church, who remains unaffected by the complaints of the queen, who prefers civil war to forgoing one Pierce de Gaveston, is not astonishing. The theme must have fascinated him. It is not simply the actual, historical events of Marlowe's own age that it reflects, namely those surrounding Henry III of France of the House of Valois, who kept a court of pretty boys, his *mignons* (who appear in Marlowe as "minions") and who was assassinated on August 2, 1589, by a Jacobin monk with a poisoned dagger. Marlowe was fascinated by the homosexual constellation. One sees that again and again in his works. We do not know how he himself was inclined. We have no report of mistresses in his life. On the other hand, all kinds of things have been said about him: that he had killed someone, that he had close associations with the London underworld, that he was a blasphemer and atheist. He was never called a sodomite. Yet that is one of his leitmotifs, alongside the theme of political immoralism, where he had a predilection for the principles of Machiavelli.[2]

In Marlowe's unfinished epic, *Hero and Leander* (first published subsequent to his violent death in a tavern at Deptford on June 1, 1593), the sexual passion with which Leander is described, much in contrast to Hero, is so unmistakable that even Marlowe's reticent biographer, Frederick S. Boas, expressly makes reference to the recurring "homosexual element."[3] Neptune is enamored of Leander:

> let it suffice
> That my slack muse sings of Leander's eyes,
> Those orient cheeks and lips, exceeding his
> That leapt into the water for a kiss
> Of his own shadow, and despising many
> Died ere he could enjoy the love of any.

Christopher Marlowe and Edward II

Had wild Hippolytus Leander seen,
Enamoured of his beauty had he been; (I, 71–78)[4]

The mythological play upon Hippolytus must have appeared to Marlowe's educated contemporaries as a kind of erotic denunciation. Theseus'
son Hippolytus refused the advances of his stepmother Phaedra. In
Racine that becomes the formal proferring of respect for the incest taboo,
which then has lethal consequences. Marlowe understands Hippolytus in
a much cruder fashion: he loves neither Phaedra nor other women, but
doubtless would be affected by Leander's beauty. Marlowe seems to have
gone quite far in his talk in the tavern in providing (re-)interpretations
regarding homosexuality.

The homoerotic interpretation of the story of Phaedra and Hippolytus
might have been well received by the humanist literati and their noble
patrons. Another, absurd and compulsive interpretation might well have
cost him his neck. Perhaps it was an assassin hired to prevent Marlowe's
being publicly executed for blasphemy. His erstwhile friend and roommate, Thomas Kyd (1558–1594), had been arrested and tortured on the
charge of atheism after a blasphemous tractate had been discovered
among his possessions. Kyd swore it belonged to Marlowe. Provisionally
let free, Kyd directed accusations against Marlowe to the authorities. A
letter written in his hand to that effect still exists. No matter what the
author of the story of King Edward and Gaveston was given to saying,
he thought the apostle Paul was a swindler, Kyd said. That fits into the
atheistic scheme of things in *The Jew of Malta* as well as in *Doctor Faustus*.

Then Kyd goes on: "He would report St. John to be Our Savior
Christes 'Alexis.' I cover it with reverence and trembling that is that
Christ did love him with an extraordinary love." Marlowe, as Kyd writes
here, had madly stylized Christ's favorite apostle, John, into the pagan
shepherd sweetheart Alexis.

Kyd apparently had invented nothing. In an almost contemporaneous
secret report of a professional police spy by the name of Richard Baines,
which likewise has been passed on to posterity, the same story is reported.
Baines knew nothing of Kyd and Kyd's letter. Marlowe must have had
a store of especially blasphemous turns of phrase that came up when he
was drunk. What they show is that the story of Edward and his minions
Gaveston and Spencer was for Marlowe not simply material like any
other, read in Holinshed's *Chronicles of England, Scotland, and Ireland*
(1577), a source used by Shakespeare for his royal plays, and then suited

up for the stage. If it is correct as is generally accepted today that *Doctor Faustus* was his last work, *Edward II* his next to last, then it becomes apparent that Marlowe's creative impulse toward the end of his life turned more and more away from interest in the material actions of a drama as in those of a Tamburlaine, say, or a Barabas, to a drama of self-revelation, as there likely was in Shakespeare's last comedies.

The history of King Edward II is such a drama of homosexual self-revelation: male–male eroticism not simply as dramatic material, but as content. One sees that in comparison with his earlier drama, *The Massacre at Paris,* which in many external aspects is quite similar, and in its construction and handling of themes is like a preparatory study to *Edward II.*

The material was taken from contemporary French history, which lay such a short time in the past that our dramatist and his political prophecies would come to be ironically contradicted by real developments. Marlowe had had the history of the religious wars end with the coronation of the Huguenot, Henry of Navarre as Henry IV, who was in league with Elizabeth of England, which is the provenance of the obligatory maledictions against pope and Catholic church. Henry swears to revenge the murder of Henry III of Valois until: "Rome and all those popish prelates there / Shall curse the time that e'er Navarra was king" (XXIII). That was probably written in, 1590. Unfortunately, in July 1593, scarcely two months after Marlowe's death, Henry of Navarre converted to Catholicism. Paris was worth a mass.

Structurally speaking, the relation of Edward to Mortimer is presaged in this earlier play about the Massacre of St. Bartholomew's Eve and its consequences. On the one hand Henry of Valois and his minions, on the other the mighty Duc de Guise, the king's adversary from the ranks of the high nobility. Here too political confrontation in the struggle for power is coupled with hatred stemming from the erotic sphere. One of King Henry's minions, Mugeroun, also sleeps with the Duchesse de Guise, who confesses, "Sweet Mugeroun, 'tis he that hath my heart./ And Guise usurps it cause I am his wife" (XIV). The mighty Guise who seeks to depose the royal house, an impotent cuckold. In *Edward II* the constellation is reversed: the queen goes over to Mortimer when Edward will have nothing more to do with her. In *The Massacre at Paris* as well as in *Edward II* both sides are ruined, both king and aristocratic adversary. At the end of both plays there is a Fortinbras to announce a new and better era: Henry IV in the one and Edward's son, Edward III, who reigned long and successfully, in the other.

The hegemony of the boys of pleasure at the court of Henry III was the subject for the first time in modern European history of a general and much bantered about scandal. Rumor and actual fact stirred up the bourgeoisie against the king, as it did the nobility who wanted to prevent Henry from distributing sinecures and estates according to pretty looks. Interests of the Church came into play as well. Henry, a Catholic and coplanner of the massacre of the Huguenots on St. Bartholomew's Eve, was murdered by order of the pope's party. Henry had, finally, been obliged to put on the play of the dutiful husband who spends his nights at the side of his queen. In Heinrich Mann's novel *Young Henry of Navarre,* which covers the same ground as Marlowe's *Massacre at Paris,* the playful shepherd-boy mischief of the mignons is brought to the fore, just as it is recorded in the chronicles. The well-staged drama of the king lying next to his queen so as to be observed by a good burgher of Paris who will inform the city of what his eyes have witnessed and so refute the rumor-mongers is there as well.

Marlowe had some sympathy for Henry, if markedly less than for King Edward of the far-off fourteenth century. It was simply the subject matter that held him fast. The mignons at the court in Paris were current, as was the scandal and the murder of the last king from the house of Valois. Henry did not lose his kingdom and come to ruin on account of his boys; his assassination derived from political calculations. (His successor, Henry IV, a great favorite among the ladies with the nickname "Vert Galant," was stabbed to death as well.)

What was only a secondary episode with the mignons in *The Massacre at Paris* becomes the precipitating event in the story of *Edward II.* The dramatist immediately gets to the heart of the matter. Gaveston speaks the first words of the play. Actually they are the words of the king in a letter to his friend. He has now succeeded to the throne after the death of his father, who had banished the young Gaveston to France. "Come back, father is dead," the letter reads, "come share my kingdom with me."

The noble lords refer to Gaveston mostly as "that base minion," whereby his common origins and common intentions may be meant, yet he was not, as later in Brecht's adaptation, some sort of muscleman from the local butchershop but the son of a knight from the Gascogne who had served under Edward I. Gaveston *fils* grew up with the son of the king; when their close friendship seemed undesirable, Pierce was sent back home to France. Now he is asked to return. He has lived at court and is on good terms with the classics.

Sweet prince, I come; these, these thy amorous lines
Might have enforced me to have swum from France,
And, like Leander, gasped upon the sand,
So thou wouldst smile and take me in thy arms.

A Leander who swims the Channel to throw himself into the arms of his regal Hero. What might have been in Marlowe's mind when composing, perhaps simultaneously with his work on *Edward II,* his verse epic *Hero and Leander?* He had imitated Ovid, knew the story of Leander from Musaeus, yet the insistence with which Gaveston in the play's opening monologue refers to that ancient ardent swimmer of the Hellespont leads one to suspect a hidden point of connection and sympathy in Marlowe for that old mythological scheme of things. Frederick Boas in his "biographical and critical study" of Marlowe points out how much Shakespeare's *Richard II* was indebted to Marlowe's *Edward,* then regrets that Marlowe never dramatized the story of Hero and Leander—which would then have been a counterpart to *Romeo and Juliet.*[5] But what if the counterpart mentioned here were to be found precisely in the history of the troublesome reign and lamentable death of Edward the Second, King of England?

That Edward's (same-sexed) eros stands at the centerpoint of the drama and makes possible the tragedy within the history becomes apparent in the manner in which Marlowe makes historical facts subservient to this end. The historical Edward ascended to the throne at the age of twenty-three, defended his friend from Gascogne against the English nobles for five years until Gaveston was finally killed in 1312. Edward himself did not die until 1327; Mortimer was executed by Edward's son, now become Edward III, in 1330.

After Gaveston's death then Edward continued his "troublesome reign" for another fifteen years. And Gaveston appears in the play for the last time, to be sure, in the first scene of the third act. Yet the historical as well as the dramatical Edward was not exclusively fixated on this one man from the southwest of France. The business was not over after Gaveston disappeared from the scene. Holinshed relates in his chronicle that after the death of his first favorite, Edward raised up the Spencers,

Christopher Marlowe and Edward II

father and son, who induced him to practice "all kind of naughtie and evill rule." The Spencers appear in Marlowe, too, and both die in Edward's service. They are here members of the English nobility, consequently no longer marked by the deficiency of the base Gaveston. Nonetheless the civil war continues. And with it Edward's *amours.* The young Spencer takes Gaveston's place. He also came close to taking the king's place in Gaveston's heart, as he tells a friend, the young scholar Baldock. Gaveston liked the boy, but held to the king, "for he loves me well/ And would have once preferred me to the king" (II, 1). Now the young Spencer enters Edward's service as mignon. The erotic constellation thoroughly resembles that of the mignons in *The Massacre at Paris.*

Gaveston was the active, male partner. He was Leander. He loved and wed the daughter of the duke of Gloucester, became duke himself, and the duchess in love with him. Simultaneously he is the king's lover, who for his sake disowns Queen Isabella and reviles her as "the French strumpet." Gaveston vacillates erotically between Spencer and the king. Spencer, also the king's lover, clings to his friend Baldock. They all go to their ruin because of it.

Gaveston is precisely depicted: the foreigner and outsider in every respect. A Frenchman, of low birth in comparison with the earls. An erotic adventurer. He is impudent, boorish, violent, but not pitiful. When he must die, he sums up cooly as he always did:

I thank you all, my lords. Then I perceived
That heading is one, and hanging is the other
And death is all.   (II, 5)

King Edward is evidently the feminine partner in this erotic constellation. The obscene way in which he dies makes it all too plain. This king is not, as later Shakespeare's Richard II, a weakling of a king, dependent even in the erotic realm, on stronger and resolute men; no, he is a king whose lovers are more important to him than everything else, so that all his actions, giving of gifts, banishments, laudations and damnations always hold in them manifestations of his sexual freneticism. This first homoerotic hero to appear in the title of a European drama is to be distinguished from that other Elizabethan eponymous hero, the merchant of Venice, by his solitariness. Shylock cuts the figure of another prototypical adversary in his relations to Antonio, so that this comedy has two centers, as it were, and takes on an elliptical shape. Marlowe's Mortimer, Edward's adversary, on the contrary, is no more than a trivial machiavellian plotter on the order of the Duc de Guise or the Jew of Malta. In the earlier *Massacre at Paris,* there was the king and his adversary, Henry III and Guise, the actions of the one and the counteractions of the other. In *Edward II* there is only this male-female king. On this account things never come to be the homoerotic counterpart to Romeo and Juliet or to Hero and Leander. Edward loves men, not one particular one. He leads an aesthetic-erotic existence. Gaveston is well aware of that and is careful to plan:

Music and poetry is his delight;
Therefor I'll have Italian masks by night,
Sweet speeches, comedies, and pleasing shows.   (I, 1)

Edward the Second, King of England and First Lord of Ireland, commences that long line of literary figures out searching for their home of Sodom, bent on dreams, power, poetry, and music, unremittingly living their lives between delusion and reality. Centuries later there appears the Baron de Charlus, a mighty man from a mighty house, who sinks down into misery. Then there is the provincial boy come to Paris who wears women's clothes—known to his friends and pickups as Divine, who meets his death in a garret. At his funeral there appears a sometime lover known as Mignon. They are figures in Jean Genet's *Notre Dame des Fleurs.* Whoever has heard and seen Marlowe's Edward already knows all of them who will come later. Marlowe had more than sympathy for his king.

I must admit that the exact opposite of this proposition is asserted by one of the great connoisseurs of Elizabethan theater. In an addendum to his work *Shakespeare Our Contemporary* Jan Kott deals in some detail with the mainsprings of Marlowe's dramatic theory, starting with a juxtaposition of Shakespeare's *Richard II* to Marlowe's history of Edward. For Kott, the author of the great amoral outsiders Tamburlaine, Barabas, Edward, and Faustus is a precursor of Artaud's theater of cruelty. The moral indolence of the main figures in his plays corresponds to the dramatist's disdain for human failure, he maintains. Kott sees in Edward reviled and executed merely an object of contempt: an object of contempt in Marlowe's eyes. How well deserved his end, served up almost enjoyably in its absolute negativity!

"Marlowe equally hates king and usurper. The world he shows is naked. Human behavior is stripped bare: there no longer is faith and philosophy. Demythologization has been brought to its logical conclusion. No one of this circle has honor or even courage."[6] This thesis, however,

Christopher Marlowe and Edward II

is contradicted by Edward's actions and demeanor in the play, and not least by the level of his language during the course of his fall. Kott's inclination in his analysis of Elizabethan works to underestimate dialectical and divergent elements of character (he characterizes Thersites in *Troilus and Cressida,* for example, simply as a "lout"!) means that he views Edward, contrary to the text itself, as an object of pitiless disdain. Yet it is simply a fact that Marlowe does not at all treat King Edward and usurper Mortimer in an identical fashion. He did not even do that with Henry and Guise in *The Massacre at Paris.* Henry of Navarre spoke there of the murdered Henry of Valois almost as Fortinbras of the dead Hamlet. In *Edward II,* Edward's son sets out to avenge his father amid a universal show of approval. There is no longer any thought of Gaveston and Spencer. Mortimer's severed head, at the end of the play, on the other hand, demonstrates the thoroughly divergent "attitude" of the playwright Marlowe to his two adversaries. Bertolt Brecht's adaptation, *The Life of Edward II,* an occasional work of the early 1920s undertaken on Lion Feuchtwanger's suggestion and with his collaboration to build up the repertory of the Munich Kammerspiele, also understands the contrasting positions of Edward and Mortimer. Brecht, in contradistinction to Kott and completely in contrast to Marlowe, tries to devalue the king in favor of the usurper. And it is on this account that Mortimer's head has no place in his version, nor even the whole ruin and failure of this intellectual thrown into politics, whom Brecht allows the showpiece monologue on the Trojan War and its origin in Helen.[7]

Brecht rewrote the play along the lines of his own lyrical sensibility, anticipating the attitudes of the *Neue Sachlichkeit* amid the then universal outpourings of Expressionism: whereby he missed Marlowe's intent and Marlowe's antitheses of love and knowledge or power and death. Strangely enough, Brecht, the young author of *Baal,* for whom the tragic story and pitiful ruin of Verlaine and Rimbaud were so full of meaning, did not seem to grasp that Edward's history is in a sense an anticipation of them in both a real and a poetic sense. None other than the Bishop of Coventry, representing church and state, sums up at the play's end the lamentable history of this Brechtian king:

Thus none of those who in Westminster Abbey
Attended that man's coronation will
Witness his funeral. For Edward the Second
Not knowing, or so it seems, which of his enemies
Remembered him, not knowing what breed of men

Dwelt in the light above his head; not knowing
The color of the leaves, or the season
Or the position of the constellations, died
Forgetful of himself
In misery.[8]

He was unknowing then, an avoidable lapse on his part, not Marlowe's absolute existential alternatives. And with that, the young Brecht's Edward simply becomes one more in the row of unknowing and apathetic characters found in Brecht's early lyric collection, the *Hauspostille*.

In his study of the overreacher Christopher Marlowe, which deals with St. John's differentiations between the *libido sentiendi,* the *libido sciendi,* and the *libido dominandi* in the case of Marlowe's dramatic characters (Edward, Faustus and Barabas, Tamburlaine), Harry Levin[9] sees a clear line of connection between the personality of the man Marlowe and the stereotypical conflicts of his dramas. "Unloved, the Marlovian protagonist desiderates a companion, a minion, a deuteragonist; and here the exception that proves the rule is the Uranian Eros of Edward and Gaveston." Levin then cites a verse from Marlowe's poem on Hero and Leander, "One is no number" (I, 255), and continues: "Marlowe's dramatic heroes stand alone in their singularity and singlemindedness. Conscious at every moment of their identity, they are supremely self-conscious at the moment of death." So they are, in Levin's opinion, fashioned by the author after his own image, after his own character: "egoists, exhibitionists, infidels, outsiders."[10]

11 Winckelmann's Death and the Discovery of a Double Life

He died the morning of June 8, 1768, in the inn in which he had been staying in the Locanda Grande in Trieste, a noose round his neck, stabbed to death by a man who was then going by the name of Francesco Angelis, whose actual name was Arcangeli. Winckelmann had been born in Stendal on December 9, 1717, so was fifty when he died.[1] A world-famous man lost his life. A community of artists, scholars, and connoisseurs of art mourned him and was disquieted. Lessing in his *Laokoon* had somewhat ironically taken issue with some of the deceased's propositions, especially with some of the documentation. Now he wrote, badly shaken by this second sudden death (Laurence Sterne had died shortly before), that he gladly would have given up his own life in Winckelmann's stead. In Potsdam, Frederick II of Prussia first communicated the news to the sculptor Cavaceppi, Winckelmann's companion on the journey back to Germany, when he received him toward the end of June.

For all of them he had been the acknowledged master of his craft worthy of emulation: for his artist friends in London, the cardinals in the Vatican who lost the best man of the art collections with him, and for members of the future *Sturm und Drang* movement in Germany, from Goethe to Herder. In Herder's *Memorial to J. Winckelmann*[2] and in Goethe's later work on the author of *The History of Ancient Art*, there is reflected after the fact, even decades later, the great enthusiasm and then sudden desolation that shook those who were young at the time.

After his fashion, the later Weimar Goethe attempted to block out anything that might have contradicted his version of a happy and harmonious scholar and connoisseur of art. That was in his own essay[3] on Winckelmann's life and character that accompanied the edition of Winckelmann's letters to the privy councillor Berendis brought out by the Weimar Friends of Art in 1805, which was meant to legitimate Weimar classicism by conjunction with the great scholar of the recent past. Yet, in the end, there was the violence and murder of Trieste. Goethe interpreted it, beating it almost violently into harmonious form, in the following manner: "So then on the highest rung of happiness and fortune that he could want for himself he disappeared from the world. . . . And in this sense we can account him happy, that he rose up to the blessed from the topmost point of human existence, that a short horror, a speedy pain took him from the living. The frailties of age, the diminution of intellect were spared him. . . . He lived as a man and went forth from this world as a man in his fullness."

It was a favorite thought of Goethe's, found in his poem "Anacreon's Grave" as well, a wishful dream: to die as a man, without the pains and impairments of old age. He himself did not come to fulfill that dream of sweet death. The "cheery old one" of the *East–West Divan* lyrics may have come to think differently than the ailing Goethe of 1804, distraught by strife and civil war, who in such an imposing fashion sought to banish the disharmonies and ruptures in Winckelmann's life and death. "A short horror, a speedy pain . . ." The court records of Arcangeli's murder trial, which report in ample detail Winckelmann's slow hemorrhaging from the puncture wounds, the vigorous man's struggle with his murderer, the ugly death in a public inn surrounded by stupid and indifferent waiters and cleaning girls, know otherwise. Goethe, too, must have known otherwise.

It must have been even clearer to Goethe just how provocative (even for Winckelmann's friends and admirers) his proclamation of intact manliness must be. "He lived as a man and went forth from this world as a man in his fullness." That is well put, despite all its disavowal of patent facts of life, and even correct in so far as it sketches Winckelmann's intellectual acuity, his exactitude of sight, his speculative potency, the completely unsentimental manner of his science and his writing. But a "man in his fullness" when speaking of the deceased's sexual and spiritual aspects? Certainly in the collection of letters to Berendis edited by Goethe there are scarcely to be found counterparts to the love letters written to the twenty-six-year-old Livonian baron, Friedrich Reinhold von Berg, to whom the forty-six-year-old Winckelmann dedicated his "Treatise on the Ability to Perceive the Beautiful in Art." Among the letters to Berg is one dated February 10, 1764: "All names that I might call you are not sweet enough and do not suffice my love. . . . My dearest friend, I love you more than all other creatures, and time and accident and age cannot diminish this love."[4]

One recognizes the tone of the letters of the historian (and friend of Goethe's) Johannes Müller von Schaffhausen or of Count August von Platen-Hallermünde. So often they too are directed to young and well-formed yet insignificant Junkers whose names have remained to history only because of that mostly hopeless, sometimes (objectively seen) even half-comic passionate longing. Neither is the sulky nuance lacking in Winckelmann's love letters to young men. The older and aging lover becomes simultaneously the object of the younger man's love, his beloved, and his mother, who is desirous of protecting him from "women's wiles," in quite the same language as Sarastro's divagations in *The Magic Flute*. When Berg commerces both in Rome itself and later in Florence with "wantons and strumpets," as Winckelmann disappointedly puts it to another acquaintance, and then travels on to Paris, Winckelmann writes him that "the Genius of our friendship will follow you from afar up to the gates of Paris and then leave you there in that seat of foolish prurience. Here in Rome, however, your image will be my saint." (June 9, 1762)

In his psychoanalytical study, "The Drama of Winckelmann,"[5] the depth psychologist Gustav Bychowski characterizes such positions of a male–male mother–son relationship as being well known and "specific." This protégé of Freud's sees parallels in literature over one century later and across the Atlantic, finding Winckelmann's letters to Count Bünau or Baron Berg reminiscent of Walt Whitman's epistles to the young Peter Doyle.[6]

There is paternal and maternal care, sensual and stylized love. Much of it even in Winckelmann is a modish sentimentality: not many years thereafter the cult of friendship in the German *Sturm und Drang* movement was to be ceremoniously organized and made to fructify poetry. Despite everything, Winckelmann's life stood in deepest accord with his science and scholarship. He has no illusions, least of all with his young friends. In the same missive to Berg where he spoke of Paris as the seat of foolish prurience, he quotes Cowley's "Ode on Platonic Love"

I thee both as man and woman prize.
For a perfect love implies
Love in all capacities.

That could have been in a poem by Platen. Winckelmann does not delude himself, or others either for that matter. That is a part of his genuineness and the honesty acknowledged by all quarters as being at the center of his life and work. In the letters to Berendis edited by Goethe, he unabashedly reports he has cares with his work but not in his personal life. There, he says, he knows a young Roman—blond, good-looking, sixteen years old, half a head taller than he. But he sees the boy only on Sundays for dinner.

That the aesthetic of this art historian and scholar of antiquity was almost exclusively concerned with the beauty of the male body, loses objectivity when concerned with representations of Aphrodite, has long been noted. Winckelmann's famous early analysis and description of the torso in the Vatican Belvedere was already a hymn of exact science inspired by an awareness of male corporeal beauty. All of the later debates over the aesthetic priority of the male or female body (maliciously parodied against Platen by Heine in *The Baths of Lucca,* later eccentrically driven to absurdity by André Gide in the dialogues of his *Corydon*) are already prefigured with high connoisseurship and erotic ardor in Johann Joachim Winckelmann.

Nonetheless Goethe, who had all of this in mind, spoke of Winckelmann's manliness and happiness. He called it by name in the section on "Beauty" in his essay that prefaces his edition of Winckelmann's letters. "We often find Winckelmann in conjunction with beautiful young men, and nowhere else does he seem livelier or more amiable than in such oftentimes mere fleeting moments." That has been conceived and put differently than Heine's moral abhorrence at Count Platen's *ghazels* on the theme of friendship.

It is even more noteworthy that Goethe's interpretations were conceived in complete cognizance of the manner in which this friend of young men met his death. The proceedings against Francesco Arcangeli together with his detailed confession have been subjects of considerable discussion. The documents were first published in recent times. Arcangeli was publicly broken on the wheel in Trieste for murder. That Winckelmann, as his murderer apprises us, sought out his company, appears to correspond to the facts. On the other hand, there was no erotic relationship. That was something Arcangeli had asserted because it might have saved him had he been able to sustain a plea of "self-defense." Arcangeli was a man over thirty, and pockmarked besides, something detestable to Winckelmann, who praised the Greeks, happy because they were apparently unacquainted with that particular disfigurement. Winckelmann had been traveling incognito, a simple Signor Giovanni, and had stimulated the imagination of a fellow lodger in his hotel, Arcangeli. He had told him of a visit to the empress in Vienna, had mentioned mysterious missions that had some connection with the silver and gold medallions he showed him. Arcangeli was a professional criminal of unsteady fantasy. He began to despise this apparent wellwisher, thinking him a Jew or a Lutheran and seeking a religious opinion before buying the knife and rope he would employ as the murder intruments. Winckelmann was unsuspecting and trustful. Nonetheless the whole history of his last journey with its depressions, presentiments of death, the sudden decision to quit Germany and return to Rome seems a real-life rehearsal for Gustav von Aschenbach's actions in Thomas Mann's *Death in Venice*.

The psychoanalyst Bychowski viewed it thus: "Loving his young friends like an emotional mother left him unfulfilled since he wanted to be embraced by them as well, like a tender woman by a mighty hero. . . . Yet life, their own youth, and real women took them from him. What remained was art, the study and contemplation of which made him content. But apparently cold marble could not completely substitute for the warmth of human flesh. He reached at last in his final deadly embrace the Nirvana he had longed for, the complete dissolution of all desire." That is a questionable proposition, more strongly inspired by Romantic postulates than by the plastic rationalism that informed Winckelmann and the eighteenth century in which he lived. Despite this, the death of this scholar and representative of his epoch has remained a source of disquiet. Gerhart Hauptmann near the end of his life decided to juxtapose a darker version of his own making of Winckelmann's life and demise to Goethe's. Hauptmann chose the novel as his vehicle in which the last stage in the Locanda Grande at Trieste would provide the epic moment. The novel was never finished.

What are the reasons for this strangely fascinating disquiet? Perhaps they are to be found in the exposure of a double life, the very reason Goethe so self-determinedly tried to deny this very discrepancy and ambivalence. In his endeavor to praise the homoerotic Winckelmann as a model of manliness, to stylize his abrupt end without sweetness and light as a happy one, Goethe misrecognized the specific contradictions involved, and with them Winckelmann's ardent productivity, which remains a source of great stimulus to this day.

Modern art historians have identified one after another the curious antagonisms in the thoughts and critical judgments of this first art *historian* in a modern sense.[7] Richard Hamann, for one, has called Winckelmann's historical understanding into question. It is curious that a thinker who was able to situate and order historically the great masses of remaining antiquities conceived the central notion of his aesthetic, "nature," in a thoroughly ahistorical manner, posited absolutely the fundamental concepts of beauty, repose, dignity, which he took from works of Greek plastic art, and elevated them to an ahistorical norm. He was an art historian touched to the core by the manly beauty of Greek ephebes, who invited his contemporaries to be touched too. He was a bourgeois rationalist to whom the Idea manifested itself. He was the child of a family of miserable means in Brandenburg who set the plastic arts the task of representing human beings in quiet dignity, whereby Winckelmann naively projected back into antiquity the rules for statues imitated everywhere in the Europe of French absolutism.

Richard Hamann sharply criticized the famous definition of noble simplicity and quiet grandeur; that meant, he said, "less the return to great, noble classical art than something negative, abstract, a break from that which provided the art of antiquity and the related art of the Middle Ages and the Baroque with their content. What is left is a form without content."[8]

Goethe seems to want to suppress all this. That it did not escape his notice is evidenced by that very suppression. Without a doubt Goethe was writing about the great and ostensibly so felicitous scholar from Stendal to his own ends: the piece *Winckelmann and His Century* was a preliminary work and first attempt at later depicting in autobiographical form Goethe and his century. Winckelmann was also made to provide corroboration after the fact to the effect that the art journal (*Die Propyläen*) edited by Goethe and his Weimar Friends of Art and dissolved after two years of publication (1800) had succumbed to intrigues—say those of the evil Romantics in Jena—rather than to its anachronistic program of a "form without content." Despite all this, these explanations do not suffice. Hamann's thesis of the ahistorical historian, which had appeared as early as in Herder's memorial essay, spoke of the discrepancy between historical placement and ahistorical, aesthetic normativity. But it is just this contradiction that must be historically situated! It did not escape Winckelmann that Bünau and Berg, even more so his Roman boys, could reproduce only the contour of the ancient models of a Praxiteles or a Lysippus, not the social process reflected in Plato's dialogues or in Aristophanes' diatribes. In his *Clouds* or in *The Congresswomen,* that writer of Athenian comedy had mocked the aristocratic pederasts in the circle around Socrates and Euripides with political and aesthetic lines of argument, not with moral and certainly not with existential ones. In Austria, however, the German Emperor Ferdinand III had in the year 1656 decreed for the lands under his domain, which included Trieste, that the crime of "unnatural" sexual intercourse would be punished by death by fire at the stake.[9]

The life and thought, work and death of Johann Joachim Winckelmann reflect this schism. A lover of beautiful things who had to die in a manner at once ugly, without dignity, and full of scandal. Richard Alewyn, a Hofmannsthal scholar, has shown that Hofmannsthal's "Tale of the 672nd Night," which reports the ugly "death of an aesthete," was inspired by news of Oscar Wilde's trial. Winckelmann's end in the Locanda Grande was already such a death of an aesthete. Whether seeded by his sexuality or finding individual motivations there, that aestheticism produced a rift down the center of life in turn reproduced by social, legal, and moral norms. But its most sublime consequences are to be discovered as the contrast between the ideal of beauty and its impossibility of fulfillment, terror and comicality, in the form of thought: in the immense work of Winckelmann and the other representatives of Sodom's diaspora. What we see here is the coercion to lead a double life. A euphemism of the bourgeois era branded homosexuality an eros that dare not speak its name. That was the case for works of literature as well, including those of Marcel Proust, who takes pains to represent his friend Albert as "Albertine." This includes Wilde, who was in no sense inclined to communicate to his readers wherein the real, scandalous depravity eating away Dorian Gray's body and soul lay, though he is not miserly with certain intimations.

The revelation of a double life attendant on Winckelmann's demise at the end of the feudal era cannot be understood simply as a contrast between respectable conduct on the one hand and sensual pleasure on the other, between social upper and underworld. This dichotomy had meant nothing to the feudal lord; it was part and parcel of his libertinage. Perhaps it was the stuff of comedy but certainly not the stuff of the tragedy of life. The rising middle class, contrarily, demanded equality before the (middle class) moral codex. What resulted was the coercion to lead a double life in all sectors of society, a double life stamped by hypocrisy and self-deception, erotic conformity to the norm and also by a coercion to idealization and stylization. Such idealization is to be found in Winckelmann as the ahistorical normativity of an aesthetic formulation that was all the more passionately disseminated as it was doomed to remain anachronistic. In Platen it is found as the stylization of unfulfillable eros through strict poetic form. In Whitman as the rhapsodic hymnody that means to embrace all exceptions within the universal rule. In Stefan George as the apotheosis of a handsome Bavarian boy. In Proust as the gender changes of fictional characters resulting from the author's sexual inversion. In Oscar Wilde, once more as in Winckelmann, it is found as a double life raised to the status of aesthetic postulate. In the preface to *The Picture of Dorian Gray* one finds that "to reveal art and conceal the artist is art's aim." That was written in an age that strove for nothing more passionately than to reveal the occasional and particular self of the artist. Wilde was well aware of that. Yet that principle was not applicable to artists from Sodom's realm. There the necessary motto was to distill art out of one's double life. Which is to say, conceal impulse and motivation. Conceal the artist. By the time of Winckelmann's death a new law of life was becoming visible for his kind. Many paid dearly, as did Verlaine and Wilde, who did not hold themselves to it. When August Graf von Platen-Hallermünde transgressed its boundaries, he was confronted by Heinrich Heine.

12   The Conflict between Heine and Platen

This is once again the confrontation between the Jew Shylock and Bassanio's unhappy friend, the merchant of Venice. Once again the Jew did not actually begin the struggle.

There is a sense of unease remaining to this very day in all the observers of this feud between poets and men of letters who for reasons stemming from their personal lives and not at all having to do with their literary productions were edged into a realm to the far side of polemics, satire, and the obduracy of literary reviewing. Here outsiders were battling who did not simply care to poke barbs at the assertedly wretched poetic productions of the other but who went on to denounce the adversary's outsiderdom, which, as it happened, was different from one's own. So that it fell to Platen, mindful of his birth and baptism, to chase off the "Jew boy" from the literary scene of the German restoration period, while the "Petrarch of the Feast of Tabernacles" and the "synagogue bloat" made reply with the plebeian epithet of "pansy," mindful himself of all the bodily pains and nervous sufferings visited upon him by femininity.

Literary historians do not seem to be particularly concerned with coming to exact terms with this quarrel of the year 1829; that is especially the case with Heine scholars who have assembled the documents relating to it and have reconstructed its phases without attempting any kind of critical interpretation. All they feel is an unease. The friendship (if it was that) between Karl Immermann and Heinrich Heine, which provided the first inspiration to the ensuing polemic, went to pieces because of it. Heinrich Heine is reputed to be a "German scandal"; whenever there is talk of that one comes perforce to the mention of *The Baths of Lucca* and the accumulations of wit in it directed against boy-lovers. Heine has most recently even found a vindicator in the person of an editor of his collected works. Günter Häntzschel[1] writes in his commentary to *The Baths of*

Lucca that they simply give answer to the "vulgar, oftentimes flaccid, and weak-minded attacks of Platen" that had deeply insulted Heine, at the time in a "porous mood . . . and consequently doubly susceptible to attack." Platen, he says, had scarcely read anything by Heine or Immermann when he launched his offensive. That Häntzschel in turn interprets Heine's existential diatribe against the count as a "better-founded, wittier, but also completely damning repartee," may be right. It is hard to pass judgment on wit, and Heine's mockery was certainly "damning" in adumbrating Platen's lyrics as the product of "schoolboy assiduity, if not bottoms, in regard to content as well," certainly damning as Platen's last years (1829–1835) demonstrate. If only our Heine editor, who censures Platen's ignorance, had in turn better acquaintance of Platen's views and political stance.

There was much more involved in the unparalleled polemics between the recently baptized German Jew and literary figure and the impoverished, aristocratic son of a chief forestry officer who lived in Erlangen and sang of well-built friends. Something was involved here that fully transcended the dimensions of hitherto existing polemics. Thomas Mann recognized that in his Platen lecture in Ansbach in 1930, which he included five years later, then already an emigré, in his collection of essays, *Leiden und Grösse der Meister* (Sorrows and Greatness of the Masters),[2] signifying in that title alone that Platen's sufferings were also coupled with greatness and with first-rate poetry, so that a laudatio of one who wrote the verse "How I grow ill on account of my fatherland" did not seem untoward in times of exile and under conditions in Germany where Count Platen's "species," the butt of insults much like those provided by Heine, were being rounded up and perched in concentration camps with pink identification triangles sewn on their uniforms . . . under conditions in which, at the same time, the author of *The Baths of Lucca* had been declared by the authorities a nonperson.

Count August von Platen-Hallermünde's lyrics and eroticism brought Thomas Mann to see a spiritual correlation to the Hidalgo de la Mancha, the knight of the sorrowful countenance. There is in Platen, he says, who to all appearances is such a declared believer in classical form, in truth an anachronistic, romantic knight-errantry where love once again pits itself against death. And that is assuredly more the case there than in the all too popular verses contained in Heine's *Book of Songs*. This is why Thomas Mann says in his Platen lecture: "One is well-acquainted with the playfully macabre and significantly emphasized coupling of love and death practiced by the Romantic writers and by Heine in his Romanticizing songs and romances. Here, in Platen's poem, these concepts are bound to each other in a sense that goes far beyond a superficial and sentimental Romanticism."[3] His conclusion: "Platen—Don Quixote! An itinerant soul insufflated and driven by a divine folly, by a thankless, anachronistic, impossible, embittered nobility of spirit and courage to do battle—reviled and beaten one moment, the butt of common laughter the next—which will swear to its last living breath that Dulcinea of Toboso is the most beautiful woman under the sun, although but a farm lass—which is to say here, although but some silly student by the name of Schmidtlein or German."

Don Quixote's illness is incurable just as is every disposition of the body or spirit that does not allow itself to be "corrected" medicinally, or, along the postulates of the bourgeois Enlightenment, does not allow itself to be eliminated by rational discourse. This is why a Jew stays a Jew and why Sartre pokes fun at conservative psychiatrists who, well-meaning though they may be, advise pederasts to take greater interest in young ladies. A cured Knight of la Mancha immediately becomes a banality: a pathological exception after successfully applied therapy. Platen–Don Quixote however, remained incurable: out of the reach of officious Enlightenment.

Heinrich Heine's case was no different. Just as (in *The Baths of Lucca*) he was mistaken about Platen's politics and poetry, so was he equally mistaken about his own possibilities of really belonging, those extending beyond mere formal stipulation. Baptism, talent, and conformity of sexual drive to the norm were not sufficient. Almost with disdain Thomas Mann quotes Heine's line of justification: Count von Platen, he said, reviled the most precious thing he had, his Christianity. Two years after Platen's death in self-inflicted exile in Syracuse, the freely willed emigré Heine in Paris composed something as introduction to a new German edition of Cervantes. Platen had suspected nothing of his own position as Don Quixote; that was part of the role. Heine, on the other hand, cast a glance back at the 1820s, the decade of his *Images from Travel*, those years when he to all appearances enjoyed every success in Germany, when he was able to give vent to all his desires publicly: even the scene where the baptized Jew from Hamburg, Gumpel, now Marchese Gumpelino, is wont to moan "O sweet Jesus" from time to time, and who as a sufferer of diarrhea, pulls out a copy of Platen's poems: "On the last page was artfully penned, 'A present of our oh-so-dear friendship' and from the book there came wafting that curious perfume having not the least connection with eau de cologne—which is perhaps due to the fact that the marquess had spent the whole night reading in it."[4]

In those days it had been an incurable foolhardiness, an authentic Don Quixotism, with nothing between one and the deep blue sea but talent, a baptismal certificate, and gravitation toward the student life of Göttingen, to attempt to brush away in the same burst of enlightened laughter Gumpelino, emancipated with belles lettres and striving ever higher in literary matters, and his Jewish Sancho Panza, Hirsch-Hyazinth of Hamburg, together with the poetic Don Quixotism and unsuccessful boy cult of Count Platen. It disturbed many of their contemporaries, contemporaries, I might add, well-disposed toward Heine and not particularly inclined toward Platen, that Heine did not shrink from reproaching the poor knight from Franconia with his poverty, which is to say with his paltry honoraria. "The count . . . resolved to live from his writings and from occasional dotations from above and some few other earnings. The count's countly estates, you see, are to be found on the moon."[5]

In his *Baths of Lucca*, Heine comes to speak of Cervantes and his ingenuous hidalgo. The baptized Marchese Gumpel and his manservant Hirsch are playful imitations of that sad knight and his donkey-riding page. Yet their foolishness is curable. It was unavoidable really, at this juncture, that Heine would come to consider the original knight of the sorrowful form first in relation to his madness. Heine sees the essence of Don Quixotism in what he, together with most of his contemporaries, considered to be Platen's poetic megalomania: "I must admit that I don't consider Count Platen to be the big fool one might be led to believe he is by his puffed-up manner and incessant need to attract praise and attention. Some foolery, one must admit, is the proper part of poetry; but it would be awful if nature herself came to heap such a great portion of foolishness onto one single individual and at the same time provide him with such an insignificant amount of poetry."[6] So far all this has remained quite within the usual confines of literary polemics. Karl Immermann had, in a similar vein, given the count, who had made the dramatic character "Nimmermann" (nowhere-man) out of him, cause to reflect in one of his sonnets called "Glorious Misery":

Doch in den Versen dann, den grauen, glatten,
Der nachgefühlten Fühlung greise Weise,
Und die Doublettgedanken, ach! die matten.
Ich denk': der Bettler bleibt ein Don vom Heller,

Wenn er auch isst die magre Bettelspeise
Zufällig vom geborgten goldnen Teller.[7]*

But then, after the fun and games with Gumpel and Hirsch had served their purpose, Heine came to address in his own name and as a critical essayist, Platen's poetic substance: that death-seeking romanticism of an impossible eroticism, as Thomas Mann has put it. The Enlightenment critic Heine wanted to call the count's proclivities by name and denounce them openly, but at the same time did not want to come under suspicion of allying himself with officiously minded sneaks, as it were, attacking someone merely for his "difference."

At this crossroads Heine's polemics become as ingenious as they become dishonest. He did not want, he says, to pass judgment on Platen's pederasty but on his hypocrisy. "The noble count is for me rather an edifying phenomenon, and in his special and delicate connoisseurship I only see something not of these times, merely the dilatory, embarrassed parody of ancient hubris." Can Heine have meant what he wrote? Because Platen, a homoerotic, fortuitously came into the world as a member of the aristocracy, as Heine did a Jew, is his way of feeling and perceiving, the quintessence of his lyrics, to be nothing more than a production of aristocratic degeneracy? A degeneracy comparable to Don Juan's libertinage in Molière where, next to the reproach of aristocratic degeneracy, the reproach of hypocrisy had also been articulated. And it is precisely in that sense that Heine continues: "It is interesting in this connection what the comparison of Platen's little poems with those of Petronius shows. In Petronius there is a bald, ancient, plastic pagan openness; Count Platen, contrarily, despite all his claims to classicism, treats his object in a fashion thoroughly romantic, mystifying, yearning, clerical— and, I am obliged to add—hypocritical."

One cannot claim all of these things in one breath. Heinrich Heine was thoroughly cognizant of the fact that his exposures (which interpret poetic metaphors as the facts of real life and with the help of a mixture of information and gossip reduce Platen's poems to "what is really meant") could only hit his adversary square in the belly, in the real one and not merely in the literary one. Heine knew that. He is a polemicist

---

*But in verses then, gray, smooth, / in the fashion of old men filled up with imitated feelings, / and the thoughts in doublets, oh yes, so insipid / I suppose the beggar remains a nickel and dime noble / when he eats the food he begs / accidently from a borrowed golden plate.

who knows and panders to the sexual taboos of his age, the Catholic as well as the Protestant ones. When he discovered Platen's satire against Immermann and himself, he wrote Wolfgang Menzel (against whom, in another matter, he would later direct his manifesto "Concerning an Informer"): "Read as soon as you can the Count Platen just published by Cotta; I mean the poems; he's a real poet. Unfortunately, or better yet, frightfully! Frightfully! The whole book contains nothing more than pederastic whimperings. It turns my stomach with deadliest discomfort" (letter of May 2, 1828).[8]

How's that again? If one as a critic means to manipulate ecclesiastical, bourgeois, and literary prejudices against one's personal enemy, then one must needs reckon with their feelings of sexual unease and embarrassment. A critic of *The Baths of Lucca* who had only disdain for its author energetically put his argument against pederasty, which he only refers to as P . . . , thus: "Morals, the most fundamental moral feeling, the basic tenets of our people, yea, of all Christian peoples, demand that such transgressions, if they are ever mentioned only be treated with the sternest abhorrence." That had not escaped Heine. If his reproach against Platen in Munich in the year 1829 seems not to have played Petronius (on the face of it as argument of enlightenment against prejudice and hypocrisy), what was really going on was that the reproach of hypocrisy was being raised by a hypocrite against someone who was not one.

There was no small portion of demagogy involved. Heine knew enough about the manner of life of the impoverished count, who just managed to get by, to know that no aristocratic decadence or debauchery was involved, against which some kind of Jacobin middle class virtuousness must take to the field, but an autochthonous outsiderdom just like his own ineradicable fault of being a Jew. This is why the conflict between Heine and Platen was different from all previous and practically all later literary polemics. Compared to it, Goethe's and Schiller's dispute with colleagues over the *Xenien* was simply a potato war, as Heine put it. The shots here are meant to kill.

This too is an aspect of the Don Quixotism on both sides, an aspect of the hopelessly exceptional life of both. It was Heine's belief, in the restoration Germany of Metternich and Ludwig of Bavaria, to somehow attain to a consummate integration, to find a place for the Jew from Bolker Street in Düsseldorf somewhere between the liberals and the old-time Germanophiles, Bavarian Jesuits, and Prussian and Swabian Pietists, between the declining feudal order and a world of unborn classes—at the cost of making a compact with all the current existential prejudices, like those against the manner of life and substance of poetry of Count Platen. The count from Ansbach, for his part, had thought to amalgamate in his own life respectability with literary exhibitionism. Heine proved to him that a literary double life does not suffice in such (abnormal) circumstances. Platen does not seem to have grasped his own verse: "Only a free people is worthy of an Aristophanes." He seems to have misunderstood as well that it was Aristophanes who consistently rode hard any prejudice against outsiders; against the misogynist Euripides and the midwife's son, Socrates, who philosophized about double-sexed eros before an audience of aristocratic pederasts.

Heine returned to the topic of Don Quixote de la Mancha in February 1837, scarcely two years after Platen's death. He now saw himself and not simply Platen and Gumpelino as the incurable fool. What was foolish was not merely the anachronism of aristocrats in a world of the bourgeoisie, of books about knights in the beginnings of capitalism: "My God, I have since discovered that it is an equally thankless foolhardiness when one tries all too precociously to introduce the future into the present, and in the ensuing struggle against the dense interests of the day notices one has at his disposal nothing more than an emaciated steed, crumbling armaments, and a body just as decrepit."[9]

Who was it who had started it? The impetus quite apparently was provided by both sides at almost exactly the same time: by the progressive Romanticism of Heine and Immermann who considered themselves more closely aligned to Shelley, Byron, and Victor Hugo than to the converts around Schelling and Görres, and by the neoclassical formalism of Platen, which was elitist only in an aesthetic sense, but progressive (as would be seen after the July Revolution of 1830) in its political conceptions.

It began as so many polemics do, with an inconsequentiality. Heine was fed up with the dessicated climate of German restoration literature toward the middle of the 1820s, with dramas about the Hohenstaufens, fateful tragedies, and the soft and learned lyrics of Rückert and Platen; Immermann was annoyed by the same authors for similar reasons. They were both well versed in the controversies surrounding the *Xenien* of the former Weimar circle and decided to produce similar "Xenias" in similar cooperation. Since Heine carefully avoided "antiquifying" forms, however, he left the matter up to his playwright friend and offered him a spot in the second volume of his own *Images from Travel* where his polemical writings might appear. That is exactly what happened. As an appendix to "The North Sea," introduced by Heine's comment that these xenias "have flowed forth from Immermann's pen, my noble comrade's," one was regaled with jokes, malicious comments, and by and large well-meaning remarks directed against sentimental literary historians, Raupach, Kotzebue, the Catholic convert grown pious, Friederich Schlegel, and also against "Eastern poets," a remark directed more at the popular divan mode inaugurated by Goethe than the poetry of Rückert and Platen specifically.

"They gobble down too many of the fruits that they make off with over the garden walls of Shiraz, the wretches, and then puke up *ghazels*."[10] All of that being well within the confines of custom, graciousness, and literary tradition. Immermann, by the way, in a letter to Michael Beer of July 27, 1828, a year after his xenias in Heine's second volume of *Images from Travel,* had emphasized that "I hold Platen in considerable estimation; it is only that he, in my opinion, has to beware seduction by particularly artificial forms."

In the meantime Platen had taken a counter step in his second dramatic satire à la Aristophanes, *The Romantic Oedipus.* The first, *The Fateful Fork,* a nicely composed satire in the ancient manner directed against the playwrights of the school that had grown up around and after *The Bride of Messina* or Grillparzer's *Ancestress,* had proved generally amusing. People had simply tired of the recipes of a Müllner or a Houwald. Remarks similar to Platen's could be found elsewhere, in Hauff, in Grabbe.

What could Platen have had against Immermann, whose work *Cardenio and Celinde,* as he himself admitted, was the only one he knew at the time? Probably not much, unless it was seeing in the declared friendship of the two authors Heine and Immermann something like a league against his own works, meaning to outflank him with a seemingly daring modernity, meaning to outshine him, too, probably, at his publisher, Cotta. Heine and Platen never conversed during the time they were in Munich together. That was what Heine later claimed, and it is likely true.

In *The Romantic Oedipus* of 1829, then, Platen makes the character Nimmermann into the egregiously Semitic companion to his "comrade," the "baptized Heine," in their mercantile society of mutual praise, where the latter apostrophizes the former as Petrarch, the former the latter as "the first tragedian of our present age." Even this is not unusual, and remains within the bounds of literary tradition. The tone becomes somewhat different when Platen speaks of Heine. Not only his literature is found fault with but his very existence: that of the baptized Jew who has no business writing books. "The seed of Abraham," "The Pindar of the little tribe of Benjamin," "the Petrarch of the Feast of Tabernacles"—all that is acceptable: up to the dialogue between Nimmermann and the chorus representing the public.

NIMMERMANN: What a warm-up jump you're taking, o prize of the synagogue!
THE PUBLIC: You're right there. It's the one and only and most brazen-faced of the race of mortal men.
NIMMERMANN: I am his friend; and I'd rather not be his bosom buddy, since his kisses are impregnated with the strange odor of garlic.
THE PUBLIC: That's why he carries his snifter with him wherever he goes.
NIMMERMAN: My Heine! Aren't he and I a pair of geniuses? Who dares, my dear, to destroy our sweet dream? [11]

This is a literary controversy that is not aimed at the actions and writings of the adversary but at his very being, his blood lineage, his body, his behavior out on the street and indoors. It is incomprehensible how Platen (Aristophanes notwithstanding) can have been unconscious of the fact that such a manner of attack could only provoke real injury to himself. It is conceivable that he thought the division between "faultless" social behavior and simultaneous production of ephebic eroticism proclaimed as the content of poetry would be recognized and respected by his adversary. More likely he was of the opinion that vis-à-vis a converted Jew, which is to say an impudent intruder into the German hall of poets, no particular rules of the game need be taken into consideration.

Heine proved him wrong by throwing over other rules that not even Kotzebue had dared ignore: the peculiarities of one's sexual life had been respected, at least up to the point that it became a matter of royal favoritism as was the case with Edward II of England, Henry III of France, and the English Stuart kings. Winckelmann's enemies recognized this line of demarcation, just as did the numerous enemies of the historian Johannes von Müller, even when they saw themselves obliged to reckon him a traitor when he entered the service of Jérôme Bonaparte, the king of Westphalia. Now, however, in *The Baths of Lucca,* the lottery collector Hyazinth, the Marchese Gumpelino, and Dr. Heine debate on which is preferable: love of men or women. The doctor answers the marquess, who had been arguing along Platen's lines: "There you have man. The one likes to eat onions, the other has flutters of the heart for queer love, and I, as an honest man am forced to admit I'd rather eat onions and have a bad cook at that than the best of our little friends of beauty." The counterpoint, to use Platen's words, of "kisses impregnated with the strange odor of garlic."

Goethe had no appreciation for this squabble between two lyric poets of real (though for him personally scarcely enjoyable) talent. Heine himself was not pleased with his own actions. He eliminated the Platen polemics from the French edition of the *Images from Travel*. In letters to Varnhagen he played the republican and Jacobin fighting against aristocratic caprice, and spoke of "execution." He somehow thought that in refuting Platen's silly anti-Semitism he had pushed back a systematic campaign against him organized by Munich Jesuits. "Robert Gans, Michael Beer, and others have always, when attacked, suffered wisely with Christian patience. I am someone else, and that is good."

Yet Platen was no instrument of some conspiracy. He acted on his own account. Immermann, too, made answer to him in the same year, 1829, through Heine's publishers, Hoffmann and Campe. His reply is a play on the novel *The Cavalier Reeling in the Unreal Garden of Love* by Johann Gottfried Schnabel; he calls Platen a "cavalier reeling in the unreal garden of meter," with "a literary tragedy" for subtitle. But nowhere is the person August von Platen meant here; it is solely the writer that is in view. Very much in contrast to Heine's position one finds the differentiation between "truth and poetry" put thus:

I do not believe you when you appear
Drunken with Shiraz' wines, when you
Desire pretty boys and Aphrodite's
Golden gifts and act as if
You were warm in the sunshine . . .

Yet when you sing that you are the great one
Who has not yet found his proper century,
Then I believe you! You sing what you feel![12]

You sense almost a sadness in Immermann's reply to the Nimmermann polemics. "He will probably suffer his own judgment soon enough. Bitterness and choler are destructive muses. Another 'Oedipus' and I fear for the days of our young man." Immermann was right both in truth and in poetry. Platen was to commit an act of (self-)destruction. He could most probably no longer stay in Germany. Heine's literary credit was on the wane. Even in the well-meaning reviews of *The Baths of Lucca* commissioned by Heine himself, not to speak of those by Heine opponents, there echoes a certain sense of outrage at an inhuman polemic that had been inhumanly provoked and that pretended—as if the affair of Voltaire and Calas reborn—to strike out at a system of infamy and regression, but was simply the spectacle of one *homme de lettres* denuding another: the outsider by race against the outsider by sexual preference.

It remains to be asked in the name of just exactly what conviction Heine took such demonstrative umbrage at Count Platen's homoeroticism or even homosexuality. The sensualist Heinrich Heine, an opponent of ascetics and the Nazarenes, cannot be thought an adept of Pauline morality, neither as a Protestant evangelical or Catholic Christian.

It cannot have been a matter of Pauline moral severity. Both our authors take recourse in Aristophanes: Platen with his literary comedies; Heine, much later, in what is a decisive place—the last chapter of *Germany, a Winter Fairytale*. Aristophanes, as the author of *The Clouds* and *The Congresswomen,* poked no less gross fun at tender male loves than Heine in his *Baths of Lucca*; it is simply that he never placed the social institution of *paiderasteia* in question. He disliked its effects when he found it coupled with misogyny, as in the despised Euripides; or with elitist arrogance, as with Socrates' disciples. If his position had been any different, the respectful-ironic role that Plato has him play in the *Symposium* would be incomprehensible. Platen-Hallermünde and Harry Heine, on the other hand, authors in a period of restoration, should not have forgotten what Platen himself said in conjunction with his aristophanic satires: "Only a free people is worthy of an Aristophanes." Which can only point up that Heine must have known that he did not strike Platen in the heart of literary matters but at the heart of his social existence; his polemic was in consequence a denunciation that had as its purpose the social disgrace of a literary opponent. In the name of what ethical and erotic principles? He certainly did not take them from the teachings of Christianity. It is clear as day that Platen's great enthusiasms for young men, sublimated into poetry at that, must from the viewpoint of any representative of the Enlightenment, elicit only toleration; just as that would be the case for Heine's own Jewishness. That cannot have escaped Heine, who was neither ascetic nor religious zealot.

Precisely this erotic outsiderdom of the Frankish count must have made him aware of just how much he himself, despite baptism and the success of his books, had remained the outsider. Platen's silly satires opened up that question all over again. And in Platen, too, a similar psychic mechanism may be posited; otherwise it would be incomprehensible just why someone living on the margins of social repugnance, and barely getting by at that, would come up with this store of anti-Semitic vulgarities. It is the frightening position of one who feels: I exist only on the margin of things; insufferably cute fellow writers lead me to the door accompanied by the chatter of faint and polite obsequies (all this to be found in Platen's journals) whenever I touch upon the question of poetic friendship too intimately. Nevertheless I am Count von Platen and Hallermünde, and here is one who comes from a blemished and impure past so that even I can put him in his place.

And through Platen's provocations, an emotional, a mirror-image re-action is precipitated in Heine: I live on the margin of things, baptism as my entree into European culture was a formality merely that did not erase my outsiderdom. Yet despite all that: I love women and only women, and here is somebody who does not, so that even I can send him packing.

It is to be Heine, then, and women. Among the poems in his literary works never published during his lifetime there is one of a curious persuasion:

Mit dummen Mädchen, hab ich gedacht,
Nichts ist mit dummen anzufangen;
Doch als ich mich an die klugen gemacht,
Da ist es mir noch schlimmer ergangen.

Die klugen waren mir viel zu klug,
Ihr Fragen machte mich ungeduldig,
Und wenn ich selber das Wichtigste frug,
Da blieben sie lachend die Antwort schuldig.*

It is not without reason that Heinrich Heine's lyric poetry was imme-diately associated with unhappy and unfulfilled love. That was part and parcel, in the beginning at least, of the poetic posture of someone who loved to distill little songs out of "great sorrows." It was intimately con-nected with his own actual life, however. In an epoch of great romantic passions in artists, Heine, this celebratory hymnist of women, appears in a strangely ambiguous and frustrated form. He knew Chopin and Liszt,

---

*With dumb girls, I supposed, / You can't do anything; / But when I switched over to the smart ones, / I had an even worse time of it. // The smart ones were much too smart, / Their questions made me impatient, / And if I posed the most important ones myself / They laughed and never came up with an answer.

Alfred de Musset and Honoré de Balzac. But for him there was no
Madame de Hanska as there was for the author of *The Human Comedy*,
no George Sand as for Chopin and de Musset, nor a Countess d'Agoult
as for Liszt. Heine's much admired Rahel lived with Varnhagen von
Ense, a friend of his.

The women central to Heine's life were his mother, the adored "old
woman," and Mathilde, the "good fat child," who was mother, refuge,
lover, all in one. Contemporary sources have described her complete
ignorance (compounded by her unfamiliarity with the German language)
of who her lover was and what he was doing. Heine himself has evoked
and poeticized this whole scene with an almost passionate love of suffering, even if his own.

His mother. The mothering foreign woman. Anyone else? Flirts from
his student days in Göttingen and Berlin and Munich. In the *New Poems*
of 1844 there are lyric cycles devoted to various women with names like
Seraphine, Hortense, or Clarisse, yet they impress one on the whole as
the erotic-lyrical journal of an unhappy Don Juan in the realm of the
citizen-king, and scarcely as the poeticized documents of a passionate and
romantic lover. The curious manliness that attempts to outbid everyone
in sight, which is so proud of its own righteousness in matters sexual vis-
à-vis Count Platen and in *The Baths of Lucca* the Marchese Gumpelino,
has to do with deep, hidden feelings of its own deficiency. It suddenly
becomes apparent that Heine's polemic did not spring out of an un-
questioned, intact manliness, so to speak, when you compare to Heine's
the reaction of Karl Immermann, the most manly of men, the lover of
Countess Lützow. As much as Heine is inclined in his polemical rejoinders
to overstep the bounds of a literary dispute, Immermann (Platen's butt
in Nimmermann) restricts himself to the realm of belles lettres and its
rules whenever he responds to his adversary.

To the whole business, in Heine's feuds in general, of emphasizing the
norm and being normal is intimately connected a wide-ranging escalation
of attack. Count Platen had his soulful bosom friends; the aging August
Wilhelm Schlegel's young wife ran off after the wedding night, thereby
providing Heine with a readymade argument against the Romantic
school; Börne lived together with a married couple in a curious menage,
where the husband seemed to tolerate his wife's lover, an argument
against the writer and politician Börne. Who was it who could be taken
in by such lines of argument? Quite unmistakably Heine can only have
reckoned with consolidating the prejudices of a conservative and officially

prudish aristocracy and bourgeoisie. The child of the Enlightenment here provides the respectable businessmen's and officers' clubs with something to chuckle about: counter-Enlightenment, in a word. What he (the young Jew from Bolker Street and nephew of the millionaire Salomon Heine) undertakes and accomplishes is a kind of social mimicry.

To be found at the bottom of the dispute between Heine and Platen— Platen deeply unconscious of it, Heine painfully aware of it—is a double phenomenon of self-identification of the attacker with what he attacks. In Heine's case what gives it away is the figure of Gumpelino. The marquess has to be, according to Heine's principles of composition, both a friend of beauty à la Platen and a Jewish convert. This last guise has nothing to do with Platen's position and is consequently irrelevant. Gumpelino's Jewishness adds nothing to the story or the polemic. All the talk about Platen and love of men or women in the narrative could just as well have come from a German Christian schoolteacher from the south of Germany.

Heine, however, has doubled his polemics against outsiders in that he in one and the same move has placed the naive Jewish convert, Hirsch, who is "normal," alongside the sentimental, O-sweet-Jesus-sighing Gumpelino who is cut from the same cloth as Platen. Once again the phenomenon of "Jewish self-hate," to use Theodor Lessing's words, is manifested. A recent dissertation sees precisely in the confrontation with Platen a higher level of progressive polemics, interpreting this particular confrontation as the result of surprising sociocritical insight: "In the phenomenon of sexual aberration, Jewish capitalist of *Finanzkapital* and Catholic aristocrat come to resemble each other. They are both representatives acting in behalf of the league of *Finanzkapital,* aristocracy, and church."[13]

That is pure nonsense; using Marxist terminology, there has been *Finanzkapital* only since the advent of imperialism: what is meant here can only be the financial interests of the banks. Platen was a Protestant; his family had its origins in Rügen in northern Germany; he never converted to Catholicism. Heine's suppositions that Platen was part of a plot against him hatched by Jesuits in Munich have been disproved. Even Heine himself cannot have believed his own claim of a high and mighty aristocratic decadence that can afford to make poems in praise of boys. He knew Platen was not well off and mocked him because of it.

Why then must Gumpelino represent both the Jewish-Christian and the poetic-homoerotic outsider? Because the positions in this singular controversy were and have remained interchangeable. Platen sought to justify himself in his own eyes and in those of society by calling up the visions of prejudice against the Jewish man of letters. Heine went further still. By attacking Platen, he exhibited the "great sorrows" of his own manliness. When he sent Hirsch and Gumpelino up on the stage where, to use his formulation, Count Platen's aristophanic comedy would be "executed," he was fighting against himself. And he could not come to be victorious because of it.

13   Alternatives in the Nineteenth Century

Life in Conformity: Hans Christian Andersen

In chapter 7 of *The Story of My Life*,[1] which deals with the period 1835–1837, Hans Christian Andersen reports a curious incident in his relations with Søren Kierkegaard. Andersen, born in 1805, was in his thirties. Kierkegaard, of the generation of 1813 along with Georg Büchner, Hebbel, and Richard Wagner, was still a student at the time, but he knew all manner of people in Copenhagen, among them the controversial Andersen, a child of poverty from the island of Fyn. Andersen had just published his third novel: *The Improvisatore* and *O. T.* were now followed by *Only a Fiddler*. This third novel (1837) in as many years was well known in Copenhagen to be filled with autobiographical detail.

Andersen reports the incident, looking back, of course, knowing exactly what had become of Kierkegaard or at least what had become of him in the eyes of the official circles of Danish church and crown. He says that his novel about the gifted and despised fiddler "made a strong impression for a short time on one of our country's young and highly gifted men, Søren Kierkegaard. Meeting him in the street, he told me that he would write a review of my book and that I should be more satisfied with that than I had been with the earlier, because, he said, they had misunderstood me!"[2]

Then some time went by, and Kierkegaard came to read the book anew, this time in a far less favorable light. "I must almost believe that the more seriously he examined the story, the more faults he found, and when the critique appeared it did not please me at all. It came out as a whole book, the first, I believe that Kierkegaard has written; and because of the Hegelian heaviness in the expression, it was very difficult to read, and people said in fun that only Kierkegaard and Andersen had read it through."

There is something of a patronizing tone when he then remarks of this work that it taught him he was no poet but himself a poetical figure that at some later date a real writer would be able to employ. In Andersen's constant striving to make no enemies, he provides the anecdote with a conciliatory finish: "Since that time I have had a better understanding with this author, who has always met me with kindness and discernment."

Did Andersen for a moment comprehend that Kierkegaard's book (it was, indeed, his first)[3] negated the foundations of his creative work by exposing and denouncing as lies its kind of transformation of a wretched life into edifying literature? One doubts it. Andersen scarcely possessed the intellectual and literary requisites for understanding the full scope of Kierkegaard's work, which was in fact difficult, if not ponderous, and studded with classical citations. What he did grasp was that this young philosopher took him and his novel seriously only as a symptom of other matters and disgustedly rejected the work as a poetic creation.

The success of the novel *Only a Fiddler* was, indeed, symptomatic for that era of *Weltschmerz*. Otherwise it would be incomprehensible how such a prescient writer and connoisseur of literature as Robert Schumann could write Andersen on October 1, 1842, that the *Fiddler* was charming, certainly the best thing in modern literature, and could only be compared to Immermann.[4]

Andersen's critics centering around Johan Ludvig Heiberg in Copenhagen, with whom Kierkegaard had associated himself, rejected the literary parvenu: the man without language and a solid education. Their judgment derived from bourgeois vanity. In Kierkegaard's Andersen polemic this provincial arrogance is entirely ignored. For him a novel like *Only a Fiddler* represented an attempt by a writer to lie both to himself and the world—in an edifying and profitable way at that—that capitulation is fate, that failure to meet responsibilities is merely a bit of ill luck. Kierkegaard's work ("From the Papers of One Still Living. Published against His Will by S. Kierkegaard. About H. C. Andersen as a Novelist, with Special Reference to His Latest Work, *Only a Fiddler*") was a moral confrontation, not a literary one. Whoever sits down to read it today with Andersen's biography in mind finds all the moments already sketched out that make the case of Hans Christian Andersen an exemplary one: his attempt with the aid of seeming revelations to conceal the essential. And by that means he did, quite in fact, make himself over into a poetic figure time and time again: as the improvisatore lacking substance; as the musical genius doomed by circumstance; as the ugly duckling; as the little mermaid; as a miscast tin soldier. What did not quite succeed in the earlier novels came to life in the fairytales. It is not certain whether Kierkegaard recognized that. Nonetheless Kierkegaard's early criticism of an exemplary case of prevarication by means of literature is to this day the best means we have of unraveling Andersen and the make-believe constructions of his biographers.

This son of a mentally disabled shoemaker and an uneducated washerwoman seems all too willing to bare his insides. As the portraitist of his poverty and ugliness and the playstuff of his dreams, Andersen takes pleasure in portraying his defeats. How inclined he is to cry the tears of yesteryear all over again in the retelling! At the last, even, he makes allusions to the feminine elements of his nature. Writing of his lifetime friendship with Edvard Collin in "The Fairytale of My Life,"* he says that "he was the antagonist to my almost girlish nature." When Collin decided to marry, Andersen wrote his famous fairytale, "The Story of the Little Mermaid." Nothing had ever moved him more in writing, he confessed later. Here he had not only dared to portray himself as outsider, but as a sexual outsider. Even a palliative biographer like Signe Toksvig, who tends to leave such matters undisclosed, can find no way to avoid the subject: "the little mermaid was himself—in her attempt to win the distant beloved mortal prince, though she was handicapped in every way; a foundling, a slave, an outsider. . . . She lost the prince, saw him wed another. . . . Rather a confession of weakness it was, this feminizing of himself."[5]

It was not a confession of weakness but one of the few documents of steadfast honesty, almost of an irrepressible urge to confess. Perhaps it was a mark of Andersen's true genius that he early recognized that his attempt to ward off scandal by dredging up everything in his past—except his revulsion at the female body and his love for young men—a tissue woven of lies and self-deception, could only endanger his life as a writer. That was exactly what Kierkegaard had said. The upshot was that Andersen created in his fairy stories the possibility of speaking about himself with a minimum of subterfuge; he had in them the opportunity to intimate that his loneliness was not the result of poverty, ugliness, low birth, lack of schooling, or even a self-isolating poetic genius, but that it

---

*"Das Märchen meines Lebens," the commentary that Andersen wrote for the German edition of his writings (translator's note).

had to do with an existential outsiderdom. Beings from another element, miscast, a swan among the ducks in the lake.

Andersen successfully attained a state of complete conformity in the nineteenth-century bourgeois social order. He can be compared only with the Jewish outsider Benjamin Disraeli in that. Toward the end of his life he had succeeded in establishing for public consumption a monumental stylization of his life—the authorized version, so to speak. Andersen was the author of fairytales, consequently a great friend of children, something that he actually was not. During his last illness, when he was concerned with plans for a monument to be erected in his honor, he forbade the addition of children's figures around his own. Even close friends took his tragicomic heart-throbbing intimations of love for women seriously, his feigned courting of Riborg Voigt or Louise Collin, which was wont to begin as soon as Andersen knew his lady was firmly committed to someone else. This women's courtier remained himself a virgin, as he is said to have confided in old age to a friend and physician. What was meant was a virgin in his relationships with women.

For the rest, this Danish child of poverty had discovered the possibilities of a double life. In Andersen it becomes a sundering of his existence into the moral and inconspicuous mode of life at home on the isle of Seeland, and the incessant erotic tours abroad of one always yearning to be on the move. And for Andersen too, as for Winckelmann, Platen, Tchaikovsky of the "Capriccio italien," the Englishmen who pilgrimage to Capri, the world of Italy becomes the landscape of happiness. Yet with the strange difference manifested in Andersen's letters, that he can see his fulfillment in the South only as a kind of substitute for the missing union with his friends in Denmark. Much complaint in his oftentimes whining letters home is stylized and subterfuge, meant to distract from the delights of being away. Behind his begging for letters, nonetheless, especially from Edvard Collin, there is a forlorn tornness seeking to unite the frustrating life in Denmark with the happiness of the South.

Andersen seems never to have been able to allay fears of discovery and scandal once he had embarked on his double life. From that comes his restless collecting of unimpeachable acquaintances and protectors, from ruling monarchs on down, which in the case of an actual scandal, as later was to be demonstrated with Oscar Wilde and Philipp, Prince of Eulenburg, would have been unavailing, perhaps even detrimental. Besides, he seems to have lived in a panicky anxiety of being taken for what he was, either by other homosexuals who were less constrained by total conformity or by strangers whom he was bound to fear as malicious spies. The sculptor Bertel Thorvaldsen belonged to the first group, who received Andersen, his young fellow countryman (as Andersen reports in a self-congratulatory manner), amid a round of hugs and kisses and very likely acquainted him with bohemian Rome. In his letters, however, you feel how Andersen, though clearly flattered by his acquaintance of such a celebrity, nonetheless carefully shuns any deeper community. His coldness is embarrassing in an obituary he wrote for a Hamburg newspaper the night after Thorvaldsen's sudden death during a theater performance. Andersen and others had had dinner with him and then accompanied him to the theater before going off on their own. He died there of a heart attack. Andersen described this last meeting coldly, almost as if relieved. It was not a friend who wrote the obituary notice.

It is curious that in his autobiography, among the gigantic collection of celebrities who were all claimed as his friends, above all in Paris although he scarcely comprehended French, there is to be found listed the name of Heinrich Heine. In his letters home, on the other hand, he reports how he anxiously guarded himself against Heine's visits. For what reason? Did he fear the Jewish outsider? Scarcely. More likely he feared the polemicist and adversary of Count Platen. Andersen was acquainted with Heine's *Baths of Lucca*.

The older he got, the less he was inclined to play the poor, rejected suitor forever chasing after the favors of women. More and more, young men begin to people his travel accounts; he cannot suppress the happiness they bring. In Madrid a festive dinner is given in his honor. "One of my young friends from Manila," is there who "seems to have taken quite a fancy to me."[6]

Even in his correspondence with H. E. Scudder, his American publisher, he feels obliged to mention the young friend he found in Vienna; what makes this acquaintance all the more precious is that he is the son of the novelist Bulwer, Lord Lytton.[7] On his sixty-fifth birthday he writes Scudder that he enjoys most the company of young people. This contradicts, of course, all the perorations of friendship in his letters to old friends, particularly old bosom friends like Signe Lässö, the mother of one of his boyhood chums, but is fully credible.

His Danish contemporaries were not deceived. The vehement attacks that Andersen experienced at the outset of his career were only mitigated by the worldwide fame of the fairytale composer; the tone of displeasure at so much stylization of life—stylization whereby the misogynist gives himself to appear as a praiser of women, the avaricious old man as a goodly benefactor, the egotistical hypochondriac as a friend of children— was always in the background. That he probably suffered a nervous shock as a boy in Rector Meisling's house in Copenhagen where he was supposed to make up for his missed schooling, a shock after repeated attempts to seduce him on the part of the mistress of the house and the parlor maid, is mentioned even in Elith Reumert's palliative biography, *Hans Andersen the Man.*[8]

Only with this in mind does it make any sense that when, in his older years, the high point of which doubtless was the ceremony making him an honorary citizen of Odense, he who was so much honored, he had an irrational fear before every ceremony that something would go awry. Even before the festival in Odense that concludes *The Story of My Life* and that he took to be evidence of a guiding providence, as he says at the start of his autobiography, the honored guest seems to have vividly anticipated the trauma of a sudden awakening in the midst of scandal. Signe Toksvig in her Andersen biography asserts that immediately after his "feminine" fairytale of the little mermaid, Andersen wrote a decidedly "masculine" and political fairytale, one of his most successful: "The Emperor's New Clothes."[9] But like "The Ugly Duckling," "The Tin Soldier," "The Little Mermaid," this story too deals with the panic of conformity and being different. To be sure, the emperor parades his way amid pomp and honor; one could say he even goes back to Andersen's native Odense where they are going to memorialize him but where someone might suddenly say something, a child perhaps, allowing the truth to slip out so that everything will end in uncircumventable scandal.

In Denmark they awaited his passing away. Immediately thereafter the critic and dramatist Erik Bögh published an essay characterizing the man Andersen,[10] the public man Andersen at that, by underscoring the connection between Andersen's "feminine" nature, as Bögh calls it, and his political indifference, indeed even conservative bootlicking. In point of fact, one is flabbergasted reading the innumerable wooing letters from his travels. Whoever takes the trouble to read through this correspondence receives not the slightest inkling that their author was living in a time between two European revolutions, in an epoch when patronage by the ruling nobility meant less and less, when Denmark was twice involved in war with the Germans, which in 1864 led to a national catastrophe and in which several of the writer's close friends lost their lives. That was what Bögh demonstrated in his analysis, precipitating a flood of

Alternatives in the Nineteenth Century

literature that swept over the seeming favorite and forced the Collin family to realign the memorial. Conformity had failed in the end. It happened as in the "Emperor's New Clothes."

Looking back at Andersen's life and works, at his means of skirting all the conflicts of the time by going over to the side of those who seemed mighty, it seems all of it had been anticipated in Kierkegaard's analysis of 1838. One has to assume that Kierkegaard from the first moment on had divined in that writer a moral and existential phenomenon, not a literary one.

Kierkegaard's main thesis posits that "Andersen's own realness, his own person, takes refuge in poetical works, so much so that one is really tempted in certain moments to view Andersen as a figure that has run off from a group some writer has invented and not yet finished; it is certainly indisputable that Andersen could become a most poetical figure in a story."[11] An object, then, not the creative subject of poetry. Yet the poetical figure that becomes delineated for Kierkegaard when reading and contemplating Andersen is that of a liar and self-deceiver.

"In consequence of the ill humor and unhappiness," as Kierkegaard writes in this first book of his, "which he feels in the real world, he seeks in the despondency of his own poetic creations a satisfaction as it were for his own despondency. Exactly like La Fontaine he sits there on that account and cries over his unhappy heroes who must perish, and why? Because Andersen is he who he is. The same joyless struggle that Andersen himself has to battle in life now repeats itself in his poetical works."[12] That is a perception of remarkable acuity. Kierkegaard was acquainted with Andersen in those days only as the author of poems, little prose pieces, and three for him unbearable novels. He had yet to make the acquaintance of the fairytale writer. On that account he somewhat condescendingly calls Andersen "an author not disadvantageously known through a fairly significant literary activity."[13] Nonetheless he compares him, surprisingly enough, with the fable writer La Fontaine. La Fontaine's heroes, however, over whom he ostensibly laments as he lets them fall to their doom, are above all figures of fable and appear in the form of animals. In a series of lectures on "The Five Temptations of La Fontaine," Jean Giraudoux relates how La Fontaine tried again and again to compete with the successful authors of his day in the lyric and verse epic, always unsuccessfully, until the animals came to him and he transformed himself into their darling and poet.[14]

Andersen, the author of what one must admit is the scarcely passable novel *Only a Fiddler,* against whom Kierkegaard mounted his attack, stood at the time at a crossroads—there where a mediocre and prodigious writer after so many lies to himself suddenly resolves to find a poetic form that admits some genuineness and honesty, and who then comes to his own identity as author of the fairytales—exactly as had La Fontaine thanks to the animals in his fables.

How that worked can be seen by comparing Andersen's typical fairytales with his novel about the poor tailor's apprentice and brilliant musician by the name of Christian who pitifully meets his ruin as "only a fiddler."[15] This novel is a psychoanalyst's delight. That it was packed with autobiographical detail, even obtrusively so, was known to the reading public throughout Copenhagen, hence Kierkegaard's transferring to the author his conclusions about the figure in the novel. Andersen was generally equated with the fiddler. Yet the novel is constructed as the contrast of two life stories, one male, the other female—the female's rising, yet unhappy, the male's waning, yet subjectively, as Andersen would have it, liberating. It is in the female figure of Naomi that the author has disclosed himself far more than in the fiddler. She is the illegitimate daughter of a Jewish girl and a wild adventurer. Her Jewish blood soon surfaces. She runs off with a gypsy trick rider named Ladislaus, disguises herself as a man, and becomes this virile outsider's lover. She lets herself be chastised with a riding crop, is then taken back to the aristocratic world of her adoptive parents, marries a marquess, and is consumed by desire for her gypsy.

The novelist has rid his Naomi of any and all inhibitions: she lives out what Andersen does not allow himself. Yet her social conformity leads away from her own identity. That identity was to be found in the one episode where social outsiderdom was lived to the fullest, in scandal both enjoyed and provoked. Jewishness, illegitimacy, gypsy life, transvestism. All thrown together without any particular concern for plausibility. Andersen has summed up the phenotypes of outsiderdom. That he identifies himself erotically with Naomi will scarcely escape the modern reader. He composed here the authentic fairytale of his life.

The fiddler Christian is meant, as Andersen later claimed in "The Fairy Tale of My Life" (1847), to exemplify another variation of providence: that of Hans Christian Andersen misfortunate and without protectors. One might also add: without lies and conformity as well.

It was precisely this that embittered Kierkegaard the more he read the mediocre work and the more exactly he came to reflect on it: the equation

Alternatives in the Nineteenth Century

of unhappiness with fate, genius with failure. The result of that equation is a feeble and immoral complaisance in the conduct of one's life. Kierkegaard was at the time still self-sufficiently Hegelian and conceived genius as action and transformation. This is also the reason he gives no credence to Andersen's assertion that his fiddler Christian is a failed musical genius. "This conclusion of Andersen's," the critic Kierkegaard replies, "contains a basic misunderstanding of the power of genius and its relation to untoward circumstance (for genius is not a little wick of light that goes out in the first wind, but an inferno that the storm only whips on), and is grounded in the fact that Andersen does not show a genius in battle but more nearly a weakling, of whom it is said that he be a genius, and who has in common with genius only the fact that he suffers a couple of unpleasantnesses, to which he in fact succumbs." [16]

Between Kierkegaard's first reading of the novel and repeated later readings there falls a decisive religious turningpoint. Andersen probably reported correctly that the young student Kierkegaard had at first been filled with enthusiasm for the work and then later came to think (and write) of it in quite a different vein. At any event, this novel of Andersen's of an identity refused became for the reader Kierkegaard the occasion for the finding of an identity. And so Søren Kierkegaard's first book resulted out of it; the ephemeral occasion of Andersen was needed to enable Kierkegaard to speak of Kierkegaard.

Hans Christian Andersen had, after many mendacious attempts, to arrive at his identity as an author not by describing conditions of happiness and unhappiness but conditions of total and incurable outsiderdom—of the little mermaid, the miscast tin soldier, the swan in the duck pond who has to go on living in a pond where swans are not recognized as a higher category. So that scandal always awaits behind the scenes and can be called up by a child who sees the emperor naked.

Scandal: Verlaine and Rimbaud in Hell

From the very first moment they met, the relationship between the not yet seventeen-year-old Jean Nicolas Arthur Rimbaud from Charleville and the ten years older married man Paul Verlaine stood under the sign of scandal. [17] Simple chronology is enlightening. Verlaine had not been married for long; with considerable difficulty he had been freed from prison after the crushing of the Paris Commune despite the fact that he was suspected of harboring sympathies for, or even having worked for, the communards. Mathilde Verlaine was expecting. On October 30, 1871, Georges Verlaine was born. By that time the marriage had already foundered. On September 10 young Rimbaud had once again run away from Charleville, this time at Verlaine's request. It was the invitation of one lyric poet to another, younger, obviously greatly talented poet who had sent him verses. At Rimbaud's arrival there presented himself a big blond country boy, clumsy and cunning, strong and attractive. Verlaine may have made the homosexual's attempt at conformity with marriage and family: the meeting with the boy from the Ardennes undid everything.

From the beginning, scandal. Young Rimbaud the wrecker of marriage. When they get drunk together on absinthe, the boy can tolerate more, but Verlaine is wont to metamorphose into a bungling would-be murderer: on January 13, 1872, he nearly strangles his wife, asks for forgiveness a week later; on July 10, 1873, in Brussels he fires at Rimbaud, wounds him in the wrist, and then, crestfallen, takes him to an infirmary.

From the very start contemporaries had no doubt as to the nature of their relationship. As early as November 1871 suggestive remarks appear in the press, Verlaine being an author in the public eye. At the end of the year Verlaine and Rimbaud are obstreperously thrown out of a literary gathering. This makes all the more astonishing the prudery in Rimbaud's biographers. In his 1926 edition of Rimbaud's letters, Jean-Marie Carré energetically contested the slightest homosexuality of his "hero"; he was then obliged five years later, after having become acquainted with the police reports in Brussels, to admit the evidence in the new edition of 1931. At all events, he takes refuge in the grotesque proposition: "I should add that Verlaine's homosexuality was a matter of habit while Rimbaud's was an adventure."[18]

What is habit, what adventure? The facts speak of a passionate and stormy love affair in which the physical actions, comparatively speaking, were scarcely significant compared with the emotional aspects. Rimbaud is the man in the relationship; that has always been surmised. Verlaine submits himself, then rebels against the insolence and callboy allure of the younger man. He goes away, leaving his friend behind, penniless, receives several letters imploring him to reconsider, then sends money, whereupon the tone of Rimbaud's letters immediately changes. Endless lovers' squabbles punctuated by open reconciliations, for the sake of which one supposes they broke up. Both have a threatening maternal image at their disposal: for Verlaine returning to his marriage or living at home with his mother; for Rimbaud going back to Charleville under guardianship of his powerful mother. He has not had a paternal superego since Captain Rimbaud quit the family in 1860.

A double life here even in the midst of public scandal. By July 10 the following events had taken place in Brussels: Verlaine had once again quit London leaving behind a penniless Rimbaud, whom he then sent for. On July 8 Rimbaud arrives in Brussels. This time, however, he has decided to put an end to it and return to Charleville. Verlaine's mother is with them. On July 10 Verlaine, drunk, starts a new round of bickering on the street. In the apartment later Verlaine, according to Rimbaud's subsequent testimony, cries: "C'est pour vous, pour moi, pour le monde!" A mood as if at the Last Judgment. A first shot injures Rimbaud in the wrist, a second hits the ceiling. Sudden change to complete remorse. Rimbaud is given the gun; he is supposed to execute the evildoer. Instead they go to the hospital where Rimbaud's wound is treated; he is immediately released. Nothing would have come of it if Verlaine had not begun a new row on the street. He cannot bear to have Rimbaud leave him. Once again the revolver—until Rimbaud asks a policeman for protection. In this way everything comes to light. Rimbaud is taken to a hospital, Verlaine to prison. On July 13 and 18 Rimbaud is interrogated in the hospital by an examining magistrate. A charge of attempted murder is brought against Verlaine, for which he is subsequently sentenced to two years in prison, which he for the most part sits out.

During the course of the trial Rimbaud played it all down. Their misunderstanding had arisen on account of mutual acquaintances, so Rimbaud said, who had mistreated Verlaine. The magistrate inquired just why Madame Verlaine separated from her husband, whether it did not have something to do with Verlaine's relations with Rimbaud, whereupon Rimbaud took to the counteroffensive. Yes, there was mention of "relations immorales" in Madame Verlaine's complaint, "mais je ne veux pas me donner la peine de démentir de pareilles calomnies"[19] ["I do not wish to trouble myself with denying such calumnies"], the eighteen-year-old Rimbaud responds. The whole matter was a harmless, a simple misunderstanding. An argument between two poets with a difference in age and different tastes in many things.

Verlaine, too, was full of respect for the precepts of bourgeois morality and represented the whole occurrence as an act of drunkenness. Besides that, he had a wife and child, and could expect every protection from a mother who in the midst of these scandals astonishingly enough mostly took Rimbaud's side against her daughter-in-law. When at the end of

1872 Verlaine lay ill in London, Rimbaud having broken with him and returned to Charleville, it was Verlaine's mother who sent money to Charleville to enable Rimbaud to go to London and care for the ailing Verlaine. A bourgeois nest of vipers. They all mean for the plainly evident scandal to be transformed back into a capricious aberration from a respectable mode of life, which can then be forgiven.

Verlaine is imprisoned in Belgium: Rimbaud, in March of the following year, 1874, is off to London with Germain Nouveau, a poet, who is also enamored of the nineteen-year-old's "charisma." His mother and sister visit them there. Rimbaud gives French lessons in Reading, where twenty-one years later Oscar Wilde will be imprisoned. The next year, 1875, he is in Stuttgart learning German, then later travels to Italy and plans on going to Spain to enlist as a volunteer in the cause of the Carlist rebels. All this is described by Germain Nouveau to Verlaine, who has once more taken up residence in Paris. Rimbaud has broken with them both, Verlaine as well as Nouveau. Verlaine's visit to him in Germany in February 1875 miscarried. Did they come to blows this last time they saw each other? The reports contradict one another, but there is an account of it by Rimbaud in a letter to Ernest Delahaye dated March 5, 1875. Paterne Berrichon, who later married Rimbaud's sister and for a very long time popularized the legend of a chaste Rimbaud led astray who eventually returned to religion, claims that they fought. Rimbaud's letter gives reason for doubt: "Verlaine came recently with a rosary in his claws. Three hours later he had so denied the Lord that the 98 wounds of O. S. began to bleed anew. He stayed two and a half days, was very reasonable, and went back to Paris on my advice; from there he'll go to study out on the island."[20] That is a play on a passage in the *Season in Hell*: "Mais le Père est là-bas dans l'île." The island is England. Who is the father?

By that time Rimbaud had already renounced literature. A return to Verlaine, and with it a return to that ambulatory existence evoked by the "Vagabonds" in *Illuminations,* would not have been merely repetition of an experience with another from which all the conclusions had already been drawn, it would also have been the repetition of the attempt to transform the world, social circumstances, oneself, by means of the "alchemy of the word." What the possibilities of that are, are found summarized in the work *A Season in Hell,* which Rimbaud carefully composed between April and August 1873, and turned over to the printer in Brussels in September. It was a workingman's press, which printed it for a fee. Rimbaud's mother provided the money, and in October the author picked up his 500 copies in Brussels and immediately quit Belgium where he was under police surveillance. Author's copies were sent off; even Verlaine received one in prison at Mons.

The last text in the *Season in Hell* has the title "Adieu." Whoever is versed in literature senses that farewell is being taken from writing as a means of influencing the world, departure from all memory of scandals triggered purposely or involuntarily. "Tous les souvenirs immondes s'effacent." No more poetry; it too belongs to dire memory. "Point de cantiques." Between these two sentences there is, in a paragraph of its own, the author's last message formulated to himself: "Il faut être absolument moderne." How that is to be interpreted is contained in the last, underlined, sentence of the work: it is the simple surety "de posséder la vérité dans une âme et un corps."

It is quite understandable that Rimbaud's sister Isabelle and brother-in-law Berrichon later thought to derive the Catholic concept of salvation out of that line. Yet the fact is the work deals with hell and leaves it with the one single surety: being alive in the full sense of both body and soul.

What was this hell? Scarcely his life of disgrace, being hard-up and in disrepute. Rimbaud had sought these things ever since, after running away to Paris during the war year 1870–71, he was forced back to Charleville like "The Drunken Boat" itself. In Charleville he played to the hilt his role as the local scourge: unwashed, cynical, coarse, and boorish, ascribing to himself all manner of scandalous acts. His friend Delahaye remembered, "He got his kicks by making his money in the most repugnant of ways, and by describing various immoral acts in great detail, so that fire from heaven would have had to engulf the café."

The fire of Sodom. Delahaye meant his report in all seriousness. Modern scholarship accepts it as well, as Antoine Adam in the introduction to his exemplary edition of the collected works (Pléiade) confirms.[21] Rimbaud used to make much of himself in the Café de la Promenade for living off wealthy men who picked him up; he got money, beer, and girls for his trouble. Later on, in Paris, Verlaine did not lead any countryboy innocent astray. The painters or literary people who took in the seventeen-year-old (Forain and Germain Nouveau) well knew what they were dealing with.

Yet this is only a single aspect to consider. Psychology, once again, is not of much help. It is able to prove various motivations: his mother, the provincial small town, an aversion to women, hatred of the victors over the Paris Commune. Everything has a motivational effect in Rimbaud's acts and writings but does not "explain" them, for this youth from the Ardennes is not driven by his experiences—he activates them—is the activator of the poetic experiences as well as of the others. He makes his outlines and drafts in the period between his first return home and then later with Verlaine, in London, in Brussels, culminating with writing it down as the testimony of experiences in hell, as the attempt not simply to think out an antimorality and antiaesthetics, but also to put them to practice. The surrealist circle around André Breton knew why it looked to Rimbaud as a precedent.

In Rimbaud's concept, the setting free of the senses, the rediscovery of love transcending the "vieilles amours mensongères" and the hitherto existing mendacious couples, "les couples menteurs," fashion one part of his concept of hell. The other has to be provided by poetry, likewise the setting free of all the senses in the form of an "alchimie du verbe." Scandal and literature belong together; both have the infernal, new experiment with life in view. In *A Season in Hell* leave is taken of both. The first part of its retrospective depicts, in Dantesque fashion, the experience of Verlaine and Rimbaud as the confrontation of the groom of hell with the foolish virgin. The second part deals with word alchemy. Both have the common title, "Délires." This written text is conceived as a death announcement.

Literature and the acceptance of homosexual scandal belong together. Rimbaud's so endlessly interpreted renunciation of any kind of unifying poetic genius must also be understood simultaneously as the forgoing of scandal. Neither one brusquely took effect with the printing of the one book this author absolutely wanted to see published. He still wrote poems on occasion in London around 1874: a few pieces in *Illuminations*; and with Germain Nouveau likely still continued a bit of his callboy existence. But when Verlaine appears in Stuttgart, the whole turbulence has subsided. There was to be no return to Verlaine, to scandal, to literature.

From provocative love of scandal to provocative insignificance: that was his path until he died of an agonizing cancer in a Marseilles hospital at the age of thirty-seven. Don't attract attention; be independent with the help of money you have from your own (in this case, stringent) labors. In Ethiopia Rimbaud dealt in coffee and ivory as the regional representative of a French firm. He did not deal in slaves as has been asserted. He corresponded with Menelik II, the Lion of Judah in Addis Ababa, and with the underkings in Harar. The letters have been preserved. He made some money and was manifestly well thought of. He was linguistically gifted as well. His will mostly provides for his servants.[22]

Looking back on it all, according to his mother, he is supposed to have involuntarily disavowed that time of scandal and literature. He disconcertedly said, we are told, that at least he never did any harm to anyone. That may be only the edifying claptrap of a Catholic bourgeoise; yet Maurice Riès as well, Rimbaud's sometime boss, putting down his memories in a letter at a much later date (1929), reports conversations with Rimbaud in Ethiopia where the returnee from hell denied those episodes in his life. Rimbaud, he said, spoke of youthful misdemeanors (*frasques de jeunesse*) that he now "abhorred."[23]

The last bourgeois concerns of the dying man with an amputated leg correspond with that. Rimbaud once again in France, in a hospital at Marseilles, receives notice that he is being sought as a deserter for inattendance at a practice maneuver, the orders to which probably never reached him in Africa. The times of indolence are gone. Rimbaud hides himself in semilegality. He obliges his family to deal with the military authorities. Finally relief as the documents arrive temporarily freeing him of his duties. A good and respectable citizen who wishes integration.

Not quite with all his heart, though. His mother asks again and again, when her well-off businessman son seems well, whether he does not intend to return and get married. At first he says he has no time, he cannot abandon his business affairs (letter of April 21, 1890). Then he seems willing, but the woman must go back with him to Africa; it is out of the question to consider living in France (August 10, 1890). Finally his refusal: he has to stay free, be able to travel, stay in Africa, has fallen out of contact with Europe (November 10, 1890). Then came the outbreak of the synovial tumor and bone disease.

Hans Christian Andersen had reacted to similar letters recommending his marriage by saying that he was too ugly or too poor. Arthur Rimbaud says his business affairs and the distance to Europe make it impracticable. His erstwhile programmatic requirement of a "dérèglement de tous les sens" has long since fallen by the wayside.

In a study on Rimbaud in 1961, the poet Yves Bonnefoy no longer—as once Berrichon or Carré had done—saw fit to dismiss Rimbaud's entire homosexual theory and practice as an ephemeral episode, with Verlaine as the evil seducer, but attempts to formulate precisely its idiosyncrasy. His thesis: "Homosexuality was for Rimbaud in these first months a part of a conscious deregulation of the senses. It had only, according to this expression, the character of depravity. For the frustrated and rebellious Rimbaud it was not so important to exchange one form of sexuality for another as to confront depravity of every sort with the various forms of loving—and nonpleasure, often in the form of loathing, with all kinds of pleasure. His homosexuality originates from exile, and for a long time is one of the manifestations of exile. On that account it runs so deep in his always scrupulously honest work and is so difficult to lay one's hands on."[24]

Honest yet at the same time deep and hardly accessible. The sixteen-year-old's offensiveness and boasting in the Café de la Promenade does not intertwine with visions of Sodom in order to provoke heaven's fire, it is simply the sole possibility for his own self-acceptance. Seventy years later Jean Genet embarks on a similar course.

Rimbaud's eroticism, if one leaves aside the chronicle of scandals and the police reports and takes the poetic texts under scrutiny, is the male relationship to another man. He is hell's bridegroom. What excites him is the androgynous, the hermaphroditic mixture. Two contiguous texts in the *Illuminations* are completely candid—as is everything else in this astonishing poetic legacy.

They are the pieces "Antique" and "Being Beauteous." The first is a prose poem on the statue of a faun in the form of a loving address. It is, however, a satyr of a special sort. "Ton coeur bat dans ce ventre où dort le double sexe." A double-sexed faun, a hermaphrodite. The poem has him go out into the night. To what manner of copulation?

The English title "Being Beauteous" is taken from a poem by Long-fellow. Once again, as in "Antique," the poetic vision of a statue come to life. Is the lyrical *I*, like Pygmalion, evoking the feminine beauty of a Galathea? Some things indicate that, yet the characteristics given, the "blessures écarlates et noires," can be interpreted otherwise. Antoine Adam, the cautious commentator of the Pléiade edition, speaks of "a young woman (or a young man?)"[25] who comes to life in the vision and achieves union with the poet. The poem then has a second part—the joyous cry of "le canon sur lequel je dois m'abattre à travers la mêlée des arbres et de l'air léger!" The sense of that is unmistakable. The modern commentator has no inhibition in formulating it; it is a masturbatory vision but once again sexually ambiguous as far as the evocation of the sexual object is concerned.

In the two most important texts that represent a poetic balance of life with Verlaine, the prose poem "Vagabonds" from the *Illuminations* cycle, and the first of the "Délires" in A Season in Hell, the poetic I allows its partner to speak, only to interject short, mischievous commentaries into his garrulousness, as the bridegroom of hell vis-à-vis the foolish virgin or as one vagabond to another who is the "satanique docteur." Verlaine recognized himself in the poem and in a letter to a friend protested against being characterized a "satanic doctor."

In "Vagabonds" the meaning of Verlaine's and Rimbaud's living together in hell is laid out. It was a conscious undertaking to proceed to hell. More than that, it was the conscious undertaking of both of them together, far more than erotic decadence on the part of the older man, a letting things fall whichever way they will on the part of the younger, because Verlaine had some little money and, besides, was a respected poet in the young Rimbaud's scheme of things as well. What he reproaches Verlaine for, beyond all the instances of begging, is his (Verlaine's) metaphysical washout. He could not deal with hell. He reneged on their common quest.

"J'avais en effet, en toute sincérité d'esprit, pris l'engagement de le rendre à son état primitif de fils du Soleil." Thus Rimbaud begins the last paragraph of the "Vagabonds."[26] A devil's pact of reciprocal diabolism. The dirt of country roads, hunger and thirst and universal proscription were not meant when that other book of Rimbaud's spoke of Hell. It was not meant as metaphor. Being shut out of the social order, they sought to heighten their condition by, say, publicly embracing in Brussels and thus providing the formula for a new condition humaine that called out to be created. It was thus that Rimbaud saw the matter: out of the conscious derangement of the senses and accepted behavior a new mode of existence would shine forth: as the negation of the negation. "[M]oi pressé de trouver le lieu et la formule," reads the final line of "Vagabonds" in Illuminations. The quest for a previous existence as son of the sun—Luciferism, one might put it—was meant in all seriousness only by the man in this marriage, only by the "époux infernal." The foolish virgin Verlaine once again washed out; it was all only half-serious then when Rimbaud sought the place and the formula for the transformation.

In the famous text "Vierge Folle" in Rimbaud's book on hell, Verlaine's world and private incomprehension of their communal experiment is masterfully evoked through having it seem that only the foolish virgin speaks as she incessantly prattles on. She has a single topic: hell's bridegroom. He too speaks when she, full of lamentation, quotes him literally, a not infrequent occurrence. Rimbaud comes to speak in a double capacity: in citations of his words by the foolish virgin, and in one sentence each at the beginning and the end of the text. At the beginning the notice: Let us hear the confession of a companion in hell. Then begins a torrent of babble from the foolish virgin, a mixture of treacly pining away for deliverance, gossip, accusations, self-accusations, and pleasure in suffering. The closing word is had once again by the groom. He simply says: "Drôle de ménage!"[27]

An odd couple, indeed. There is considerable evidence, in the opinion of Rimbaud scholars, that the text had already been composed before the pistol episode in Brussels: as a taking stock, which at the same time provides the reasons Rimbaud no longer wanted to support their risky common venture. Doubtless it is too simple to see in the foolish virgin merely Verlaine, in the husband Rimbaud. A modern interpretation emphasizes that what gleams through from behind is an inner dialogue between the earlier, devout Rimbaud and the present theoretical and practical patron of Satanism. The text is to be interpreted, accordingly, as an inner dialogue of Rimbaud's with an earlier self.[28] Nevertheless it is not permissible to remove Verlaine from the interpretation. Too many personal characteristics of his are indicated; the "drôle de ménage" is a real marriage comprising two partners, of whom the one, the foolish virgin, has taken on the woman's role. The decisive proposition uttered by her against the bridegroom captures the essence of her whole position: "C'est un Démon, vous savez, *ce n'est pas un homme.*" That was indeed Verlaine's opinion. He had not grasped the fact that Rimbaud really did mean hell, not merely a symbolistic metaphor. In precisely that same vein Verlaine's sonnet on the death of Arthur Rimbaud (November 10, 1891) begins: "Mortel, Ange ET démon, autant dire Rimbaud."[29]

Paul Verlaine never overcame his capitulation in the sight of hell where all recantations and reversals back to bourgeois conformity, "with good conduct," become meaningless. The memory of Rimbaud haunted him ever after. He distorts that memory when he attempts to fixate it as erotic gratification. Rimbaud, on the other hand, evoked, as Verlaine well knew and then came to express in his poem, the purity of an absolute quest and of a quest for the absolute at the dregs. Therefore the appearance again and again of the word *pure* when he, the other, is to be apostrophized. Moreover, it was probably Verlaine himself who, after the meeting in Stuttgart, broke off from Rimbaud. In a letter dated November 27, 1875, Verlaine informed Ernest Delahaye that he no longer intended to read Rimbaud's letters. It would seem, then, that he still must be

Alternatives in the Nineteenth Century

receiving some to read. A last encounter may have taken place in October 1878 in Roche, as Rimbaud was preparing to go to Italy on foot, and from there to sail to Cyprus. By that time, however, Verlaine had already established himself as the fatherly friend of Lucien Létinois.

Rimbaud never again mentioned his partner in the *drôle de ménage.* Verlaine's later poetry cannot survive without the diabolical bridegroom. His long poem "Laeti et Errabundi," whose title betrays a counterversion to Baudelaire's *Flowers of Evil,* is actually Verlaine's counterattack to Rimbaud's text "Vagabonds."[30]

It first appeared in a periodical on September 28, 1888, which is to say during Rimbaud's lifetime. Verlaine subsequently included it in his collection of poems, *Parallèlement,* as part of the "Lunes" cycle. The news that Rimbaud was dead had been circulated in Paris to which the lyric *I* of the poem makes answer:

On vous dit mort, Vous. Que le Diable
Emporte avec qui la comporte.
La nouvelle irrémédiable
Qui vient ainsi battre à ma porte!

The devil here is simply a cliché, a word gone to spoil. This is neither a good poem, even if masterfully rhymed, nor a reminiscence capable of attaining the height that Rimbaud had demanded—whose diagnosis in "Vagabonds" is only corroborated by this poem of Verlaine's. An embarrassing comfortableness and self-satisfaction suffuses it. Those were the days! A disregard of women and the founding of an antiethics and antiaesthetics in a male league: that was the goal of the diabolical pact that the boy from the Ardennes had established. Verlaine never saw in the experiment anything more than physical pleasure, inspiration for new poems along old lines, a delight in provocation.

Le roman de vivre à deux hommes
Mieux que non pas d'époux modèles
Chacun au tas versant des sommes
De sentiments forts et fidèles.

But it was exactly this that Verlaine had been incapable of: strong and constant feelings amid the scandalous experiment. He remained the foolish paramour of hell's consort, and as "foolish virgin" never comprehended why everything had to founder in the end. Yet he himself unknowingly provides the answer. This answer, as the whole of the poem, is directed at the far-off Rimbaud now believed dead:

Pardonnâtes-vous aux femelles?
Moi, j'ai peu revu ces compagnes,
Assez toutefois pour souffrir.
Ah, quel coeur faible que mon coeur!
Mais mieux vaut souffrir que mourir
Et surtout mourir de langueur.

That could literally be part of the blather of the foolish virgin in *A Season in Hell*. In all of the excesses of the voyage to hell Rimbaud remained strangely pure. It was not only the partner who thought so, the poetic texts give proof of it. Verlaine is obscene and enjoys the situation. More than that: he is strangely lascivious. In his collection *Parallèlement* there is another poem on that order, "L'Impénitent":[31] a self-portrait with Rimbaud as the imagined partner. "The impenitent" has once again put away his rosary and acknowledges his sexual peculiarities.

Les nez te plaisent, gracieux
Ou simplement malicieux,
Etant la force des visages,
Etant aussi, suivant les gens,
Des indices et des présages.

Indeed: from the shape of a nose one can plainly deduce many a thing. When they issued out of hell's gate they went off in different directions. Verlaine for the time being to prison in Mons. Rimbaud to bourgeois conformity with mother and sisters, after that with business partners, profits and losses, business correspondence, even documentary reports—but without literature. Paul Verlaine spent the rest of his life staging new provocations and penitences, with a Létinois instead of a Rimbaud, later on with elderly courtesans. It all could be made use of for his poems. Although it is true that his application for admission to the Académie Française was first denied, he was admitted in August 1894, after the death of Leconte de Lisle, as the "prince des poètes." He had attained what he had sought: scandal and conformity simultaneously. Which is to say, nothing. Rimbaud had died on November 10, 1891, at the age of thirty-seven, of an agonizing cancer.

Ludwig of Bavaria and Peter Ilich Tchaikovsky

When King Ludwig II of Bavaria found his death in Lake Starnberg in June 1886, taking with him Privy Councillor Gudden, a specialist in

Alternatives in the Nineteenth Century

mental disorder, there was scarcely a report that did not mention the name of Richard Wagner. The composer of *Tristan* had died three years earlier in the Palazzo Vendramin in Venice. The completion of his work, *The Meistersinger,* the Ring tetralogy, *Parsifal,* the idea of the *Festspiel,* would have been inconceivable without that one king of Bavaria who now it was assumed left this world as murderer and suicide.

Among those who saw things in this light was Paul Verlaine.[32] He had discovered Wagner's magic art shortly before and at the beginning of 1886 had published ten sonnets in Wagner's honor, most of them having to do with *Parsifal.* It should be mentioned that Wagner's Catholicizing left him cold, yet he was well prepared, this sometime companion of Arthur Rimbaud, to sing the praises of the Pure Fool victorious over Kundry and the flowergirls. "Parsifal a vaincu les filles, leur gentil Babil et la luxure amusante." The poems were printed in the *Revue Wagnérienne.*

When news of King Ludwig's death reached Paris, Eduard Dujardin, the editor of that Wagner review, asked Verlaine for another poem in memory of the event. Verlaine sent it to him on July 6. In an accompanying letter he asks Dujardin's indulgence on account of the delay. The text is "vaguement loufoque," somewhat topsy-turvy, but that, he continues, is understandable in view of the circumstances. The poem appeared on July 8 under the title "La Mort de S. M. Louis II de Bavière." Verlaine later incorporated it into his lyric oeuvre with a slightly corrected text, under the title "A Louis II de Bavière." What had begun as a news event ended in a dedication.

It is manifestly an occasional poem, perhaps not even meant seriously, as the cover letter to the editor of the French Wagnerite review gives one reason to believe. Nonetheless, the sonnet is most noteworthy. It was born out of the spirit of an elective affinity.

A Louis II de Bavière

Roi, le seul vrai roi de ce siècle, salut, Sire,
Qui voulûtes mourir vengeant votre raison
Des choses de la politique, et du délire
De cette Science intruse de la maison,

De cette Science assassin de l'Oraison
Et du Chant et de l'Art et de toute la Lyre,
Et simplement, et plein d'orgueil en floraison,
Tuâtes en mourant, salut, Roi! bravo, Sire!

Vous fûtes un poète, un soldat, le seul Roi
De ce siècle ou les rois font si peu de chose,
Et le martyr de la Raison selon la Foi.

Salut à votre très unique apothéose,
Et que votre âme ait son fier cortège, or et fer,
Sur un air magnifique et joyeux de Wagner.

Much in this poem is curious. As a lyrical construction it is without significance, although or perhaps because Verlaine had not wanted to compose a cold, summarizing epitaph but instead wanted to express a deep sympathy with the man and the manner of his death. It is not even "loufoque" or simply meant to be taken tongue in cheek. That passage in the cover letter was likely there to mollify the editor. All glorifications, namely, and all negations in sonnet form had become a part of Verlaine's poetic inventory since Rimbaud had left him.

The individual reason at work in this regal artist, Ludwig, is brought to a confrontation with the reason of men of science. A man of the despised sciences, in the person of the medical officer Dr. Gudden, penetrated the dream realm of an artist, come to investigate, classify, and destroy it all: prayer, music, art—all of it for him but the plunkings of the Muses. King Ludwig did away with this intruder in order to be able to conclude the dream of his own demise. Verlaine busily, knowingly, applauds with cries of bravo. As early as the seventies he had occasionally manifested royalist sympathies. They were scarcely to be taken seriously, the whole of his political activities, from his inflammatory speeches during the Paris Commune to the clerical edifications (and I do not mean Verlaine's religious lyric poetry), to the rhymed diatribes against the Third Republic. Despite all that, the occasional monarchist Verlaine never made much of the hereditary house of the now deposed Bourbons. They are certainly in view when he honors Ludwig of Bavaria as the one and only monarch worthy of the name. A martyr, above all, of an aesthetic religion trampled by the dissecting reason of the technocrats.

Ludwig is apostrophized as soldier, poet, king, and martyr, all of these terms having a special meaning alongside their usual one. A martyr in the cause of a menaced artistic totality; a soldier for accepting the task of killing at the point of his own death; a poet for poeticizing it; Ludwig, a poetical existence incarnate. Verlaine's sonnet sees itself as partaking of the general apotheosis, accompanied by funeral music by Wagner that will be "magnifique et joyeux."

The nearness to the "real" King Ludwig demonstrated here is questionable at best. Verlaine incorporated as verities conjectures he found in the press, according to which the king strangled the good doctor in order to be able to kill himself. He decided that that must have been the fact of the matter. He, the lover of Rimbaud, Lucien Létinois, and others, could not have known what lay behind Ludwig's virginal solitude. That Ludwig's life was not comparable with any other (neither royal nor bourgeois) could only have been patent from the start. Even more peculiar that Verlaine considered this uniqueness of the king's reason enough for his transfiguration, and not simply his friendship with Richard Wagner. The obituary notices on Ludwig in the year 1886, a decade after the first *Festspiel* in Bayreuth, probably had their impetus in the fame of the *Meister*. The royal patron was thanked mostly with a "Well, he tried."

Verlaine honors King Ludwig on his own account, as a poeticized life, the culmination of which is a beautiful and brutally fulfilled death. A self-abasement resonates in the poem that Verlaine here as elsewhere manages to enjoy to the full. How often had he himself toyed with suicide! "As far as kicking the bucket is concerned, I know you," Rimbaud wrote him from London on July 5, 1873. "You are going to wait for your wife and your death, play the lunatic, wander around lost, get on peoples' nerves." The diagnosis continued to prove correct over the years. Verlaine had no great illusions. He enjoyed his weakness, intoxicated with the desire for death palmed off into more banal intoxications.

Ludwig had constructed a dream life culminating in a dream death that was directed into reality like everything else in this royal life, which was always rigidly formal and was expected to remain so. A threefold solitude: the formal life of a monarch, of an artist who is unable to create except for the architectural fantasies, of a homosexual who is a king and a Catholic and who is therefore unable to lead a double life. One senses in Verlaine's sonnet that he had sensed much of that. He himself had made a try at both integration and a scandalous nonintegration. He failed at both; in the first try he had lost wife and son, in the second the unforgettable Rimbaud. And with the third possibility, the intoxication of death, he had scarcely ever been serious.

Under the conditions of puritanical nineteenth-century bourgeois society, next to either total conformity striven for in despair or consciously provoked scandal, there was a rare third possibility for homosexual existence: an intoxicated self-extinguishing. It is not something to be confounded with the usual motivation for suicide as end to a condition of life grown intolerable. That is something that has to do with a no more. The other, however, has in view the (futile) annihilation of one's own existence from its very inception—Faust's exclamation at seeing the murderess Gretchen: "Oh, were that I had never been born!" This consciousness of oneself as a botched being forced to go on living is not limited to homosexual existence. It can be found in Kleist; but was he free of homoerotic feelings? It was felt and analyzed in exemplary fashion by Otto Weininger. A work on the order of *Sex and Character* proceeds from the desire of self-annihilation, transforms it into a theory of culture, and follows up with a pistol shot in Beethoven's death chamber in Vienna, putting an end finally to a botched, miscreated being after twenty-three years of existence.

The homosexuality of Ludwig of Bavaria and Peter Tchaikovsky is no longer contested. Whether they died as suicides is the subject of controversy that will very likely never be settled. Verlaine seems to interpret the struggle at Lake Starnberg as the king's desiring death, which the good doctor tried to prevent, whereupon the younger and stronger man, to carry out his aim, was obliged to kill the other as well in order to be able to die himself. But the medical reports could well have been a varnishing over of the truth. A king in a Catholic country as murderer and suicide? That is not the decisive aspect.

It is equally uncertain whether Peter Ilich Tchaikovsky[33] on November 2, 1893, a Thursday, five days after the premiere performance of the "Symphonie Pathétique" in St. Petersburg, drank a glass of water in the middle of a cholera epidemic accidentally or with an inner intent. His brother Modeste reports Tchaikovsky to have answered, upon being reproached for drinking the water, that one cannot go through life on tiptoe for fear of death. Then he collapsed. That evening he said, "This is the end." He died in the night before Monday.

The supposition that he deliberately infected himself does not seem improbable. It was a manner of suicide that avoided all scandal, albeit depending to a great extent upon chance. Tchaikovsky was well versed in the arrangement. One evening in the first week of October 1877, shortly after his marriage to Antonina Miliukova, a pretty, vacuous, nymphomaniac woman who later became mentally ill, Tchaikovsky, in despair, possessed by the notion of strangling his wife, went out into the freezing waters of the Moscow river. They were shallow. Tchaikovsky, soaked through, his features distorted, returned home and claimed he had fallen out of a fishing boat.

Alternatives in the Nineteenth Century

His probable intent was to contract a fatal disease and thereby to avoid the ignominy of scandal. The disease did not appear, and Tchaikovsky was at wits' end. His brothers and friends took him to St. Petersburg, forced through a separation from his wife, and now comes the moment for the wealthy Nadejda von Meck. Tchaikovsky is endowed with liberal amounts of cash, is able to give up his teaching position at the Moscow Conservatory (thereby reducing his fears connected with the maintenance of respectability), is free to travel and compose his music. Antonina is taken care of. Tchaikovsky is without exception respectful whenever he mentions her; he blames himself alone for the dissolution of their marriage.

That first, indirect attempt at doing away with himself unlocked creative urges. Shortly thereafter he wrote his Symphony no. 4 in F-minor, which according to his own commentary begins with a "motif of fate" containing all manner of manifestation of joy for life, drunkenness, and vulgar festivity, as he explains to Mme. von Meck in a letter analyzing the score, and returns to culminate in an intoxicated victory of fate.

The lyric scenes in *Eugene Onegin* originated in that period as well. The story of a man approached by a woman seeking marriage—just as Antonina Miliukova, then a student at the Moscow Conservatory, had once written to Professor Tchaikovsky. Onegin refuses and attempts to make clear to Tatiana the reasons making marriage with her impossible. Tchaikovsky had in his time given in to the wooing, but Antonina was no Tatiana.

Sixteen years came between that first liberating attempt at suicide and the later episode with the glass full of cholera bacillae in early November 1893. Tchaikovsky had in the meantime become world famous. He had been celebrated in Berlin and Paris, London and New York. Despite his Sixth Symphony in B-minor, opus 74, receiving no more than a polite reception at its St. Petersburg premiere as well as some consternation over its unusual sounds, the composer himself even then, independently of his work, had been thoroughly extolled. Yet Tchaikovsky must have felt that this symphony, the "Pathétique" (and here we have the testimony of many) represented some kind of finale that would not admit any new, creative impulse. It was quite unusual and not simply to be explained away by any new self-confidence that this composer who had always been unsure of his own work and was even given to despising it was in this case inspired with the greatest of confidence by the score. It was not only his best work, he confessed, it was also honest. In a letter dated October

30, just two days after the premiere, Tchaikovsky wrote to his publisher, Jurgenson, that "something strange happened with this symphony; one cannot say that the audience disliked it, but they were certainly confused by it. I am prouder of the work than of anything else that I have written." And he asks that on the title page of the score there appear the following:[34]

Dedicated to Vladimir Lvovich Davidov

No. 6

Comp. P. Tch.

Even this dedication, decided upon two days after the premiere and a week before the composer's death, is one more of the curiosities attendant upon his life's finale. A symphony haunted by death; suicide through the help of cholera; the feeling of having attained the pinnacle of all that music is capable of expressing. Added to that comes the intertwining of life and work in a dedication to the solitary human being whom Tchaikovsky still loved. Vladimir Lvovich Davidov, the beloved Bob of his letters and diaries, was the son of Tchaikovsky's sister; twenty-two years old at the time, he was, Tchaikovsky literature simply takes for granted, the lover of the man who made him his sole heir. Tchaikovsky's younger brother Modeste Tchaikovsky, himself homosexual, mostly avoids any immediate commentary on the matter in his biography and edition of the letters, yet the journals and other reports leave no room for doubt. The Soviet edition of the letters makes note of various suppressions of text it has undertaken; yet the originals themselves are accessible as well. Scholars who have studied them have noted that the suppressions in every case have to do with homosexual episodes. Bob Davidov shot himself in 1906 at the age of thirty-five.

The intoxicated amalgamation of homoeroticism and death as it is evoked, both in the realm of art and in life, in Peter Ilich Tchaikovsky's Sixth Symphony has again and again stimulated the imaginative faculty. Klaus Mann's novel, *Symphonie Pathétique,* sets out to represent the end of this life and creative effort as embedded in such a constellation.

The symphony in B-minor, which subsides at the end in the darkness of life's dissolution, probably bears the title "Pathétique" without justification. It is not at all certain that Tchaikovsky agreed to it. One has only Modeste's account to speak for it, that he recommended the description *pathétique,* which, he claimed, immediately met with an enthusiastic re-

sponse on the part of Peter Ilich. Tchaikovsky's letter to his publisher
mentions only the dedication to Bob and says nothing of pathos. Nonetheless is was Modeste's account that was to be decisive to the printed
score after his brother's death. The symphony, however, is not pathetic,
for pathos is suffering given form. Here suffering evoked in the first
movement is transcended. Everything is as if only recalled in memory:
even the bright and cheery sequence in irregular 5/4 time. The composer
shrank before the adagio lamentoso at the end, wherein all pathetic
suffering is left far behind and only the sounds of an intoxication with
death remain to take on animated form. Filled with care he confided to
N. D. Kashkin of the Moscow Conservatory that he wanted to wait and
see what the effect would be at the rehearsals; if it was negative, he would
do away with the movement and write a new one. On this occasion
Tchaikovsky once again spoke of presentiments of death. They had
become a part of his life. In his diaries he calls them his "feeling."[35]

This symphony in B-minor is uncanny. It represents an overstepping
of demarcations. In that it is reminiscent of Kleist's *Prince Friedrich von
Homburg*; and in Offenbach's "Tales of Hoffmann" as well the appearance
of Dr. Miracle, who signifies death, brings in his train something of such
a transcendence. In all three cases the works are also the last stage of a
life.

Homosexual love tied the fifty-three-year-old Tchaikovsky to a young
man of twenty-two who was his nephew. This love could not be lived out.
Tchaikovsky, fearful and easily intimidated, lived his whole life in fear
of scandal. His intention to marry very likely resulted from fearfulness
and conservatism. The creator of the noisily czarist "1812 Overture" was
demonstratively loyalist and affirmative of the existing social order. He
was an anti-Semite who in his diaries finds "the Jews" disgusting, but
does not mean the likes of Rubinstein, who was baptized. He admires
Tolstoy but considers his notions of social reform childish. He cannot
stand Zola but is acquainted with all of George Eliot's novels and loves
every one of them. Did he sense the affinity to outsiderdom there? The
Greek Orthodox liturgy again and again moves him to tears. That he
lived his life in a country of anti-Enlightenment absolutism that was
despised in Western and Central Europe for its methods of domination
never entered his consciousness. The rebellious artists, writers, and thinkers in nineteenth century Russia, ranks of men like Belinski, Chernish-
evskii, Dobroliubov, the Narodniki and the social revolutionaries, the
assassins of Czar Alexander II, never seem to have reached him. He sees

the composers around Balakirev, Moussorgsky, and Borodin simply as technically unfinished yet musically talented dilettantes. He did not discover the political stance.

A thoughtful Tchaikovsky, then sixty-five, would have reacted to the Russian revolution of 1905 no differently than Hans Christian Andersen in 1848 and 1864. One is reminded of the Dane by Tchaikovsky's resolve to lead a double life. This thoroughgoing conformity and labor at bulwarks against scandal, but then too the solitary walks in foreign cities on the lookout for "attractive" young people, which he unfailingly records in his journal. Andersen for his part, however, mystifies and prevaricates. He plays at being all complacency, as if buoyed up by divine providence. Tchaikovsky is disconsolate, forever tossing and turning, but sincere in his art. In the case of the "1812 Overture" he has no illusions. When the decision is made in Frankfurt not to play the work, he immediately accedes.

His music is supposed to possess all the straightforwardness that the composer is incapable of bringing to bear in his own life; had he in fact acted otherwise, it would probably have meant his end as a respected composer and his works being struck from the repertory. Verlaine was able to risk scandal as a poet; a composer who wants his music to be played has no such latitude. August von Paten too had known an infatuation with death as an amalgam of homoeroticism, social respectability, and artistic uprightness. "Who with eyes gazes upon beauty," as his sonnet "Tristan" begins, has in the process already fallen into the hands of death. Thomas Mann in his address on Platen identified this erotic-aesthetic correlation with utmost precision. It was also the sphere within which Peter Ilich Tchaikovsky's life moved. It is life led as a double life, productively and in the real world, but with only one thing in mind: death.

Ludwig II of Bavaria is another with the same strivings. Nadejda von Meck must have sensed it.[36] She had corresponded with the king and had the astonishing capacity of being able to discern the unusual people behind the exaggerations that adhered to them and their legendary wealth. In Paris she engaged a young French student with whom she wanted to play music for four hands and set him the task of writing the score. She took him along to Russia with her. He wanted to marry one of her daughters but was turned down. He was Claude Debussy. It was she who commissioned and paid for Kaulbach's famous portrait of King Ludwig that shows him in Lohengrin's white cloak. This picture of the king of Bavaria hung over her writing table. Here Mme. von Meck formulated her letters to Tchaikovsky. In a letter dated March 30, 1877, she speaks of her five-year-old daughter Ludmilla, who a year previously had accompanied her mother to the opening of the festival in Bayreuth and had seen his majesty. She knows, Nadejda continues, that her mother has taken the king into the circle of her household deities. Now the child demands to know to whom her mother is writing. "On my answering that I am writing to you because I like you very much, she asked me, 'et pourquoi est-ce que tu n'écris au Roi de Bavière?'" Nadejda von Meck then added, "Similarity of feeling suggested this question to her."[37]

Whether the daughter actually felt like her mother is open to question. During her last illness, tuberculosis, she who had brought eleven children into the world remained isolated and alone. Nadejda von Meck doubtless felt a "similarity of feeling" when she wrote the king of Bavaria or the composer of *Eugene Onegin*. Ludwig's social shyness was known to everyone, yet Nadejda writing him from Moscow could scarcely be aware of the king's proclivities that lay at its root. That she as a woman was so deeply attached to these two men who both reacted to the physical presence of the female body with aversion (the story of the king's engagement and Tchaikovsky's marriage) may have to do with the decidedly manly aspects of her character. The portraits show, according to the conventions of the nineteenth century at least, a most "unfeminine" woman. She, too, is one who makes the decisions. When she abruptly writes Tchaikovsky, now become famous in his own right, who no longer has need of her and who lets that come through in his mandatory epistles to her, that she has lost her fortune and can no longer supply him with money (the pretence being easily found out), that is a peculiarly male way of putting an end to a relationship grown to be a nuisance. Indeed, an inversion of the usual positions characterizes their correspondence.

Nonetheless this does not suffice to explain that similarity of reactions between Nadejda and Ludwig. It was a similarity that did not simply spring up out of the desire to break out of an all-too-evident loneliness. Nadejda was well-disposed toward music, yet it was the music of Peter Ilich Tchaikovsky to which she had succumbed, not that of Richard Wagner, although she did not share the rather ill-shod negations of the master in Bayreuth voiced by Tchaikovsky in his letters and critiques. It is not known whether Ludwig had ever taken notice of the composer Tchaikovsky. At any rate, Ludwig was, one can only suppose, of a much less musical temperament than his correspondent in Moscow.

It must have to do with an intuition of death. It was evident from the start that the builder of the castles and palaces Linderhof, Neuschwannstein, and Herrenchiemsee fully intended to live outside the bounds of his own time. Perhaps he actually did. It is not enough to call it all mental illness and so dispose of it as one individual's aberration. The nostalgia for the Middle Ages that led Ludwig to Wagner (better: that led him to Tannhäuser and Lohengrin), had devolved upon him from the German Romantics. Moritz von Schwind's frescoes in the great hall at the Wartburg are essentially only *technically* better than the Middle Ages style profusions in Neuschwannstein. The magnetism that emanates from this imitation bastion of defiance, "in a far-off land, unapproachable to your steps," and which strikes visitors of all sorts, from the Expressionists to Andy Warhol, forces the thought to dawn upon one that Ludwig felt here in a representative capacity for others, and built for them as well as for himself.

What was solely his own was his enthusiastic if not fanatical fancy for the French absolutism of Louis XIV. When a constitutional Bavarian monarch in the latter half of the nineteenth century signs his name "WE, THE KING!" and means to have erected at Chiemsee a new, even more opulent mirrored gallery than at Versailles, then that is as much connected with an individual's neurosis as with a singular, and in point of fact, impotent megalomania. During the last night at Neuschwannstein before he was forcibly transported to Berg Palace, Ludwig is said to have commanded the arrest, torture, and execution of the government officials and doctors who had come from Munich. The affinity of this "virgin" king to the world of Versailles is singular as well, to that world dominated by mistresses and courtesans (their very name referring to the royal court). If all this in the end is nothing more than a concretization of Ludwig's political aversions more than any kind of actual inner elective affinity (Versailles being for Ludwig France—not the German Empire; absolutism, not middle class codetermination; Catholicism, not Prussian Lutheranism), it is nonetheless, all of it, typical to an artist's dream in the latter nineteenth century. His desire to flee from the hideousness of the bourgeois order into a realm of pure knights of the grail, or royal despots, is in its essence not so very far removed from Gustave Flaubert's reaction, who sought consolation from the provincial miseries of Madame Bovary in the north African sun, in dreams of Carthage and Salammbo (what he called his "Carthago-chinoiseries.")

Ludwig lived as an artist; that which the decadents at the end of the century had put down in writing or painting he tried to build and live out in his own life. And like them, he negated the present, stood frozen without hope before a future imagined without exception to be hideous, and so in his desires and dreams he had no recourse but to the past, that is to say, to death. He is an artist who possesses no artist's craft. He is, besides, a monarch who is prevented from leading a bohemian double life not so much out of fear of scandal as from a deep sense of dignity. Where he does make an attempt at it, if under the sign of an overblown pathos in imitation of Schiller, as on the trip to Switzerland with the actor Josef Kainz, everything ends in the grotesque.

As he sat interned, looking out over Starnberg Lake from his cell, the thought of Wagner's Tristan may have surfaced in his mind. That was where it had all begun: Wagner, Cosima, Bülow, the first powerlessness and the first deceit. Tristan's desolate day now at the very end. Put an end to both the erotic and political impotence. A yearning for death, culminating in the tragic concatenation of killing and dying.

That was how Verlaine had understood it: writing in his own turn from a sense of elective affinity. That this King Ludwig, this artist without an art, nonetheless no dilettante, had as his only instrument his own life, where Tchaikovsky could create a moving form in sound, does nothing to change such an affinity. It was not the search for another homosexual's tragically ending existence that prompted Klaus Mann after the completion of his novel about the Symphonie Pathétique to write a short story, "Barred Window," in which Ludwig's end was depicted.[38] The strange elective affinity between Bavarian king and Russian composer may well have had its root in eros. Nonetheless it remains noteworthy as the attempt to circumvent those two other choices so rigidly fixed by the age: hopeless conformity or impotent scandal—the alternatives represented by Andersen on the one hand and Rimbaud and Verlaine on the other.

14   Concerning the Typology of Homosexual Literature

Oscar Wilde, *The Picture of Dorian Gray*

Oscar Wilde's own fate is so well known that the assertion the only novel he wrote, *The Picture of Dorian Gray* (1891)[1] is a homosexual story, seems credible. Nonetheless, everything in the text appears to speak against it. The scandals that isolate the aging Dorian Gray from society, so that members of the high nobility leave the club when Dorian appears there and houses once open to him now remain obstinately closed against him, are nowhere exactly specified. Wilde portrays rumor and its effects; he does not communicate the reasons for the alienation between Dorian, who continues to remain beautiful and young and his sometime world. It is not permissible to equate the rumors surrounding Dorian with those rumors and bits of gossip that attended Wilde even years before his lawsuit against Lord Alfred Douglas's father.

That Dorian might have had sexual relations with Lord Henry, or even with his portraitist, Basil Hallward, whom he later murders, seems excluded by the text. No matter how Basil and Lord Henry explain the fascination they feel for Dorian, a rigid separation evidently exists between the sexual and the erotic spheres. Somewhat later, André Gide wrote in his confessions that he always held fast to that rule separating sex and eros, even if not always successfully. The structure even of his homosexual novel *The Counterfeiters* presupposes such a sundering.

To be sure, Wilde's insistence that Dorian is so beautiful, his beauty being continually evoked, is somewhat odd. Yet it is no stranger than Balzac's hymnic descriptions of the beautiful Lucien de Rubempré in his novel *Lost Illusions,* which is certainly no homosexual novel, even if the reader is given to understand that the criminal Vautrin, who takes in and loves the failed Lucien, proceeds from a desire to possess his darling.

The conclusion to *Lost Illusions* reads like a pact with the devil. Balzac composed here and in the continuation in *Splendeurs et misères des courtisanes* (A Harlot High and Low), a homosexual constellation but not a homosexual novel. Oscar Wilde, responding epigrammatically to the question of what had been the deepest sorrow of his life, answered: "The death of Lucien de Rubempré." The difference between Balzac and Wilde is that in *A Harlot High and Low* there is a homosexual relationship presupposed between Lucien and Vautrin without which the continuation of the story could not be explained but which has no more significance than a daring erotic motif. Lucien is loved by Vautrin, while he himself loves the courtesan Esther. Vautrin wants to make him happy through this woman. Dorian Gray, contrarily, loves nothing but his own portrait. He is Narcissus. If he is loved by men like Basil and Lord Henry, then it is without sexual consummation. Was he the seductive downfall of young men of the nobility who are then rejected or who elect suicide? One is left not knowing.

Yet hints and suggestions dropped here and there in the novel give one to suppose that the scandal encompassing Dorian Gray has more to do with drugs than with homosexual practices. The pub in the London underworld where Dorian is supposed to be assassinated by Sibyl Vane's brother is evidently a meeting ground for opium smokers. Yet the addiction to opium had been an almost reverently acknowledged tradition in London society and English literature since the beginning of the nineteenth century, from Thomas de Quincey's *Confessions of an English Opium-Eater* through Coleridge's poems conceived in narcotic delirium. It was clear to Wilde why in one of his essays he resurrected the memory of de Quincey.

What gave cause for so much umbrage in the story of Dorian Gray and made the novel a cause for scandal immediately upon its appearance four years before the outbreak of real scandal surrounding this book's author, is not to be derived from any offensive episodes but from the message it contained, which Wilde consciously propagated. It is the image of the world reduced to a purely aesthetic totality. It appears that this proposition is retracted during the course of the novel, in that all those guilty of aesthetic idolatry succumb to suicide and loneliness or are murdered, yet this seemingly moralistic finale is simply there for the sake of effect. It is none other than an aesthetic ending, if it is not interpreted as a disdainful concession on the part of the author to his public. The Victorian reader, at any rate, seemed to understand it in this fashion.

The Typology of Homosexual Literature

The existence of the homosexual outsider in the bourgeois society of the nineteenth century is conceivable only as an aesthetic existence. The proposition is not reversible in the sense that every attempt at an all-encompassing aestheticization of life would have to be interpreted as the sublimation of drives having homoerotic components. As evidence I can cite the book that according to Dorian's own confession "poisoned" him, by all accounts Joris Karl Huysmans's *Against the Grain*. Pater, Ruskin, Huysmans, and d'Annunzio, the writers of the nineteenth century upon whom Wilde sought to base his aesthetic theory and practice of life, were not viewed as inhabitants of Sodom. It was the homosexual writer and artist alone who was condemned to play a certain role, which is to say, condemned to an aesthetic existence. Either he acted the part of the ideal husband and father, forgoing any fulfillment of his drives and desires, a role Verlaine and Wilde had both tried and one at which Tchaikovsky too had made an effort; or, sometimes even taking up a kind of counteroffensive, he played the exact opposite role of total outsider and vagrant. That was the path Verlaine chose when he wandered off with Rimbaud, just as it was the way for so many figures in Jean Genet's novels, if perhaps not for Genet himself. It is always the playing of a role; that is to say, it is the aesthetic mimesis of reality. Refusing to play the role does no good whatsoever. The finding of one's own identity through self-acceptance changes nothing in the situation of the homosexual vis-à-vis his environment. When the homosexual Daniel in Sartre's fragmentary tetralogy of novels *The Roads to Freedom* decides to reveal himself to his friend Mathieu with the words, "I am a homosexual," he has decided on his own life, in Sartre's sense, but his gratuitous confession only calls up in Mathieu a polite disquiet.

Oscar Wilde in *The Picture of Dorian Gray* has attempted to describe an equally aesthetic intermediate realm where one has neither to wear the mask of respectability nor opt for scandal. It cannot be denied that in the process scandal is summoned up, as if a spirit constantly resting just below the surface of things and recognized as being there. It is from this vantage point that Wilde's novel must be understood as a homosexual creation. And to this extent it also has a programmatic intent, as outlined in Wilde's famous preface. It is a program of total aestheticism and immoralism on principle—whereby it heavily influenced, as he himself admitted, Gide's later "immoralisme." But it has more in view than the usual aesthetic decadence and all the striving, starting with Flaubert, to oppose the middle class world, daily growing more and more hideous, with the beauty of invented things. The homosexual components in Wilde's aestheticism, in the preface and in the elements that correspond to it in the novel itself, consist in the hopeless attempt to avoid the role playing lying between bourgeois mask and scandal by expunging one's own existence in an aesthetic totality of life made over into a work of art. It is only in this sense that the famous and paradoxical beginning of the preface can be understood: "The artist is the creator of beautiful things. To reveal art and conceal the artist is art's aim."

How is it that Oscar Wilde, of all people, proposes that the aim of art is to reveal art and conceal the artist? Yet that is exactly what is meant. This proposition recurs word for word in chapter 9 of the novel in a revelatory context. The artist Basil curses his portrait of Dorian Gray in conversation with him. It reveals too much of the artist who painted it, he complains, namely, the passion of the painter for his model, who is another male. "I grew afraid that others would know of my idolatry. I felt, Dorian, that I had told too much, that I had put too much of myself into it. Then it was that I resolved never to allow the picture to be exhibited." Basil was afraid lest the portrait once exhibited allow conclusions to be drawn about its creator: the portrait of a beautiful young man as evidence of forbidden sentiment. The artist, then, speaking further, comes to a conclusion: "It often seems to me that art conceals the artist far more completely than it ever reveals him"—precisely the formulation of the preface. It is the wish fulfillment of a man who does not want to be recognized for what he is. Basil Hallward quotes Oscar Wilde. It is a homosexual wish fulfillment, and Wilde was not to be allowed to attain it.

If, however, one's self-extinguishing through integration into an artistic totality ends in failure, and mask and scandal are to be avoided, one then lands, not in Wilde's dreamed of intermediate realm, but once again in the dilemma of Dr. Jekyll: the double life. And in this as well *The Picture of Dorian Gray* is a homosexual book. In Stevenson's famous story, Jekyll both fears and longs for the transformation into Mr. Hyde. In this same vein Wilde describes Dorian's emotions at the beginning of chapter 15. A short time previously, before leaving home, Dorian had seen to it that the chemist Campbell, his erstwhile schoolboy friend, now the victim of his blackmail, had disposed of the body of the murdered Basil Hallward: "But the thing that had been sitting at the table was gone." Now it is time for dinner and Dorian, exquisitely dressed, wearing a large buttonhole of Parma violets, is in Lady Narborough's drawing room. They are about

The Typology of Homosexual Literature

to dine; Lord Henry would join them later. Dorian wonders at the calm that suffuses him, "and for a moment he felt keenly the terrible pleasure of a double life."

Dorian's world is an integral male world. Not in the sense of the American dramas that developed after the Second World War, equally propelled by homosexual intent, filled with longings for the comradeship of war, boarding school, or the playing field, but in the sense that whatever happens takes place between men. Or to be more precise: between Dorian and his aesthetic and Platonic lovers and admirers. The female figure of Sibyl Vane is not a failure because Wilde was incapable of portraying women convincingly. One need only look at his comedies to disprove that. It is simply that Sibyl Vane is an artistic character of reduced, secondary dimensions amid artistic characters. Dorian loves her art, or Shakespeare, not the woman herself. It is for this reason that she dies. Dorian's erotic adventures with women that Wilde mentions do not result from any richness of the female figure. They remind one more of a double life, once again, this time behind the mask of a Don Juan who does not particularly care for the women he seduces. And in such women's disappointments and discoveries is perhaps the source of the rumors that surround Dorian.

Lord Henry is acquainted with the business. When Dorian appears inconsolable over Sibyl's suicide, he tells him he should view the event as a part of theater, as a strange lurid fragment from some Jacobean tragedy. "The girl never really lived, and so she has never really died." Dorian has been returned now completely to male society sufficient unto itself. It is, to be sure, a world on the defensive. And in this too Wilde's novel is a homosexual work and not simply the work of a homosexual—in its incapacity to conceive women other than as odious creatures. Wilde begins a whole genealogy of fearsome and hateful female characters to be tolerated by the male world, all of them breakers of the peace, shrill, imperious, lewd, treacherous. Homosexual literature cannot afford it any other way. So many in this typology: Laura in Gide's *Counterfeiters*; the figure of Signe in Hans Henny Jahnn's novel *Perrudja*; the cat on the hot tin roof in Tennessee Williams; Martha in Edward Albee's play *Who's Afraid of Virginia Woolf?* Only the older society women in the novel, who pose no erotic threat, are described with ironic affection. All the other women are unpleasant, loud, stupid. There is no paucity of descriptive adjectives. The women's voices in the theater box are "shrill and discordant." The brief episode where Dorian goes to Lord Henry Wotton's and to his great surprise meets Lady Wotton, depicts the woman as an abominable caricature. Her voice too, naturally enough, is "shrill," she has a "silly laugh," and talks nonsense about "dear Lohengrin," which she likes because it is so loud one can talk through it without anyone being able to eavesdrop. This marriage is no more than a masquerade and probably was never anything else. An earlier paramour is described by Henry as a tactless neighbor at an official dinner. She seized upon that opportunity, he tells us, to rampage in the past and accuse him of having destroyed her life. "I am bound to state that she ate an enormous dinner, so I did not feel any anxiety." That is both mean and stupid, as are most of Lord Henry's maxims, apparently so highly regarded by the author. I should add that the principle of Wilde's comedies comes to be applied here: the aestheticization of moral problems. Speaking of Sibyl, Lord Henry says, "No, she is better than good—she is beautiful."

It is, moreover, a parasitic world. No one works, yet there are everywhere domestics of the cruder and finer sort. The money one has is mentioned only in connection with debts or the amount of one's annuity.

Wilde is more cautious than Marcel Proust after him. The servants are not yet drawn into the homoerotic nexus. Nonetheless, *Remembrance of Things Past,* which sports the title "Sodom and Gomorrah" for one of its most important parts, is, seen as a whole, not a homosexual novel and not only because it attempts to establish and maintain philosophical and psychological causalities but more nearly because its whole task is to hoard memory and depict all sexual fulfillment as a matter of the past. The aesthetic eroticism of the homosexual novel, in contradistinction, knows only the present. Since the erotic relationship between men must be posited as fundamentally ephemeral, and the beauty of youth vanishes, so then is this literature scarcely familiar with a past. Only rarely does one learn something of the antecedents of the lovers in such texts. Here is only the factor of fascination. Without future, for one is unfaithful and grows old. In André Gide's homosexual novel about the counterfeiters this becomes all too evident.

But if all art, as Wilde claims at the end of his preface, is quite useless, and only beauty counts (whatever is to be understood by that—for Wilde perhaps Sèvres China and asphodels), then one inhabits a world without past and history. Other literary motifs are incorporated in Wilde's novel, from Wagner's Tannhäuser to the pact between Faust and Mephistopheles, so that James Vane comes to act out the preordained role of Gretchen's brother. Yet the dominant symbolic motif is Wilde's own creation: the picture that grows old in place of him depicted in it. The literary sources in Poe and Balzac's *The Fatal Skin* are well known. Yet something new and original is at play. The portrait demonstrates the fruitlessness of the unmitigated and self-sufficient homoerotic world. There is no stopping growing old, even if it is only the image in the portrait that changes. One can never fully aestheticize the moral universe, for it too remains preserved in the portrait. By negating the image in the portrait, by hiding it, by covering it over, one accepts the rules and rites of the others, on which one to all appearances at least had so arrogantly turned one's back. The first consistently homosexual novel, *The Picture of Dorian Gray,* demonstrates at once the dead end of a genre that can repeat itself but is unable to develop.

André Gide, *The Counterfeiters*

The Picture of Dorian Gray was the only novel Wilde wrote; *The Counterfeiters* is the only narrative work by André Gide that he acknowledged as having the rank of a novel. In questions of poetic genre Gide was utterly scrupulous; he differentiated with utmost precision between *récits* and *soties.* Not even *The Caves of the Vatican,* which has all the characteristics of a novel, including length, was recognized as such. Only in the dedication of *The Counterfeiters,* "à Roger Martin du Gard je dédie mon premier roman en témoignage d'amitié profonde," is the reader given to understand that this is a novel, the author's first. It was to be Gide's only novel. That was the plan from the start.

The Counterfeiters[2] is as singular within the body of Gide's work as *The Picture of Dorian Gray* within Wilde's. They are further comparable in that a secret satanism is at play in both novels, introduced toward an artistic end but never fully dissolved in aesthetic function. Both epic constructions are meant to portray extremes. In the very nature in which it is done a certain unease remains with the reader: What will these authors be able to write after this? Both in the most curious of ways after ending these works quit the realm of a literature that sought to unite fiction and confession to make art. Both novels are not simply high points, they are endpoints. Certainly Wilde, in the four years that lay between *The Picture of Dorian Gray* and his trial, continued to write, producing essays, well-honed theater pieces, fairytales. But compared to the dimensions of the novel, it was ephemeral stuff. Then came the hour for lyric poetry and confessional prose. Then came muteness.

After *The Counterfeiters,* the storyteller and dramatist Gide produced only minor works and these very painstakingly. One can read in his *Journal* how arduous, unproductive, and filled with doubt his work on Thésée was. He had written *The Counterfeiters* obstinately and filled with confidence.[3] His doubts had had to do with artistic considerations and were not scruples about the sense of writing the work. For Gide as well all later deeply moved and moving work sprang from autobiography and criticism. In the twenty-five years remaining to him it is only the *Journal* that counts and is meant to count.

Five years before the appearance of *The Counterfeiters* Gide had allowed his tractate "Corydon" (1920) to be published. It was an explanation and apologia for pederasty written in imitation of the Platonic dialogues. That he was speaking for his own person as well was not left in doubt. On the contrary, even here he insisted upon exactitude. He was not a homosexual, he later explained not without a bit of coquetry, because he felt no attraction toward handsome men. Not a homosexual then, but a pederast. It is the beauty of the ephebes to which his desire is directed. It is fully unthinkable that Wilde in Victorian England might have written something in a similar vein, let alone publish it. What Dorian does in the night in the London underworld remains a matter of conjecture. That Olivier in Gide's novel, in conjunction with Count Passavant and later with Edouard, commits what the law terms unnatural acts, the reader has every right, following Gide's sense, to suspect.

Two novels by homosexual writers, then, that possess a confessional character. Both are homosexual novels. And that means something entirely different than that their authors inhabited the city of Sodom. Works of homosexual writers like Proust, E. M. Forster, or Somerset Maugham are not at all to be characterized as "homosexual novels" though a central section of *Remembrance of Things Past* is specifically entitled "Sodom and Gomorrah" and Jupin's *établissement* is none other than a male brothel. Somerset Maugham's *Of Human Bondage* approaches the typology of homosexual narration insofar as Maugham or his character Philip Carey in his sexual dependency on the waitress Mildred once again describes, and here with horrifying exactitude, the hatred and anxiety of the pederast in the face of feminine eros, making a lasting impression on English literature. Yet the novel in its basic conceptions resembles far more the bourgeois *Bildungsroman* for it to be accounted to the specific category of the homosexual epic.

It was not Gide's sexual inclinations that make *The Counterfeiters* a work of this modern and peculiar genre. Nor is it the couple of erotic scenes that Gide hints at. What *The Picture of Dorian Gray* and *The Counterfeiters* have in common is that they circumscribe a closed cosmos: a fenced-off male world, averse to women, socially homeless, parasitic.

The writer Edouard stands at the focal point of Gide's novel. When the book first appeared, all its critics were at one in interpreting him as André Gide himself: the character of a novel as key to the author. Gide protested naturally, but let things take their course. Nowadays it is a commonplace that one must sharply differentiate the two. Edouard is drawn into a counterfeiting affair as he is forming the plan of writing a novel with the title *The Counterfeiters*. Edouard's diary provides a running commentary on how the novel is progressing—or not progressing. Gide carefully brought the story, which suddenly breaks off, to the point where the reader would have to surmise that Edouard will never complete his novel.

Gide, however, is successful where Edouard failed. One of the themes of his novel, one that has become a literary topos since making its first appearance there, is the failure of a novelist depicted as a novel. Nonetheless, many of Edouard's aesthetic considerations in *The Counterfeiters* can be interpreted as Gide's own maxims.

Is that also true, however, for the following confession of Edouard the novelist? He makes the admission, "As soon as I must put clothes on my figures, decide on their rank in society, their careers, the amount of their income, particularly as soon as I have to create an environment for them by inventing parents, friends, families, then I've got to close up shop. I see each one of my heroes, as I am obliged to admit, as an orphan, an only son, a bachelor, and without children [orphelin, fils unique, célibataire, et sans enfant]."[4]

What is immediately striking is the restriction to the male sex; the heroes of novels are for Edouard male: only sons, bachelors, without parents, without wives, without children. It seems as if through this the profound difference between the novelists Edouard and André Gide is accentuated, for in *The Counterfeiters* there is a carefully worked out reservoir of familial ties. Olivier has a mother who is Edouard's half-sister and a father; he is the middle son of three. Bernard too has a family; even Count Passavant lives in a house with his dying father, whose death he makes known to his young friend in an artfully trivializing expression only when asked. They may be all sorts of things, Bernard, Olivier, Vincent, Georges, Caloub, even Boris; one thing they are not is orphans and only children. Here as well Gide could do what Edouard could not.

Nevertheless the novelist who wrote *The Counterfeiters,* if in an incredibly subtle fashion, has worked along Edouard's lines. His world too is a monad. It is the world of young people. Older people have one sole function and that is to get in the way. Bernard and Olivier, Georges as well, and to his dismay even Boris, attain an identity only in dealings with those of their own age. The world of parents acts as an instigator or modifier of action. Right at the start of the story Bernard's exodus from his parents' house sets the entanglements and confusions of this epic comedy of intrigue and mistaken identities in motion. The cosmos here, at any event, is of young people.

Young males at that. Like older people, women get in the way. They are either hated or scorned. And in this, Gide's novel once more fulfills the premises of the homosexual model. Laura is a victim, a lover who gets in the way of a world without a past. Lady Griffith, superficially seen at least, seems to be a member of that dynasty of pretty, aristocratic female bringers of ruin familiar from eighteenth-century European literature. A distant relative of the Marquise de Merteuil from Choderlos de Laclos's *Les Liaisons Dangereuses.* She is satanic; together with Passavant, she is the incarnation of all that is counterfeit in morals, art, and love. Gide breaks off her last letter to Passavant once its intended effect upon the reader has been achieved, an evocation of the ugly, distorted features of a waning love affair between man and woman. That Vincent then murders her in Africa without the least concern being evoked is part and parcel of the complex of hate and scorn in which she is embedded.

A world without a past, wherein the future is conceived simply as a permanently extended present, or better still as an ever new (and thus libidinous) present. The relationship between one man and another, between a desirous older one and a desired younger one, can be posited only as something of limited duration. If it lasts a long time, it becomes a posterotic tie, whether from fear of loneliness, or out of habit, or for convenience' sake, or from boredom. In *The Counterfeiters,* on the other hand, the homosexual situation finds a pure incarnation as the permanent extension of the present moment. From Vincent to Olivier to Georges, the older man awaits with expectation the maturation of the younger boys. The novel began with Bernard's conflicts; it ends with a fanciful look at Bernard's little brother, Caloub. "I am very curious to know

Caloub," Edouard jots down. Everything can be present all over again. It is the last sentence in this homosexual novel.

A parasitical cosmos. It is not, to be sure, that of the rich English aristocracy as it was in Wilde; here it is the world of the bourgeois French upper stratum of judges, government bureaucrats, well-off writers living on their annuities, solid and middle class like Edouard (or Gide) or luxuriant and filled with hauteur like Count Robert de Passavant. This patent parasitism is served up, however, quite in the fashion of *Dorian Gray,* as an aesthetic phenomenon. The characters write books but could just as well leave off writing. A literary magazine is founded that has no program and no visible function unless it is to instigate intrigues, attract young men, pass out favors, and rebuke those fallen from grace. And with this the conflict between Edouard and Passavant becomes the focus of the book. It is the *agon* of two homosexuals for the favor of a youth desired by both. Once again, to all appearances at least, Basil Hallward and Lord Henry fight for Dorian Gray. The pattern has been inverted, however, in that in Wilde the cynic was victorious, for a while at least, while he who was smitten with love went to his doom. Gide has written a comedy in which the erotic and literary counterfeiter (Passavant) has only intermittent success, whereas Olivier, at the end, goes to live with his loving Edouard until further notice.

Edouard's victory over Passavant is meant in all seriousness. It is Gide and not merely the character Edouard who represents their union as fulfillment. Olivier is supposed to see things in exactly the same fashion. He is convulsed by joy, as the motivation of his attempted suicide is portrayed. A *Liebestod* after the highest, so long delayed fulfillment. A homosexual novel along the lines of a genre comedy. At first the mismatched lovers; now, at the end, the true lovers make their way to each other. Yet one thing should be noted: it is a comedy without women.

At this point a look at the autobiographical context of *The Counterfeiters* is unavoidable. Gide based the family Molinier and its sons upon the Allégrets. Marc Allégret played a role in his life similar to the role Olivier played for Edouard. It can all be read, scarcely disguised, in Gide's *Journal.* Marc Allégret, afterwards a very successful film director, remained close to Gide until the very last.

Yet the young Allégret, for whose sake Gide in 1917, a man of forty-eight, let his marriage founder, was also attracted by the intellectual charm and seductive powers of Jean Cocteau. On December 8, 1917, Gide notes in his diary after a return from Paris, he experienced "an enormous and singing joy," and continues: "Despite all this, the day before yesterday, and for the first time in my life, I experienced the oppression of jealousy. M. did not come home till ten at night. I knew that he had been at C.'s. I was dumbfounded. I felt myself capable of the most terrible of insanities and in my fears could measure the depth of my love."[5]

Gide was almost fifty at the time. He was one of those who had met Wilde and Alfred Lord Douglas in the Tunisian oases. Cocteau was around twenty years younger, at the time a successful snob and literary figure of twenty-eight. Almost every one of the entries in the *Journal* that have to do with Cocteau is both angry and nasty. The portrait of the young Cocteau at the start of the war in 1914 and during the battle of the Marne is appalling but very likely true to life. During the course of 1918 one finds the comment: "Nothing is more alien to me than that concern for modernism, so noticeable behind all of Cocteau's reasoning and conclusions . . . I do not wish to be a child of my epoch; I wish to transcend it."[6] That could just as well be found in Edouard's diary in *The Counterfeiters*, referring in that case to the Comte de Passavant.

On January 16, 1923, at a point when *The Counterfeiters* is gradually reaching completion, Gide notes his impressions of a Cocteau production of Sophocles' *Antigone*: "Suffered miserably from the ultramodern sauce in which this marvellous piece was dished out. It remained beautiful— but more nearly despite Cocteau than on account of him."[7]

Cocteau and Gide both are admitted homosexual (or pederast) writers. And they also want to be understood as such. An erotic rivalry at a decisive moment in their lives brought them up against each other. Maurice Sachs in *The Sabbath*[8] has incisively described how the young men of that era saw these two men from Sodom as alternatives and wavered between them; in his own case, I might add, as in *The Counterfeiters*, he came finally to favor Edouard/Gide.

A banal, everyday story with its elements of intrigue, jealousy, differences in age, seduction and resistance. It was no less usual by virtue of the fact that it took place in a world of men only and that two (or three) illustrious names were connected to it. André Gide, however, transcended this real situation by making it over into the model situation of *The Counterfeiters*. It was thus inevitable that all the artistic strands of the dramatic action were spun out to their end only out of a sense of conscientiousness after the catharsis had been reached and the ephebe landed where he apparently belonged. Until further notice—as always in homosexual literature.

Pornography

The breach of misunderstanding between literary production and interpretation could scarcely be greater than in the area of what is termed pornography. I say what is termed pornography, because the term itself is derived from moral and aesthetic considerations, in the antinomy of cleanliness and filth and is consequently inadequate. The matter itself is what it is: namely, pornography.

Of interest here are booklet productions available in adult bookstores at a cost of a few dollars. With photographs or drawings they are somewhat more expensive. It is a business based on solid marketing principles, from the conceptualization by author and publisher to the distribution methods. Needless to say, it is a phenomenon of serialized mass production. Certain buyer classifications have been worked out. Their specific visions in the realm of the erotic (rather: in the process of autoeroticism) are expertly serviced. The lists of works available make it altogether evident. One publisher—who can substitute for any number of others—has arranged his series, one each, according to the various sexual special proclivities. "Redlight Books" services those enamoured of Lolitas, with titles like *Little Girl, Big Man,* or *Never Too Young* and *Passionate Children.* Dreams of incest are dealt with in the "Zorro Books" line. The market is apparently open to expansion, since from time to time other serialized products are moved into areas of family life formerly held under taboo. Whether living conditions in American slums or the isolation of farm families far from town provoke such incest erotism would be a subject for further investigation. The demand, however, cannot be overlooked. Titles like *Daddy Knows Best, House of Incest,* and *Mother Loves* are produced by the hundreds and devoured by a hungry market.[9]

Alongside the specialized (and popularized) wants and desires of sadomasochism, *S & M* in street talk, next to a gargantuan heterosexual pornography, which for its part divides its labors according to positions or practices, there is also to be found, spread among the various publishing organizations, a competitively viable homoerotic pornography—homo porn. Sometimes the firm names are reminiscent of Paris; for the most part, however, they seem keen on resurrecting notions learned in history class in high school and college where, apparently, homosexuality was interpreted as the speciality of Greek antiquity. Titles are made tempting with Greek connotations. Whole series of homosexual pornography are advertised as "Trojan Classics" or "Spartan Classics," supposed to be classic in both a historical and literary sense since the booklets themselves are called "classics."

The criticism and sociology of literature are of little help in dealing with such phenomena of literary mass production and consumption. Debates over obscenity and pornography in international cultural politics, legislation, and jurisdiction are still oriented to individual, for the most part well-known writers and individual literary works. The disputes are for or against *Madame Bovary* or *Lady Chatterley*, *Ulysses* and *The Tropic of Cancer*; they course around a Genet or a William Burroughs. Whoever today reads through the court ruling in the obscenity trial dealing with Arthur Schnitzler's *Reigen* (Berlin, 1921),[10] soon sees that the debates in the legislative chambers in Bonn or the U.S. Supreme Court in Washington, when the subject is the impoundment or release of pornographic publications, still move within the confines of a bourgeois liberalism that perceives itself the friend of art and artists. That is entirely unsuitable insofar as here we are dealing with a mass production of literary commodities not written by individual writers as literature but by writing teams (as can often be demonstrated by stylistic analysis) who under someone's name not taken seriously by anyone, even if it is not bogus, have no other than the avowed purpose of sexually stimulating the buyer/reader. Any talk of creative impetus, of the artistic character of the product, or even—as in Schnitzler's case—of a secret moral intent, is manifestly pointless. The term *pornography* is questionable. The matter itself is not. It is frank and means to be nothing more than illusion. And it sticks to its promise.

An anthology of essays on the subject, published in 1970 and edited by Douglas A. Hughes, *Perspectives on Pornography*,[11] is a good example of just how little such facts of modern literary life are taken into consideration. Writers of note assess the topic: fiction writers like Alberto Moravia and Anthony Burgess, critics and literary historians like Harry Levin and George Steiner, the English playwright Kenneth Tynan and the psychologist Ernest van den Haag. The result is disappointing. Whether the contributors argue for censorship or, as in Tynan's case, postulate the release of de Sade's writings, one thing remains constant: these are all analyses of an aesthetics of production and are fixated to the aura of the individual literary work of art. Neither the aspect of reception nor that

The Typology of Homosexual Literature

of mass production based on marketing research is ever a matter of consideration. This anthology, so honest in its intentions, so highly original in its thematic, is disappointing because it scarcely uncovers anything more than the disparity between production and interpretation: which is to say, anachronism.

Susan Sontag's article, "The Pornographic Imagination"[12] is an exception. Here the author rightfully argues for necessary differentiations within the realm of the pornographic. The three proposed by her, however, are not subdivisions of this body of writing but are critical means of procedure: from a sociological, psychological, and literary vantage point. Sontag analyzes the forms of pornographic imagination. She too immediately falls into the trap of applying the traditional modes of literary criticism to an area that does not necessarily fall under their sway. The question is posed correctly: whether connections are provable between "high" literature and its epigonal and degraded derivatives. Naturally *Fanny Hill* belongs to the realm of English realistic literature, just as Dracula and Frankenstein to Romanticism. A class conflict like *Love and Intrigue* degenerates 150 years later into Lehár's operetta. This kind of argumentation, however, scarcely strikes upon the specific differentiating characteristics of modern mass pornography. And it is for that reason that Susan Sontag puts more weight on the discussion of the reverse question: whether a genuinely pornographic work can at the same time be a work of literature. Proof is not wanting, naturally, especially with examples drawn from authors like Georges Bataille or the pseudonymous Pauline Réage. But this attempt to describe the pornographic imagination also takes all of its criteria and categories from the "normal" production of established publishers and authors—in order to prove that even in producing pornography they cannot help but produce literature. One expected as much.

Susan Sontag's essay controverts Theodor Adorno's contention that a pornographic narrative has no structure, having neither beginning nor middle nor end.[13] That is disputed here, yet both argumentations are themselves inadequate, Adorno misunderstanding pornography simply as bad literature in the exact same way that Hanns Eisler repudiated jazz as poorly composed music. But when Sontag attempts proving the contrary, her own contention fails at a decisive spot: the pornographic imagination, which she simply subsumes as a part of a more generally envisioned literary fantasy.

For the same reason Sontag fails in her polemic against Gore Vidal.

He had denied the assertion that pornography is merely impersonal narration without sharply delineated characters. Sontag means to controvert that just as she had controverted Adorno's criticism of the structurelessness of the pornographic narrative. Gore Vidal's logical analysis, which first appeared in *The New York Review of Books,* is interesting. In his study on the pornographic "Halfworld," Felix Pollack as well, quite in Susan Sontag's sense, takes the matter up once more.[14] Vidal argued as follows: "Yet by abstracting character, and by keeping his creatures faceless and vague, the pornographer does force the reader to draw upon personal experience in order to fill in the details, thereby achieving one of the ends of all literary art, that of making the reader collaborator."[15]

Vidal's claim is correct, yet it too takes its argumentation from the sphere of established literature, the thesis being that pornography too follows literary conventions and consequently must also be literature.

That is a terminological game that takes no account of the specific characteristics (here: anonymous/pseudonymous) of pornographic writing and not the accessory works of an Apollinaire or a Bataille. Pornography has a genuine narrative structure, which is misconstrued if one, like Adorno, operates with the containing forms of bourgeois realism. Its purpose, naturally, more than any other form of literary work, even the culinary theater, is the active "participation" of the reader, as Gore Vidal asserted. This collaboration is the sole purpose of its existence. The task at hand is not to redeem pornography and those who write it and pass them on to purgatory; more pertinent is grasping the nature of the literary hell they have created.

In analyzing homosexual pornography, its structure and technique, it soon becomes evident that it has taken over familiar narrative forms; all the typological characteristics of homosexual literature established in *Dorian Gray* or *The Counterfeiters* are met once again. The writers are well versed in such matters: they are certainly not always themselves homosexual, something it is possible to sense from time to time from behind the scenes in their writing, yet they too routinely operate with the same interior world and consciousness evoked by Wilde or Gide or Proust and Cocteau. It is simply that homosexual pornography for marketing and sales reasons is seriously constrained; literary affinities, story, and technique must be subordinated to the pornographic purpose.[16]

As in the narrative world of Wilde and Gide, so too is the cosmos of homosexual pornography composed of a closed society of men hostile to women. The world of homo porn knows women only as contrastive interlopers: the nymphomaniac who wants to escape and ends in Sodom, the waitress whose flirtation routines are malignantly depicted, the prostitute with whom the boy who has not yet recognized his real drives would like to "get it on like everybody else," fails and is ridiculed. Stereotypical situations and characterizations. And it is for the most part a motherless world as well. A certain *deus ex machina* appears again and again to allow the tielessness of the central male figure as he appears in every homo porn, and thus the possibility of untrammeled promiscuity— namely, the parents dying in a car crash. Brothers appear, either as killjoys or as seducers in early incestuous pairings.

Women in these stories speak just as shrilly as they did in Oscar Wilde. They are always pushy and possessive: the reader can only be relieved when they, either letting loose some vulgar epithet or receiving one, leave the stage and thus no longer disturb the action of homosexual consummation. After the disappearance of the contrastive figures, the exclusive male–male world is constituted once more. In these booklets everybody is "that way." For the most part they are aware of it and wish to be what they are; variants are a late discovery of sexual identity through the aid of what one would call emotional education. It is reported of Marcel Proust that after having made great progress in writing his epic work, he came to the astonished realization "Ils le sont tous!" They are all that way. He himself, however, had set them up that way so that is was only surprising for Proust himself to come across Robert de Saint-Loup toward the end in the same male bordello that is financed by his Uncle Charlus. In Proust's work, though not with the exclusivity of Wilde's or Gide's novels, one inhabits a womanless world insofar as woman incorporates the erotic sphere. The woman Odette has her life only in Swann's thoughts, the girl Gilberte in those of the narrator, Marcel. When it is necessary to portray women Proust is brilliant, just as Wilde was or Norman Douglas in his novel set on Capri, *South Wind*— that is to say, brilliant in the portrayal of older, deeroticized women, the trusted friends of the people of Sodom.

Just as pornography with lesbian tendencies striving for realism, which is to say, a stimulating credibility, situates its dramas in the pertinent milieu (the women's prison, the girls' school, the backstage dressingroom, or even the ladies' "powder room"), so too does the pornographer of Sodom's affairs try to make the frequency of sexual play credible through the surroundings in which it takes place—the exclusively male world of ships' cabins, barracks, the lockerroom, the gay bar, the ambience of the hustler.

Like all pornography, the homosexual variety robs its figures of all epic individuality and reduces them to their sexual activities. The story begins with some name, some Tom or Steve who is so hazy in the narrator's mind that time and again in these little booklets the names get mixed up. Mark, in the middle of the action, suddenly says sentences that should have been said by Larry.

Pornography is purposely unrealistic literature, notwithstanding the precision of its copulatory descriptions, to the extent that it has reduced its characters, as in Expressionist drama, to their functions. Pornography shares with Expressionism a certain predilection for parataxis as well. All these stories are evocations of stages along the way. The hero counts the stages not only as so many beds with so many constantly changing partners, but often enough as sociological progressions in his life from—depending on the story—down-and-out hustler to the happy favorite of a millionaire or from the little rich boy to the disinherited, aging model in porno flicks. Even homo porn can end from time to time like Wedekind's *Pandora's Box*.

The decision whether the story is to be written from the viewpoint of the provocative outsider or from that of the homosexual, in all ways but this a lawabiding and conformist male, is decided in nearly every case for assimilation. The partners are macho in their voices and demeanor; transvestite or effeminate males are always depicted without sympathy and are mostly despised: the porn writer speculates on the homosexual self-hate of his readers.

For this reason the demonstrably moralistic and idealistic structure of homosexual pornography is not so unexpected. Where the reader's expectations determine the flow of narration, the pornographic writer must head for happiness at last. He who has despairingly sought so long now finds at last in the true love of a young man the longed-for partner, friend, and heir. Homosexual pornography borrows its clichés from the *Bildungsroman* and even from the gothic romance. Thumbing through its productions by the hundredfold one swiftly recognizes that almost all stories end with a happy monogamous relationship after so much willy-nilly promiscuity. Elements of the *Bildungsroman* are to be found two ways in almost all these productions. First as the process of sexual self-discovery: the boy is shown at the beginning to be filled with contempt for any perverse doings but is then, step by step, brought to realize his own secret erotic impulses, is brought to his own identity. Then too the actual pornographic realm is closely connected with the process of education: The hero learns to accept all manner of homosexual activity.

These cheap hard-core little books essentially end no differently than André Gide's *Counterfeiters*—in the happiness of final union. Olivier in the arms of sugar daddy Edouard. The moment becomes eternity. The task given the pornographic writer, for which he delivers the goods so proficiently—namely the consolation of loneliness—only manifests the real and material unhappiness of the reader of so much literary final joy.

15 The Alternatives of Klaus Mann and Maurice Sachs

Both of them were born in 1906. The one, Thomas Mann's eldest son, came into the world in Munich; the other, the Parisian Maurice Ettinghausen, went by the name of Sachs. Klaus Mann committed suicide on May 21, 1949, in Cannes; Sachs was shot to death in Germany on April 14, 1945.[1]

Sachs, who had formerly been an agent for the Gestapo and was now their prisoner, found himself toward the end of the war in Fuhlsbüttel Prison in Hamburg. On April 12 Fuhlsbüttel was evacuated by order of the SS. Everyone was to march to Schleswig-Holstein. The commandant, Tessmann, ordered stragglers to be shot. The first day they covered about 30 kilometers; on the second they reached the vicinity of Neumünster; on the morning of the third day two prisoners said they could not go on. They were the Frenchman Sachs and a German policeman convicted of bribery. They were taken aside and shot by a Flemish SS trooper by the name of Vouth. The death certificates do not mention the cause of death. Formalities were seen to by Ortsgruppenleiter Francke from Gadeland. The bodies were taken by truck to Neumünster where they were interred without coffins in the East Cemetery. A French writer in a North German grave.

It would be absurd to compare the two biographies for their political content unless one means to take them as polar opposites. We have the political emigré Klaus Mann and the French half-Jew Sachs who in Hamburg in 1943 under Ettinghausen, his father's name, entered the service of the secret police as operative G117 for the weekly remuneration of 80 reichsmark.

Exile forced the antifascist writer Klaus Mann to relinquish many of the intellectual frivolities of his literary beginnings. He tries organizing a "collective" of exiled authors around his magazine *Die Sammlung*; he falls into a despairing rage when the U.S. military for the longest time ignores him when he volunteers. Finally inducted, he fights in the invasion of Italy, returning to Munich as a member of the forces of occupation. He was bitterly serious with his collection of antifascist writings, which seemed to many of the contributing political protagonists merely a strategic instrumentality. Klaus Mann had taken part in the founding congress of the Soviet Writers' Union in 1934. In the typescript of his *Notes from Moscow* is to be found a sentence reacting to Karl Radek's speech, a comment subsequently deleted in the published version: "What does Karl Radek mean when he speaks the word *literature*? Does he mean that broad front of the spirit that affirms the future, illumines what is around it, and remains aware of its great task and responsibility in these times? Or does he mean a propaganda instrument of the Third International?"[2] The posing of this question, as its author, who immediately censored it, knew, already contained the answer.

This honest striving after community and "progress in the consciousness of freedom" likely drove him to his death. The stories, novels, and essays show that Klaus Mann from his early years on was on close terms with that romantic enchantment found in the consonance of beauty, sensuality, and yearning for death. Suicide was a thread running through the fabric of his life. How little can one be surprised if Klaus Mann—after Alexander of Macedon—chose the heroes of his historical novels from among suicides, those whose "self-carting away," as Thomas Mann once put it, was accomplished indirectly: Tchaikovsky and Ludwig of Bavaria. A third was to come to die by his own hand as well, no less indirectly than the others: the protagonist of the novel *Mephisto*.

Despite all this, Klaus Mann's end in Cannes in the year 1949, which had been preceded by an attempted suicide, was a political death. Klaus Mann died in and of the Cold War. His writers' collective had failed. "When then the teacher and founder Stalin clambered up happily out of the ruins of a war he nearly lost," as Solzhenitsyn sarcastically puts it, "he sat himself down to ruminate on the welfare of his subjects." All the Communist central committees were called on to bind over the unmasked traitors and agents of the Anglo-American secret services, who after torture confessed to everything during trial, were thereupon sentenced to death, and were unspeakably abased until being shot or hanged. In Budapest, in Sofia, in Prague, the desired sacramental purge was consummated. It did not get beyond a few beginnings in East Berlin—arrests, deportations to Siberia—for Stalin died in 1953. And there was the especially strategic situation there to be taken into consideration as well.

The sacramental counteraction in the United States was called Mc-Carthyism. Its "contact with the sacramental and demonic" Joseph Gabel, a Hungarian, analyzed and dialectically set into relationship with the Communist ritual of the proscription of renegades, in an article in *La Revue Socialiste* in 1954.[3] A play like Sartre's *Dirty Hands* takes its substance from that ritual. On that account Aleksandr Fadeev, in his platform address to the Congress of Intellectuals for the Defense of Culture in Breslau in August 1948, an address coauthored by Andreii Zhdanov, simply calls the author of this "anticommunist" play "a hyena at the typewriter."

Klaus Mann, who had himself spoken at the first Congress of Intellectuals in Paris in 1935, did not go to Breslau but nonetheless closely followed its debates. He was stunned. In his own programmatic essay in turn, "Europe's Search for a New Credo,"[4] Fadeev himself is not mentioned by name, but one does find quoted Ilia Ehrenburg's laconic characterization of Anglo-American literature as a "flood of opium." These were all symptoms for the antifascist litterateur Klaus Mann of an almost universal "trahison des clercs," to use Julien Benda's expression, an expression Klaus Mann analyzes at length and puts to repeated use. He probably did not know at the time that Julien Benda himself had been one of the speakers at that congress in Breslau and had called for a critical community against anti-Enlightenment cliched thinking. His speech did not have the slightest effect.

Then comes the fateful and disquieting conclusion to that essay of Klaus Mann's that served in its fashion as his last will and testament. It first appeared in English in the June 1949 issue of *Tomorrow* a few weeks before Mann's suicide in Cannes. The essay's conclusion calls for nothing more than the concerted mass suicide of European intellectuals: to bring public opinion in the world, in the integrity and autonomy of which he quite clearly still believed, to its right senses. "A suicide wave among the world's most distinguished, most celebrated minds would shock the peoples out of their lethargy, would make them realize the extreme gravity of the ordeal man has brought upon himself by his folly and selfishness."[5] Was his own action, carried out soon after that was written and published, thus in accord or disaccord with this belief? It will never be known for certain.

The arguments and historical examples Mann cites in his cultural critique could just as well support a case for disaccord. The essay analyzes the condition of the postwar era circa 1949 as the result of failure on the intellectuals' part. "The intellectuals delved too daringly into the secrets of the human soul, of society, of nature. What they brought to light from the depths was as dreadful as that gorgonian face whose glance is said to turn the beholder to stone." He names names. They all stand for an existential isolation through madness or erotic heterodoxy. Nietzsche, Strindberg, Wilde, Tchaikovsky, Verlaine and Rimbaud.

In this last text Klaus Mann speaks as one from their ranks. Even in the early essays written in the twenties and then in his last long autobiographical work, *The Turning Point* (1942), his favorite authors were counted and lovingly celebrated. The writers from Sodom predominated: Hermann Bang, Rimbaud and Verlaine, Whitman, Radiguet and Cocteau, Spender and Auden. They had been read and recognized as his own.

Since his earliest beginnings as a writer, as a boarding school student at the Odenwaldschule, Klaus Mann had made no secret that his were the works of a homosexual writer. The alternatives of the bourgeois nineteenth century were no longer to be in effect, neither total conformity nor scandal. Smaller upsets might be provoked. The Weimar Republic was only moderately tolerant. In it too the chronicle of murder and scandal continued with Haarmann and Röhm and many hushed-up suicides. *The Criminals,* a play by Ferdinand Bruckner, operated with familiar material in a familiar vein. Gustav Gründgens had his first great success in Berlin in it. The fiction writer Klaus Mann, even the essayist Klaus Mann, usually avoided such topics. He was not interested in a theoretical apology for homosexuality à la André Gide's *Corydon.* He sought community with the (heterosexual) others but without conformity: mimicry, in a word. He had no success in it. His last essay finds him in a community all right, but it is with his own kind. This amounts to the same thing as saying that there was no communication, for the inhabitants of Sodom live like monads, like Strindberg and Nietzsche and van Gogh, whom he quotes.

It is here that the political engagement of this author broke apart. He could never be anything but a fellow traveler, either tolerated with good will or the butt of jokes, depending on the circumstance. Comrade Klaus Mann: he had no intention of serving up that drama. What might happen in moments of the slightest insubordination had been learnt in the example of André Gide. Gide had been received with high honors in

Klaus Mann and Maurice Sachs

Moscow, had experienced certain disappointments that he reported upon his return, cautiously and in the spirit of comradeship he had every reason to believe. The result was foreseeable. In an essay, "The Controversy Surrounding André Gide," which appeared in the emigré periodical *Die Weltbühne* in Prague in 1937, Klaus Mann wrote that even people on the order of Kisch, Rolland, and Feuchtwanger thereupon treated Gide "not only as a traitor, but as a mentally incompetent, pleasure-seeking old sinner, whose sellout is abominable but scarcely of intellectual consequence."[6]

Klaus Mann had no intention of letting the same thing happen to himself. The result was that he was spared abuse of that sort all right but then became the source of umbrage for the counterritual of the other side. In the eyes of McCarthyism he took on the shape in his last years more or less of an abominable agent of the Reds. He perished on account of it. In the end he lived only between negations. Neither Comrade Mann like Louis Aragon and Anna Seghers nor anti-Communist like Arthur Koestler, neither convert to Catholicism like Eliot and Döblin, and too old to play anymore with the aging Cocteau. Neither symbiosis with the others nor with his own kind. That had been the lesson taught him by the person to whom he felt spiritually (and probably existentially) closest. It was thus that he had interpreted André Gide's example in his own life. Yet it proved not strong enough to keep him alive.

Would it have been possible otherwise? In the preface of his *Nourritures Terrestres,*[7] Gide addresses a young person whom he does not yet know, his imaginary reader, to whom he gives the name Nathanael. The teaching of a book on earthly nourishment, he says, would have to be "que mon livre t'enseigne à t'intéresser plus à toi qu'à lui-même,—puis à tout le reste plus qu'à toi," the counsel of an outsider to someone who will not be one: Read my book but then discard it. You are more important to yourself than my book is. Later, however, everything else must become more important to you than you yourself. The author, Gide, was unable to follow his own advice. All his attempts at interesting himself more in everything else than in himself ended in failure.

Klaus Mann had grasped this. His one monograph dealing with the sum of an entire life and the works of that life was about Gide. That work, *André Gide and the Crisis of Modern Thought,* comes to the conclusion that with Gide's instruments and moral thought the crisis can indeed be analyzed but not solved. One cannot even emulate the man Gide. A few months before the final May 21, Klaus Mann lectured on Gide in the

Hebbel Theater in Berlin. He answered a question in the debate on his "hero's" experience in Russia quite coolly—by saying it is just as pointless to go off to Moscow full of positive preconceptions as it is to return full of negative prejudices.

In Maurice Sachs's case too, the sole monograph analyzing one author's life and works was written on Gide. He had read him yet had taken no heed of the warning not to follow and found himself, on the first visit on his twenty-first birthday, refused admittance. He felt himself "rejected" but not without secret pleasure. "I was in a state of despair," he wrote in his book of confessions, *The Sabbath,* "but my more unconscious elements were secretly glad now, finally, to be able to get back to their loathsome deeds—this time with a valid passport and a good excuse."[8]

In a strange way there are parallels in the origins of Klaus Mann and Maurice Sachs. Ettinghausen/Sachs also came from a family of famous artists and writers. From his youngest days it was as easy for him as it was for Thomas Mann's son to meet those who appealed to him or who could be of assistance. His grandfather was a friend of Jaurès and Anatole France and had been a cofounder of *L'Humanité.* When he divorced his wife, she took her daughter (Sachs's mother) and remarried. Her second husband was Jacques Bizet, Georges Bizet's son. He was to be for the child Maurice a first hero and role model.

It was only Klaus Mann who as a fledgling writer enjoyed the security of comfortable family wealth, however. When his father was awarded the Nobel Prize for literature in 1929, he arranged for Klaus and Erika Mann's debts to be taken care of. Maurice Sachs had been forced to make his own way in life from the age of fifteen. Nonetheless he too aspired to be a man of letters if at all possible. He had connections and talent, which would soon be manifested even if he was lacking a sense of form and elegant traditionalism—something Klaus Mann had demonstrated even in his little writings as a boy. As the son of Thomas Mann and the nephew of Heinrich Mann, he had "natural" counsel immediately at hand. Ettinghausen/Sachs bore no illustrious name; from his idol, the composer's son, and from Madame Bizet-Strauss there was much to be learned in matters of society and pleasure, but not the technique and function of literary labor. That he fell under the sway of Jean Cocteau at the beginning of the 1920s and in Paris was probably unavoidable. In his book *The Sabbath* Sachs writing with shrill contempt for Cocteau, breaks off from him once more after the fact. Since Jacques Bizet had died by his own hand and Maurice's mother abruptly deserted husband

and family, the fifteen-year-old was left to his own devices. He was filled with the seed of poetry and art. A school chum takes him to Cocteau's. "I already believe that Cocteau is the greatest poet alive today, and one of the greatest of all time." Later on in the same book he writes: "One day one will no longer understand why this author was so inordinately loved. And one will finish up by quoting Wilde and saying of Cocteau that he put his genius more into his life than into his work."[9]

Cocteau was a man of wealth and property, as was Gide. Yet he had no reputation for generosity like Gide. A criminal matter ended the affair between master and disciple. But before that came to pass, Sachs, wanting to emulate his model in all ways, converted to Catholicism. In Cocteau's case an edifying literature had resulted: the correspondence with Maritain. Sachs, however, constantly confused reality and literature. He decides to enter the monastery and is admitted as a novice to the Carmelites, but the experience ends abruptly in scandal as was to happen again later, with a concatenation of eroticism, financial dealings, fraud, and self-deceit at this stage of his life as in all the others. Since he has good command of English he goes off on a lecture tour to America a few years after Klaus Mann had done the same. He lectures in every conceivable place on all kinds of subjects about which, as he later admits, he knows nothing. As a homosexual who is able to entertain an erotic relationship with women, he transforms himself for the sake of a woman into an American Presbyterian, marries the daughter of one of the leading men of this church, then leaves her and returns to France.

He wrote a short sketch of his life while a prisoner in Hamburg, a condensed version, so to speak, of *The Sabbath,* in which he says: "Sachs handed his existence over to intrigues and enthusiasms, farces and *malheurs,* tricks and amusements that drove him from country to country and occupation to occupation. Journalist, actor, monk, civil servant, salesman, critic, factory worker; illustrious lecturer in America then obscure beggar; a man of the metropolis and of country living; a guest in many salons, praised in many professions, disowned in others, he has seen and experienced much; yet he knows well what price he has had to pay."[10]

In the end the price was his life. Sachs was not a forced laborer in the German Reich. As a Frenchman and half-Jew he had volunteered for work in a German armaments factory. Then came a game with the highest stakes: selling his services to the Gestapo, which must soon have become dissatisfied with him. He was imprisoned in Fuhlsbüttel. *Derrière cinq barreaux* (Behind Bars), his account of life there, was smuggled out of prison in manuscript form and sent to France. It was published by Gallimard in 1952 under the "Nouvelle Revue Française" imprint, a reminder that Maurice Sachs, at one of the many disparate stages in his life's way, had worked as a reader in that house.

The biographies of Klaus Mann and Maurice Sachs, and the positions they took as writers, reveal more than simply the political antagonisms of the political refugee on the one hand, and of the collaborator and police spy on the other. In an eerily mediated fashion the antitheses of the nineteenth century once again repeat themselves: the alternatives of conformity versus scandal. It is certainly correct that Klaus Mann's conformity no longer had anything to do with self-disavowal, not to mention that mendacity characteristic of Andersen. It is merely that he wanted to be one in the ranks struggling for progress and a larger humanization of life, as others were who were not outsiders by virtue of their existence. Just as the Jew Bronshtein/Trotsky thought himself to be one more Communist among so many others. When the death wish gained the upper hand in Klaus Mann's life, this outsider of goodwill realized that he had lost.

Maurice Sachs entered adult life as an outsider in every respect: branded by family scandals and poverty, resentment, and his own unscrupulous activities as a swindler, and as a homosexual besides, who enjoyed what he could get. So there was nothing but the path of manifest and obvious scandal. Infidelity becomes the maxim of life. At first he cheats and embezzles; Cocteau is one of his victims. At the last this Frenchman who is nothing whole, not Jew and not French, cheats the country that means nothing to him.

France is not Sodom, but Sodom is no home. This French homosexual who made common cause with the German master race was no unique phenomenon. In the third part of Sartre's (unfinished) series of novels *Roads to Freedom,* the homosexual Daniel is described readying himself for a life of debauched dishonor in occupied Paris, which is to say, of treason interwoven with promiscuity. In Jean Genet's novel *Funeral Rites,* a narration in the first person, this same pattern becomes the central motif.

Sachs's letters to friends in France refused to reflect on the reasons for his "unnecessary" treason and voluntary exile to Germany. If he had confessed, he would have had to say that here he had, consciously and secretly deriving pleasure from the fact, made antimorality into his ready and everyday mode of behavior. So the twenty-one-year-old Sachs, disappointed with Cocteau, seeking shelter with Gide, as Olivier from Uncle Edouard in *The Counterfeiters,* rejected, makes out of this rejection a cause and excuse for the scandalous and shocking life that ensued.

The scandals were not long in coming, and they outlasted him. It was thought scandalous that two years after the liberation of France, a book like *The Sabbath* should appear (1946). It was the era of reckoning with collaborators. The paradox is completely conceivable that had Sachs survived the end of the war in Germany he would have been executed in France.

Both of them, Sachs and Klaus Mann, accepted their existential outsiderdom. They each thought to live out and enjoy a love life in conformity with their natures. That immediately released hidden powers and abilities to play the parts of comic actors, for this eros knows no tomorrow: erotic praxis necessarily becomes here a drama of escapades. Sachs placed frenetic activity, consequently infidelity, above all else: even above literature, which he seemed to love so dearly. His confessional works are the product of a preceding defeat as lover and as comedian.

Klaus Mann, on the other hand, where Sachs had chosen scandal, had striven for an unequivocal either/or, attempted a wide-ranging unification of opposing elements. Eroticism and aesthetics were to be united with a political and moral stand in life. He believed in this prospect. What supported him, in comparison to Maurice Sachs, was a much broader and technically better-founded talent as a writer. Nevertheless, the longed-for synthesis did not come about. Klaus Mann must have known that at the end.

When the final version of Klaus Mann's most important autobiographical writing, the revised German edition of *The Turning Point,* appeared in 1952, clearly this author's best and most authentic work, the real countertext to Sachs's *The Sabbath,* the critic Friedrich Sieburg questioned the success of the synthesis Klaus Mann had aspired to, the synthesis of an isolating eros and the moral will to communicate. He denied it had ever worked. Sieburg was writing three years after Klaus Mann's death at the moment the revised edition of *The Turning Point* appeared.[11] As one who knew what it meant to get stuck between fronts and associate with those with whom one has nothing in common, he is essentially sympathetic. Yet he has a sharp, critical eye. Before it, Klaus Mann's life seems to fall into a few good and harmonious years, with nothing but senseless agitation and writing both before and after. These good and happy years were, he says, the years of exile during the war. Thomas

Mann acts as chief witness: "Hitler offered the great advantage of inducing a simplification of one's feelings, the NO which has no doubts, the clear and deadly hate. The years of struggle against him were good years."

They were also good years for Klaus Mann. He felt at last that he had found a place with acceptance on both sides. As an antifascist he stood in the general phalanx. That had been closed to Maurice Sachs, as he well knew; there was no such thing as a community of collaborators. A famous collaborator and writer who survived the year 1945, Louis-Ferdinand Céline, describes it in his account *Castle to Castle*.[12]

But then the community precipitously broke apart again once the task of defeating Hitler's Reich had been accomplished. Sieburg sees what then happened thus: "Klaus Mann recognized this and his despair may have sought a final rest when he saw that the turning point, namely the destruction of the dictatorship, returned to him the power to lead his own life, a life in which he did not know what to do anymore."[13]

What was there to do and write after that? The autobiographical report, but what then? What did Wilde produce after *Dorian Gray* and Gide after *The Counterfeiters*? After Klaus Mann wrote *The Turning Point* he was once again alone. There follow a few speeches, essays, travel. And then at the end the moving and frivolous *idée fixe,* to raise up a new community, a new communality consecrated to death. The community and collective tie to be forged by collective suicide. Heinrich von Kleist had preceded him in that same conclusion. For a long time before his end at Wannsee he had sought a companion in his last act. He found a lonely and dying woman. Klaus Mann died alone. Maurice Sachs was shot by someone who was not even his enemy, as a simple victim of circumstance. And with that his good years too had ended, those he had spent behind bars at last alone with himself, the past, and literature, when there was nothing left to experience, only the writing of accounts.

16   The Turning Point of Jean Genet

Sartre and Genet

One can tell the story of the convicted felon and writer Jean Genet in very different ways.[1] One way would even satisfy François Mauriac, his Catholic adversary, who, after reading the first works of the "poète maudit" Genet, publicly beseeched him who was supposedly damned and forlorn, to stop writing or at least to stop publishing so as not to lead others to their damnation. Yet Genet's story has all the marks of a legend out of the Golden Book, including edifying moral purpose.

He was the child of a prostitute, it is generally supposed, who was abandoned by his mother and put in the charge of the French government welfare program. The public assistance authorities sent the baby, who was born in Paris, to foster parents in the country. His first years there must have been unremarkable. Nothing out of the ordinary happened, no bodily infirmities, no mental disturbance. One farm boy among others. In *Our Lady of the Flowers*[2] Genet described the village childhood of the little Culafroy, the later "Divine" of Montmartre. Presumably his own memories were worked in.

The child begins to thieve, apparently in all innocence and out of predilection, not out of need. At the age of ten he is caught, branded a thief, and ostracized. A series of thefts follows and the first sentences. Then he is sent to the penal settlement for juveniles at Mettray, subsequently disbanded. Genet describes its world, both the interior, spiritual aspects and the physical, exterior ones, in *The Miracle of the Rose*.[3] Whoever leaves Mettray has concluded his criminal apprenticeship. What follows are a thief's wandering years as a journeyman. They are recounted in *The Thief's Journal*:[4] hunger and being thrown out of places, prostitution and theft, the first planned burglaries, and occasional work as a police informant ratting on his cronies. A European and North African world, depicted from the viewpoint of the male hustler and professional thief—Prague and Warsaw, Germany and Austria, hustling in Barcelona and on the Place Pigalle. From time to time he can live rather well on his spoils, without relapse even. Now and again he runs into benefactors of both the selfish and the unselfish variety who help and want to get him started "on the right track." Then comes their turn to be swindled and blackmailed by their protégé. Prison sentences follow. He edges closer and closer to a life sentence for professional criminals.

When Genet reaches thirty, twenty years after the first punitive actions, France is at war. In despair, awaiting a final incarceration, he begins to write. The texts attract attention "on the outside." People like Sartre, Cocteau, and Picasso support their publication and their author's release from prison. They are successful at both, though the books have to be sold under the counter and are seized by the police. The first German translation of *Querelle de Brest,* published by Rowohlt in Hamburg, leads to court and a judgment against the publisher. Yet critics everywhere are one in praising the prisoner's literary genius. Genet is pardoned; his plays are produced; he publishes new books that now no longer turn out to be especially "pornographic." Jean Genet is from this point on an integral part of literary history, an allowable subject of doctoral dissertations, as he is informed. The famous author is not recidivous; at the most he travels illegally to the United States with the help of certain blacks despite his having been refused a visa. But that is American bureaucracy for you, echoes the immediate refrain from the literary establishment. Even his sexual practices seem to undergo a transformation: no trace of Divine's attraction to tough pimps is left. In his book on Genet, Sartre reports that the sexual relationship to a young man has changed into "friendship," the protector having found the boy a wife now takes pleasure in being the friend of a growing family.

That is a fine story that ends well. The individual facts might very well be correct; it is simply that their causal and psychological linkage is utterly confused. Guilt and expiation; or better: guilt and clemency; or better yet: freedom through work and genius. That is a nice bourgeois success story. Please keep in mind: even if everything could be causally connected in the manner just sketched, an impossibility in itself, the works of the man who was pardoned sharply contradict any edifying purpose. They were conceived not as texts of resurrection but of damnation.

Neither can one load the history of the convict and writer with a charge of social criticism. This life has its origin in failure and breakdown. What followed is scarcely reminiscent of the children's miseries found in Charles Dickens's novels. Many of the later crimes naturally were commited in situations of acute need by the tramp, the illegal alien and confirmed thief whom no one would employ. Nonetheless Genet has always put great emphasis on the aesthetic moment of his thievery. Stealing not from need but for pleasure and the cultivation of an aesthetic sense.

Besides: Genet's books are the exact opposite of a literature of indignation and rebellion. This author has no intention of making accusations or unmasking society. He is a true believer in the bourgeois order, not a critic. From the depths of the social hierarchy he legitimates its structure and upper reaches. On account of this, Walter Heist[5] has concluded that Genet is permeated with fascism, a bogus conclusion in this case based on uncareful reading and a misapprehension of the aesthetic play, the luxuriating provocation of Genet's works. Even his antagonists have never asserted that Genet collaborated with the German army in occupied Paris, as he reports in *Funeral Rites* in first-person narrative.[6] Maurice Sachs became a collaborator, but not the "real world" Genet. Nonetheless, all of his books manifest a passionate sexual propensity for uniforms, might, powers of execution, for reckless domination. And so there comes to be again and again, most artfully developed in the *Querelle,* a political-erotic bond between criminal and policeman.

Even here one could try to salvage the Golden Legend by deriving such servility from fear and impotence. Brecht upon occasion employs such devices to portray workers as servile and piously loyal to established authority. In *St. Joan of the Stockyards,* where this occurs at length, Joan Dark reflects their situation in her response to the capitalist Mauler by saying he has not demonstrated the baseness of the poor to her, but only their poverty. The simple fact is Brecht never glorifies treachery, the abandonment of solidarity, even in a community of thieves. Genet, contrarily, desires, practices, and praises treachery. With that the Legend breaks to pieces, and that is also this man's and author's intention. His thieving: the result of an unhappy childhood. His pederasty: the result of rape at an early age, necessity, and certainly inclination as well. His treachery: here the matter becomes the turning point of Jean Genet.

A completely new line of attack is necessary. That Genet was able by writing to free himself from the external constraints he had interiorized and thus attain his identity, is unmistakeable. The phenomenon is not unusual and has by now become almost a commonplace. It is not by accident that Jean-Paul Sartre, in the nigh 600 pages of his book on Genet, *Saint Genet: Actor and Martyr,* offers the first attempt to delineate the salvation of a man by the act of writing, by his existence as a writer. It was not to be Sartre's last work treating this existential conflict. His own autobiography, *The Words,* has no other purport. Once again, as the two divisions "Lire" and "Ecrire" demonstrate, we find the childhood of a writer, who by reading and then writing, however badly and plagiaristically, attains to his intellectual identity. It is simply that Sartre this time has become the subject of his own experiment. After the example of Genet there now follows the example of the young Sartre. A third attempt is underway: the example of Gustave Flaubert. The organization of the three volumes of *L'Idiot de la famille* that have appeared so far are arranged entirely according to the rules of disposition in the book on Genet.

Genet chooses himself by writing and as a writer. That is not unusual and, besides, is morally neutral. In Genet literature presents itself simultaneously as autism and as negation of values. The two belong together. Genet's literary autism or solipsism designs only one reader: the author. That may have been modified in the later plays like *The Balcony* or *The Screens,* but at the beginning of his process of emancipation through the act of writing (in his prison cell, probably forbidden by the authorities), that was the fact of the matter. Genet makes no secret of it; *Our Lady of the Flowers* and *The Miracle of the Rose* operate through the device of an author summing up accounts, who evokes memories, lets them sink away once again, interweaves past and present, and who knows himself to be the omnipresent reader—the only one there is. What is envisaged here is a literature for masturbation. The text integrates this situation and function as one of its moments. Such a literature has no message and desires no communication.

Since it presupposes isolation, in life and in writing, it must interpret all the events of the past that have led here, to the prison cell and to acceptance, as the necessary conditions, the consciously necessary conditions, of its development. That occurs through a no less conscious negation of values. "In his all-out effort to commit the greatest crime, Genet breaks all records," writes Sartre in his book on Genet. Sartre represents that process as a Kafkaesque trial. The catchword is "metamorphosis," and recalls Gregor Samsa who awoke of a morning a giant insect. The child Genet metamorphoses into a criminal who is caught

The Turning Point of Jean Genet

and ostracized; the criminal accepts first the rules of behavior, then the linguistic forms, finally the specific countervalues of a so-called underworld in its relation to the overworld and ruling orders. It is simply that this counterworld still very much belongs to the ruling universe, as hypocrisy does to virtue.

From here on in Genet breaks camp and goes off on his own. That is what Sartre meant with "all-out effort." Before him, in the middle of the Victorian era, Oscar Wilde had ventured a bit down that same path by flirting with crime, murder in particular, as a realm of the fine arts. There was more to it than a coquettish paradox. Wilde was once again practicing demoralization in the form of aestheticization.

Genet is more consequential—and grimmer. For his own part, he drives morality from all theory and practice. Only the beautiful ritual has meaning, the beautiful action, the beautiful body. Even the deaths of the murderers Pilorge and Harcamone under the guillotine are a beautiful, poetic ritual. What has been left behind is the ugly (and moral) world of the bourgeoisie. Genet is certainly not the only one who has instigated an abrupt and utter negation of the dominant legal structure and modes of behavior for the sake of something that can only be termed an aesthetic normativity. Flaubert had done no different. In his case the aesthete, struck by the Paris Commune, rapidly returned to belief in the world of the bourgeoisie: just as Genet in his precipitous aestheticization of life will never forgo contact with the prevailing powers in state and society. One can, and this is all to be read in Genet's works, just as well celebrate the policeman, the fascist militiaman, the SS trooper, and the hangman of Berlin next to the criminal for their beauty in deed and being. André Breton's and the Surrealists' rejection of Genet was less unexpected than Sartre seems willing to admit.

Genet attempts but never attains to a fundamental isolation in society. He is not the one individual. The counterworld remains within the world just as countermorality remains within morality. Even the aestheticization of treachery, that is to say, the one action that spurns society and isolates the most, was not able to sever the social bohnd. Sartre, whom we must assume to be knowledgeable, is not really convinced of the "real" Genet's treacheries.

The autism of the writer writing in his cell had its hour, which then passed. The writer Genet who is released and who continues to write is obliged to communicate and in the end desires to, with the Algerians, then with American Black Panthers. The negation of bourgeois values with the help of values that have been negated in turn by bourgeois society does not provide a way out of that society. It assumes a relationship like Nietzsche's atheism to Christianity or Gide's immoralism to Protestant moral philosophy, or the antitheater to the theater. The printed yet illegal books bearing the countermorality came to be the objects of police actions; yet soon enough the action against the book *Querelle de Brest* became a literary and historical test case along the lines of *Madame Bovary* before it, Joyce's *Ulysses,* and finally Henry Miller's *Tropic of Cancer.* At its conclusion, the paperback edition could be bought everywhere.

The thief Genet, with a cult of treachery, the saint of a one-man religion of satanism, was fetched back to literature, and with that to social communication. His had merely been venial sins after all. One does not become an absolute outsider so easily. The significance of Jean Genet's experiment, with all the alarm that continues to proceed from it, lies in the relationship of the homosexual Genet to homosexual literature. Here a turning point was reached. And here too comes to the fore, temporarily at least, something like a benign tolerance. Gide the Nobel Prize winner; Jean Cocteau, member of the Académie Française. Nonetheless, every new authoritarian regime that makes an appearance in the world soon enough remembers those with the inner pink triangle, the emblem their fellows were forced to wear in the concentration camps of the Third Reich. When there was scarcely any opposition left to Stalin, he had the liberal laws of the Soviet Union regarding homosexuality changed; Gorki stood at his side and discovered the moral degeneracy of a Verlaine. Fidel Castro organized a majority against the suspect outsiders of sexual behavior who apparently are different in their very existence. The cry for law and order always means order in bed and injustice toward this minority.

On this account Jean Genet's works mark a high tide that has indeed receded but that can hardly be exceeded. In his book on Genet, Jean-Paul Sartre traces the genealogy of the homosexual author and defines the exceptional case of homosexual existence in bourgeois society as follows: "The drama of the bourgeois pederast is a drama of nonconformity. How is he able to maintain his culpable originality within a society where family, profession, money, education, and religion all strongly work to integrate him?"[7] Over and over, the case of Andersen's botched integration, that of Verlaine and Rimbaud as failed provocation, the longing for death of Ludwig of Bavaria, Tchaikovsky, Lorca, Klaus Mann repeat themselves.

Genet has rejected all these alternatives. The decision to survive, the rejection of suicide, is strongly manifest. Conformity, which may have been conceivable at first, is thwarted by circumstance: both internal and external. The scandal was provided objective form by the courts and penal institutions; thus Verlaine's dilettantism, his conventional and lewd "sanctimoniousness," could be avoided. Proust attempted to out-trump the conflict between outsiders and society by making everyone over into outsiders. "Ils le sont tous," he concluded, relieved. Swann's jealousy was as much a destructive and ulcerous cancer as Baron Charlus's horniness for pretty young men. The Calvinist André Gide placed his bet on two lottery numbers simultaneously: on the divine omnipotence that had created his own species and on the creative powers of nature, which know all manner of species and variation.

As a case that parallels Genet's, Sartre mentions the life of the French Catholic writer and Nazi collaborator Marcel Jouhandeau. After the war Jouhandeau attempted to interpret the choice of evil as a conscious religious choice for damnation. Sartre quite acerbicly portrays the case as one of moral duplicity: "I shall put it quite clearly: this dialectic stinks. First of all, that is a lot of circumstance to surround a couple of acts of masturbation, whether alone or à deux. Such a big deal! Where is the crime? Among pederasts human relations are possible as between man and woman. . . . It was certainly better to go to bed tenderly with a young boyfriend than to go traveling in Nazi Germany when France was overrun and strangled."[8] In Sartre's interpretation, Jouhandeau remains the timid French provincial who has to fear the scandal that Proust's Baron Charlus could haughtily ignore.

Of all of them and their attempts at a balance between outsiderdom and bourgeois integration, Genet distinguishes himself through the unity of literary subject and object. Here a homosexual is writing homosexual literature. He does not transform his lover Albert, as does Proust, into an Albertine. He also does not separate, as did Gide composing his tractate *Corydon,* the real *I* of the writer from the written narrative. He does not play the rueful sinner whom society finds so sweet and conserving to forgive, as was the case for Verlaine, for Maurice Sachs in his cell in Fuhlsbüttel Prison, for Jouhandeau. Genet never had James Baldwin's opportunity, if it ever was one, of incorporating his sexual outsiderdom into a larger outsiderdom, that of being black. Genet's play *Les Nègres* failed on account of it.

In Jean Genet's books a pederast speaks as pederast about pederasty, without asking for forbearance, without asking for understanding, without retrospection, and without objectivity, which would be impossible. Without confession as well, for confession aspires to a partner to whom one entrusts oneself: from that friend to whom Daniel in Sartre's novel quite gratuitously and without the least effect suddenly confides that he is a pederast, to the larger community of readers of Gide's journals. Each attempt at a seemingly courageous frankness conceals secret dishonesties. Hans Christian Andersen developed this procedure with virtuoso technique, with every confession necessarily bringing a new and supplementary confession in tow.

Genet does not confess. Who would there be to hear it? He also does not glorify himself as does Allen Ginsberg. Most assuredly he would not integrate himself into any movement for "gay power." Whoever has reached a turning point can never go back again. But neither can he go forward. Jean Genet's silence, that of the writer Genet, can be interpreted privately as the capstone to a process of self-realization. What has to be taken more seriously is an objectivizing interpretation, which from the point of view of the works produced, is able to recognize only a single lethal alternative: repetition or regression. Genet's silence seems to suggest that he rejects this alternative as well.

Genet, Bukharin, and Trotsky

From here on the specific instance of Genet broadens into a representative social process. The case of Joan of Arc never repeated itself in bourgeois society. The spy Mata Hari and those real life models for female commissars in the Red Army who were adapted for Vishnevskii's *Optimistic Tragedy,* the Nobel Prize winner Marie Curie and the British queen: not one of them is proof against being aestheticized and consequently integrated into modern society and its mass media culture. All three of these women outsiders are merely the stuff for more films. The case of Marilyn Monroe offers an extreme example: the life of an outsider at once dismantled, made palatable and transfigured by film as a preliminary step to a final apotheosis. Latching onto homosexual outsiders in the selfsame fashion is as little practicable as the aesthetic evisceration of a Shylock, even if the American dream factory makes every effort to serve up everyday Jewish life as folklore and tries to defuse it all the way up to the pogrom. It is the *Anatevka* method. Filmed pogroms, played by stars. But that was a long time ago. Or was it perhaps only yesterday.

The Turning Point of Jean Genet

Nowadays things are different. The appellations for homosexuals, Sartre points out, which derive from the Biblical Sodom or the planet Uranus (Uranians!) fundamentally strive for a geographical and chronological distancing. Long ago; perhaps even yesterday. Nowadays things are different.

The express aim of the works by Simone de Beauvoir and Jean-Paul Sartre that have appeared since the end of the Second World War has been to combat such defusing and evisceration. Books like *The Second Sex,* on the representative significance of Genet's turning point, on the Jewish question after Auschwitz, all complement one another. It is logically consistent then for Sartre to explicate the universal significance of a Genet by juxtaposing him, the homosexual outsider, to the Jewish one. Once again Shylock and Antonio, Heine and Platen, the integral outsid erdom of a Walther Rathenau. In the concluding chapter to his book on the actor and martyr, Saint Genet, Sartre calls another juxtaposition to hand. He compares Jean Genet with Nikolai Ivanovich Bukharin, that is writing as self-liberation and speaking as self-incrimination in one of Stalin's trials where everything is agreed upon from the start—guilt, condemnation, and execution.

Bukharin was not a homosexual. Sartre calls up the constellation of Genet–Bukharin at the end of his book where it becomes necessary to demonstrate the universal significance of a Genet beyond any question of individual emancipation. The matter of erotic proclivities has long since fallen by the wayside. "I have no police record," Sartre writes, "and no inclination for boys. Yet Genet's writings have moved me. If they move me it is because they concern me. If they concern me it is because I can benefit from them."[9]

With that Genet's case takes on parabolic dimensions, like that of N. I. Bukharin. Sartre sees in the publicly confessing Bukharin of the trials someone attempting a system of simultaneous denial and admission, and who is entrapped in this hopeless dialectic. He attempts it because he at one and the same time just as hopelessly both accedes to and refuses to recognize the court and Stalin's mandate. The connection of the book on Jean Genet (1952) with another work of Sartre's, *Anti-Semite and Jew* (1946),[10] is overlooked. But the case of the homosexual Genet and the case of the Bolshevik Bukharin belong together.[11]

Stalin's trials were traditionally proceedings against Jews. Naturally Iosif Vissarionovich Dzhugashvili, in the trials of the 1930s under the direction of the state prosecutor (and later Foreign Minister) Vyshinskii, was seeking to rid himself of his most prominent political opponents. It is simply that the Zinovevs and Radeks, the Kamenevs, Tomskiis, and Rykovs were Jews. The trials were from the very start an anti-Semitic ritual undertaking. Just how much Stalin and his aides-de-camp adhered to the trusted formula can be seen in the trials of the late 1940s. In Hungary: the Jews László Rajk and Tibor Szöni, the pattern not being altered in the least by the fact that it was a Jewish strongman, a Jew who went by the thoroughly magyarized name of Mattias Rakosi who had prepared these proceedings, which were to end in particularly cruel scenes at the gallows. In Prague: Rudolf Slansky and others who were Jews almost to the man. Arthur London, a survivor, has reported the situation in the court room and in the cells and interrogation rooms below. The trial in Prague, more so than any of its predecessors, was emphatically anti-Jewish. In the meantime the formula had been discovered whereby one could practice anti-Semitism, by attacking not "Jews" this time but merely the "Zionist elements." In the German Democratic Republic, the trial, which had been prepared on instructions from Moscow, but never took place because of Stalin's death and the uprisings on June 17, 1953, would have been along similar lines. Leo Bauer and Bruno Goldhammer, the prospective defendants, would have provided the requisite supply of Jewish traitors. The proceedings failed to develop to a holocaust; neither did the last imaginings of the ailing Stalin come to be carried out: actions against Jewish doctors accused of having cured Gorki into his grave, in addition to the obligatory accusations of having perpetrated attacks on the life of the father of the peoples. Just how much the mechanical principle continued of selecting from among outsiders the defendants for show trials whose purpose was intimidation, from among those who were already existentially guilty as it were, can be seen in the trials in the GDR after the Hungarian uprising of 1956—four years after Stalin's death. When Wolfgang Harich, who was not unknown, and therefore known in the sense of the complaint, but too little known in the world, was arrested as the symbolic intellectual for having caused difficulties, the state prosecutor general, Melsheimer, had seen to it that among the four other conspirators there was a Jew and a homosexual.

Both live lives of isolation. That is something that ever threatens individuals in society and in the case of outsiders seems to be inescapable. In the transition from Genet to that of the shipwrecked Communist Bukharin, Sartre concludes that "true solitude is that of the monster given short shrift by Nature and Society. He lives out to its conclusion, to very impossibility, the latent solitude that we all know and attempt to pass over in silence. One is not alone if one is in the right, for Truth will out; nor if one is in the wrong, because then it suffices to admit one's errors for them to scatter. One is alone when one is *simultaneously* in the right and the wrong: . . . right as subject . . . and wrong as object because one cannot simply reject the objective condemnation brought against one by all of Society." [12]

That is precisely the situation for Bukharin and Genet both. In the fashion in which they arrange themselves or have placed themselves in this solitude, they become antagonists and alternatives to each other. If Bukharin had won out politically in his struggle with Stalin he would have been able to appeal to historical necessity vis-à-vis future generations. High treason if bungled becomes a crime against the state; high treason if successful means the emergence of a new legality and legitimacy: namely that of the victor and the greater strength. By failing, Trotsky as well as Bukharin were guilty of high crimes from the viewpoint of Soviet legality. Nonetheless an essential distinction seems to escape Sartre by confronting Bukharin only with Genet and not with Leon Trotsky.

In his struggle against Stalin as before in exile, with the exception only of a short span of six or seven years when he had a share of power, Trotsky was and remained an unmitigated naysayer. He was fought, exiled, slandered, assassinated at the end by a hired killer; yet he always remained the strict adversary, an autonomous subject, the vanquished yet still threatening opponent. At no time did Trotsky become an object to be degraded, reified, made into something to toy with. Bukharin became just that, was toyed with for a while in court under a cross examination that was then broken off as planned in advance. Naturally the methods of the secret police played a role in bringing Bukharin to sign his "confession." Nonetheless the distinction between Trotsky and Bukharin is to be found in their fundamentally different ways of grasping the role of outsider. Trotsky, who is supported here by his Marxist, Enlightenment stand, does not view his Jewish parentage as a determining factor in the fate he is served up. He reacts to Stalin's anti-Semitism with the greatest contempt. He sees in it a nationalistic aberration, a form of revisionism. Bukharin, one expects, saw things similarly.

Both were wrong. Stalin's theoretical failing was his practical and political strength. The "Jewified Bolshevism" of the Lenin period, as the fascist propaganda of the time was wont to characterize the Soviet Russia of Trotsky, Zinoviev, and Litvinov, was not on a footing that promised duration. Stalin represented the exact opposite position for the country, that of the nonexile, the nonintellectual, the non-Jew. Within such a situation, only Trotsky's position was logically consequential: protest, opposition, a return to outsiderdom—out of this nonlegitimacy the distillation of a theory of destabilization of the revolution, of permanent revolution.

Bukharin neither dared such a position nor thought it legitimate. In this manner he became an object. Sartre interprets Bukharin's position thus: "Since he can appeal neither to his former comrades, who condemn him, nor to his enemies, whom he despises as much as ever, nor to posterity, which will perhaps absolve him of the charge of treason only to rank him among the bunglers and unfortunates of history, he is alone. He senses in himself only emptiness and failure. . . . His last act consists of self-destruction. . . . He confesses to treason. That is one possible stance: the solitary escapes his solitude by means of moral suicide; rejected by men, he makes himself a stone among stones."[13]

A second stance and possibility, according to Sartre, is that taken by Jean Genet. "For Genet is the Bukharin of bourgeois society." He is the citizen of a society that rejects him. But here is where the difference begins. Genet may worship the system of bourgeois power, including its fascist forms, but nonetheless will proudly attempt to assert his own outcast subjectivity. Bukharin abases himself; Genet chooses pride and noncommunity. In his study on humanism and terror,[14] Maurice Merleau-Ponty presents an analysis of the Moscow trials and of the untenable position taken by Bukharin, who confesses and at the same time tries to disprove at least the charges of espionage and sabotage. He is nothing more than a vanquished member of Soviet society, a traitor in consequence. Merleau-Ponty, in a now famous formula, put it thus: "Tout opposant est un traître, mais tout traître n'est qu'un opposant" (Every opponent is a traitor, but every traitor is only an opponent).

Genet, however, if one follows Sartre and characterizes him as a "traitor and opponent to bourgeois society," belongs more at the side of Trotsky than at that of the semitraitor and semiopponent Bukharin. Genet accepts himself as a monster, just as Trotsky established himself as a communist outside of the Soviet Communist party establishment. Here, however, differences immediately become visible that make an approximation of Genet to Bukharin à la Sartre impossible and thwart any integral parallelism between Genet and Trotsky. These differences have their source not so much in the characters of the men involved as in the differing positions of their outsiderdom, above all in the dissimilarities between a restorative bourgeois society and a revolutionary doctrine like Marxism.

Genet is a member of the opposition in a bourgeois social order who is not permitted full membership. He is obliged to withdraw himself, on account of his sexual outsiderdom, from social integration, and in the end this withdrawal increasingly becomes a conscious process. In so doing he only legitimates the existing social order and its moral norms. Sodom was destroyed and can never be rebuilt. The Sodomites must live (and even want to live) in the diaspora. From that derives their aversion to meeting in normal society one of their own kind. Jean Genet establishes the maxim of nonintegration. Yet that can never become the foundation of a constitution for Sodomites. What he attempted, in life and then later in literature, was something akin to what the young Rimbaud had envisioned. Even monsters can be integrated, externally at least.[15]

Merleau-Ponty's criticism is not applicable to Trotsky. He is a vanquished opponent within Soviet doctrine and a traitor as well. Yet through the position of naysayer he is able to reverse the ideological positions. He denounces Stalin's treason. The most important of his political books is entitled *The Revolution Betrayed*. Genet praised treason, but within the scheme of bourgeois society. That was the protest of an outsider, an acknowledgment of nonintegration in a much admired yet unattainable social hierarchy. Bukharin admitted an act of treason that he did not commit and so became an object and a victim, but not a martyr for posterity.

Neither did Trotsky become a martyr. There is no religion that could canonize him. That has nothing to do with the success or failure of "Trotskyism." It has far more to do with his Jewishness, which he disdainfully would register in his own mind only as a problem of nationality. He was never conscious that he lived as Comrade Shylock.

The inequality of women could be given a smart trim by a process of transfiguration. The inequality of sexual desire might oscillate between the futile conformity of an Andersen or a Tchaikovsky and the equally futile monstrous stylizations of a Rimbaud or a Genet. But for Shylock the alternative has been again and again: Auschwitz or Israel.

Shylock

In Siegfried Kracauer's writings on the philosophy of history, there is a chapter headed "Ahasuerus, or the Riddle of Time." In explanation he writes:

It occurs to me that the only reliable informant on these matters, which are so difficult to ascertain, is a legendary figure—Ahasuerus, the Wandering Jew. He indeed would know first-hand about the developments and transitions, for he alone in all history has had the unsought opportunity to experience the process of becoming and decaying itself. (How unspeakably terrible he must look! To be sure, his face cannot have suffered from aging, but I imagine it to be many faces, each reflecting one of the periods which he traversed and all of them combining into ever new patterns, as he restlessly, and vainly, tries on his wanderings to reconstruct out of the times that shaped him the one time he is doomed to incarnate.)[1]

With that, however, the philosopher of history Kracauer in truth degrades the Eternal Jew, to whom he reckons so much symbolic power, to an observer of universal history. Ahasuerus stands then far more for the permanently hopeless undertaking of conceptualizing and transforming into secondary literature the irreversible course of history, than becoming himself the incarnation of real history. It must be clear that this seeming paradox is connected with the idiosyncrasies of Kracauer's philosophical-historical mode of inquiry, yet at the same time it manifests a peculiarity of this "legendary" (as Kracauer puts it) figure itself. It is indeed astonishing enough: the Eternal Jew is a thoroughly un-Jewish figure. He signifies a crystallized past that surfaces again and again in whatever present there happens to be: oftentimes with comic effect, as in Wilhelm Hauff's *Satan's Memoirs,* where Ahasuerus, partaking of an aesthetic high tea (perhaps, even, in the Jewish salon of a Rahel Levin or a Henriette

Herz?), grows bored and falls completely out of character. Incarnated in him is time gone by once and forever, yet he does not incarnate any particular Jewish life, even if illustrations since Reformation have always had him appear in Jew's hat, caftan, and with forelocks. In the literature where he appears he is seldom scorned or made fun of. Enveloped in a distant aura, he appears both venerable and uncanny. This Jew is least of all a Jew. For him immortality is a curse; his companions in this fate are non-Jews. Heinrich Heine, in his *Memoirs of M. de Schnabelevopsky,* where he outlined the story of the flying Dutchman, thereby unknowingly prefiguring Richard Wagner's libretto, called the Dutchman an "Ahasuerus of the Ocean." But the Dutchman is no Jew, and the curse that fell upon him occurred in modern times and is not implacable. Ahasuerus stands for a provocation to which there is no remedy. That is not the case for the Dutchman, nor the Kundry in Wagner's *Parsifal,* who can be absolved by dying.

Even the name is non-Jewish. Biblical scholars who meet the name Ahashverosh or Ahasuerus in the book of Esther and in Ezra IV, 6, understand a Persian king, in other words an adversary of the Jews more than not.[2] The spelling seems to be a Hebraicized form of the name Artaxerxes; historically speaking, Xerxes is probably meant. Hans Joachim Schoeps writes that the name "according to rabbinical interpretation [signifies] a man of calamity and misery."[3]

The legend of the eternally wandering Jew marched in pace with Christianity across the Mediterranean. The name itself varied from place to place. In Italy he is called Buttadio: he who is struck by God. On the Iberian peninsula he has the conciliatory name of Juan Espera en Dios.

Anti-Semitic elements first appear in the German versions, as in the *Short Description and Explanation of a Jew with the Name Ahasver,* a tract first published in 1602. In all the chapbooks about the eternal wanderer, the curse is traced back to a cobbler in Jerusalem spurning Jesus on his way to Golgotha. In a similar fashion, Wagner establishes the curse on Kundry:

I saw—Him—Him
and . . . laughed:
then his gaze pierced me!
Now I seek him from world to world,
try to meet him once again.

(*Parsifal,* II)

From Ahasuerus to Shylock

The figure and mythology of Ahasuerus is of Christian contrivance. It has in mind and is aimed with particular mockery at the Jewish Parousia, which never took place. The Jewish Messiah appeared but was not recognized by the chosen people. Ahasuerus belongs to the imaginative world of the builders of the Gothic cathedrals, along with the foolish virgins and the blindfolded synagogue. Naturally he is the incarnation of his people, the diaspora, the wandering without rest, a grudging hospitality among alien peoples.

But the Eternal Jew never signifies a particular Jew. He stands rather for a theological fatum, not for the particular life of any one, single Jew. For that reason, Ahasuerus is no scandal, not even in an eschatological sense. Scandal presupposes someone who actually exists, implies a single individual in time and space: on the Rialto, under the palms of the wise Nathan, as leader of the Tories in the House of Commons, in the Jockey Club, as Jewish Foreign Minister in Weimar. The phenotype for the Jewish emancipation that failed is not the immortal Ahasuerus, but the character of a dramatist: Shylock, the man without a forename, the Jew of Venice.

18   The Jew of Malta and the Jew of Venice

They were scarcely based on real life, these Jews: Marlowe's unfathomably rich Jew Barabas of Malta and Shakespeare's propertied and prospering Shylock who lends money on the Rialto.

The councils of the Catholic Church since the eighth century had forbidden the faithful the practice of lending out money at interest but had left it open to Jews since, in the opinion of the canon lawyers, they were a people excluded from eternal salvation and one sin more or less for them would be inconsequential.

In England since the close of the thirteenth century at least, however, this duality of Jew and non-Jew did not even exist in society. After the celebration of a string of rumors in the city of Lincoln in the year 1255, as everywhere else in Europe and the Near East during the Middle Ages, about ritual murders, after riot, plundering, and murder, a ritual in its own right, the Jews of England in 1290 were ordered to leave the realm. That was two hundred years before the Spanish and Portuguese Jews were similarly expelled. Very few were permitted to return. After that time Jews in England were mostly creatures of rumor and invention, as they still were for the great poets of the Elizabethan age, Marlowe and Shakespeare. Whatever real content existed was the subject of hearsay, propagated in rumors, coalesced in reports of travels by those who had seen real-life Jews in Germany or Italy. What was noted down and passed on was what seemed to go along with the ogre's image of a strange and threatening exotic people. The incomprehensible rites and holy books in an incomprehensible language and alphabet; caftan and prayer bands, forelocks and ritual head-coverings; the despising of the pork so popular in Northern climes; Sabbath instead of Sunday churchgoing; a high scriptural learnedness and medical skills, something that until well into the Renaissance and Reformation caused a good deal of apprehension.

In his preface to the German translation of Marlowe's *Doctor Faustus* (1818), the Prussian Junker, Romantic poet, and anti-Semite Achim von Arnim noted this connection. It demonstrated, he said, the convergence of the Jewish and the Faustian trauma.[1] Magic books and a wondrous healing power: they were attributed to, as subjects for reproach, both Faustus, as a monstrous exception, and the whole of the Jewish people, as a monstrous collective. "The priests," Arnim wrote, "mysteriously consecrated, stood at a great height over the race of men; their fall was all the more terrible then. This, in connection with their possession of the sciences, of which natural history in particular gave rise to the reputation of magic, was the reason why so many monks, even bishops, fell into suspicion of having a pact with the devil." One need only call to mind the story of "Cenodoxus," the heretical "Doctor of Paris."

The contractual eternal damnation stipulated by such a pact with the devil corresponded, in the case of the Jews, to a much more confusing (because it could not be reduced to any one individual's act of volition) preestablished exclusion from salvation and damnation of Jewry. One sees that the sculptors of the Strasbourg Cathedral provided the blindfolded female figure who represents the synagogue with an aura of gracious sorrow, far more touching in comparison to the proud and exulting figure of the Church militant; yet the fact was that for the princes and the townsfolk, the farmers and clerics of the Middle Ages and Renaissance, the outer strangeness of the Jews, whether real or depicted in tales, remained an overt sign of their damnation. Martin Luther was not one to change any of this. He was no humanist like Johannes Reuchlin or Erasmus of Rotterdam; on the contrary, he eschewed any humanistic laxness in matters of faith. What had been the anti-Semitic conciliar practice for the Roman theologians and canonical jurists was now, in the Lutheran catechism, deduced from the spirit and letter of the New Testament, with analogous results.

Besides, concupiscence has a hand in all this as well. The sacred has always had to do with sanctification and infamy, salvation and damnation, white and black magic at one and the same time. The French usage of *sacré* preserves the ambivalence up to the present day.

And cupidity and desire were evoked twofold by the strange and damned existence of the Jews: in the hoarding of gold and in the puzzling beauty of their women. That an expression like "une belle juive" is still used today in France, not without some feeling, almost lip-smacking and eye-rolling, was noted by Sartre in his observations on the Jewish question. Literature is crammed with such beautiful Jewesses; particularly the theater, with confrontations between one and a non-Jewish lover, who may be a king or prince or artist but who always falls under the thrall of a mystifying and sinister sensuality, usually by subterfuge, under which he suffers and is made to suffer. This reaches from Lope's and Grillparzer's *Jewess of Toledo* and the beautiful Jewish princess Berenice in Racine, to the emotionally bewildering Jewess Hanna Elias, who in Gerhart Hauptmann's play drives the painter Gabriel Schilling to his watery death.

The beautiful Jewess and the Jew's gold: neither Marlowe nor Shakespeare can do without them, though the play about the Jew of Malta in the posthumous printing of 1633 is entitled *The Famous Tragedy of the Rich Jew of Malta,* while *The Merchant of Venice* is accounted one of Shakespeare's comedies. But in both of these Elizabethan dramas—and internal evidence suggests that the author of *The Merchant of Venice* was familiar with Marlowe's play—the ingredients from all the tales of Jews have been put to good use. Nothing is painted from nature; everything is legend and third-hand report. So much so that the Jew Barabas in Marlowe and Shylock in Shakespeare have been punctiliously robbed of all characteristics that might provide even a precarious community with their surroundings. Even Hamlet and Malvolio, even the black Moor of Venice, are all at least partially integrated into society, no less so Doctor Faustus and King Edward in Marlowe. The two Jews, on the contrary, signify nothing but aliens and alien being.

Shakespeare endows his figure with a greater concreteness as Jew than Marlowe his, who has little use for specific coloring. Antonio, the merchant of Venice, spat, as Shylock remembers, on the Jew's caftan, "on my Jewish gabardine." Launcelot Gobbo, Shylock's Venetian swindler of a servant, can make report of the Jew's behavior at home, while Ithamore, the slave bought by Barabas on the marketplace, only reports or carries out crimes, but provides no sense of the world of his unbelievably rich Jewish Machiavellian master, the world of a man who has lost his wife and is bent on revenge.

The Jew of Malta in Christopher Marlowe's play does not demonstrate the tragedy of Jewish existence but the immoralism of a man of the English and Italian Renaissance on the further shore of religion and morality. Cesare Borgia in a caftan. The dramatist needs the hero to be a Jew for two reasons, one dramatic, the other conceptual. The "rich Jew of Malta" signifies the dual phenomenon of immeasurable wealth, yet a wealth constantly threatened. It is here that the exposition of the tragedy coalesces: the Turks are requiring tribute from the knights of Malta that is in arrears; the Jews of Malta are required to come up with it or convert to Christianity. This gesture, following Marlowe, is nothing more than a contemptible act of hypocrisy since the Christian governor counts on the Jews' allegiance to their own religion and consequently on legal expropriation.

Jewry here, fundamentally nothing more than a mechanical device of the plot, is the basis of Barabas's acts of vengeance, and consequently for a whole suite of crafty and sensuously arrayed murders. More important is the second, conceptual side of this Jew's tragedy. Marlowe needs Barabas's Jewishness for the triadic construction of the play, which is intended to be a drama of the three religions. Malta offers the confrontation of Moslem protectory power with Christian knights. To that is added the Jew, at first as the most influential member of the Jewish community; yet Barabas soon separates himself in thought and deed from any kind of Jewish solidarity. It is this isolation from all communality, even from the members of his own faith, that yields the tragic solitude Marlowe means to fashion: isolation both by origin and by individual decision.

The idea of *The Jew of Malta* strikes one as a diabolically perverted prefiguration of Lessing's *Nathan the Wise*. In the parable play by the German protagonist of the Enlightenment, there is set before one's eyes in Palestine, where the play takes place, an Islamic protectory power, protected Jews, and captured Crusaders. Three religions in one finally converging action. In the parable play by the Elizabethan, the disintegrating function of simple membership in any one of these religions is made evident. No common humanity connects the three warring creeds. Quite the contrary: the Jew, the Christian, the Moslem are united only in their readiness to commit utter inhumanity. No religion, Marlowe's message appears to be, opens the view to a humanity of common care. Barabas, by virtue of the logically consequent lawlessness of his actions and sufferings, is the incarnation of a categorical imperative of immorality, of "Machiavellianism" as Marlowe interprets it. He acts precisely as all the others would act if they were reduced to such total outsiderdom. As a person of great wealth and a Jew in Malta he acts out the principles of a general Maltese lawfulness.

And from this tragedy, as well as from Marlowe's *Tragicall History of Doctor Faustus*, there emanates the taint of atheism. The three religions do not allow, as later for Lessing in the parable of the rings, the postu-

The Jew of Malta and the Jew of Venice

lation of a *religion naturelle* behind all their specific differences, but instead point to the connection between the secret intellectual and religious mode of thought of this dramatist who was killed in such an equivocal fashion and the arguments presented in the mysterious tractate, "De tribus impostoribus," concerning the three huckster founders of religion: Moses, Jesus, and Mohammed. For that reason Barabas is not the title figure of a "tragicall history" like Doctor Faustus. His demise is caused by a single act of renunciation. He forgoes consequential Machiavellianism. He secretly brings the Turks to Malta; the Christian governor who confiscated his property is now his prisoner. The prevailing principle of action would be to do away with the adversary. He lets him live and is then in turn cunningly murdered by the Christian who acts precisely as the Jew of Malta did. Confrontation of three religions in total alienation.

Where there are no ties and no restraints, Machiavellianism alone reigns. The author of *The Prince,* who died in Florence in 1527, belonged to Marlowe's century. He is made the speaker of the prologue to *The Jew of Malta.* Marlowe has the dead man's ghost appear on the English stage after a sojourn in France in a metamorphosis as the duke of Guise, the organizer of the massacre of St. Bartholomew's Eve (to whom Marlowe had dedicated another play, *The Massacre at Paris*). But now he appears in England in the introduction to the history of a Jew.

> I∙come not, I,
> To read a lecture here in Britain
> But to present the tragedy of a Jew,
> Who smiles to see how full his bags are cramm'd;
> Which money was not got without my means.[2]

The ghostly prologue, however, immediately provides the dramatist the opportunity of putting clearly and openly what is meant to be said. If the author is then taken at his word, which was the case, he could always explain that it was only Machiavelli who put things thus. Namely:

> I count religion but a childish toy,
> And hold there is no sin but ignorance.
> Birds of the air will tell of murders past:
> I am asham'd to hear such fooleries.

Yet Barabas ends, like Mozart's Don Giovanni, in decided acceptance of his law as monster and freely "takes up into his will" his monstrous, exceptional life as a Jew:

Shylock

Then, Barabas, breathe forth thy latest fate,
And in the fury of thy torments, strive
To end thy life with resolution.

Damn'd Christians, dogs, and Turkish infidels!

Marlowe needed the Jewish outsider to portray an essentially political world where all aspects of private life, even the facts of economic power, are only of significance as the props of an absolute decision making: the decision made being that of life or death. At any event the rich Jew of Malta, despite all his plans, fails the first moment he has to utilize immediate political power instead of mediated economic might. The life to come for the later Jewish bourgeoisie in Western Europe, looking back now in hindsight, can already be read in this first monumental stylization of a Jew in European literature.

Barabas is the figure of tragedy. Shakespeare's Shylock, despite all his overshadowing the gaiety of Belmont, even endangering it, has been integrated into a comedy. If the harmony of the spheres is predetermined, as Lorenzo explains to Jessica on Belmont, as the music of things, then even Shylock's dark harmonies have their place in the whole, just as does the melancholy and platonic erotic existence of Shylock's adversary, the merchant who has provided the title to this Shakespearean comedy.

The characteristics of the Jew of Malta can scarcely be called Jewish. His Machiavellianism might have been as well represented by a Christian or a Moslem; open and intimate talk with his coreligionists is unthinkable; he loves neither his daughter Abigail nor the Jewish faith. As part of his scheming and hatching of plots, he orders her to convert to Christianity and enter a cloister.

Shakespeare's Shylock, on the other hand, has been fleshed out with many real characteristics of Jewish historical life. It is a historical fact that an act of Parliament in 1522 forbade Christians in England the taking of usurious interest, while some few Jews expelled from Spain and let into the country were admitted to that occupation. It is historical fact as well that one of them, Dr. Lopez, once again Jew and physician in the infamous "Faustian" concatenation, was charged at the time Shakespeare was staying in London, an imaginary charge to be sure, of having planned to assassinate Queen Elizabeth with poison. He was subsequently racked and hanged.[3]

The stage figure of Shylock underscores this connection of rumor and scarcely understood reality. Nonetheless the wealth of individual and national traits in the rich Jew and usurer of Venice is surprising. He is proud of his religion and despises the Christians and their faith. He hates Antonio, who as Christian and Venetian merchant "lends out money gratis." He entertains relations with the other Jews of Venice and does not wish to be unworthy of them. His famous lament before the do-nothing parasite Salarino on the mocked and persecuted Jewish nation (III, 1) is neither Machiavellian nor egocentric: it is a universal Jewish lamentation. His hatred for Antonio is proxy for his whole race. "He hates our sacred nation," or "Cursed be my tribe if I forgive him." He, the widower, loves his deceased Leah and sentimentally holds in high honor the turquoise ring she once gave him, now stolen by their daughter and traded for a monkey. That he loves his daughter Jessica, who finds her vexed and avaricious father's house a hell, is patent. Her flight and betrayal first conjure up the real possibility of the strange contract with Antonio and its perfidious content: now to have revenge once for all! The outsider, spat upon, buffeted, and cheated by society in a monstrous manner, now transforms himself into a monster in his own right. And in this fashion the fateful transformation takes place: heretofore the Jew and usurer of the Rialto had been more or less a Jewish Everyman. Now he becomes a singular monster. He becomes Shylock.

In so doing, however, he becomes the mortal adversary of another man who for his own part cannot pretend to be a Venetian, Christian Everyman. Antonio is a Venetian merchant who has grown wealthy in the sea trade but who, as good Christian and law-abiding citizen, lends money out at no interest. A burgher, apparently, who consorts with young and extravagant noblemen. The man who he loves is for him always "Lord Bassanio."

The merchant of Venice is a monster as well, in the disguise of the decent burgher, who lives in solitude and spreads it about himself, a burgher and provider of money among profligate aristocrats. As Bassanio's loving friend he is supposed to help the young dandies attain their ladies. The question of mime—how Shakespeare could conceive this figure who speaks so few lines and scarcely has a "great scene" as the eponymous hero of his comedy—is wrongly put. It is the confrontation between the two outsiders, Antonio and Shylock, who have no other course, who are irreversible, to use Sartre's terminology—that is to say, robbed of all possibility of freedom of decision, since the one cannot stop

being a Jew and the other cannot "switch over" his feelings and love—
that makes possible the structure and dimensions of the play.

The merchant Antonio belongs to Shakespeare's androgynous stage
figures found in the comedies: Orlando, Sebastian, Patroclus. A lyrical
character from the proximity of the sonnets. By his very existence a
melancholic, unlike Jaques of *As You Like It,* who affects melancholy
merely because it is in vogue at court. To him belongs the very first line
of the play: "In sooth, I know not why I am so sad." The young fops
whom he takes into his confidence mistake sadness for sorrow, care for
fear. This merchant fears for his ships! The very first scene of the play
thereby confronts the outsider with the "man in the street," one who
feels and argues like all the rest.

Antonio too has his moment of liberating self-expression: just like
Shylock, who reveals himself to Salarino but who in court, when asked
the reasons for his suit, expresses only a concealed and stylized hatred,
not the eruptions of before.

Antonio had spoken openly in his letter to Bassanio, where Lord
Bassanio is suddenly addressed as "Sweet Bassanio" and is reminded of
his love (and debts). Now when everything seems lost, he is obliged to
cast off the stylization of feeling but to preserve the tone of amity wherein
"love" could mean everything at once, or nothing at all:

Give me your hand, Bassanio; fare you well!
Grieve not that I am fallen to this for you;

Commend me to your honourable wife:
Tell her the process of Antonio's end;
Say how I lov'd you, speak me fair in death;

And, when the tale is told, bid her be judge
Whether Bassanio had not once a love.   (IV, 1)

In a decidedly important analysis of *The Merchant of Venice,* W. H. Auden
not only interprets Antonio and Shylock as real adversaries but also
contrasts the two of them in diverse ways with all the other characters.[4]
Through the antagonism of these two incurable and real monsters the
magic of the arcadian world of Belmont is irretrievably and inescapably
dissipated. Its music is suddenly the production of mere musicians; verses
cannot negate the real misery of the Jew and of the hopeless lover; all of
Lorenzo's adjurations invoke mythology and play the coquette with the
great infidelities of the past: Cressida's, Jason's, Aeneas'. These, however,
have long since been committed. Antonio and Shylock both become the

The Jew of Malta and the Jew of Venice

killjoys of common happiness. Both are excluded from the bright world of Belmont. Antonio appears there of course, but as a superfluous, essentially ridiculous best man and "fatherly friend."

When Bassanio chooses the lead casket, by which he wins Portia's hand, he had trusted to the inscription, "Who chooseth me, must give and hazard all he hath." He won by pride, as it were, as one who admittedly despises the gold fever of the crowd and the silver pieces of day-to-day commerce. Auden is right to remark that it is actually Shylock and Antonio who dare at once to give and hazard all they have: "Shylock, however unintentionally, did in fact hazard all for the sake of destroying the enemy he hated, and Antonio, however unthinkingly he signed the bond, hazarded all to secure the happiness of the friend he loved." Auden continues and closes his analysis with the reflection that "it is precisely these two who cannot enter Belmont. Belmont would like to believe that men and women are either good or bad by nature, but Shylock and Antonio remind us that this is an illusion: in the real world, no hatred is totally without justification, no love totally innocent."

In Marlowe, the Jew Barabas fell himself into the abyss he had intended for his enemies. His was a kind of descent into hell, as the dramatist gives us to believe, reminiscent of Doctor Faustus's end. But both of them, the Machiavellians and the scoffers at religion, continued to enjoy the dramatist's almost openly expressed favor. The Jew of Malta had to embody many things at once: magic, the solitude of great wealth, the unscrupulous tactics of the immoralist, the monstrous existence of the Jewish outsider.

In Shakespeare, the Jew Shylock acts out his part in a cheerless comedy, which particularly on the account of his dark epiphany throws into question all the apparent happiness the others take in beauty, landscape, love, music. Even the Christian merchant Antonio gets in the way and spoils things for Belmont. One can imagine (the play being a comedy) how both go to live out their days. There is no community, not to speak of solidarity, for outsiders.

The comic figure Shylock in Shakespeare is related to his adversary Antonio as, in Marlowe, the Jew of Malta coursing to hell to King Edward, brutally yet not entirely uncomically murdered, who persisted in loving his Gaveston. In *The Stranger in Shakespeare*, Leslie Fiedler does not end his analysis with Shylock's demise (baptism and expropriation signifying execution), but proceeds to the cruel consequences of the complicated story in seemingly harmonious Belmont. Fiedler simply dismisses the seriousness of Portia's speech on mercy since Portia is almost always a liar—which is why Shylock is so wary. After the revenge taken on Shylock, there follows the revenge taken on Shylock's victim, Bassanio's friend and lover. The ring was meant as a tie between Bassanio and the merchant of Venice: "an effort doomed from the start, since the ring, by long tradition, stands for marriage and for female sexuality itself."[5] Thus Antonio, in solemn reacceptance, must put the ring on Bassanio's finger: the outsider marries off his beloved and remains behind, alone. Perishing, as Shylock.

19 The Wise Nathan and the Bandit Spiegelberg: The Antinomies of Jewish Emancipation in Germany

The reciprocal relationships between early capitalism and Puritanism are clearly demonstrated in the events surrounding Shylock's return to England in the immediate wake of the bourgeois revolution of 1648. When the rabbi, printer, and diplomat Manasseh ben Israel applied to Oliver Cromwell for permission for Jews to enter the Lord Protector's Puritan republic, he produced strangely chiliastic arguments and citations that made a marked impression on Cromwell: according to messianic promise (Daniel XII, 7), the return of the Jews to their homeland in Palestine was prophesied for a time after their complete and utter dispersion throughout the world. But since England far off in the north refused so long to become a part of the Jewish diaspora, it was thereby obstructing the messianic promise. This was developed in Manasseh's work *The Hope of Israel,* which appeared in English translation in London in 1650.

Various writings by Puritans had preceded it, like that of the parliamentary secretary, Edward Nicholas, who in the year of the Stuart king's execution (1649) published in London "An Apology for the Honorable Nation of the Jews, and All the Sons of Israel." There now began to flourish a strange, extremely "philo-Semitic" literature of tractates and broadsheets, which in unabashed biblical faith and fervor, equated a manifest interest in the importation of Jewish capital with the discharge of divine precepts.[1]

From now on Shylock was English reality, not simply a stage figure put together out of rumor and poetry. At the same time a thoroughly new, realistic interpretation of the comedy about the merchant of Venice and his Jewish adversary could be envisioned. Shakespeare had, without knowing a great deal about Jews and their specific manners (providing Tubal, a Jew, with a thoroughly un-Jewish name, for example), nonetheless created a dramatic character concrete enough to be played and now to evoke the Jews of London in the Strand or Haymarket.

In the third of his letters from England, Georg Christoph Lichtenberg reports on December 2, 1775, on a performance of *The Merchant of Venice* with the actor Charles Macklin, an equal in fame to Garrick, as Shylock. Two things are to be deduced from this portrayal: that reality has now caught up with Shakespeare's vision and that in consequence the bourgeois proponent of the Enlightenment, Lichtenberg, is immediately confronted with all the contradictions called up by a monstrous outsiderdom of real Shylocks in a real England.

Lichtenberg perceives a schism between his Enlightenment creed and all his rationally uncontrollable feelings when he is riveted by Macklin's performance of Shylock and must admit that "seeing this Jew is more than sufficient, even in the most stalwart man, to reawaken all over again all the prejudices of childhood against this people. Shylock is not one of the talkative little sharpers who can spend an hour discussing the merits of a golden watch fob made of brass; he is unhurried, taciturn by way of immeasurable cleverness, and, where he is at one with the law, righteous to the point of evil."[2]

Apparently this theatergoer felt himself at a far remove from any sphere of the poetically wondrous, as people were wont to put it in the eighteenth century. For him Shylock is reality, Jewish reality, whose own particular mode of existence can be differentiated from the other well-known types common to Jewish life. He is not one of the only too familiar hawkers of secondhand goods and door-to-door peddlers, the little people among the Jews. Shylock, you see, is "unhurried" as a gentleman is wont to be, and "taciturn" like the respected and respectable businessmen among the Christians of England. Yet his polite distance, as Lichtenberg feels rather more than he distinguishes intellectually, is contrary to that of a wealthy and secure Everyman in every aspect. The similarity of his modes of behavior reveals all the more poignantly the utter divergence between Shylock in London and his English partners and adversaries.

In the play of his intuitions, feelings, opinions Lichtenberg only repeats embarrassingly cliché-ridden constructs. So once again "the prejudices of childhood" well up in him. The "stalwart man" catches himself in the theater suddenly mirroring the child's aversion for the Jews of the market square or in Jews' Alley, an aversion not merely against this clearly malignant Jew from the Rialto, as Lichtenberg does not fail to specify, but against "this people."

That is precisely the matter at hand: Shylock signifies in perpetuity a whole people in the condition of outsiders. The fear and repugnance of the theater audience—even if presented with a "noble" Shylock who rouses one's sympathy, a Shylock on the path of restitution as is not uncommon with modern productions of *The Merchant of Venice*—even here the pathetic and cheap emotions in Shylock's lament for Jessica are not directed at a single strange Iago or King Richard, but at a whole people: Shylock and his brethren.

Through Shylock the second fundamental contradiction of the bourgeois Enlightenment, next to the disparity of formal and material equality, gapes wide open: the dialectic of origins and transformation. If the Enlightenment actually means to act on its fundamental postulate of equality for everyone "with a human face," then it must accept the Jews in their differentness as a people with their own social heredity. This must occur along the lines of universal law, as the bourgeois legally constituted state would have it, whereby swindlers would be brought to trial as swindlers, not as Jewish swindlers.

The theory and practice of the Enlightenment was to attempt to solve the problem by raising the issue of Jewish assimilation. This meant renunciation of one's origins in favor of transformation, the reduction of a people to a religious community at best, total amalgamation if at all possible, just as the young Karl Marx set forth in "Concerning the Jewish Question." But this theory and practice has only repressed this dialectical contradiction, not resolved it. On this account *Nathan the Wise* could never supplant and counteract Shylock; it only demonstrated the inability of even significant bourgeois literature to displace the Jew Shylock from the consciousness of the enlightened European bourgeoisie. Lichtenberg's emotional reactions stand in witness.

It was only logical that the attempt to confront Shakespeare's figure with its literary opposite should come about in Germany. Jews, despite the recurrence of pogroms and expulsions, had always been a reality there, a consequence of the open borders to the East and the multitude of German ministates. In a speech on Germans and Jews delivered before the Jewish World Congress in Brussels in 1966, Gershom Scholem noted that "up until the second half of the 18th century, to some extent even beyond, Jews in Germany led essentially the same kind of life as Jews everywhere. They were clearly recognizable as their own nation; they possessed an unmistakable identity and their own history throughout the millennia."[3]

Yet in Germany two extreme social positions imprinted the general consciousness with its notions of Jews: the Jews at court and the Jews who received stolen goods. "But the economically strongest elements, as they manifested themselves in the phenomenon of Jewish factors at court, and the lowest groups communicating with the German underworld, had both to do with Germans in a way that constantly risked life and limb," Scholem continues.[4]

Appended to a book printed in Strasbourg in 1558, the *Liber vagatorum*, is a vocabulary "in *Rotwelsch*, a glossary of thieves' argot." It begins with the words "*adone* equals God" and "*achelen*—food." Two Hebrew terms for immediate use.

The curious philo-Semitism of the seventeenth century remained confined in Germany, much in contradistinction to England as might easily be deduced from the fundamentally different economic conditions, to an inconsequential theological and philosophical debate among scholars. The image of Jews as a social reality, on the other hand, was impregnated by the social triad of Jews at court, a petty bourgeoisie in the ghetto, and an impermeable German-Jewish underworld. This well-known scheme of things left its tracks in German literature up to the heyday of nineteenth-century liberalism, up to Gustav Freytag's novel *Debit and Credit*.

What was of more consequence, indeed dominant in the so-called Age of the Baroque in Germany, was not an abstract philo-Semitism, but an exceedingly concrete anti-Semitic malediction. A bitterly comic example in literature is found in *Die wunderbarlichen und wahrhaftigen Gesichte Philanders von Sittewald* (The Astonishing and True Visions of Philander von Sittewald), 1643, by Johann Michael Moscherosch. Moscherosch was war councillor in Hanau, a member of the consistory, a member of one of the philological societies, a satirist of Germanophilia (cf. *Sittewald*). In the ideology of the Germanophile Sittewald, shot through with yearnings for an restoration of the Middle Ages, there is a diabolical duality of Christian "commissarius," or merchant, and Jew.

Ein Kommissarius ohn Lohn
Ein Jud ohn Spott, Meineid und Hohn
Sind zwei Buben in einer Haut,
Der dritt, der diesen beiden traut.[5]*

---

*A commissarius without profit / a Jew without perjury, mockery, scorn / are two rascals of one mind / the third being him who trusts them both.

Comically enough, the evidence brought forward by the Baroque scholar Curt von Faber du Faur suggests that Moscherosch, who claimed descent from an ancient Spanish line of aristocrats, was operating with a faked family tree. Rather more likely it was a Jewish family, Rosch (head), the family Mosche ha Rosch, later converted to Christianity in Alsace, not that Moscherosch was ever ignorant of his real family origins! Faber du Faur therefore notes somewhat sarcastically that "this lineage of Moscherosch's has a most curious relation to his decidedly anti-Semitic vein. But then he possesses a wealth of such divisions; indeed, a contradiction between appearance and actuality, between ethical mandate and practical behavior is fundamentally characteristic of his being, even his Germanophilia is always somewhat forced."[6]

A strange case of Jewish self-hate, in the middle of the seventeenth century, a counterpart to the actions of the baptized Jew Pfefferkorn at the beginning of the sixteenth, against whom Johannes Reuchlin rose up in anger. Again and again the outsiderdom of the Jewish people came to be manifested via the typical reactions it provoked, as rational but impotent affirmation of the individual and irreducible particular; as emotional aggression; as a confusion of feelings in the individual who finds himself ejected into such an anomalous existence, something that can lead to self-hatred, a forced conformity, or to the acceptance of one's peculiarity.

No German writer of the Enlightenment occupied himself to greater purpose and with such logical consequence with this dialectic of the Enlightenment that Gotthold Ephraim Lessing. In his case there was no visible discrepancy, as with Lichtenberg, between the rational and emotional spheres. No one manifested a more rigorous goodwill or sharper acuity. That was particularly true for his play about the wise Nathan. "Out of gratitude for this high song of tolerance," Theodor Lessing wrote in his memoirs, "various Jewish families in those days in Prussia, Hannover, and Bavaria adopted the name Lessing."[7]

Just how much the play *Nathan the Wise* was interpreted, not only in Germany but in the broad reaches of Eastern Europe where people understood and were wont to read German, as the incarnation of Enlightenment, tolerance, and Jewish emancipation, is shown not only by the disfavor into which this work and indirectly its author fell from 1933 to 1945. As complement to that, immediately after the end of the war were the reactions in the four zones of occupation, when theater directors invested there, that is to say those who were not politically suspect, immediately set on the program, as if to cleanse and rededicate the house, this work with its ominous parable of the three rings, which had been silenced for so many years. Thus it was performed first for the men of the Soviet military administration in Berlin; Max Reinhardt's Deutsches Theater was provided absolution with Lessing's didactic drama of "pure tolerance." Elsewhere in the defeated and occupied *Reich* the same idea was popular; it was varied at times by substituting Goethe's *Iphigenia in Tauris* for Lessing's work but in no less bald miscomprehension of the work and the historical moment.

Lessing's earlier attempt at dealing with a Jewish thematic was entirely eclipsed by the fame he won with his play about the wise Jew, Nathan. Yet his *Lustspiel, The Jews,* a reflective comedy which bears the notice "composed in 1749" (when he was twenty) is anything but an insignificant piece of juvenilia to be relegated to graduate seminars and read there only because of the author's general importance. It is far more the case that this one-act play written by a young man who understood there could be no Enlightenment without including a foreign people who wore caftans, lent money, sold goods at the fair, and received stolen property, was more far-reaching and more acutely argumentative than the play about the wise Nathan. Young Lessing conceived it as a *Denkspiel,* an intellectual drama confronting ideas. His own emotion was not (yet) heavily invested. His acquaintanceship with Moses Mendelssohn did not come about until 1754, a consequence, to a great extent, of that play about the Jews. Lessing's *Lustspiel* has one act, in correct dramatic understanding that a static situation on the stage—one of the characters is a Jew, the others are not and are much more nearly openly anti-Semitic—has to be unfolded and exemplified in a single action without distraction and secondary plot.[8]

A one-act play that is a *Lustspiel.* Lessing's technical naiveté arises far less from his lack of stage experience than from a profound misconception of the Jewish question as a central theme around which the dialectic of the Enlightenment has to be worked out. A consequence of his misconception is that the dramatist treats his material as if he were dealing with a mental or emotional outsiderdom in the manner of the French comedy of types. The miser, the hypochondriac, the inveterate liar, the misanthrope or misogynist, the bookworm or boastful man of letters: the comedy of types has, since Molière, been in the habit of announcing in the title the particular manner of outsider who is going to be the butt of universal wit and who in the course of a predestined turn of events with servants, nurses, reasonable and unreasonable people, is to be brought to surrender his eccentricities.

That was how the young playwright Lessing handled his *Free Thinker*, which was also written in 1749.[9] The concluding point of *The Jews* is to be found almost word for word in this other play, which also deals with struggles against prejudice and confronts an "inauthentic" libertine with a no less inauthentic, thoroughly enlightened and tolerant cleric. The free thinker Adrastus is shamed: "Heavens! If I err everywhere as I have with you, Theophanus . . ." If only all clerics were so openminded. Theophanus's answer is in the same vein: if only all free thinkers were as sensible in recognizing the errors of their ways as Herr Adrastus.

The Jews concludes with: "Oh, how worthy of respect the Jews would be if they only were all like you!" The baron and anti-Semite says that. To which the nameless traveler rejoins: "And how amiable the Christians, if only they all possessed your character!" Behind all of this is more than an Enlightenment schematism that would just as soon subsume all exceptions in one general principle. A most personal characteristic of Lessing's, his Aristotelianism, becomes manifest in the rejection of all excessive intellectual and spiritual positions, in the return to the mean, which encompasses both the one and the other. But the attempt to deal analogously with libertinage and the problematic of the Jews, with the help of stage demonstrations of the supposed outsiders' exceptional behavior, whereby their integration into the community of the "rule" is facilitated, is erroneous. The outsiderdom of the Jews is not a mental spleen, still less an emotional idiosyncrasy, as was the case, say, with the young Lessing's *Misogynist*. It was an existential given in the society of those days and consequently unresolvable.

After the traveler relinquishes his anonymity and brings to naught any possibility of marriage and friendship with the simple sentence, "I am a Jew," the unsuspecting baroness, who loves him, is alone in stammering "Oh! What does that mean?" She is immediately reprimanded by her lady's maid, "Tush, Miss, tush, I will tell you later what it means."

Indeed, it means a great deal. Not least dramatically by having this bright one-act play, set up by Lessing, wrongly, after the fashion of a comedy of types, end as though "en queue de poisson"; there is nothing there of the obligatory marriage, that time-honored recipe for ending such *Lustspiele*; there are laws, you see, which formally interdict marriage not only between bourgeois and aristocrat, but particularly between Christian and Jew.

The dramatist could not fail here with his properties taken from the world of the *Lustspiel*. The speculative proponent of the Enlightenment, Lessing, on the other hand, has at the same time accomplished an astonishing task. By revealing against his will how little "the Jews" can be integrated into a communality with the other exceptions, he makes it evident that any endeavor on the part of the Enlightenment toward Jewish emancipation has got to distinguish between *general prejudice* against Jews, nourished by the sight of those who live in the *real* ghetto, and the rigorous postulate of universal equality and the equality of rights of all men, including Jews. Lessing is incapable of placing the Jewish hawker from the ghetto on the stage as an object of demonstration, who is then the speaker and actor of perfected human love, as was the case with his traveler.

The conflict is only heightened by Lessing's seeking to diminish that figure's reality as "a Jew who does not look like one and who is not taken for one." Recent scholarship has rightly pointed to the parallels between Lessing's *The Jews* and Max Frisch's parable play *Andorra*.[10] In Lessing someone who is a Jew is not taken for one, something that makes possible all the *Lustspiel* entanglements that are without solution. In Frish someone who is not a Jew is taken for one and treated correspondingly with fatal consequences.

Yet another astonishing anticipation is to be found in the young Lessing's one-act drama: the sober presentation of the social conditions under which alone the postulate of Jewish emancipation could be realized, namely via property and education. The traveler has both: he is educated and rich. In him, Lessing has outlined the intellectual prototype of the bourgeois Shylock later so well known to the nineteenth century. Thus all later social contradictions, especially the conflict between Jewish master and Christian servant, have already been anticipated.

"Ten years ago when someone said people don't notice that I'm a Jewess, you shot back, sure they do. That's what's so good about it, the clarity." This is the Jewish wife speaking in her interior monlogue with her "aryan" husband in Brecht's *Fear and Misery of the Third Reich*. It is this clarity that Lessing avoids. The path Shylock and his brethren had to traverse from the eighteenth to the twentieth century, through bourgeois Enlightenment and counter-Enlightenment, can be measured from here.

It remained for the author of *The Jews* to be convinced soon after the publication of his early theatrical works, that one-acter among them, that his attempt to broaden the thematic of the comedy of types with its scheme of making prejudice ludicrous, in truth had arrived at the outer limits of bourgeois illumination, at least in Germany.

J. D. Michaelis, a professor of oriental languages at the University of Göttingen, father of the later Karoline Schlegel, colleague of Lichtenberg's, friend of Georg Forster, and helpful patron of Carsten Niebuhr's explorations of *arabia deserta,* was certainly a proponent of the Enlightenment as much as Lessing and Lichtenberg and anything but a man of prejudice and vulgar collective emotions. His criticism of Lessing's one-act play has to be weighed, therefore, very seriously. It has to do with exactly what welled up in Lichtenberg's emotions vis-à-vis Shylock that day in the theater: the appearance of the monstrous in any attempt at Jewish emancipation.

As a reviewer of Lessing's plays, which he generally finds inordinately well done, Michaelis, in an article in the *Göttingen'sche Anzeigen von gelehrten Sachen,* critically dissects the figure of the Jewish traveler. It naturally does not escape him that Lessing had once again been inspired by a literary model, not by another author's play for a change but by a most successful novel of those days that gave rise to many tears, *The Life of the Swedish Countess G . . . ,* by Christian Fürchtegott Gellert. Lessing had become acquainted with it when he was still in Leipzig, where the book appeared in 1746–1748, a year before *The Jews.* In Gellert's work as well one finds the description of the exemplary humanity of a noble Jew, here living under marvelously adventurous but scarcely credible circumstances in a far-off Siberian camp where he is held prisoner. Michaelis does not hesitate in his review to raise the objection, against both Gellert and Lessing, that through their excessive idealism they more likely than not damage the case of universal brotherly love. Lessing for his part, when he undertakes writing a detailed reply in 1754, cannot refrain from citing Michaelis's objections at length in order to refute them. Lessing's tone, as Michaelis's had been, is friendly, trusting, almost hearty: Professor Michaelis is a comrade of the spirit, not a Professor Klotz or a Pastor Goeze.

Michaelis had objected that

the unknown traveler is in all respects so thoroughly good, so nobly minded, so careful to do his neighbor no wrong, . . . educated, so that while it is not impossible, it is exceedingly unlikely that such a noble temperament could have come to be formed among a people whose fundamental beliefs, way of life, and education color their dealings with

Christians all too noticeably with animosity, or at least with a decidedly cold reckoning against Christians. This improbability is a hindrance to our pleasure, the more so that we wish this noble and lovely image had truth and reality to it. But even run-of-the-mill virtue and honesty are so rarely to be found among this people that the few examples that are in truth to be found cannot diminish as much as one would like the hatred felt against them.

Lessing cites everything openly and at length when he makes reply in 1754 in his magazine *Die theatralische Bibliothek*.[11] He considered this text, "Concerning the *Lustspiel The Jews* in the Fourth Part of Lessing's Works," important enough to be included in the collected works. His argumentation goes after Michaelis's two critical points: the figure of the traveler lacking concreteness and his immanent improbability. Lessing counters with respect to his faithfulness at depicting reality, by adjoining a letter that one Jew wrote another Jew about the play. This document shows "that there do exist and can exist such Jews as the traveler." The letter was authentic. Moses Mendelssohn had written it to the physician Aaron Samuel Gumpertz in Berlin.

More important is Lessing's argumentation concerning the possibility of a Jew, under the given conditions of Jewish life, developing into a philanthropist after the manner of the traveler. Here he argues via wealth and education. He cannot, of course, contest the fact that the Jews find themselves in a condition of "contempt and suppression" and are prevented by law from living by any other means than commerce. Yet does that mean it is inconceivable for someone to free himself from this condition and act in ways similar to those of the traveler in *The Jews*? Lessing answers: "Would it be the case, not a necessary consequence, that this improbability disappears as soon as the conditions that give rise to it cease?" Already we have the manner of argumentation of the wise Nathan (and of many Jewish thinkers) and of Lessing: to pose the answer to a question as a counterquestion. But how would a Jew come to be in a position to raise himself up over the necessities of general Jewish life?

Lessing's answer to Professor Michaelis in the year 1754 already has all the earmarks of subsequent bourgeois Enlightenment in Germany: the forgoing of any larger solution for the sake of an individual one; one's own direction taken toward the wealthier bourgeoisie; a league between the upper bourgeoisie and the intellectual elite. It finds its articulation in the following: "What else is necessary to this end but wealth? And the proper application of that wealth, needless to say. One has only to look to see if I have not brought both into play in the character of my Jew. He has means; he says it straight out that the God of his fathers has given him more than he needs; I have him travel; indeed, I exempt him from ignorance, in which one might suppose him, and the companions of his voyages are his books."

It is part and parcel of Lessing's concept of education and that of the proponents of European Enlightenment in general, that books, if they are to produce bourgeois education, are for the most part understood as works of belles lettres. On which account the unlettered Christian servant of the Jewish traveler makes fun of the heavy bags of so-called fine letters.

The conclusion? Wealth and education, as in the case of the traveler, are a means of emancipating Jews from that sphere where they are met with prejudice and suppression. As someone who knows Jews well, Lessing believes himself able to hazard the conclusion: "To be sure, one must, in order to believe this, be better acquainted with Jews than simply with the ragtag riffraff that pokes about on fair day."

A bourgeois Shylock is postulated; he becomes the purpose and task of individual emancipation. The other possibility, that of changing the laws relating to Jews, thereby motivating them as a whole to find other social realms for themselves, does not cross the mind of either the Göttingen professor and proponent of the Enlightenment, Michaelis or his partner in dialogue, the author of *The Jews*, Lessing. How appropriate, since even formal and legal emancipation in the course of the French Revolution turned out to be a conjunction of Jewish equality of rights and the economic necessity for Jews to take charge of the economically indispensable functions of commerce and finance. The Polish kings and Russian czars as well did not support the immigration of Jews in order to bring craftsmen or large-scale farmers into the country, but only to entice an easily tapped capital that would not be bound up with all the difficulties presented by tapping the capital of the propertied independent bourgeoisie resident in the cities.

If the faith in wealth and education on the part of German proponents of the Enlightenment corresponded to general rationalistic premises that admitted no doubts of successfully coming to terms, even with the strange exceptional existence of the Jews, by means of the general antitheses of prejudice and rational persuasion, then in hindsight, the Jewish impulses to emancipation can be seen only as an ambivalence of hope and fear. The Zionist Jochanan Bloch has provided an almost brutally hard, yet historically not unrevealing, analysis of these premises.[12] The thesis that reason is capable of bringing about reconciliation was the starting point from which the goal would have to be reached, "even if there were again and again aberrations originating in the sensually chaotic and unreasoned class." Indeed, such argumentation is to be found not only in *The Jews*, but even more broadly in *Nathan the Wise*: the reasoned dialogue of Sultan, rich and wise Jew and aristocratic knight Templar, who is both things at once, Christian and Moslem, Oriental and German, the quintessence of tolerance and material serenity. What is excluded from this communion is the patriarch's orthodoxy and the servant's rustic simplicity.

Jochanan Bloch counters that "this belief fully ignores the direness of the oppositions involved. It is in consequence evolutionary, aspires to no revolution, and lacks the minutest sense for the advent of catastrophe and its fateful necessity. Yet for all its modesty it is arrogant vis-à-vis the dimension of concrete reality over which it has so little control and understanding. To its credit I would add that this arrogance has its origins in fear." Such diction may not be pleasant. And the line of thought does not necessarily stand on a surer footing with "concrete reality" than was the case with those Jews who succeeded to Moses Mendelssohn in abandoning—more and more consciously and totally—Jewish identity for the sake of German nationality. That the alternatives today bear the names Auschwitz and Israel should not mislead one into believing that in the eighteenth century Jews in Germany ever had a real, "concrete" alternative between bourgeois-German emancipation and Jewish messianism. The phantasmagorias of Moritz Spiegelberg in Schiller's *Robbers,* something I shall take up presently, proffered no antitype to Nathan and Lessing's message of tolerance.

And yet, as early as 1779, the year it appeared, a close and attentive reading of the dramatic poem *Nathan the Wise,* beyond all musicality and humanity, would have discovered the friability of its argumentative and social premises.[13] Nathan, too, just like the traveler from the repertory of the very young Lessing, is rich and wise at once. Daja, in all her simple prejudice, is aghast that the Jews speak so much of Nathan's wisdom and not of his wealth. To which the knight Templar (himself as yet prejudiced) sarcastically replies: "Rich and wise is to his people/Perhaps the same thing" (I, 6). Property and wisdom make Nathan the partner of sultan and knight. But perhaps only on the very surface of things? At the operatic apotheosis at the end, where everyone seems to be the close relation of everyone else, a unified humanity under the sun of reason, Nathan is left empty-handed. He is related to no one. Saladin and Sittah, Recha and her brother: all blood relatives spanning Orient and Occident. The Jew Nathan is a friend, he has their gratitude, he will always be welcome, yet he remains an outsider—like Shylock in Venice.

The dramatic technique of this poem for the stage, as surprising as it may seem, compares favorably to the threefold religious division found in Marlowe's *Jew of Malta*. The Jew Barabas in Malta possessed the sole function of accommodating the third of the world religions to the atheist Marlowe's all-encompassing distrust of ideology. He scarcely could distinguish himself with any peculiarly Jewish characteristics. Lessing's Nathan is also to a large extent simply abstraction; only his famous narration of a pogrom (IV, 7) conjoins his life to general conditions of life for Jewry; otherwise Nathan represents the Enlightenment generally, not any particular Jewish version of it. His characteristic means of expression in question and counterquestion is something he has in common with his author. Above all, Nathan's Jewishness is interpreted by Lessing, something intimately connected with the central concept of the play, as religion and not as nationality. Whereby a *petitio principi* has occurred: at the beginning of Jewish enlightened emancipation Lessing, in the figure of Nathan, has already anticipated the desired end result. Nathan is a Jew purely as a matter of religion, and he himself considers this religion fortuitous and interchangeable:

> Both of us
> Did not choose our people.
> Are we our people? What does people mean?
> Are Christian and Jew more Christian and Jew
> Than they are human being?   (II, 5)

Saladin expostulates:

> I have never demanded
> That one bark grow round all the trees.   (IV, 4)

What Nathan does, meant for the eyes of the Templar, this agent of Christian action, is what he himself sees as the manifestation of a Jewish ethics.

The interchangeability that is posited as toleration, as pure tolerance, is at one only in the skepticism common to sultan, knight, and rich and wise Jew vis-à-vis the social relevance of the established religions. This is precisely the significance of the parable of the rings. On this account the dramatist Lessing was obliged to choose a form that very artfully juggles reality and possibility. The dramatic poem about the wise Nathan is simultaneously a fable and a parable. In its interpretation Günther Rohrmoser has asserted: "Tolerance is for Lessing a concept of struggle that makes it possible for him to break through a situation of theological sterility into a realm that is religiously productive."[14] Yet it is simply the case that the positions taken by Nathan and his partners provide no vindication for such a thesis. Rohrmoser is in the right, however, when he remarks of the dramaturgy of *Nathan the Wise*: "Only by means of a unified ordering through the form of the dramatic poem is the fable able to preserve its character of reality; if it is taken into view independently of its function, then its character as parable, as possibility, comes to light."[15]

But even in Lessing's artful attempt to represent as already accomplished what still waits to be done, to present anticipation as reality, there again and again come to the surface signs of the difficulty of the task, originating not merely in the plebeian incomprehension of a Daja or the prejudice of the patriarch, but in the conflict between reason and one's own private interest. The Templar provides a sobering example. He had agreed to a compact of toleration with Nathan out of respect; now intrigue gives him to understand that Nathan has apparently acted contrary to the Templar's own best interests.

> He is discovered.
> The tolerant mumbler is discovered!
> I'll set upon this Jewish wolf
> In philosophical sheepskin
> Dogs to tear his hide! (IV, 4)

Whoever reads this passage or hears it declaimed from the stage and is not thoroughly jolted in the light of subsequent experience, but lets all his attentions be captivated by the aria of the ring parable, diminishes the generous and hopeless attempt by Lessing to extricate Shylock (as Nathan) from his extraordinary life with the help of wealth and educated humanity and transform him into an Everyman who merely happens to practice a somewhat antiquated though venerable religion. Then indeed pure tolerance changes over into its repressive variety.

In the didactic fairytale of *Nathan the Wise,* in the ambivalence between reality and possibility, all societal concreteness is purposely left out. One finds oneself among wealthy people who manifestly practice tolerance only among themselves. Herbert Marcuse speaks of the "background limitations of tolerance," which in the societal process transform all "pure" tolerance into a repressive instrument of domination as long as tolerance is unable to be practiced with no distinction and with the same effectiveness "by the rulers as well as by the ruled, by the lords as well as by the peasants, by the sheriffs as well as by their victims."[16] Lessing's greatness here stems, as in the fairytale cheerfulness of *Minna von Barnhelm,* as in the theoretically and practically flawed plan of the *Hamburg Dramaturgy,* from the necessary breakdown of his attempt. He established Jewish emancipation as an irrevocable constituent of the Enlightenment. Insofar as he also understood such liberation and equality to be one of wealth and education, he was simply acting in compliance with the requirements of capitalist evolution on the one hand; on the other, he founded tolerance on a postulate of intolerance. That is to say, equality for Shylock and his brethren is conceived only at the cost of abandoning their nationality, the ground of existential individuality in European society since the beginning of the Christian era. Historical development has given Lessing the lie both in his sundering of reality and rumor in *The Jews* and in his concept of the interchangeability of religions under the sign of reasoned discourse among the wealthy and ruling class (*Nathan the Wise*). Shylock, however, embodies no problem of a religious nature, but together with his kind, stands at odds to the bourgeois Enlightenment. He can neither be incorporated nor done away with by Lessing's and Kant's "humanity." What he signifies for all formal Enlightenment is a blurred and blurry phenomenon.

In a curious yet for him typical misapprehension of Lessing's drama of compromise, of a universal tolerance as well as its evasion through presupposition, Friedrich Schiller criticized the dramatic poem about the wise Nathan for being a tragedy that has failed. In his treatise *Concerning Naive and Sentimental Poetry,* he says disdainfully: "Here the frosty nature of the material has frozen the whole work of art. . . . Without the most fundamental changes it would scarcely be possible to rewrite this dramatic poem as a good tragedy; but with only accidental changes it might make a good comedy."[17]

It is evident that Schiller has missed Lessing's intention. The form of the drama, he says, is only appropriate to tragedy, yet Lessing as a tragic poet "has had the fancy . . . to work on . . . a theoretical material." When Schiller passes judgment on *Nathan* as a failed tragical conception, we seem to be learning more about Friedrich Schiller's poetics than anything else, for the moment at least. What is of considerable note is the chronological interval between the composition of *Nathan the Wise* (1779) and the appearance of Friedrich Schiller's treatise in 1795.

Not even two full decades lie between them, yet all the phases of the French Revolution from the storming of the Bastille to Thermidor are encompassed there. In this passage of time the metamorphosis of one of the cornerstones of the bourgeois Enlightenment apparently took place; I mean Jewish emancipation into a phenomenon of only aesthetic relevance. Schiller grasps *Nathan the Wise* exclusively as "a theoretical material" like any other. A not especially good dramatic subject: unsuited for tragedy; in a pinch, but not without essential formal changes, utilizable in the realm of comedy.

This process of aestheticization must not be interpreted as an individual response on the part of Schiller to Lessing. What we see here is a new social declaration. Lessing's deism appears obsolete to one who has read *The Critique of Pure Reason*. Legal and apparently also social equality for Jews had been achieved in France as early as in the beginning of the Revolution. Schiller was in full agreement with that process, whereby for him the essentially tragic substance became lost to the material. Historical thinking was not the forte of the historian Schiller. In his reflections on history, as elsewhere, his pleasure in tragic objects proved an impediment.

That was, however, all the stranger in the case of *Nathan the Wise,* since Schiller at the start of his career as a writer had shown himself not at all untouched by the peculiarities of Jewish life in the Germany of those days. This critic of Lessing and of his dramatic poem himself as playwright had essayed a confrontation between Jewish monstrosity and Christian social rule.

The youthful Schiller's enciphered yet scarcely mistakable attempt to confront Moritz Spiegelberg in *The Robbers* with both the *ancien régime* and the protest movement of the *Sturm und Drang* can be taken as a literary concretization of the Jewish alternative to Nathan, namely, the antithesis of Jewish messianism to the emancipatory tenets of the bourgeois Enlightenment.[18]

It is quite unmistakable that Moritz Spiegelberg, the only one of the robbers who is mentioned by both first and last name, has a "Jewish coloration," as Gerhard Storz puts it.[19] The strange, apologetic attempts of earlier scholarship to deny it remain unconvincing if one follows the text closely, especially if one takes to hand the "suppressed quarto" which has been accidentally preserved, and which contains the original version of the first scene between Karl Moor and Moritz Spiegelberg. Moritz was a name typical for assimilated Jews, retaining at one and the same time an echo of the original form Mosche or Moses.

In the exceedingly harmonious architecture of *The Robbers,* in that ordered balance from Kosinsky to Karl, from Spiegelberg to Franz Moor, there grows up out of all preformed proportions the strangely opaque Moritz who is uncommonly difficult to situate socially, religiously, and, in particular, intellectually. Twice in the final introduction to his play Schiller speaks of the three extraordinary people who "cannot be laid bare within a space of twenty-four hours, not even by the most prescient and acute psychologist." And then only two of them are extensively analyzed, Franz and Karl. Who is the third extraordinary person in the play? Only Spiegelberg can be meant. But here the young author guards against any nearer definition.

Although in the printed version the first talk between Karl and Moritz "in a tavern on the border of Saxony," confronts the *Sturm und Drang* proponent Karl with his "ink-splotching century," Spiegelberg remaining reduced to a few scurrilous interjections and ripostes, playing more the funmaker than evincing any intellectual partnership, the scene as it was originally written is completely the reverse.[20] Spiegelberg there pawns a stolen watch with the innkeeper to order Hungarian wine for his table, and a drinking bout with Karl commences; from the very beginning there is a buildup of biblical motifs, particularly from the Old Testament, to fuel the progress of the scene: from the "scribblings" on the tavern wall about the prodigal son, to the biblical motif of Tobias, to Spiegelberg's grotesque depictions of a new state of Israel. "We will once more come together in the valley of Jehoshaphat, chase the Turks out of Asia, and rebuild Jerusalem. All the old customs will be taken out of storage. The Ark of the Covenant will be glued together again. The New Testament will be voted out. We will all wait for the Messiah, either you, or I, or one of the two of us. . . ."[21]

Karl's laughter is warded off; Spiegelberg is serious. "We'll put a tax on pork; whoever wants to eat the stuff can pay, and pay through the nose. In the meantime we'll have cedar cut in Lebanon, build shops, and hawk old selvage and clasps, all of us."

Karl Moor immediately understands that the ambiguous phraseology about the future messiah does not have an alternative in mind but means to evoke Moritz Spiegelberg as the Messiah. On which account he replies dryly: "What a pristine nation! What a pristine king!"

It is a dialogue all helter-skelter. The cultural worlds and the resultant images used by the two student companions, the count's son and Moritz (who is possibly already baptized, yet "strangely circumcised in advance") diverge to their very foundations. Moor bases himself on Plutarch's great men, on the rebellious Satan from Milton's *Paradise Lost,* on the classical rebels of antiquity and the Renaissance as seen in his day: Catiline and Cesare Borgia. Spiegelberg does not acknowledge the devil as an adversary of equal rank as in the poetry of the English revolution, he sees him only as the horned and goat-footed creature of popular superstition.[22] His dreams are retrogressive: he wishes to rebuild the biblical kingdoms of Israel and Judah in the valley of Jehoshaphat, but reckons, in a peculiar mixture of chiliasm and political-economic realism, with the Turks, with legal and military maneuvers. Ultimately the plan for banding together as robbers derives from the wondrous mind of this man whom Schiller decks out with many Jewish characteristics, yet, not even between the first and second printed version, without ever clearly declaring him.

In his study "The Strange Case of Moritz Spiegelberg," the American Germanist Philipp F. Veit has pointed to the function of this Jewish messianism in a play that again and again and on all levels, alongside the underlying phenomenon of revolt and libertine excess, incorporates theological concepts stemming from the circle around Albrecht Bengel.[23] In these theological concepts of eighteenth-century Germany, the tenet of a common Christian and Jewish salvation assumes decisive importance. In such visions of salvation, understood as socially real so that secret correspondences tie Pastor Moser to the robber chief Moor, only Franz Moor and Spiegelberg (ignoring the caricature of the Catholic curate) are excluded from the spiritual communality. That is to say, only the atheist and feudal libertine and the chiliastic Jew are excluded. Spiegelberg is anything but a caricature. Veit alludes to his prototypes in the Jewish adventurers, illuminati, and bandit chieftains in the eighteenth century, particularly in southern Germany. The messianic adventurer Jakob Frank, who had many adepts among both Christians and Jews, died in Offenbach in 1791.[24] Lessing's brother Karl, in a letter of October 26, 1769, apparently alluding to Frank, refers to such "ecstatic confusions of a Polish Jew."[25]

Spiegelberg is no caricature but, rather, a figure caught in the conflict of speculative daring and physical anxiety, the equality of fellowship in the tavern with the count's son and the voluntary/involuntary jester's role of the foolish outsider. His chiliasm is nourished by the longing for a return to Jerusalem and the resumption of ancient custom. The question being, what will they do after their victory there? "And hawk old selvage and clasps, all of us."

If only our broken-down libertine and subsequent bandit had at least been seriously fixed to his postulations of a rebirth of Jewish messianism. But as he vacillates between books, between religions, between places where he might belong in society, so too does he vacillate between the excesses of messianism and those of bourgeois assimilation. Spiegelberg's dreams do not merely encompass the notion of a savior in the Orient; he is evidently thinking of a messiah for both Christians and Jews since the New Testament will be "voted out." At the same time he is dreaming for himself the career of a Jewish adviser to the mighty in the oriental world: "And Spiegelberg will be the name in East and West, and in the mire with you, you yellow bellies, you toads, while Spiegelberg with outspread wings soars up to the temple of fame and posterity" (I, 2).

A double succession is insinuated here that is only conceivable as an either/or. It was characterized in the seventeenth and eighteenth centuries by the two unhappy Jewish figures Sabbatai Zevi and Jew Süss Oppenheimer. Spiegelberg means to consummate both at once. Schiller portrays with dramatic logical consequence, quite without antipathy, more likely fascinated by the case, the miserable end of one who turned into a bandit and murderer only to be eliminated by his own kind.

The dramatic poem of the wise Nathan ended with serenity, arialike. Nonetheless Nathan stayed on the outside. Spiegelberg, in all his phantasms, stood closer to Jewish reality than Nathan. That is to say, he was not rich. So he vacillates between a Jewish/messianic existence in the nation where he was born and a sensational upstartism with the others. The wise Nathan and the robber Spiegelberg: in such confrontation, at the very beginning of the bourgeois Enlightenment in Germany, the perspectives are set for Shylock in the European bourgeois world of the nineteenth century.

20 The Bourgeois Shylock

Rothschild and Heine

In his own interpretation of the *Lustspiel The Jews,* Lessing had made the assimilation of this foreign people and religious community dependent on two preconditions: education and property. Those concerned were already cognizant of the matter. Prosperity was widespread in the German Jewish enclaves, which is to say in the ghettoes and not merely among the factors at court and those Jews protected by royal or imperial decree. The stringent commandments of compassion and charity in Mosaic law made sure that even the little peddlers, including the tramps, had a bearable life. The enjoinder for education was also taken seriously in the Jewish community. The passage from prayerhouse and schoolhouse to an intense occupation with German letters and science as emphasized by Moses Mendelssohn took place without difficulty.

The conditions for Jewish emancipation posited by Lessing were all too easily fulfilled. When in the wake of the French Revolution and the Code Napoléon with its stipulations of equality for all citizens, extensive debates on the quantity and quality of Jewish emancipation were held, culminating in the deliberations of the National Assembly in the Paulskirche in Frankfurt (1848–49), new arguments became public that saw in Lessing's premises more a hindrance than the precondition of a possibility. Lessing as philosopher and dramatic writer had always considered the danger of tragedy to be where what is in itself praiseworthy exceeds its bounds and becomes excessive. The too exaggerated bravery of Hercules, the too passionate need for knowledge of Dr. Faustus, even the too great virtuousness of Sara Sampson or Emilia Galotti.

Now German Jewry, from the start of the nineteenth century assuming the habit of the bourgeoisie, represented a double excessiveness. The stipulation of prosperity was met by a hypertrophy of wealth and property. The precept of learning was fulfilled and overfulfilled in excessive fashion—hypertrophy of knowledge and intellectuality. There soon coalesced in Germany a polemical antitype, that of the too rich and too clever Jew. Even Moses Mendelssohn's daughter, Dorothea Veit, later Dorothea Schlegel (Friedrich Schlegel's wife and a convert to Catholicism), encountered this hatred and scorn. Objections were raised against Friedrich Schlegel's novel *Lucinde* by churchmen and laymen alike that it was immoral because of its open and honest dialogue of letters between two lovers who are manifestly not married; in addition there arose an emotional argument, which said: besides, the female partner of this regrettable correspondence is of Jewish extraction.

The National-German, Christian, and petit bourgeois reservations vis-à-vis the principles of Enlightenment and Jewish emancipation found their consummate fulfillment when Harry Heine debuted as poet and polemicist. Armed with nothing more than a baptismal certificate, an immense talent, and a no less immense faith in the validity and persuasive powers of the maxims of the Enlightenment, he immediately encountered enemies along the way who multiplied without cease, even long after his death. In the case of Heinrich Heine, every contradiction to bourgeois Enlightenment in Germany broke open. This writer came to learn that not only the sometime forces of reaction—monarchy, aristocracy, Jesuits, Lutheran pastors—were arrayed against him. As with Lichtenberg in London viewing Shylock on the stage and finding his true feelings at odds with the well-meaning yet scarcely anchored principles of the Enlightenment, so then did the phenomenon of Heine bring confusion into the camp of the progressive bourgeoisie. Even the adherents of Young Germany, who were wont to define themselves proudly as the carriers of the *Zeitgeist,* became unsure when they read Heine's writings. Was the Jews' emancipation at all well advised if it meant such excesses by a Jewish talent?

It always pleased Heine, and he had need of this simplification as an article of his Enlightenment faith, to attack and denounce the anti-Semitism of the Germanophiles (*Deutschtümler*) as simple social and political reaction. Yet he was mistaken. The dialectic of the Enlightenment manifested itself in a Germany of declining estates and unborn classes (to use Marx's description) in that students' and gymnasts' movement as well. Progression and regression were to be found simultaneously in that mixture of Christian German Romanticism and embittered Francophobia. The controversy over anti-Semitism and "Germanomania" that came to the surface soon after the Wars of Liberation* was symptomatic.

This controversy is bound up with an otherwise forgotten Jewish writer, Dr. Saul Ascher, whom Heine knew personally and has mentioned in a friendly fashion. Ascher's work *Germanomania* (1815)[1] can be seen as the first attempt after the defeat of Napoleon, in all of Germany, but particularly in the Protestant North, to counter the strains of a fashionable Romantic Germanophilia with the arguments of an ideology of tolerance. Lutheran Christianity and Germanic-messianic missionary zeal espied in the non-German, especially in the Frenchman and Jew, antitypes to be zealously combated. Once again progression and regression at the same time. This was a movement encompassing Germany as a whole and was consequently directed against the particularism of the ruling princelings who in the period of the Rheinbund, with their bootlicking toward Napoleon in the Erfurt Congress, had once again presented themselves as an impediment to a politics of national unification. The cult around the prebourgeois Middle Ages (as they were understood then at any rate) and of a supposedly pro-German and antiuniversalist Lutheranism (which had actually first made that particularism of the princelings possible) was contravened by the modern Enlightenment with its abstract demands for equality for all people, as well as by the nascent, no less abstract, money economy. Jews had a part and interest in both. The ideological, political, and military liberation movement against the French occupation, in consequence, was hostile to Jews and Enlightenment from the start. The formulas of the Virtue League of 1814, the students' and gymnasts' movement after 1815, like the slogan "All traitors to the Courts for Summary Justice!" (*Feme*), were assumed in the twentieth century into the verbal and ritual inventory of the SS.

Ascher proposed to work against this flood of what he took to be a German feverishness, or Germanomania. His work was read and furiously rejected by the youthful followers of *Turnvater* Jahn, the founder the German gymnastics movement. The famous, or infamous, Congress of Germanophiles on the Wartburg in October 1817, where the jubilee of the Lutheran Reformation of 1517 was celebrated and the victory over Napoleon at Leipzig (October 19, 1813) memorialized, had as its high point an auto-da-fé of reprehensible books, notwithstanding the Catholic ritual nature of such zealous burnings. Here too an ambivalence in the

---

*Against the French occupation and hegemony established by Napoleon (translator's note).

points of view taken. A cane used for flogging in the army and a pigtail were consigned to the flames in rejection of the princelings' mercenary armies and in acknowledgement of civil rights for all and as a memorial to the notion in revolutionary France of a nation at arms. At the very same time, however, the Napoleonic law books were also thrown onto the pyre, the quintessence in those days of a modern codex of human and civil rights.

Ascher's little book *Germanomania* also went up in flames amidst catcalls because, so they claimed, he had asserted in it that the German victory over Napoleon had been won only with the help of Jewish volunteers. That was something easily scorned and mocked. Ascher, arguing against a Germanophile by the name of Rühs, had simply written that Rühs as a fanatical Germanophile had neglected to take into account that "Germany's armies lost in the war against France until the Jews took part in it," he forgot that the German armies first tasted victory only after "the Jews from Russia, Poland, Austria, and Prussia came to stand in their ranks."[2]

Even a more exact reading of Dr. Ascher's argumentation would not have helped his cause. He was probably not aware how much he, precisely as a proponent of the Enlightenment, was doomed. How so? Ascher cavils against the notion of German unity but for his own part does not for an instant hesitate to speak of "the Jews from Russia, Poland, Austria, and Prussia," conjuring up, it would seem, a national and not merely religious community—just as the Germanophiles, but with exact contrary valuation, were forever positing.

He must have noticed the schism himself, for three years later, in a pamphlet meant to counter the incidents on the Wartburg, he returns to the subject. "The Festivities on the Wartburg in View of Germany's Religious and Political Atmosphere"[3] is more cautious in its formulation: "I simply represent the Jew, not the Jews, just as it would be permissible for me to represent man but not all men. One should not believe that I absolve my people of all guilt. They are human beings, replete with all the virtues and vices that heaven has implanted in the breast of the whole species."[4] It is certainly not a matter of quibbling to say that Ascher's text can only be called remarkably unclear; it all serves rather as confirmation of the antinomies already present in Jewish emancipation in Germany in its decisive early stage. On the one hand, he forgoes any claim to speak for a Jewish community, however that is to be defined; on the other, the formulation "my people" presupposes a national community anew.

The Bourgeois Shylock

Ascher provides evidence enough in his new work of the obstacles facing Jewish emancipation in everyday life. In Frankfurt a Germano-phile bookdealer protested against bookdealer concessions being given to "people of the Jewish faith." Ascher does not even dare to specify the city of Frankfurt by name. In Dresden 150 Jewish families were granted permission to take up habitation in the city, "but not a single means of livelihood has been granted or assigned them."[5]

Ascher's new work is especially impressive in its concluding section, which critically appraises the Romantic school. In contrast, Heine's book, which appeared more than fifteen years later, directed its arguments from the standpoint of a new literary and political position following the July Revolution of 1830 (and judged in retrospect from the higher terrain of a new, engaged, halfway "Young German" literature), Ascher forms his arguments amid a nostalgic turning back to the literary Enlightenment of the age of Lessing. Wieland, Lessing, and Moses Mendelssohn, who is always mentioned in conjunction with them, are his models. In compar-ison with them even the "genuinely German" Schiller, above all Goethe, but certainly the actual Romantics like the Schlegels, Tieck, and Zacharias Werner, a convert to Catholicism, are mentioned very circumspectly and are mostly deflated as literary models.

Heinrich Heine cordially praised "Doktor Ascher" and adopted into his own prose writings Hans Ferdinand Massmann,[6] the instigator of the book burning on the Wartburg, as a polemical stereotype and portable backdrop to his barbed wit (Massmann even makes an appearance in *Germany, a Winter's Fairytale*). Unlike the author of *Germanomania*, how-ever, Heine argues, as he had learned from Hegel, from a historical-philosophical viewpoint. In Ascher as well there is to be found the thesis of Heine's later book *Concerning the History of Religion and Philosophy in Germany*, that "Lessing continued the work of Luther." It is simply that Heine is careful not to posit the Enlightenment of the age of Lessing absolutely. It is unfortunate that in Heine's grand project to draft a comprehensive historical-critical work on Germany, precisely the section that would have provided a history of literature in Germany from Luther to the Romantics remained unwritten. The reasons why can be recon-structed.[7] Heine is, in any event, at a far remove from Ascher's dogged insistence on retaining abstract postulates of emancipation. Through this Heine necessarily became the opponent of Ludwig Börne, who tried more seriously and more acutely than anyone else to realize the synthesis of Jewish emancipation and German patriotism.

Shylock

On the Wartburg in the year 1817 Saul Ascher had been symbolically done in by youths. At the Hambach Festival on May 27, 1832, Dr. Ludwig Börne, coming from Paris, appeared as the main speaker. The Heidelberg students serenaded him.

That seems to evince progress and a closeness to reality: Börne as a more cautious, even more morally imposing Saul Ascher. Heine, however, mistrusts this seeming harmony. His conception of history has no place for the antinomies between Germans and Jews that Ascher had analyzed or for Börne's emancipatory syntheses. Heine rather sees in a strikingly intuitive all-encompassing vision the parallelism between Jews and Germans, as both being outsiders in common. On this account he is less fixed than Ascher or Börne on emancipatory citizenship for German Jews and more for striving to overcome their common outsiderdom through recognition of their affinities. Through recognition—and then by German universal revolution.

The opposition between Heine and Börne culminates in their entirely diverging interpretations of Shylock. Börne dualistically and moralistically distinguishes the monied Jew from the oppressed Jew: "We despise the money-devil in Shylock; we commiserate with those who are downtrodden, but we love and admire him who revenges inhuman persecution."[8] Shylock is brought into juxtaposition with the Rothschilds, the "great Shylocks who display the ribbons of Christian orders on their Jewish roquelaure." The antithesis at work is one of noble or ignoble humanity. The moralistic point of view has a concealing effect and is both noble minded and frivolous at once.

Heine as well appears to come to frivolous terms with Shylock. He goes the roundabout way via Portia, yet his interests center on the old man of the Rialto and not on the lady of aesthetical existence at Belmont. He too does not refrain from alluding to Shylock's cousin, "Monsieur de Shylock of Paris," who has become the "mightiest baron of Christendom."[9] Yet he avoids any dualistic manner of thinking. More than that, the moralizing distinction between noble and ignoble Jew is seen by Heine, who has spent his life's efforts trying to overcome the antitheses of Nazarene and Greek culture, as a typical Shylockian attitude. Using Shylock as pretext, he analyzes, particularly in his book on Börne (1840), the synthesis of Judaism, Christianity, and ascetic spiritualism, which, he says, is also the German synthesis. In the work on Börne this receives its programmatic formulation: "However that may be, it is quite possible that the mission of this people has not been fulfilled, and this may also in fact be the case in respect to Germany. Germany too is awaiting a liberator, an earthly messiah—the Jews have already blessed us with a heavenly one—a king of the earth, a savior with sword and scepter, and this German liberator is perhaps the same one whom Israel is awaiting as well."[10]

In the context of Heine's intellectual development, such a thesis, formulated a decade after the July Revolution, after the disappointment with the failure of Saint-Simonism, can only mean universal revolution—the action from the thought, the deed of the man holding the lictor's axe from *Germany, a Winter's Fairytale,* which appeared four years later. Revolution transcends the limitations of Kant and Robespierre, Jewish-Börnian moral rigorism as well as the nationalistic partial rigorism of the anti-Semitic Germanophiles. The emancipation of the Jew in the world can be reached only through "the liberation of the world from the Jew," Karl Marx's formulation during the period of his acquaintance with Heine in Paris, in his study "Concerning the Jewish Question" (1844). This Hegelian formulation means that if Jewish existence is to be equated with the modern money economy, culminating in the Rothschild syndrome, then Jewish emancipation must be equated with the liberation from this money hegemony. A qualitative leap has to be undertaken: from Shylock the bourgeois to Comrade Shylock.

Heine, as is known, failed in this qualitative leap. Much has been written on Heine's relations to socialism and communism,[11] with some few letters between Marx and Heine the target of ever overzealous interpretation. That Ferdinand Lassalle came to play a greater role in Heine's life than Marx will be discussed further on. All too often the topic of Heine and capitalism is set aside in embarrassment. Heine himself found it an embarrassment. What he personally chose was connections with Baron Rothschild's offices and salons in the rue Lafitte.

Heine and Rothschild: they belonged together and thought of each other (I mean here particularly the youngest of the five brothers from Frankfurt, Jakob, called James Mayer Freiherr von Rothschild—born May 5, 1792, in Frankfurt, died November 15, 1868, in Paris) as partners and parallel phenomena through the hypertrophy of education and possessions. Rothschild was a phenomenon of the real world that busied the writer Heine without cease. When he went to the rue Lafitte he was tantalized and dismayed at once. Franz Grillparzer once had dinner with him there and noted his impressions in his autobiography: "As much as Heine impressed me when we were alone, he distressed me when a few days later we were invited to dine at the Rothschilds'. It was clear that our hosts feared Heine, and he took advantage of this fear to poke fun at them at every turn. Yet no one is obliged to dine at someone's he does not care for, and if someone despises someone he does not need to dine at his house. Our relationship did not continue from then on."

In the two volumes of Egon Caesar Conte Corti's courtly history of the house of Rothschild,[12] in which the rise of the house and the "period of its blossoming" is piously described (avoiding any association of "rise and fall"), the relationship between Heinrich Heine and James Rothschild remains a subject of considerable import. It was a connection easily taken up after Heine, following the July Revolution, began residing in the French capital. The Rothschilds were business partners with Heine's wealthy uncle Salomon Heine. Besides, Betty Rothschild, the "pretty Jewess," very likely acted as an additional inducement to the poet, after an unhappy love affair, to pay a call at the rue Lafitte. Not only the drawing rooms of the banker were there, but his comptoir as well. Many times over Heine has described those rooms and the scene of rich or poor debtors waiting to be admitted. That Heine was occasionally graciously included by Rothschild in business transactions is something we know from his letters. Karl Kraus, under the headline "The Enemies Goethe and Heine" (*Die Fackel*, October 1915), wrote his own interpretation, that of a man forever pondering "Heine and the consequences." When Heine reported he strolled down the street "arm and arm" with James Rothschild "quite famillionairely," Kraus rejoined that it had likely been "arm in wealth" instead.[13]*

Even more remarkable than the intimacy between them or Heine's emotional ambivalence is their social congruity, something both James Rothschild and Heinrich Heine sensed with utter clarity. They roamed, the minstrel with the king, at "the pinnacles of humanity" (*auf der Menschheit Höhen*). Here the minstrel trafficked with the millionaire who had long since ceased to be millionaire and had become king of kings, especially in concert with Amschel Mayer Rothschild in Frankfurt, Salomon Mayer Rothschild in Vienna, Karl Mayer Rothschild in Naples, and Nathan Mayer Rothschild in London.

Heine confirmed what was only a matter of the selective principle of high capital, that only the stars of each trade were admitted to the rue

---

*An untranslatable pun: arm in *reich* instead of arm in arm, playing on the dual meaning of *arm* "poor" in German (translator's note).

Lafitte. Or better yet: only those "capacities" the House of Rothschild deemed unsurpassable. Among composers it was Rossini but not Chopin. Among painters Heine mentions Ary Scheffer but not once Delacroix.[14]

Heine's fascination for the Rothschilds has to be understood as a fascination for power. In his book on Börne (who of course never appeared at James Rothschild's since in his "Letter from Paris" of January 22, 1832, he had sarcastically written that at Louis-Philippe's coronation Rothschild should act the part of archbishop) Heine called this banker and leveler, who destroyed the great estates and organized the system of abstract investment incomes, one of the "great revolutionaries" of all time with greater power than Richelieu or Robespierre.[15] And so Heine finally arrived, notwithstanding his sympathy for the utopian socialists, at the thought of a great duality: Rothschild and Heine as the cooperation of progressive capital with progressive literature.

And the family of Rothschild for its own part—at least as of September 27, 1810, when the first of its ranks and father of five sons and five daughters established the firm "Mayer Amschel Rothschild & Sons" in Frankfurt, making his five sons coowners of the business—had become simultaneously legend and social scandal. The firm's initial capital of 800,000 gulden was in no sense phenomenal; Jewish court factors of the seventeenth and eighteenth centuries, who had long since taken over the functions of the Fuggers and Welsers, had far greater sums at their disposal:

Looking over the history of the court financiers in the epoch of early capitalism, their line can be traced via the names Fugger, Oppenheimer, and Wertheimer in Vienna; Liebmann, Gomperz, Ephraim, Itzig, Isaak in Prussia; Behrens in Hannover; Lehmann in Halberstadt; Baruch and Oppenheim in Bonn; Seligmann in Munich; Kaulla in Stuttgart; and Rothschild in Frankfurt and Vienna. At the beginning the Fuggers are the great financiers; at the end the house of Rothschild represents the greatest potency of capital. Just as the first great court financier Fugger with his support of the Habsburgs determined the course of world history, so too did the house of Rothschild when it placed its financial might on the side of the allies in the war against Napoleon. The history of court finance in Germany runs from Fugger to Rothschild.[16]

Perhaps it was two peculiarities, aside from the personal abilities of Mayer Amschel and his five sons, that led the court factor and financial adviser to the wealthy Elector of Hesse to surpass all the other Jewish financiers despite having begun with smaller means. For one, Mayer

Amschel Rothschild in his first and most successful phase of advancement consummated a Christian-Jewish symbiosis. His alliance with Carl Friedrich Buderus, the Hessian privy councillor born in 1759, later to become Buderus von Carlshausen, cemented the new unity of faith in capital and pointed beyond their own semifeudal era. All the more so since Buderus had a strong sense of family ties; his brother was to found the Buderus'schen Iron Works in Wetzlar.[17]

And with that I have come to the second peculiarity in the rise of the Rothschilds: the adaptation of the earlier Jewish court factor to the new perspective of a bourgeois society and economy that is no longer founded on the special privileges granted by a ruling prince to a protected Jew but on the Enlightenment postulate of equal civil rights for all. Since nearly the very beginning of their financial-political influence in European history, the members of the house of Rothschild, thanks to the hypertrophy of wealth, could lay claim to the ideological as well as the material advantages from the charter of human and civil rights. They could afford to refuse to pay the entrance fee to European civilization, as Heine called it once, namely, baptism. Heine became a Christian and stood watch—half in earnest, half in jest—over his Christianity. Felix Mendelssohn-Bartholdy, Moses Mendelssohn's grandson, adopted into his intellectual and artistic credo the articles of faith of Lutheranism. A Reformation Symphony, a symphony as Protestant Te Deum: "Praise God all ye who have breath!"; in the later work assuming an almost disagreeable inclination, as for example in the second piano trio in C-minor, opus 66, to want to outdo the musical score with choral edification from another sphere. Ludwig Börne was another who went to the baptismal font, and in Trier judiciary counselor Marx's son Karl Heinrich. But not the Rothschilds. The Disraeli family joined the Anglican Church. The son of Heymann Lassalle of Breslau, contrarily, remained a Jew. So did the son of the Cologne cantor Offenbach.

The Rothschilds had no need of government offices: they stood above them. The history of their house shows that even their peerage had not been sought but for the most part was tendered by the monarch. That is what Heine means when he simultaneously praises, fears, and derides the Baron James in Paris as a true revolutionary, more consequential still than Robespierre.

For all that, the nephew of the wealthy Hamburg banker Salomon Heine and Salomon Heine's business acquaintance, James Rothschild, had already come to be associated in the minds of their contemporaries. A peculiar literary document, scarcely noticed and even today still somewhat puzzling in its motivations serves as evidence.

Honoré de Balzac in *The Human Comedy* associates the two, the banker Rothschild and Doctor Heinrich Heine, by quite subtle means.[18] In the section "Scènes de la Vie Parisienne" of this enormous epic work, two mediocre little stories have each a studied, precisely formulated dedication. The story "Un Homme d'affaires" is dedicated "A Monsieur le Baron James Rothschild, Consul Général d'Autriche à Paris, Banquier." There is no conclusive or simply polite wording that might allow some conclusion as to the motives for the dedication. One might even take it for a sneer and parody through the association of *banquier* in the dedication with *homme d'affaires* in the title. The story itself, however, contradicts any such suspicions: it is a Parisian game of masked identities between aristocratic debtors and bourgeois creditors. At precisely this juncture Balzac cannot resist bringing up the figure of the Baron de Nucingen, the well-known, clumsily horny, mostly swindled banker, whose miserable Frankfurt French is always rendered phonetically; it is unmistakable that Nucingen has to do with the Rothschilds. Yet the story "Un Homme d'affaires" does not actually lead to the *comptoirs* of the rue Lafitte. It is a very banal and ponderously told fable, which attracts attention only because of the mysterious dedication to Rothschild meant apparently as some kind of signal.

The story that follows next in Balzac's "Scènes de la Vie Parisienne" is entitled "Un Prince de la Bohème." This time the dedication is extensive, cordial, and signed:

My Dear Heine: I dedicate this study to you; to you who represent in Paris the spirit and poetry of Germany, as in Germany you represent the vivacity and wit of French criticism; to you who understand better than anybody how much criticism, humor, love, and truth this may contain.[19]

De Balzac.

It seems completely clear yet becomes confusing as soon as one thinks it over. The cordiality and admiration in this dedication are unmistakable. That Heine is associated with a story about a prince of bohemia must have been every bit as allusive as the dedication of "Un Homme d'affaires" to James Rothschild. Yet the prince of Bohemia whose story is clumsily told here through the medium of two confusing cornice stories has not the least thing in common with any kind of bohemian way of life on the part of Heine in Paris. Heine's debts grew out of control—that is common knowledge made public by Heine himself—far beyond the little discords that one associates with the notion of bohemia.

Balzac, to be sure, defines his Bohemia in an entirely different manner than later, say, Murger in his lacrimonious story of Montmartre. Balzac uses the term to signify "young people between twenty and thirty years of age, each ingenious after his own fashion, not at all well known, who are going to become so." He seems to count himself among them. He bitterly contrasts, as did Stendhal in the story of Julien Sorel, the prospects for this youth under Napoleon with the preferential treatment accorded bureaucrats and seniority under the citizen king.

Then this prince of bohemia is introduced: Rusticoli with nine Christian names, comte de la Palferine, from an ancient Italo-French line. A great lord and accumulator of debts, full of possibilities and no money, of usurpatory arrogance who takes recourse in the superiority of the aristocrat and his notorious good looks. Balzac reports the arrogant repartees of this superman from bourgeois-royal Paris with the greatest admiration. In so doing he makes this prince of bohemia (unconsciously so) as insufferable as Oscar Wilde had made his supposedly so irresistibly spiritual Lord Henry in *The Picture of Dorian Gray*.

The story is simple. Palferine, who incidently also has a part in the "Un Homme d'affaires" story, wishes to rid himself of a mistress. He announces he will admit her again only if and when she appears with spectacular equipage, distinction, and a title. Claudine accomplishes this task. She drives her older and unloved lover, then husband, to higher and higher and more and more ambitious undertakings until he becomes a peer of France and very rich. She herself, a former dancer at the opera, is now a lady of high society. The real Balzac of this rather commonplace story surfaces for a moment only toward the end of the piece, to proclaim a melancholy morality and ask whether the unloved and mediocre playwright Du Bruel, who had been driven so by his wife to fame, title, and wealth, had not really been duped. "Without his wife's conceits he would have remained a man of light theater, whereas he sits now in the chambers of a peer of France."[20]

The poet Nathan says this. He may have a few elements in common with Heine; yet there is just as little immediate point of contact between Heine and the story dedicated to him as between Rothschild and the "man of affairs."

That notwithstanding, Balzac must have believed in some such affinity. In his dedication to Heine he writes, "you who understand better than anybody how much criticism, humor, love, and truth this may contain." But where is the criticism to be discovered alongside the obvious foolery, love, and truth about life? Palferine inappropriately provides the title to the story. His whims give it impetus, but it is not his story. And yet Balzac seems altogether too fascinated by the aristocratic grossness of the haughty pauper for the story to be interpreted as a criticism of bohemia. Where then should Heine, the mediator between German poetry and French wit, as Balzac's dedication puts it, seek to discover truth and criticism in the story of the count and his mistress?

A satisfactory answer can be provided only if Balzac's concept of bohemia is understood as positive through and through, as a collective name for the society, literature, and art of tomorrow. That the narrator of these two stories of Parisian life takes the side of the authentic aristocrats, the lovers, the little people, and young men of talent, is just as evident as his aversion to bourgeois aristocracy, money bags, and bureaucrats. The antithesis of the "two poets" from Balzac's grand novel *Lost Illusions* is present everywhere here. On the one hand is the tamed intellectual who is all too complaisant and comes to honors under the bankers' regime of the citizen king Louis-Philippe, like Du Bruel. On the other hand is the unaccommodating intellectual, often unsuccessful, debt ridden, nonetheless the man of tomorrow. If one does not have the strength to live through this condition, the result is tragedy, as in the case of Lucien de Rubempré, who had genius and was beautiful but who as lover and writer perished in the world of the Nucingens and Rothschilds.

Balzac sees in Heinrich Heine a friend and ally. For him the world of bankers and that of bohemians are to be understood as polar opposites. Rothschild belongs to the one; Heine to the other. It is astonishing how in this scheme of things—which is not simply Balzac's idiosyncrasy but is characteristic of attitudes vis-à-vis the "noxious money economy" (Börne) of the realm of the citizen king—that outsiders should be made representatives. Psychologically, perhaps, this curious constellation in Balzac was influenced by the inauthenticity of his own aristocratic predicate. Balzac's royalism devolves from the consciousness of his own illegitimacy. Even the signature to the dedication to Heine, "De Balzac," is too obtrusive. (Sartre in his study of Flaubert has described a parallel occurrence in the novelist Flaubert's reaction to the real aristocracy of one Alfred de Vigny and his [Flaubert's] antibourgeois fulminations.)[21] Balzac too sees himself as an outsider; consequently he names the outsider Heine, the Jew among Germans, the German among Frenchmen, the poet in the kingdom of bankers and a secondary line of Bourbons, the admirer of the Saint-Simonites, and guest at Baron de Rothschild's parties, to be the representative of the intellectual and material might of the coming new day.

Lost legitimacy can be reestablished as little as lost illusions. The neo-legitimacy derived from the bourgeois revolution for Bonapartism and the monarchy of the citizen king knew itself to be illegitimate. In consequence, the illegitimacy of the first order needed another, second illegitimacy against which it could discriminate in turn. Under the class hegemony of the bourgeoisie in the nineteenth century, this function is taken by the bourgeois Shylocks, particularly in the manifestation of a hypertrophy of material success and intellectual capability. Heine and Rothschild are to be understood as phenotypes. The Rothschilds, naturally, are socially "integrated." Yet even when they are permitted to be members of the Jockey Club in Paris or of the English House of Lords, they nonetheless remain integrated only until further notice. French history after 1940, the doctrine and practice of an "Action Française," serves as evidence. A popular argument against Pompidou was not that he had come to success as a banker but that he had worked for the Rothschilds.

Heinrich Heine as a German scandal is a case in point: even in Nietzsche's enthusiasm for Heine or in the Heine pullulations of the Austrian Empress Elizabeth, the desire for provocation is manifest. Heine remained a source of vexation and scandal. The nonintegratable writer among the German poets, the elegant revolutionary, the Goethean who was ignored by Goethe. Heine knew all of this. His writing is never authentic whenever he tries to suffer like everyone else in a poetry of the pangs of love. Heine's greatness as a writer is always assured where prose and verse reflect in endless repetition Shylock's manner of life in the world of the bourgeoisie. It is clearest in the numerous cases where Heine places himself in immediate relation, as in his studies on Shakespeare, to the Jew of the Rialto. His unsureness vis-à-vis other outsiders of talent and bad reputation has nothing to do with faulty judgment but with identification, as in his relations to Platen and Lassalle.

Benjamin Disraeli and Ferdinand Lassalle

When the thirty-three-year-old Benjamin Disraeli finally after four-time defeat was elected as a conservative member of Parliament from Maidstone on July 27, 1837, he was greeted by opponents on election eve with the cry "Old Clothes!," the cry of the itinerant streethawker. They also yelled "Shylock!" at him.[22] When he died in his seventy-seventh year, on April 18, 1881, as ex-Prime Minister and Earl of Beaconsfield, only invited guests took part in the funeral ceremony at his country estate, Hughenden. Queen Victoria, according to the protocol of those days, which did not permit her to take part at the burial of one of her subjects, sent flowers and wrote a letter of honest sympathy for her favorite minister. The Prince of Wales had attended as well as the Duke of Connaught and Prince Leopold. To the close circle of Disraeli's friends who had been admitted there belonged Sir Nathaniel de Rothschild, subsequently the first Lord Rothschild. Sir Philip Rose and Nathaniel Rothschild were named executors of the estate under the terms of Disraeli's last will and testament. The Rothschilds supposedly later settled the encumbrances on Hughenden to make it possible for Disraeli's nephew to inherit it. One of the stipulations had been that its heir bear the name Disraeli. Today the erstwhile Tory prime minister's estate is a museum and part of the National Trust effectively administered by Lord Rothschild.

The association of the names Disraeli and Rothschild has nothing to do with an intimate business or speculative tie: Disraeli's money matters were up to the very end anything but satisfactory. He had never been particularly energetic in his investments, and had never enriched himself in office, something his numerous adversaries would have immediately seized upon. The tie between the conservative statesman and the banker with the magic name is not at all comparable to the transactions between the Reich Chancellor Bismarck and his Jewish banker, Baron von Bleichröder.

As Disraeli/Beaconsfield at the apex of his European fame at seventy-four years of age led the English delegation to the Congress of Berlin, celebrated as "the lion of the congress" and spoiled by the German princess royal, the daughter of his Queen Victoria, his diplomatic counterpart Bismarck exclaimed admiringly: "That old Jew, he is the man."

That is what he remained: that old Jew. Yet in his basic political stance and in his individual manner of work he was astonishingly similar to Bismarck. Disraeli's biographer Robert Blake has observed shrewdly:

Bismarck, like Disraeli, had been a Byronic romantic in the past, and thought in those terms still. Both men loved sweeping phrases, high-flown generalities, cynical asides. They were impatient of detail, bored by the humdrum. They shared the same broad views on policy: at home the preservation of an aristocratic settlement, Junker supremacy in Prussia, the ascendancy of the landed class in England; abroad the bold assertion of those national interests of which they seemed to be the incarnation in their respective countries. Bismarck admired Disraeli's courage, power of decision and refusal to be bogged down in details.[23]

Nevertheless the comparison does not take root. The identification with some sort of "national" interest or even interests of a general social nature takes place in two completely divergent fashions in Otto von Bismarck-Schönhausen and in the son of Isaac Disraeli and Maria Basevi, who came into the world on December 21, 1804, in his father's house in King's Road, Bedford Row, London. The Israelis, then D'Israelis, finally Disraelis, had come to England from Italy; the claim that they were a Sephardic family with an aristocratic Spanish background was likely a fanciful fabrication on Disraeli's part. On the other hand, the Basevis on the maternal side, as members of the Cardoso family and with Spanish antecedents had immigrated to England in the seventeenth century. This is of note on account of the social and ideological background that was to project Benjamin Disraeli as the most successful conservative politician of the Victorian era and a staunch supporter of the British aristocratic capitalist and imperialist class. Thanks to the son of the literary man and popular writer Isaac Disraeli, the queen of the United Kingdom of Great Britain and Ireland could add the title and real power of "Empress of India" to her prerogatives.

As Bismarck after each victorious war, with the backing of Kaiser Wilhelm, rose higher in the nobility—first count, then prince, finally duke of Lauenburg—he remained in his original milieu, loyal to the convictions of his caste and its social rules of conduct. The path that took Benjamin Disraeli to be Lord Beaconsfield, however, entailed a qualitative leap. It was not a matter of the baptism to which he submitted in 1817 at the age of thirteen, together with all the other members of Isaac Disraeli's family. Neither was it his successful election to Parliament. Baptized Jews were not unusual in the House of Commons in the eighteenth century, David Ricardo being the best known. What was of legal concern was one's religious affiliation, not one's racial antecedents. Until 1829 only Anglicans were permitted to sit in Parliament; after that members of other Christian denominations, Catholics in particular, were administered the oath of office "on the true faith of a Christian." Only in 1858 did the House of Commons begin to admit members of the Jewish faith. The

Anglican MP Disraeli had argued in behalf of that move, but not by appealing to the Enlightenment postulate of universal tolerance as one might expect. Ten years before, when such admission was voted down, Disraeli had argued before Commons that "the very reason for admitting the Jews is because they can show so near an affinity to you. Where is your Christianity if you do not believe in their Judaism?"

A curious line of argument for a baptized Jew who addresses the genuine Christians of the House as "you," exempting himself, apparently, from their Christian community. "Your Christianity," in a word. And his own? It seems almost grotesque when he, who had fallen out of the role of a Christian member of Parliament, seeks to slip back into the skin of the good Christian. "Yet it is as a Christian that I will not take upon me the awful responsibility of excluding from the Legislature those who are of the religion in the bosom of which my Lord and Saviour was born."

And so too from Disraeli's very beginnings when he entered upon financial transactions bringing no success, was reluctantly bailed out of growing debt by his father, thereupon as conservative MP helped a conservative government fall, to which he had vainly offered his services, the question of his credibility came to be posed again and again. What was England to him, Christianity, the nobility, the Tory party, the Empire, the Queen even? He never concealed his interest in the fortune of a wife twelve years older than he. He patiently bore her indiscretions in society and was the model of a courteous husband. They had no children. With Mrs. Disraeli, whom he had elevated to Lady Beaconsfield shortly before she died, without at that point even slightly considering making use of the title Lord Beaconsfield himself, for it would have meant the loss of his seat in the House of Commons, he staged an act for two characters from the start.

And Bismarck too, the Iron Chancellor with weak nerves and a falsetto voice, played roles, called up from time to time the inner disposition of a man of letters, enjoyed writing and wrote well—at first court memoranda, elegant gossipy letters, later thoughts and memoirs. That he identified Prussia and the house of Hohenzollern with himself and his own interests has been proved. His behavior after his demission makes it all too apparent. Yet even in that he remained a Junker from Brandenburg-Prussia. Disraeli, on the other hand, was a conservative whose bill was footed by others, a political/diplomatic agent for the great landowning aristocracy. His estate, Hughenden, did not even suffice for a baronage.

On this account skeptics' doubts vis-à-vis this conservative by volition and not by real social interest never subsided. Even modern historiography does not ultimately discharge him from suspicions of political charlatanism. Spurned as "Shylock" at the beginning, the friend of lords and gallant of aristocratic ladies, the author of love and society novels and novels stimulating social discussion, which were widely read, no man of files and details, a successful orator and polemicist, upright and dependable, an advocate of tradition and from time to time an eccentric: did he also play as prime minister a role of artifice?

The affinity between Benjamin Disraeli and Oscar Wilde has often been commented upon. Wilde found himself anticipated in the epigrams, vital maxims, and cynicisms of the Victorian elder statesman. The name Dorian Gray is in faint homage to Disraeli's novel *Vivian Grey*. The author of the comedy *On the Importance of Being Earnest,* Bunbury, grew up in a world of "Beaconsfieldisms," as Disraeli's serious detractors were wont to characterize that form of stage-mannered politics. Wilde did not pay sufficient heed to this stern aspect of puritan and bourgeois respectability. Disraeli was the Jewish outsider in the role of conservative prime minister, which was synonymous for many with license, libertinage, aesthetic dandyism. Capitalist England in the Victorian epoch was essentially bourgeois-virtuous; stolid, not playful; moralistic, not aesthetic. Even as a politician Disraeli had remained an outsider in social life. His like would not be seen again. Where the Jewish outsider Disraeli had succeeded, the erotic outsider Wilde would founder and be shipwrecked. It is of course sheerest speculation to imagine Disraeli during the time of the trial against Wilde. He had died in 1881; Oscar Wilde was brought to trial and then sentenced to Reading Gaol in 1895. Might it have come on Disraeli's part to repetition of the confrontation between Platen and Heine? One tends to think—to Disraeli's credit—not. Disraeli has remained one of a kind. His contemporaries and those coming after have ceaselessly occupied themselves with him, this bourgeois Shylock like no other. When in 1970 Jonathan Miller staged a production of *The Merchant of Venice* at the National Theatre in London, Laurence Olivier played a nineteenth-century Shylock in cutaway and pincenez, immediately evoking the shade of Benjamin Disraeli.

There was no repetition. Walther Rathenau was at as far a remove from Disraeli as is imaginable. Perhaps because he lived within himself a double outsiderdom: Platen and Heine, Wilde and Disraeli at once. We are given no reason to believe that Her Majesty's prime minister ever, aside from the external difficulties of his career, bore his Jewishness as wound and mutilation. Quite the contrary, Rathenau suffered from Jewish self-hatred; his thinking was tinged with irrationalism and hostility to Enlightenment; he was enamored of the opposing world of the supposedly "German" as an industrialist who despised the bourgeoisie but loved artists and Junkers. As theoretician and enthusiast he stood strangely close to the mental world of his murderers.

What differentiates all the bourgeois Shylocks of the nineteenth century in such a startling fashion from their Shakespearean progenitor is their greedy aristocratism. The moneylender of the Rialto wanted nothing in common with those of Belmont or with the aristocratic dandies of Venice. Business, yes, but not eating and drinking. The ostentatious bourgeois Shylocks of the bourgeois nineteenth century felt compelled, after equal citizenship, to attain total integration. The leftovers of the *ancien régime,* aristocratic salons, and narrow-minded Jockey Clubs were made to serve this purpose. Heinrich Heine created such a symbiosis for himself in Paris with the active aid of the baron and accredited diplomat Rothschild. The Rothschilds in Paris, Vienna, and London, were able to maintain at one and the same time their Jewish religion *and* a barony. Benjamin Disraeli, the literary figure and adventurer, Tory and lord, names the ennobled Rothschild to be executor of his estate. Rathenau in the officers' club is adviser to the German kaiser. Marcel Proust is the member of exclusive and anti-Semitic clubs and guest and critic of the Faubourg Saint-Germain. Hugo von Hofmannsthal, the "difficult" aristocrat, is the biographer of both Maria Theresa and Prince Eugene.

To the archetypical phenomena of the bourgeois Shylock in the nineteenth century there belongs, alongside the incarnation of excessive talent in Heine and excessive property in Rothschild, a figure complementary to the role of English conservative played by Benjamin Disraeli, namely, the role of workers' tribune played by Ferdinand Lassalle.

The nearly 900-page monograph by Shlomo Na'aman (1970) on the founder of the General Union of German Workers (Allgemeiner Deutscher Arbeiter-Verein) calls itself in the title to the preface "a new political biography."[24] That is an allusion and battle position at once. It was Hermann Oncken who in 1904, forty years after Lassalle's death in a duel, first published a critical life, which after the third edition in 1920 bore the title *Lassalle: eine politische Biographie* (Lassalle: A Political Biography).[25] Na'aman did not choose his subtitle as a polemical gesture. In his notes to the bibliography he calls the works by Bernstein and Oncken "classic" and means this qualification in the sense of "a reflection of the consciousness of the times."[26] Nonetheless this *new* political biography represents a qualitative leap. What is new is taking seriously (and mastering) Hegelian philosophy, so crucial to an understanding of the early Lassalle; then comes the solid familiarization with Lassalle's so very divergent activities as interpreter of the philosophy of Heraclitus, historiographer of law, as the (bad) dramatist who wrote a play called *Sickingen,* which has in any case retained its topicality on account of the Sickingen debates between Marx, Engels, and Lassalle.

Above all this new political monograph is concerned with arriving at new political valuations. It avoids the mistakes of earlier works, which were fixated on either Bismarck or Marx, Lassalle's two great adversaries. Even the suggestive methods of individual psychology are scarcely taken up. The Israeli historian writing in German is distanced from his hero, yet he writes not without warmth of Lassalle's crises and failures. At all events he sees Lassalle's efforts to establish and unify a German workingman's movement as an unsuitable attempt with unsuitable means to accomplish something on an unsuitable object. "The man who throughout his livelong days entrusted all practical business matters to his father does not even find his way clear in the day-to-day goings-on of his own association. He does not know how many members the union has, how much money is in the treasury, and he is in no position to know."[27]

This political biography, well-disposed toward Lassalle as it is, demolishes with a detailed analysis of the political actions of a man who died at the age of thirty-nine, precisely those activities of Lassalle's that even his adversaries had recognized. They had rejected his history of philosophy as a compilation (Marx spoke of his *Heraclitus* as a work having more bulk and show of learning than content); they criticized his historical studies of jurisprudence as amateurish. The man himself they despised as an adventuresome charlatan of dubious talent, yet they took the orator and labor leader in utter seriousness. It was out of the unification of the Marxist Eisenachers and the so-called Lassalleans that the German Social Democratic Party had its origins. Workers sang well into the twenties of our own century the battle song of "the way which Lassalle has taken us." Georg Herwegh had written the verses for him of the man of labor who should awaken and flex his power: "All the wheels will stand still if your mighty arms ordain."

What consequence all this had and yet what a failure from the viewpoint of Lassalle's own notions and desires. The somewhat confusing conclusions of this biography, supported by a great mass of detail, make it clear why this so very versatile and talented, hard-working and discerning man again and again drove those he dealt with from admiration and discipleship to hatred, scorn, and fear. An outstanding example marking off all the phases involved is Heinrich Heine's short acquaintanceship with the twenty-year-old Lassalle. At the beginning a letter of introduction for Lassalle to Varnhagen in Berlin: "My friend, Mr. Lassalle, who has delivered this letter to you, is a young man of remarkable intellectual gifts—he possesses the solidest scholarship, the broadest knowledge, the greatest acumen that I have ever encountered. He combines a rich talent for descriptive prose with an energy of will and *habilité* in action which astonish me." Heine scarcely ever wrote something like that about anybody else, certainly not about Karl Marx or Friedrich Engels. To be sure, he could hardly expect from them, as he could from Lassalle, help in settling the dispute with his cousin Karl Heine about their joint inheritance.

On March 6, 1846, two months later, Lassalle was dropped. Varnhagen had reacted disapprovingly: "I wouldn't give a tuppence for your friend Lassalle's judgments." Heine withdrew from his young and brilliant friend all power of attorney. That which Lassalle was planning in his (Heine's) business matters belongs "more to the realm of Sue's novels than to my situation," which is to say: it is criminal, sensational rubbish. "I often think of you and your future with the greatest concern; but I do not speak about it to you, still less to others. I am too experienced and clear in my mind for that. How much you will continue to be buffeted about."[28]

This is an extraordinary document. It is a great deal more honest than that ambivalent, hymnic letter of introduction. On the one hand, Heine breaks with his young business confidant. On the other, he draws with exceeding acuity a parallel between himself and Lassalle. That is quite unique in Heine's life and correspondence. Not one of the many young, highly talented Shylocks striving to get up in life who crossed his path in those days—from the Hegelian Eduard Gans to Moses Hess, from Börne to Marx—did he, the author of *The Rabbi from Bacharach*, ever compare in such a fashion to himself. He sees with his strange visionary sight that this Ferdinand Lassalle's course of life is determined in a similar fashion to his own: a chain of seeming successes and permanent defeats. He was to be right in the general contours of his vision, though not in the details.

Heine was at one and the same time a European phenomenon and a German scandal. It was not simply a matter of poetic genius but of the unconditionality he always brought to bear, defying all the disruptions and disappointments he called up whenever his own work together with all its material and spiritual underpinnings was placed in question. Heine was a writer and tambour of the enlightening word. He was deadly serious in this. Lassalle remained a man of many talents without any such connecting center of purpose and self-realization. He could do everything and anything, too much so. In consequence his name never became famous beyond German borders. His books found neither readers nor disciples, since their real purpose had never been aimed at Heraclitus or a "system of received law" but served only to demonstrate that he could do this too. And so he became a German scandal, more so than anyone else since Heine but without Heine's poetry. The labor leader to whom laborers were at bottom repugnant "possessed nothing, nothing at all, of a man of the people. He suffered physically in having to go into a pub, breathe the heavy, smoke-filled air, and shake sweaty hands."[29] The parallels to many of Heine's stances, in the preface to *Lutetia*, say, is astonishing.

Time and again the confidence man. "Who is Louis Büchner?" he asks of an acquaintance in a letter dated one April 9, and is given an answer, that this materialist philosopher is Georg Büchner's younger brother. On April 13 he writes Büchner as if "he had for years followed that man's works with the greatest interest."[30]

It was a life without trust, either in others or in himself, with all too many tasks to be accomplished, yet without one genuine one. Scarcely any of his political analyses, particularly in foreign affairs, was verifiable. There is no doubt that Jewish self-hate played a role when Karl Marx referred to Lassalle in his letters to Engels as "Junker Itzig," or "little Jew Braun," or "His Excellency Ephraim Alltoobright." Yet what was at work here was more than anything the profound mistrust on the part of the ponderous public speaker and thoroughgoing scholar against Lassalle's fluid diction and inexact methods of work—inexact because never inspired by the matter at hand. The respect, even of his enemies, for the honorableness and uprightness Marx incorporated in his life and work was considerable. Bismarck, as Marx reports in his letters to Kugelmann, probably undertook his attempt at corrupting him only half in earnest. He knew that he would have no success in it. With Lassalle, on the other hand, the Prussian cabinet president played a regular game of cat and mouse in interviews and police protocols before the Danish war of 1864, but especially after the Prussian victory at the bulwarks of Düppel. Such relations quite intentionally helped to compromise Lassalle as a man without principles, since they could only become the subject of wide speculation.

The outward occasion that brought Lassalle to an audience with Otto von Bismarck-Schönhausen on October 24, 1863, was curious enough. Lassalle went as a supporter of universal suffrage. Bismarck may well have been interested at the time in hearing the various arguments. But more important was Lassalle's need of help with the police after his brochures on the economic reformer of the petite bourgoisie, Schulze-Delitzsch, had been confiscated. Bismarck was in accord and even made the cynical proposal that the district attorney's office could be officially informed, something, of course, to which Lassalle could under no circumstances agree.

Behind all this stood Lassalle's curious conception of an alliance between aristocratic regime and the organized proletariat, aimed against Lassalle's real enemies in the liberal-democratic bourgeoisie. Such alliances were not unusual. Occasional traces are to be found later in Franz Mehring and are part of Mehring's hidden, lifelong Lassalleanism. That the author of the brochures against "Bastiat-Schulze," a supporter of such an unholy alliance of Junkers and workers, abandoned with that move all the principles of the *Communist Manifesto,* despite all verbal claims of accord, is evident.

Lassalle was not only familiar with Jewish self-hate, he used it for purposes of agitation. A litterateur who hated litterateurs. A Jewish anti-Semite. A Shylock who denounces Shylock. Sociologically this seeming paradox is part of the role of the bourgeois outsider from a well-to-do family who is neither able to be a capitalist (even if he dilettantishly speculates on the market and advises Heine in such matters), nor is publicly recognized as an intellectual through academic position or success with his books or official function. Eduard Bernstein, the later reformist Social Democrat, was obliged to come to the defense of his uncle, Aaron Bernstein, who as editor of the Berlin *Volkszeitung* had been attacked by Lassalle as "a man who isn't even capable of writing German, but an idiosyncratic mishmash instead, which he spoons down the gullets of his readers, your so-called Jewish-German—not a sentence without grammatical mistakes—which slowly but surely corrupts the language and genius of the people."[31]

That is not to be found in a polemical newspaper article but in a brochure for the political agitation of German workers. Lassalle's biographer Na'aman concludes: "It is quite another matter to take this manner of speaking to the masses and arrogate it to a socialist program. Here it is a matter of professional negligence, something which is a characteristic of the whole of Lassalle's work during the period of labor agitation: improvisation on a dangerous scale. Nothing can excuse it. Conceptual weakness on account of improvisation is a historical liability." [32]

The son of Heyman Lassalle from Breslau and brother-in-law of the Jewish capitalist Ferdinand Friedländer, later ennobled as Ferdinand von Friedland (one of the targets of Heinrich Heine's hate-filled barbs), paid for these existential contradictions with his life. At the age of thirty-nine he was killed in an absurd duel. He was no Russian aristocrat like Pushkin or Lermontov whose fate he shared. He was a Jewish parvenu, a labor leader who wanted to wed an aristocrat's daughter, Helene von Dönniges, but who, with the fine manners of the bourgeoisie, was frightened off when he blatantly compromised the girl, was rejected in consequence by the family, which was in no position to ally itself thus with the notorious litterateur. They were themselves merely government officials who had been titled, Frau Dönniges coming from a Jewish family in Berlin at that. What had attracted Lassalle was precisely what repelled the other side. Two outsider positions faced off against each other. The more secure of the two won out. Lassalle got a bullet in the abdomen, put there by a young man from Wallachia, of the nobility at any rate, to whom Helene von Dönniges had affianced herself. He lived on a few days after the duel, dying on August 31, 1864, in Geneva. Lassalle was buried quietly and without incident in his native Breslau, much to the relief of his brother-in-law von Friedland, who saw to it that various papers were destroyed.

Ferdinand Lassalle, together with Heinrich Heine, James Rothschild, and Benjamin Disraeli, belonged to the prototypes of the bourgeois Shylock in the nineteenth century. No Jewish artist, intellectual, writer in that era of the victorious bourgeoisie and seeming equality of rights for all citizens managed to avoid the intrinsic contradictions between abstract demands for emancipation and concrete inner disunity and strife. All the individual attempts are typical, each after its own fashion. Felix Mendelssohn-Bartholdy's Protestant inwardness while composing the "St. Paul" oratorium and his high-minded aid to an endangered Robert Schumann, which did not preclude anti-Semitic remarks in the secret journals of Robert and Clara. Marx's internationalism coupled with Jewish self-hate: one need only juxtapose the prose of the "Introduction to a Critique of the Hegelian Philosophy of Law" to the text on "The Jewish Question." Ludwig Börne's democratic, German patriotism coupled to his profoundly irritated polemics against the questionable outsider Heine. The continual back and forth between internationalism and Zionism in Moses Hess. The inward South-German small town idyll in Berthold Auerbach. A Prussian, Lutheran, elitist philosophy of state in the Berlin professor Friedrich Julius Stahl, who reappeared in quotations during the Third Reich as Joel Joelsohn. In all of this there is the manifestation of excess. A hypertrophy of education and wealth, of enthusiasm for the landscape, of conservatism, church music, internationalism, bourgeois ideology, and antibourgeois ideology.

Lord Rothschild, who is in a position to reject the concession of conversion. Lord Beaconsfield, who leads the conservative party, is well-acquainted with great aristocrats, the darling of the queen, who makes Rothschild the executor of his estate. Jacques Offenbach, who strikes up a tune to power while at the same time intoning a final galopade. Marcel Proust between the Faubourg Saint-Germain and the underworld, who sees through everything, even himself, by letting Charlus take his course, and Bloch. Hugo von Hofmannsthal, who is buried in the cowl of a Franciscan monk. Walther Rathenau's philosophical irrationalism conjoined with an incisive, capitalist organizational talent. Typical cases of the alliance between Jewish millions and Prussian, English, French aristocracy. Each time the "stringent happiness" from Thomas Mann's epic comedy *Royal Highness*. And even in his own case the marriage into the proudly bourgeois Pringsheim family in Munich (and soon thereafter the anti-Semitic moral to the first version of the short story "Wälsungenblut").

Ferdinand Lassalle is here, far more than Rothschild and certainly Heinrich Heine, the consummate phenotype. No one did more to fix the image of the Jewish intellectual adventurer than he. It was Lassalle who was called up in the reader's mind by that Moses Freudenstein, later Dr. Theophile Stein, in *The Starving Parson*, whether Raabe intended it or not. Georg Brandes in the Scandinavian world was of a similar decisive significance. The reader of Danish literature comes across him again and again; he is met for one last time in the twentieth century in the novel about the lucky dog Lykke Peer by the Danish Nobel Prize winner Henrik Pontoppidan, not by accident one of the favorite books of the young Georg Lukács and the young Ernst Bloch.

Shylock's bourgeois phenotypes in the nineteenth century confute Lessing's high-minded premise that emancipation is possible by education and property. Lichtenberg felt otherwise when he saw Shylock on the stage in London. Even Moses Mendelssohn, writing in Hebrew, must not have recommended conformity without misgivings. Heine and Rothschild, Disraeli and Lassalle demonstrate the irreparable provocation in education and property, in conservative and socialist politics. The twentieth century would come to create new phenotypes in bohemia and in revolution.

The Parallelism between German and Jewish Lives

The use of counterpoint in life stories was from the beginning one of the working principles of the bourgeois novelist. In Germany this goes back to the sixteenth century to Jörg Wickram, a burgher born out of wedlock, master craftman and *Meistersinger,* in whom all the essential recipes of composition are already assembled. In his novel *Der Jungen Knaben Spiegel* (Mirror of Young Boys) of 1554, there is already to be found the antithetics of a rising and a falling course of life juxtaposed one to the other. Schematic sequences of a later age are anticipated and very clearly so in counterpoint already possessing a class nature. The good burgher son rises; the lazy and imperious Junker goes to his ruin. It is an anticipation of Gustav Freytag 300 years before his time. To the degree, however, that the burgher class and its literature separate themselves from an opposing feudal world through successful emancipation, the parallelism between lives becomes doubly interiorized. The conflict now takes place totally within the bourgeois world. It is a process analogous to what transpires on the tragic stage of the bourgeois theater, which in Schiller's *Love and Intrigue* was based on a feudal-bourgeois antagonism but which sixty years later, in Hebbel's *Mary Magdalene,* puts on the stage, to use the author's formulation, only "individuals incapable of any dialectic," those of the petite bourgeoisie, to be precise.

The second form of interiorization manifests itself in the transformation of social antitheses into (seemingly) inner bourgeois, moral ones. The course of rise or decline takes place as integration or nonintegration within the bourgeois realm: the one prospers while the other goes to a "bourgeois death," as people used to put it, something that could take place in any number of ways, from no longer being invited to the homes of others to judicial deprivation of civil rights.

This recipe was as familiar to the successful, literarily ambitious novelist of the eighteenth and nineteenth centuries as it was to his despised competitor in popular light fiction. Everywhere the original scheme of the prospering, virtuous burgher (who is never a plebeian!) and of the worthless scion from the aristocracy becomes transformed into the antithesis of the prosperous and moral bourgeois who is confronted with the contrastive figure of the unsuccessful ne'er-do-well. That such a process takes place in Fielding as the parallelism between the foundling Tom Jones and the hypocritical Master Blifil in the realm of the landed gentry, offers no contradiction to this bourgeois system of categories. Fielding's world and that of his landed gentleman Allworthy is bourgeoisified society.

The process of a double interiorization, by total reduction to the bourgeois realm and by total moralization, allows an interesting variation to come to the fore, so that the parallelism of lives seems like the cliché stemming from the feudal world: the antithesis of the good and the bad brother. That was an aristocratic topos, based on the frustration of the younger sons of the nobility, magnified in Shakespeare to the exemplary action of Richard Gloucester, who had been predestined by nothing to ascend to the throne as Richard III. In Fielding this aspect of bourgeoisification has been incorporated as well: Jones and Blifil are cousins. Schiller adopts the scheme, along the general lines of which other *Sturm und Drang* writers had operated before him, for the antagonism between Karl and Franz Moor. Here as well a bourgeois and moralistic antagonism despite all aristocratic overlay.

Again and again variations on the same theme. In Thackeray's *Vanity Fair,* a century after *Tom Jones,* a parallelism of women's lives is inaugurated in Amelia Sedley and Becky Sharp. The model of rise and decline is artfully rounded off with the help of reversals. At first the intellectual and only semi-bourgeois Becky, half Frenchwoman at that, seems to proceed on the path to glory while the honest and sentimental Amelia has to endure humiliation and deceit. The ironist Thackeray, critically describing the early Victorian world, carefully avoids any identification on his own part with the mores of English society. Nonetheless even this novel about an almost total demolishing of bourgeois behavior and modes of conduct concludes by opposing respectable and unrespectable behavior, which is to say that even Thackeray, who has not only written about snobbism but does not wish to appear a snob himself, draws a line between people whom one invites to one's house and the others.

German bourgeois narrative literature was constructed on these designs as well. Initially, as with Wickram, in anticipation of and later in consolidation of the bourgeois emancipatory movement. Here the parallel biographies were still of the utilitarian bourgeois and the unproductive Junker. In Gustav Freytag's bourgeois-liberal epic novel of the German merchant, *Debit and Credit,* this sociologically and ideologically fertile model was continued. The barons of Rothsattel, socially unaware and yet overindulgent in their consumption, meet their ruin; the German merchants Schröter and Wohlfart inherit their property: not by storming the Bastille or by proclamation of a national convention but by a solid system of economic credit. Misalliances are at all events to be avoided here: baron marries baroness, bourgeois bourgeoise.

For all that, the German novel has its own entirely typical variant under the sign of parallel biographies, which is to be found neither in Dickens or Thackeray, Melville or Thoreau, nor even in the great Russian narrators of the nineteenth century. Thomas Mann, speaking here of his own starting points as well in an address in 1939 before the students of Princeton University on "The Art of the Novel," summed up most skeptically the German contribution to the bourgeois novel of the nineteenth century: "The great social epics in the novels of Dickens, Thackeray, Tolstoy, Dostoevski, Balzac, Zola, Proust make up the monumental art of the nineteenth century. These are English, Russian, French names. Why are German ones lacking?"

Whoever tries to answer this question will come to refer to all kinds of factors, all of which derive from the underlying phenomenon of backward social conditions in Germany. Deriving from this is the strange inclination of the German novelist, almost without parallel in English and French literature, to flee from the bourgeois world and the city back to the small town, to the village, from national literature to regional literature, from secularized Enlightenment to prebourgeois Protestant orthodoxy. It is a German epic leitmotif: the longing for a prebourgeois state that, strangely abstract, is not imagined as a transfigured feudal world as it was to some extent by the Romantics but that displays all the marks of a petit bourgeois village idyll off somewhere undisturbed.

This became the favorite cliché of the German reading public and the bourgeois novelist between 1840 and roughly 1920. Gustav Freytag and Wilhelm Raabe, a good deal of Theodor Storm's orgies of reminiscence, the young Hermann Hesse's *Peter Camenzind,* whose eponymous hero the author thought he had portrayed as a cranky outsider only to discover that he had sung their own life's melody to a broad spectrum of German readers. Ernst Wiechert on top of that. At the end, the simple life, the nostalgia for the "growth of the earth," is subscribed to by Knut Hamsun in Norway at a time when the German literature of the Expressionists and the writers of the *Neue Sachlichkeit* come to consider more and more boldly the phenomenon of the modern metropolis.

This socially immature epic form draws its sustenance from a threefold animosity shared by its readers. Hatred of the modern big city with its threatening proletariat is first: Berlin is chiefly meant here after, even in Thomas Mann, Munich had been fleetingly dallied with as a positive contrast to negative, Prussian Berlin. Hatred of enlightened bourgeois intellectuals is next. Finally a hatred of Jews that encompasses the whole lot at once: the metropolis, which is to say uprootedness; Enlightenment, which is to say atheism; equality of rights, which is to say taking seriously the bourgeois revolution and emancipation. Conjured up is the ideological prototype of a friend/foe: the Jewish big city intellectual, who is disdained, depending on circumstance, as asphalt litterateur, coffeehouse bard, finally as cultural Bolshevik. His adversary is portrayed, again depending on circumstance, as the solid German merchant, the parson, the teacher in the little village schoolhouse, the brave officer, the colonial politician in South Africa filled with care for "the people without space" (Cornelius Friebott in Hans Grimm's *Volk ohne Raum*).

This uncommonly widespread epic form, eagerly lapped up in the houses of the German middle class and in the manors of well-to-do farmers, is a constellation entirely typical of German conditions, once again with the scheme of parallel lives. Yet this time as the antithesis of German/"Aryan" life to Jewish life. Here too rise and decline. The Jewish riser finally falls; the modest German receives his rightful due despite all his troubles. Irony, to be sure, as in Thackeray's case, can break up the too bald antithetical structure. Hans Unwirrsch, the starving parson in Wilhelm Raabe's novel, is rewarded by an internal rise to contentment and familial serenity. Seen externally, that reward is the mean, subsistence parsonage in Grunzenow on the Baltic. The young Jew, Moses Freudenstein, on the contrary, alias Dr. Theophile Stein, suffers decline in external glory: "In Grunzenow they did not again take notice of Dr. Theophile Stein, who in Kröppel Alley went by the name of Moses Freudenstein, till in 1852, he, despised by those who used him, despised by those against whom he was used, received the title of Privy Councillor, dead to his fellow citizens in the most wretched sense of the word." "Dead to his fellow citizens" Raabe had put in italics. Glory and wretchedness, rise and fall, the highly honored spy for the administration, perhaps one day to become Dr. *von* Stein. This seemingly insignificant detail only displays the more crassly the critical ideological position in such epics of German and Jewish lives. Wilhelm Raabe wrote as a liberal bourgeois, his *Starving Parson* originated in the final phase of the monarchial restoration after the defeat of the bourgeoisie in 1849. Dr. Stein is dead to his fellow citizens; he has become a nonperson in their eyes since he hired on to the restored princes' police ministries as confidence man and spy, for which he is amply rewarded in money and titles. Bourgeois liberalism chooses him as its contrasting figure to the "rising" starving parson. Raabe's most successful novel is an amalgam of German-Jewish antagonism and bourgeois interiorization. Hans Unwirrsch's victory over the intellectual and Young Hegelian Moses Freudenstein is one of such interiorization. *The Starving Parson* lets loose all at once all of the contradictions of the bourgeois Enlightenment in Germany: liberalism but at the same time anti-Semitism; bourgeois loyalties but an inner rejection of any form of literature or thought that might burst the bounds of the existing system. In the place of the formula that had interested Kant of a possible religion "within the boundaries of universal reason," what goes on in Raabe amounts to the boundaries of reason being set within universal religion. The starving parson's hunger for Enlightenment degenerates in the novel into clerical cravings. In the face of Shylock/Freudenstein, Wilhelm Raabe is one more who like Lichtenberg feels uncanny revulsion when he has to compare the real Jew on the stage with the abstract postulates of universal emancipation that includes Jews as well.

Concerning the Good and Bad Jew

This much-praised and highly successful narrative literature works into its every detail the antithetical cliché that is unhesitatingly transferred from the world of bourgeois experience to literature. The parallel lives of the little German and the little Jew make their debut on the school playground, either as a genuine friendship from the start or as a curious and singular German/Jewish friendship that does not hold up later on account of the Jew. Freytag and Raabe are bourgeois liberals; they posit

German/Jewish friendship as being possible. Such a friendship comes into being according to the following scheme: the brave German boy comes to the aid of the oppressed, weak, and probably cowardly little Jewish boy.

In *Debit and Credit* the scene is set in the East, in the Silesian Ostrau. Anton Wohlfart and Veitel Itzig are the friends. "Itzig was not of noticeably nice-looking appearance; skinny, pale, with reddish, kinky hair, in an old jacket and defective trousers he looked as if he would attract a gendarme's attention more than any other traveler. He came from Ostrau and was a chum of Anton's from schooldays. Anton had had the opportunity in earlier days, through courageous use of his tongue and little fists, of protecting the young Jew from the abuse of mischievous schoolboys; from that day on Itzig had shown a certain attachment to him."

In *The Starving Parson* the little town of Neustadt where Hans Unwirrsch and Moses Freudenstein come into the world in the year 1819 has probably got to be imagined in the German North. "Moses Freudenstein stood amid his tyrannizers and with suppressed tears and a tormented smile passed his hand from one to the other, into which each of the young Christians and Teutons spat with a sharp yelp of disdain. . . . Now it was his turn to spit into the extended hand of the whimpering little Jew, and it struck him like lightning that a great act of vileness and cowardice was being perpetrated." Hans Unwirrsch thereupon turns against the crowd of his fellows. "He cried out wildly that they should leave Moses alone, he—Hans Jakob—wouldn't stand for it if they did him any more harm. His fist fell on the first nose that insolently pushed its way in. There was blood—a tangled mess of blows!"

From the very start the parallelism is provided in the social cliché of the brave German boy and the weak little Jew. It is adopted without scruple even up into the time of the Weimar Republic, in Ernst Gläser's novel *Generation of 1902*. This parallelism is from the very start unreal. What is lacking in the sense of Enlightenment dogma is equal opportunity. All of the Jews in Freytag or Raabe do not merely strive for equal civil rights, that which sends Itzig and Wohlfart to the same school and allows Unwirrsch and Moses to attain their preparatory school diplomas together, but a complete social integration, which is withheld. And withheld by these two German writers of bourgeois liberalism as well. Freytag was a National Liberal of the first water. Raabe gave his future starving parson Hans Jakob Unwirrsch, consciously, as he explains, Jean-Jacques Rousseau's first names as his own; in referring to the little town of

Neustadt, the little towns of Eisleben, Kamenz, and Marbach are mentioned in turn and honored. The towns of Luther, Lessing, Schiller.

What was taking place here was a literary and idealist Enlightenment of a very modest sort, not at all feudal regression. The scene of reviling the little Jewish boy is introduced feebly yet unmistakably with the words: "in those bygone days a disdain for Jews was widespread—particularly in the smaller towns and villages—which one no longer finds in such virulent forms nowadays." That is looking back to the year 1829, approximately, from the vantage point of 1861 when *The Starving Parson* was written. Raabe's novel, however, is in entire opposition to the foregoing sentence. In the figure of Moses Freudenstein, alias Doktor Stein, the Jewish intellectual and proponent of the Enlightenment is denounced. Hans and Moses both go on to the university to study. Hans studies Lutheran theology, Moses philosophy. "From the philosophy of Friedrich Wilhelm Hegel he could 'make use of a few things' and frequently made his friend Hans confused and uncomfortable by subsuming him and everything he had with him under some heinous category. With great eagerness he attended all manner of courses in jurisprudence as well; above all he occupied himself exhaustively with constitutional law: Machiavelli's *The Prince* and *Reineke Fuchs* were at this time two books that scarcely ever strayed far from his desk." A Young Hegelian; a political opportunist à la Machiavelli, whereby Machiavelli is completely portrayed in the sense of the childish prejudices of bourgeois anti-Machiavellianism, and Goethe's *Reineke Fuchs* becomes a handbook of fraud and unprincipled opportunism.

How inevitable for Heinrich Heine to put in an appearance here as well! Moses brags about patriotism and Jewish cosmopolitanism. "Individual fools among us would like to give up this ideal position and bother themselves to death with an adopted fatherland à la Loeb Baruch, known to you in German as Ludwig Börne; my friend Harry Heine in Paris remains, despite the white gown of the catechumen, a real Jew whose Semitic blood isn't to be flushed from his veins with all the baptismal water, French champagne, and German Rhine wine there is in existence! Why shouldn't he make fun of German disgrace with a touch of melancholy? Every stupidity and vile act committed on this side of the Rhine is a feast of the gods for him!"

That the narrator sees things in a completely different light than Freudenstein is evident. For Börne and against Harry Heine. To the cliché of parallel and yet not really parallel lives and to the topos of the little German who takes the little Jew under his wing, this literature of a profoundly insincere Enlightenment, which always reneges where it should be steadfast, adds the no less successful mental construct and image that would have its own consequences: the dualism of the good and bad Jew. Seen on its surface, it seems to present itself as a moral antithesis. Wilhelm Raabe formulates it as a concurrence with Börne and rejection of Heine. That is political-ideological confrontation, personalized in the feud of the two German-Jewish literati.

In the traditions of the English novel following Benjamin Disraeli and in Gustav Freytag's German epigones, the contrast was wont to be conceived as one of property and possessions to none. A subtler form of discrimination for the Jew emancipating himself in the sense of the formula of education and wealth. The stand taken by Lessing in *The Jews* continued to hold sway. Manifold forms of discrimination were conceivable. The educated and wealthy German Jew according to the hypothesis could be emancipated. Wealth without education resulted in the despicable Jewish parvenu. Education without wealth was caricatured in the coffeehouse litterateur who lives by sponging off others. At the very bottom, as totally unassimilable, was the poor and uneducated Jew.

In the face of him a second discrimination took place, this time undertaken by assimilated Jews themselves: that of the German Jews who seemed in every way qualified for wealth and education and "the Eastern Jews" they despised. That this constellation of a failed Jewish emancipation in Germany continued on in the history of Zionism and in the existence of the state of Israel with its "gecks" is well known.

In the novel *Debit and Credit*, which Freytag deliberately composed as a *juste milieu* avoiding any social and moral extremes, the Jewish positions seem nearly traced out with ruler and compass: Veitel Itzig, Hirsch Ehrental, Bernhard Ehrental, the progressive Germanization of their names is drawn not only as a process of emancipation but all in all as a moral progression. Veitel is emancipated least of all and is an undependable lout. Ehrental *père* hardly speaks the Jewish patois anymore, but as a sentimental usurer leads a life of doubtful moral purpose. Bernhard is a Jewish *bel esprit* and idealist whom education and wealth might almost have predestined to equality. The Baron von Fink comes to his house to take tea. Unfortunately Bernhard dies with a curse against his father on his tongue: against his origins.

To the trio of novels enjoying great popularity with the German educated reading public and its petit bourgeois clientele, there belongs next

Jewish Figures in the Bourgeois Novel

to Freytag's novel (1855) and *The Starving Parson* (1864) a novel by the legal historian and historicist Felix Dahn, which—multivolumned, circumstantial, filled with childish, moralistic antitheses—under the title *Fight for Rome* projects the problematic of German society back into late antiquity. It is similar to Freytag's subsequent novel, *The Forefathers*, which climactically conjoins ancient Teutonic-Germanic history with the National German liberalism of the nineteenth century. So too Dahn transports without reservation the crude ideological antitheses of German virtuousness and non-German tricksterism, loyalty and treachery, blond Nordic and swarthy Southern mentalities, into the world of the Ostrogoths, Romans, and Byzantines under Emperor Justinian and Empress Theodora. This epic-historic monstrosity originated in the period between 1859 and 1876 under the sign of German and Italian unification "from above," after the victorious crushing of the Second Empire and Napoleon III and empress Eugénie, blood and iron, war and victory. It is the conscious sense of German victory that long after the fact takes a belated literary revenge for the demise of the Ostrogoths.

Jews must not be wanting in this program of epic prophecy delivered after the fact. Since Felix Dahn like Freytag is a National Liberal, more nationalist than liberal to be sure, he too adopts the dualism of good and bad Jew. The bad Jew Jochen is cowardly, of course, and his physiognomy plainly bears all the "calculating cunning" of "his race." The good Jew, patriarch Isaac, remains steadfast and loyal to the Goths. The noteworthy lasciviousness that again and again, here as in so many other places, spurs desire for the "beautiful Jewess," gets its due both in Freytag with Ehrental's sister Rosalie and in Dahn in the figure of Miriam.

In a precise study of "The Image of the Jew in German Popular Literature," the American historian George L. Mosse, a relative of the sometime Berlin newspaper dynasty, investigates the influence of Freytag and Dahn, but curiously seems to leave out Wilhelm Raabe.[1] Mosse points to the apparently (but only apparently) curious situation that *Debit and Credit* as well as *Fight for Rome* were much esteemed even in the homes of assimilated Jews in Germany and were certainly not rejected as being anti-Semitic. "There was scarcely a Jewish household in Germany in whose library Dahn's and Freytag's books could not be found. The acceptance of this stereotype, and reading these popular authors, became a sign of Jewish assimilation."

And on the side of the German Jews there was no resistance against this stereotype of good and bad, German and non-German Jew, found readymade in literature and social life. The frankly anti-Semitic portrayal of Jews who practice usury and dupe peasants in Wilhelm von Polenz's novel *Der Büttnerbauer* (1895), is said, according to his own testimony, to have "opened the eyes" of the later Führer of the Grossdeutsches Reich. German proselytes were being prepared here through the obtrusive and stereotypical figures of Jews in bourgeois fiction. Not everyone had come across German or "non-German" Jews; but one was nevertheless put in the know by Moses Freudenstein and Veitel Itzig and Jochen. This manner of superstructure proved to have an activating power of its own.[2]

In Charles Dickens's Old Curiosity Shop

Reading on in Mosse's study on Jews in the German novel, one finds the following sentence: "Surely one can read Freytag or Dahn and remain unaffected, just as one reads Dickens's *Oliver Twist* without absorbing the anti-Semitic stereotype of Fagin."[3]

At first sight it appears as if Dickens created in his novel *Oliver Twist* the cruelest and most virulently anti-Semitic figure in all the fictional works of the bourgeois nineteenth century in the form of the gangster chieftain Fagin. Stereotypical associations of physical and moral ugliness seem to be made use of to portray a Jew who can lay claim to no extenuating circumstances and who, as the reader is asked to corroborate, is rightfully delivered to the hangman for execution.

"A very old and shrivelled Jew, whose villainous-looking and repulsive face was obscured by a quantity of matted red hair." Red-haired as well! Shylock's caricature could not be more exaggerated. The author Dickens, who had attained fame at the age of twenty-four with the publication of *The Posthumous Papers of the Pickwick Club* (1836–37), was twenty-six when *Oliver Twist* appeared in 1838. The moral and social success of the novel was immense, as is well known. The English Poor Laws were influenced by it as well as public opinion in everything that had to do with poorhouses, child labor, and combatting criminality. Oliver is simply a focal point of overlapping social constellations. He is of significance only insofar as his childlike helplessness lets the machinations and villainies to which he is subjected as victim or accomplice appear all the more despicable.

Dickens knew what he was talking about. Roaming loose in London in the 1820's, with his father in debtors' prison, then as clerk in a law office, later parliamentary stenographer, he had come into contact with those figures, conflicts, intrigues of which he in connection with Messrs. Twist, Nickelby, Chuzzlewit, and Copperfield again and again came to give report as witness of the poor and helpless, exploited children and sewing girls.

Even Fagin may be conceived as a real figure. The connection between Christian thief and Jewish fence, on account of Jewish non- or semi-emancipation, has had historical continuity since the Middle Ages wherever Jewish settlements were allowed. Bourgeois England, even before the Victorian era, was well acquainted with an array of Jewish activities from Rothschild to the criminal Fagin.

Dickens writes in an English literary tradition depicting picturesque gangsters, a tradition reaching from John Gay's *Beggar's Opera* to the underworld sequences in Smollet's and Fielding's novels. The master snatchpurse Jack Dawkins, the brutal burglar Sikes together with his mistress Nancy are at one and the same time figures seen and experienced in their author's youth as well as character masks in a tradition of English epic realism.

Fagin is of a different sort. One sees that even in the fashion in which Dickens has him meet his end. Nancy is killed by Sikes; he himself dies in flight; others are deported, end as rueful citizens or die in prison like Oliver's roguish half-brother, Monks, who in so doing joins the illustrious ranks of the malevolent brother who absconds with the family inheritance, a tradition reaching back to Fielding's *Tom Jones*. The Jew Fagin goes to the gallows.

Between *Oliver Twist* (1838) and the last novel Dickens finished, *Our Mutual Friend* (1865), there lie twenty-seven successful and imaginative years of storytelling and lecture giving, years of fame at home, in America, and on the Continent. Charles Dickens as the literary conscience of the bourgeois reader; as speaker on behalf of the downtrodden and mistreated, particularly of the speechless. Once again in this novel about "our mutual friend" the proven mixture of sensationalism, will to discovery (a dead man who is not at all dead), and martyrdom. More than in his earlier novels, Dickens falls upon the nouveaux riches snobs, aristocratic do-nothings, and pious Christian usurers, as if he wanted to step into the shoes of his great rival Thackeray, who had died in 1863.

Once more Jews are in the background. Mr. Riah Aaron manages the money matters for the firm of Pubsey & Co., St. Mary Axe, London. He has a bent over gait, a large-brimmed low-crowned hat and long-skirted caftanlike coat, but is "a venerable man, bald and shining at the top of his head, and with long hair flowing down at its sides." The venerable old man is in remarkable contrast to the red-haired, repugnant Fagin. Twice, one time after another, Dickens shows him to be a compassionate and reserved benefactor with the best of manners who is treated by younger Englishmen who are either thoughtless or without scruples as Shylock on the Rialto was by the Venetian playboys.

When Riah comes to the aid of Lizzie, who has been betrayed by her selfish brother, Lizzie's admirer Eugene tries his best to get rid of the irksome Jew.[4] His effort is not without a certain amount of impudence: if Mr. Aaron would be good enough to relinquish his charge of Lizzie and repose all further concern for her in him "then he will be quite free for any engagement he may have at the Synagogue." He has no success at this since Lizzie resolutely stands by Riah.

The usurer and bill broker Fascination Fledgeby is worse. When Riah goes over to his place one morning on business,[5] one anti-Semitic taunt after another results. Fledgeby accuses Riah and Jewish businessmen in general, unjustly so as Dickens demonstrates, of just those tricks he himself practices. When the nasty cuts from the man with whom he must do business do not cease, Riah suddenly remarks that Fledgeby apparently confuses the role that he, Riah, must play in his employ with that of his own actual character. Young Fascination answers coolly. Riah's appeal for justice is spurned, whereupon he asks for generosity, to which Fledgeby answers: "Jews and generosity! That's a good connection!" Riah is bidden continue with business and leave off the "Jerusalem palaver."

The contrast between Riah and Fagin could not be greater. The archetype of the red-haired abhorrent wretch: mean and cowardly, ruling by the power of money and business acumen over a gang of hired thieves and killers. In the illustrations that accompany the novel like Dickens's others and that participate in the effect of the whole, Fagin is depicted in an archetypical manner essentially the same as the depictions of Jews in Wilhelm Busch, very much like the drawings in the SA journal *Der Stürmer*. The representation of Oliver Twist's first meeting with Fagin culminates in the contrast between childish innocence and guilt laden ugliness.

Riah is more abstract, which is to say never sharply delineated. The kindly old Jew of unpretentious appearance and constant goodwill. Spurned by those who are his inferiors. A cliché from melodrama and trivial literature. That Dickens, in this no different from Balzac, does not

Jewish Figures in the Bourgeois Novel

simply adopt the moralistic antitheses of his readers' fantasy, but consciously reproduces them, is evident. On that account both these writers have little success with their Jewish characters. Fagin like Riah is equally unrealistic, even if there may be Jews who act exactly like the Baron Nucingen/Rothschild with the German accent in Balzac's *Human Comedy*.

According to this, the conclusion would be that the duplicity of German-Jewish lives in Raabe or Gustav Freytag and later still in the early Heinrich Mann corresponded to a greater integration of Jews in bourgeois German society, while the epic realism of a Balzac or Dickens produced in their figures of Jews nothing other than moral antitheses and (depending on the occasion) tragic or comic episodes—total nonintegration, in a word.

Yet the exact opposite is correct. Fagin is neither the product of an anti-Semite nor Riah the ideal figure of a sentimental philo-Semite. Neither is there in Dickens any process of maturity or even refinement between *Oliver Twist* and *Our Mutual Friend*. Fagin and Riah are for Dickens not social outsiders but representatives of extremities in moral behavior, which signifies total social integration. These Jews are part of a middle class totality, even if in an extreme sense of morality or immorality. The author of these extremities, however, does not deduce them from their religious or social outsiderdom. Nonetheless, it soon becomes apparent, both in Balzac and in Dickens, that the epic integration of the Jewish figures failed. They were, all of them, never a part of common bourgeois life. Whether extremely evil or good, comic or cruel is all one: they are not comparable to the other, non-Jewish, figures in Dickens's world. Uriah Heep in *David Copperfield,* a non-Jew, is eccentric without transcending the confines of the socially given. And Jonas Chuzzlewit is a murderer and unscrupulous criminal but without the horror of outsiderdom.

By the way, the Jews in Dickens's epic cosmos are without family. In Raabe and Freytag the strangeness of the Jewish milieu with its junkshops or usurer's counting room, strange eating habits, and beautiful Jewesses was part and parcel of a strange foreignness. Dickens wanted to moralize social divergences and thus integrate them. The Jewish milieu could not be used there. It might have brought about disintegration once more. By trying to prevent just that, Dickens substantially brought it about.[6]

Eliot's Daniel Deronda, or the Zionist Variant

Between Lessing's youthful *Lustspiel The Jews* of 1749 and George Eliot's last great novel completed in 1876 lie 127 years. At first glance it seems nonetheless as if time had stood still. In both instances the noble Jew, educated and wealthy. In both instances he is obliged to destroy all hopes and expectations with a single sentence: "I am a Jew." The young baroness in Lessing who had naively thought that made no difference is immediately given to understand otherwise by her lady's maid. Gwendolen Grandcourt in Eliot's novel, who is hopelessly infatuated with Deronda, having taken him to be an English gentleman but having been apprised of the true facts, answers in the end: "What difference need that have made?" Yet before that she had taken the news in a somewhat different fashion. "A *Jew*! Gwendolen exclaimed in a low tone of amazement, with an utterly frustrated look, as if some confusing potion were creeping through her system."[7]

This time it is Deronda who breaks with her. He considers himself a Jew and wants to marry a Jewess. The author Eliot, an English free thinker, a friend of Herbert Spencer, vaguely sympathetic with the positivist philosophy of Auguste Comte, can only give her Gwendolen advice in the sense of an ethical "meliorism," as Comte's followers used to call it: making use of the disappointment as a stimulus toward moral self-education.

The reader's reaction as well seems analogous to that to Lessing's early, dramatic one-act play and this new, impatiently awaited novel of a famous and much read woman author in Victorian England who cannot be invited to one's house, to be sure, since she lives in common law marriage but whose books enjoy a favored place in the library of Her Majesty. Professor Michaelis in Göttingen, a proponent of the Enlightenment as Lessing, had made the reply: there could not actually be Jews of such noble nature. The Victorian male reader (not to mention the female one) reacted similarly to the almost Christ-like figure of the noble Deronda. Indeed, even the *Encyclopaedia Britannica* speaks, catechizing the prevailing literary judgment, of a "less convincingly realized hero Daniel." The unflinchingly noble, tactful, selfless manner of this young English gentleman Deronda, who does not know his parents and who grows up under the care of his "uncle," Sir Hugo Mallinger, a member of an ancient English noble line, whose illegitimate son he secretly takes himself to be, who wanders through the eight books of the novel without ever encountering any situation of conflict that might call his fine notions into doubt, is in point of fact enervating. Yet Victorian readers had no objections to noble and exemplary characters in novels, neither in Dickens nor in George Eliot, when they were well-bred, if perhaps simple people of unmistakably English origin and type. Queen Victoria would not, of course, receive the author Mary Ann Evans, who wrote her books under the name George Eliot, but was quite taken with an exemplary figure in Eliot's first novel, *Adam Bede,* that of the stalwart Mrs. Poyser. The Queen even commissioned two paintings to capture the noble scenes from *Adam Bede*; and they have indeed been captured, in the treacly aptness of the painter E. H. Corbould.[8]

The noble Daniel Deronda, in contradistinction, was a Jew as it turns out. Immediately the old arguments flared up that had once squared off Michaelis against the young Lessing. Much in this later work of George Eliot's was conventional: the popular story of the alluring young man with unknown yet apparently respectable antecedents; the no less popular story of the alluring and pretty girl who has respectable parents, but parents who have neither means nor any sort of entree into society, and who aspires with all her might to a marriage into the higher orders. To be sure, Gwendolen Harleth, to whom this function falls in the novel *Daniel Deronda,* ends neither in glory and inner frigidity nor as a déclassée, the alternatives since Thackeray's day, but as a penitent in the sense of an ethical positivism that sees itself as the successor to Christianity.

Yet what distinguishes *Daniel Deronda* among the contemporary works of belles lettres, and not simply those in England, is its demonstrative, almost obtrusive philo-Semitism. The noble Riah in Dickens's *Our Mutual Friend* was a character on the margins of exoticism just like the master criminal Fagin in *Oliver Twist.* It would not occur to anyone to equate Fagin with any real, actual Jew. Leon Trotsky reports in his autobiography just how much enthusiasm greeted the novel *Oliver Twist* in his parents' house, among Jews in the south of Russia.

But the Cohen family in George Eliot, to which belongs Mirah, who was saved by Deronda from drowning in the Thames, is an authentic part of the Jewish quarter in London around 1866, the novel taking place at the time of the Austro-Prussian war and the Second Napoleonic Empire. The meeting of Daniel and Mirah is apparently fortuitous. The Jewish quarter is entirely unfamiliar to him. But there again and again he is taken for a Jew and causes disappointment when he in firm conviction denies it. The course of the novel represents Deronda's path or return home as a form of predetermined finding of identity. The very real horror that gripped so many apparently well-integrated members of bourgeois society, particularly in Germany after 1933, when their hushed-up full or half-Jewishness was discovered, is in George Eliot's case something involuted with strange playful facility into a positive good. Daniel is relieved, all aflame, when his mother informs him that he is the issue of a Jewish marriage who was brought to England as a small child after his father's death and despite his grandfather's wishes to be raised as a gentleman. He feels cheated out of his heritage by his mother. But now he can be a Jew and marry Mirah, a Jew marrying a Jewess.

The novel *Daniel Deronda* played for English Jews in 1876 a role similar to that played by *Nathan the Wise* for Moses Mendelssohn's coreligionists in Germany a century earlier. Where non-Jewish readers grew ill at ease with Deronda's or Nathan's moral and intellectual superiority, Jewish readers saw the possibility of identification that would, so they hoped, make possible further enlightened integration.

Here, however, the novel of 1876 sharply differentiated itself from the emancipatory models of the younger and older Lessing both. Despite all apparent sameness of the literary topoi, high-mindedness and discovery of one's true roots with wealth and education, for both devolved upon Deronda, the fact of the matter is that the novel *Daniel Deronda* negates Jewish emancipation and integration. George Eliot had translated David Friedrich Strauss and Feuerbach's *Essence of Christianity* into English. During a journey to Germany with her husband, the Goethe scholar George Henry Lewes, she had met together with Strauss in Cologne. She was to some extent familiar with the intellectual positions of the Young Hegelians. Later in London she also met Louis Blanc and the other proponents of utopian socialism, possibly even Marx. The notion of George Eliot meeting with Moses Hess is particularly appealing. But she seems to have her good acquaintance with Jewish customs from her dealings with Emanuel Deutsch, a Talmud scholar who died in 1872 and who had visited her on occasion to read Hebrew with her and discuss the return of the Jews to the Near East. That Deutsch served as the model for the figure of Mordecai Cohen, who acts as Daniel Deronda's instructor in Jewish matters, is as unequivocal in Eliot scholarship as the Jewish composer and pianist Anton Rubinstein's being used as the basis for the figure of the musician Klesmer who loves a rich English heiress and is simply dismissed by her embittered mother as "a Jew or a Gypsy."[9] But instruction in Jewish matters signifies for Daniel Deronda and consequently for the author who penned him, who was not a Jew, the negation of a possible total emancipation that both George Eliot and Daniel Deronda hold to be neither desirable nor realizable. "The idea that I am possessed with is that of restoring a political existence to my people, making them a nation again, giving them a national center, such as the English have, though they, too, are scattered over the face of the globe,"[10] Deronda says.

That is the Zionist variant in the bourgeois novel. Desiring for his people "a national center" Eliot/Deronda is making strange comparison of Jews with Englishmen since both are scattered over the face of the globe; it is strange, of course, because the English in their scattering suffer no loss of national homeland. This is part of Deronda's discussion with his woman friend Gwendolen whom he never thought of marrying and whom he as a Jew now rejects as marriage partner, just as non-Jewish families had so often found a prospective Jewish partner unacceptable. "I am a Jew." With that everything is at an end. That is once again documented in the year 1876 in the novel *Daniel Deronda* and at the same time demonstrated to be an unchanging, unalterable scheme of things.

George Eliot has her Deronda, to everyone's discomfiture, finally come "to see," to use Brecht's terminology, unlike the half-Jewish Proust and the Jesuit schoolboy Joyce. The emancipation of the Jewish snob in Proust seems to succeed so perfectly that only the relentless dissecting on the part of the narrator can diagnose failure where Bloch himself felt success. Leopold Bloom, finally, Joyce's Judaeo-Irish Ulysses, exists in an ambiguity similar to Deronda's at the first, between Orient and Occident, lotus eaters and Cyclopes: as a Jew living in Ireland who suddenly, hate-filled, lets fly with the words "dog of a Christian!"

Marcel Proust and Albert Bloch

Marcel Proust—or his narrator, who is also named Marcel—is one more who immediately seizes upon Shylock of Venice when it is necessary to characterize an old or elderly, not particularly pleasant Jew. Albertine is dead; Robert de Saint-Loup fallen at the front; more than twenty years separates the world of the Faubourg Saint-Germain at the time of the First World War from the Dreyfus affair. Marcel comes once again, accepting an invitation only because it had the name Guermantes on it, to visit the house of the Prince of Guermantes, a newly constructed place on the Avenue du Bois, as the guest displeasedly notes. Lost and rediscovered time in one. And he sees his boyhood friend Bloch there for the first time in years.

"Bloch came in with a leap, like a hyena. 'He is now to be found in salons to which he would not have been admitted twenty years ago,' I thought. And he was twenty years older. He was closer to death. What did he reap from it all? Seen at close quarters in the transparency of his face, in which I, from afar and with poor lighting had espied only sunny youthfulness (because it had survived there, or because I had conjured it up), there was the almost frightful, fearful face of an old Shylock, made up, waiting in the wings for his cue and already half-audibly mumbling his first verse."[11] Shylock/Bloch in the salon of an anti-Semite and former anti-Dreyfusard also grown old who did not wish to receive Baroness Alphonse de Rothschild and had a friendship with Swann despite his Jewish antecedents, simply because he, a Jewish Catholic and son of a Catholic, was said to be somehow illegitimately descended from one of the Bourbons. Albert Bloch had behind him a long and successful march upward. Successful? "What did he reap from it all?" the narrator repeats the question to himself. Bloch had "married into it" in the sense meant by Karl Kraus when he translates monogamy as "marrying into something." Bloch père is dead. His son honors his memory almost as a cult: good Jewish familial piety, which by the honesty of its feelings fundamentally distinguishes itself from the familial piety of the dukes of Guermantes or La Tremoïlle, which has only genealogy in mind: not the individual carriers of famous names.

At the beginning of the novel/flood on lost time, Bloch was introduced in a not particularly glorious fashion. Young Marcel is given permission to invite his much admired schoolboy friend to Combray for the holidays, even though his grandfather, a not especially philo-Semitic liberal, objects that the Blochs are not exactly the cream of the Jewish bourgeoisie. Young Bloch for his own part, aware of being an outsider, does everything to stylize his condition. Manners, speech mannerisms, apparent disdain for convention out of an exaggerated inner veneration for it: all of this makes him into an unbearable guest.

According to his fashion and in all mastery, Proust introduces the young, educated, rich, and seemingly so unsociable Jew by means of his expressions and manner of speaking. Bloch speaks about literature (how could it be otherwise) but in a fashion reminiscent of a police report on the one hand and the epithets of the Homeric epic on the other. Alfred de Musset, as if in the testimony of some swindler, becomes "le sieur de

Musset," "the herein named Racine" is spoken of with like suspicion. It is put thus: "Mistrust," he apprises his friend Marcel, "your somewhat base predilection for Musset. He is a particularly noxious sort and coarse and gloomy. I must admit, incidentally, that he and even a certain Racine once made during their lives rather good rhythmic verse, which besides, and this is for me wherein their highest merit consists, expresses nothing whatsoever. I mean 'La blanche Oloossone et la blanche Camire' and 'La fille de Minos et de Pasiphaë.' These verses, which exonerate the two idlers, were made known to me by an article by my dear teacher, Father Leconte, whom the immortal gods look upon with favor."[12] Nothing here is further from the spontaneous disrespect of an impudent young student. Everything is planned and stylized. A perfected convention of nonconvention. Debunking venerable Classical and Romantic writers; a montage of various linguistic levels, from the language of the police report to the epic; this young Jew's very dear teacher who is a priest; praise for an extremely artistic formalism. Bloch swears "by Apollo" or "by Zeus," calls his friend Marcel "cher maître" and expects the same in return.

Bloch's manners have been brought into strict conformity with his manner of speaking. A perfect convention of nonconvention. Invited to dinner, he appears one and one-half hours late, coming in muddied and dripping wet from the rain and not only does not excuse himself but admonishes his bourgeois hosts that 'I never allow myself to be imposed upon by the goings-on in the atmosphere, nor by the usual modes of counting time. While I would like to return the opium pipe and the Malay kris to general esteem, I ignore the much more dangerous and no more than humdrum bourgeois instruments of chronometer and umbrella."[13] At any event, Bloch is not invited back, so that Marcel for the time being cannot ask him why the greatest merit of verse consists in "expressing nothing whatsoever."

That was how things started out. The Duchess of Guermantes ignores him; her brother-in-law, Baron de Charlus, inquires of Marcel whether Bloch is young and good-looking but refers to him as a foreigner. Replying to the answer that he is French, Charlus, who unlike his entire family had defended Dreyfus, says: "Oh, is that so, I thought he was a Jew."[14] Charlus's argumentation in favor of Dreyfus, incidentally, is more sinister than naked anti-Semitic negation. Dreyfus could not have committed an act of treason against France, he maintains, but only against "Judea." If indeed the charges against him proved objectively correct, he should be punished for "criminal acts against the hospitality accorded him by the French nation."

Proust skirts about the immediate confrontation between Bloch and Charlus. It would only have proved once again the antagonism between Shylock and Antonio or between Heine and Platen. Yet in the structure of the entire novel it assumes the place of an important constructional element. No less important for an understanding of the *Remembrance of Things Past* than the "intermittences du coeur," than the act of memory and philosophy of lost time and time won back again.

Antithetics and intermixture are the narrator's means of representation. By melting down all seemingly frozen, antithetical positions in the passage of time, so that the servants consort with their masters and can finally become their masters, Proust allows the Don Juans to make their way to Sodom, irreproachable wives to depart for Gomorrah, and Jewish outsiders to become the bulwark of the aristocratic and anti-Semitic Faubourg.

In all of this Bloch and Charlus are certainly the purest exponents of an absolute outsiderdom in that society of French aristocrats, bourgeois, plebeians, and domestics: as the friend/foe relation of Judea and Sodom, yet there is an exceedingly ingenious system of fusions and overlappings. Swann remains, even if on the highest level of assimilation, reckoned a member of Shylock's clan. He does not wish to admit to it, evades the subject, diverges when mention is made of Bloch, whom he as a member of the Jockey Club must needs despise, but which he as "one from the Jews' camp" cannot do. Recourse is taken in art history. Bloch? "Oh yes, the boy whom I saw here once who so much resembles Mohammed II in Bellini's portrait."[15]

Heine's concatenation of Sodom and Judea is to be met in Proust as well. Just as in *The Baths of Lucca* Heine had presented the marchese Gumpelino at one and the same time as Jewish/aristocratic assimilee *and* as bosom friend of count Platen, there are in the epic of the *temps perdu* the most astonishing and humorous cross connections. During the summer holidays at the ocean at Balbec, for example, Bloch's sister executes in plain sight a lesbian scene with her actress girlfriend which brings two officers staying with their wives at the Grand Hotel de Balbec (Baalbek!) to lodge a complaint with the manager and demand the ladies' departure. In vain, one must add. Bloch's uncle, M. Nissim Bernard, is one of the most prominent seasonal guests at the hotel, because Sodom is here for him, in the form of a hotel page. Bernard is more important to the hotel than the two officers staying over one Sunday. The ladies are merely urged to avoid public exhibitions.

Bloch himself reacts as a good Jewish brother and nephew. In his erotic life he may feel only strangeness toward Sodom and Gomorrah; but their conjunction in the community of Judaism and family proves stronger. For his own part, he remains in all purity the *Jewish* outsider in society, just as Charlus, who can trace his line back to the crusades, remains in all purity the *erotic* outsider and in the end wishes to remain so.

The paths they take assume in the passage of time more and more of a centrifugal course. To the degree that Bloch grows into the society of the aristocratic salons, Charlus is unremittingly expelled. What happens to him and repeats itself is the course of events that overcame his friend Swann. In the case of the latter, the coquette Odette de Crécy; for the former, the plebeian musician Morel. The shadow thrown on the aristocratic Odette's social luster no longer originates from parentage or trade but from her liaison and marriage to Swann, the intimate of the dukes. The arrivé Morel, who has the baron to thank for everything, expends great labors in making that patronage forgotten.

Bloch, on the other hand, climbs and climbs. He was a dramatist and wrote a book on Philip II of Spain; a sometime Dreyfusard (at times a Jewish anti-Semite as well) he changed during the war first to a chauvinist, then to a pacifist. Now he is established as a writer and has sought and found his new milieu: the Faubourg Saint-Germain. And he is now called Jacques du Rozier, having simply transformed his nom de plume into a family name. He wears a monocle. The kinky hair of yesteryear has been straightened; the exaggerated nose might seem a characteristic of ancient French aristocracy. "Behind the mirror of his monocle he had arranged himself so haughtily, intimidatingly, smugly, as if it were a mirror with eight reflexes, and in order to accommodate his face to his straight hair and monocle, his facial expressions from now on were empty of any significance."[16]

He now has admission to the princess of Guermantes. Yet Proust's readers have long since known that the incumbent carrier of that name is none other than the entirely bourgeois and inordinately wealthy Mme. Verdurin. The passing of time makes it all possible: Mme. Verdurin as princess, Bloch/du Rozier as litterateur in the aristocracy's salons. For the young and "authentic" dukes of the new generation, both have always been there. He himself in matters of religion remained a Jew: perhaps out of respect for the paternal superego, or from pride in irrevocability, like the Rothschilds. His daughter marries a Catholic.

The figure of Salomon's son Albert Bloch illustrates for Proust, a half-Jew who for all his social equality of station always sensed a pressing illegitimacy that could then inspire his artistic work, at one and the same time the absurdities of the passing of time and the unreliability of human, "intermittent" memory. For him Bloch at the end of the novel when the task is to rediscover lost time by means of writing is as legitimately installed in the world of the Guermantes as all the others, namely, illegitimately. As legitimately as the Duchess of Broglie, Mme. de Staël's daughter, the granddaughter of the bourgeois banker Necker. (Proust himself fell upon this comparison.)

For Proust there takes place in all of this, through the passage of time, wealth, and property, literary activity (which he characterizes in Bloch's case as mediocre and usurpatory) and general forgetfulness, a successful Jewish emancipation. Shylock has his salvation by means of the passage of time and bourgeois-capitalist legal and financial equality.

The question remains of Bloch's identity with himself. Proust views this figure purposely from the outside; he is interested in Bloch's behavior, and scarcely in his motivation. Yet Bloch remains in his own eyes—even if he had been invited by the "authentic" Duchess of Guermantes instead of simply by her middle class cousin, the Princess of Guermantes, who married into her position—an intruder who by means of monocle and lack of expression means to counteract an excess of definition. His new stylization of extreme conformity corresponds exactly to his erstwhile stylization of permanent provocation, as apparent nonconformity. The great du Rozier who so extravagantly thanks the Jewish actress Rachel in the salon of the false Guermantes (disturbing the entire audience in the process) for declaiming badly and wrongly several verses by La Fontaine, is practicing the same game the young Bloch played who had not scorn enough for the idlers Racine and Musset. It was the convention of unconvention at that time; now it is the convention of convention, yet practiced by someone who protrudes from all convention. A snob? Only insofar as he has no choice. But perhaps that is snobbery as well. Shylock does not have the mettle to be a snob.

Leopold Bloom as Odysseus

Why a Jew, Mr. Leopold Bloom, who lives at no. 7 Eccles Street, Dublin, is an "advertisement canvasser" by trade, and appears in James Joyce's

Jewish Figures in the Bourgeois Novel

novel[17] as the wandering Odysseus, has often been commented upon. General references to Ahasuerus, eternal wandering, restlessness, a longing to return home, do not get one very far. In the twelve episodes that divide up the day, June 16, 1904, of this Judaeo-Irish Ulysses, from morning tea for the unfaithful Penelope to the late night return home after a stay with a Circe by the name of Mrs. Bella Cohen, the famous dangers to the homeric hero are very precisely—if degraded to the milieu of the petite bourgeoisie—distributed across Leopold Bloom's day. One is obliged in consequence to proceed from the assumption that Joyce understood the Odyssean adventure, both in Homer and here in the Irish capital at the beginning of the twentieth century, as trials undergone by Jews.

A reference that the author of *Ulysses* provided Stuart Gilbert, one of the first interpreters of the book, seems to help this matter along.[18] In his hesitating and suggestive fashion, Joyce, according to Gilbert's report in the 1950 preface to his commentary, made mention of a work by the French classical philologist Victor Bérard, *Les Phéniciens et l'Odyssée*. His reading of Bérard's voluminous work provided the interpretation of the *Odyssey* as an originally Phoenician, which is to say, Semitic logbook. The Greek rhapsode known to us as Homer then put the work into the Ionic language and gave it its artistic form.

Gilbert cites Bérard's conclusion:

The Ulysseid ('Οδύσσεια) appears to be a Phoenician periplous (logbook) transposed into Greek verse and a poetic legend according to certain very simple and typically hellenic principles: anthropomorphic personification of objects, humanization of natural forces, hellenization of the raw material. By these methods, to which the Greeks owe so many of their myths and legends, was woven on to a stout, if coarse Semitic canvas that typically Greek masterpiece the Odyssey.

This passage in Bérard has been worked into Joyce's material as well: the "hellenization" of the raw material at hand. Mulligan speaks of this to his friend Stephen Dedalus as a praiseworthy Irish task.

The structure of *Ulysses* in its duplicity as the course of a day for Dedalus and Bloom who miss meeting each other so often until they finally converge late at night in the hospital, could be understood on that account as the separate, then joint, day voyage of a Semitic Odysseus and his Greek-Irish Homer. Whereby this Jewish and sensuous/melancholy Odysseus, driven from here to there, seems in ironic refraction almost the creation of his Irish epic poet, Dedalus. Stephen reappears in the novel in continuation of Joyce's earlier self-portrait, the *Portrait of the Artist as a Young Man*. The figure of Bloom meets his inventor, for Stephen bears the name of the first and archetype of all inventors, the Greek Daedalus. To be sure Bloom, the Jewish stranger in Dublin, proves himself to be the protector of his young, future Homer.

Both are outsiders. Stephen is Irish and a Catholic but he breaks out of that community; his books and poetic visions alienate him from his surroundings. He tries to shake loose from the community in drunkenness and blasphemy.[19] With the chant of the Introit he enters Circe's bordello. The great concluding talk between Dedalus and Bloom that recapitulates the story of Bloom's boyhood and youth takes place in the question and answer of the Catechism.

Leopold Bloom, with a name harking back to the Hapsburg Empire where the emperors were occasionally named Leopold and the Jews at the beginning of the nineteenth century, in consequence of bourgeois emancipation, were passed out schematic names of flowers and animals, or metals, or even colors, like Schwarz, Roth, Weiss, or Blau, cannot sever himself in his inner monologues from being Jewish. He is proud of Mrs. Marian Bloom, the singer, whose amorous escapades he excuses in makeshift fashion with her Spanish-Jewish blood: Spanish Jews, the Sephardim, are nobler than the German and East European Ashkenazim.

Jewish circumlocutions and curses surface. Drunk at the Circe's, suffering Walpurgis Night visions, Bloom suddenly cries out, "dog of a Christian!" Even as early as the morning, his mind had been moving toward the Orient. The episode with the lotus eaters finds him musing: "The far east. Lovely spot it must be; the garden of the world, big lazy leaves to float on . . . Flowers of idleness . . . Water-lilies." Once more metempsychosis plays a role, the transmigration of souls, as Bloom, who is somewhat educated, explains to his Molly, who reads metempsychosis as "Met-Him-Pike-Hoses," of course.

On the other hand, Bloom is a firm believer in his Irishness. When the nationalistic and anti-Semitic Cyclops, an Irish Polyphemus, who has no name in Joyce, but is simply referred to as "the citizen," in personification of the anonymous, yet established and sedentary mass vis-à-vis the wandering Ulysses, asks this intruder into the pub after the manner of the Cyclops for his name, the following dialogue ensues:

"What is your nation, if I may ask?" says the citizen.
"Ireland," says Bloom. "I was born here. Ireland."

The citizen said nothing only cleared the spit out of his gullet and, gob, he spat a Red bank oyster out of him right in the corner.[20]

Then the conversation in the pub jumps to Irish antiquities; some anti-British sentiment is evinced; a new round of drinks is brought on. At this point Bloom continues his talk, which is no more actually than a supplementary reminiscing monologue.

—And I belong to a race too, says Bloom, that is hated and persecuted. Also now. This very moment. This very instant.
Gob, he near burnt his fingers with the butt of his old cigar.
—Robbed, says he. Plundered. Insulted. Persecuted. Taking what belongs to us by right. At this very moment, says he, putting up his fist, sold by auction off in Morocco like slaves or cattles.
—Are you talking about the new Jerusalem? says the citizen.
—I'm talking about injustice, says Bloom.

This is a dialogue all askew since no one is listening to anyone else, with the exception of Bloom, who remains a stranger and wanderer driven from place to place since he cannot claim any kind of communality with the Cyclopes in the Dublin pub. No resonance follows from him when Joyce unfolds one of his cataloging lists. In this instance an Irish one, extravagantly mixed with saga, history, geography, and business, as for example: "Glendalough, the lovely lakes of Killarney, the ruins of Clonmacnois, Cong Abbey, Glen Inagh and the Twelve Pins, Ireland's Eye—the brewery of Messrs Arthur Guinness, Son and Company (Limited)—Isolde's tower, the Mapas obelisk—"

Then a car with officials from the castle arrives. Bloom has gone out to relieve himself. His thoughts even here are fixated on the discrepancy between what he would like to be and what he is. In the meantime the Cyclopes at the bar confer about the strange events surrounding this Bloom, who apparently is no relation to the dentist Bloom. One of the officials, Martin by name, knows it all. "He's a perverted jew, says Martin, from a place in Hungary and it was he drew up all the plans according to the Hungarian system. We know that in the castle." The government knows everything. Bloom's name, he adds, is actually Virag.

Then the confused debate switches over to Jewish messianism, for which one as a good Irish Catholic can only have disdain. At the sound of a church bell there flows an epic stream, endless masses of monks' orders and middling to unprepossessing saints, a St. Leopold among them. Bloom returns, the Cyclopes clamber into the car to drive off, the "citizen" who represents Polyphemus and wears a patch over one eye suddenly bawls out: "Three cheers for Israel!". At this juncture Bloom can no longer refrain from offering a catalog of his own devise in turn: "Mendelssohn was a jew and Karl Marx and Mercadante and Spinoza. And the Saviour was a jew and his father was a jew. Your God."

Bloom is once again bifurcated even into his very expressions. He speaks of "the Savior," but then says "your God." Martin attempts to underplay the new outburst so that they can finally be off, but the "citizen" smells a new chance for a fight and retorts, "Whose God?" To which Bloom responds: "Your God was a jew. Christ was a jew like me." Whereupon Polyphemus plunges back into the pub. "By Jesus, says he, I'll brain that bloody jew man for using the holy name. By Jesus, I'll crucify him so I will."

The irony of the situation is consummate. The language stands as witness and corroborates Bloom's supposed blasphemy when he claims Jesus for himself as a Jew. Now the blasphemer on that account, by Jesus, at least in the words of the Cyclops, is going to be crucified!

This Ulysses had wanted to remain nameless like his Homeric predecessor in Polyphemus' cave: Outis, no name, nobody. In this he has no success. He is obliged to acknowledge his own identity. It breaks to the surface time and time again. "Dog of a Christian!"—that is an oriental circumlocution. There is no pride felt in the "lovely lakes of Killarney" or in Isolde's tower. Bloom sides with Mendelssohn (the grandson and composer, of course), Karl Marx and Mercadante and Spinoza. And with the Savior.

The Cyclopes at the bar had brought up the curse on Ahasuerus when Bloom was outside occupied with his thoughts and fluids. Precisely in the epic structure of the scene with the Cyclopes in *Ulysses* it becomes clear that Joyce does not view his Odysseus Bloom legitimized through the superficial myths of the Jew Ahasuerus alone.

The sea-voyager Odysseus was for the classicist Bérard a Semite, but his Homer was Greek and a poet. They complemented each other. In the sixteenth episode (Eumaeus) where Bloom takes in tow the exhausted Stephen, who has no place to sleep, the communality of the outsiders is underscored: once again in ironic paradox, as with the behavior of the Cyclops Polyphemus.

It is precisely the restless and itinerant Bloom who takes it upon himself to return Stephen Dedalus, the son of the respected Simon Dedalus, to settledness and home. In this sense his question to the prodigal son who is a poet: "but why did you leave your father's house?" "To seek misfortune was Stephen's answer."[21]

Later, when they are having coffee and a roll, a sailor comes up to their table, but addresses Stephen only. He discovers his name despite Bloom's attempt to prevent it. Stephen is simply not Ulysses. It does not enter his head to present himself as "Nobody." The sailor is curious when he hears the name Dedalus. He knows Simon Dedalus, his father. Does Stephen know him? He has heard of him, he says.

He's Irish, the seaman bold affirmed, staring still in much the same way and nodding. All Irish.
All too Irish, Stephen rejoined.[22]

Now Stephen suddenly seems to know that all-too-Irish man, his own father. And the name Dedalus itself is apparently all too Irish. They belong together as the catechetical question and answer in the penultimate (seventeenth) episode of this Odyssey demonstrates. Everything is fully divergent. Bloom was baptized three times, once as a Protestant, twice as a Catholic. Stephen only once, by the same priest who admitted the grown Bloom the last time to the community of the Catholic Church. This son of Rudolf Virag, later Rudolf Bloom, made his way from Szombathely in Hungary to Vienna, Budapest, Milan, and London to Dublin. Dedalus mère and père have for origins only Cork and Dublin.

Stephen is a poet in an unpoetical world; he sets out as a prodigal son and disbelieving Catholic to seek his misfortune. Bloom comes from misfortune and seeks a place of security and rest that is unattainable despite baptism and linguistic/behavioral conformity to the Dublin milieu. Bloom and Stephen remain on the outside. They embody the simultaneity of leaving home and returning to it. The leaving of home on Stephen Dedalus's part in *Ulysses* does not lead away from Dublin. And Bloom's return home to his dreaming Penelope is none at all.[23]

The matter is well known. Its formulation, self-hate, is found in a book by Theodor Lessing that appeared in 1930 as one of the publications of the Jewish Publishing House in Berlin.[1] Under the title *Jewish Self-Hate,* Lessing, a psychologist and professor of philosophy who had resigned his position at the Technische Hochschule in Hannover in disgust four years previously, variously intimidated by anti-Semitic and Nazi students and faculty, sought to define the two phenomena constitutive to his life and thought: hatred of Jews and Jews' own self-hate. That the obduracy of his inquiry possessed a traumatic origin was fully realized by this author of a book called *Untergang der Erde am Geist* (The Decline of the Earth in Spirit). Lessing was haunted by the early shattering of his long-time friendship with Ludwig Klages that reached back to their boyhood school days together in Hannover. Klages subsequently never mentioned the name Lessing again; nonetheless the exceptionally shrill anti-Semitic excesses in his frightening introduction to Alfred Schuler's posthumously published writings, for example, can be taken as an equally traumatic reaction on his part to Lessing.[2]

The book about Jewish self-hate falls into a Zionist phase of Lessing's. The Jewish Publishing House in Berlin was a Zionist enterprise. On the other hand, Lessing himself all too often incarnated precisely such Jewish self-hate. In his autobiography, *Once and Never Again,* he mentions it with great hesitation, even embarrassment.

Just how much anti-Semitism and Jewish self-hate can be tied up in each other is shown by an affair in which Lessing became entangled in 1910. In the affair, which has become a bit of literary history, two Jewish writers were joined by a third writer of non-Jewish origin but married to a woman of Jewish origin, who from time to time was not disinclined to let loose with little anti-Semitic barbs. Thomas Mann in his polemical article "Doctor Lessing" decidedly took the side of the Jewish critic Samuel Lublinski (1868–1910), who was from the little hamlet of Linde near Pinne in the province of Posen and was in consequence for the Hannoverian Lessing an "Eastern Jew." Lublinski, and this is noteworthy, was the first to grasp *Buddenbrooks* in its international literary significance and provide a clear notion of its author's preeminence. His book *Balance of the Moderns* (1904), which he followed four years later with *The End of the Moderns,* is interesting on account of its early use of the later so widespread concept of modernity and its high estimation of Thomas Mann's work.[3]

Whatever might have brought Theodor Lessing, six years after the first appearance of Lublinski's book, and, coincidentally, several months before Lublinski's death, to write a polemical article entitled "Samuel Draws up the Balance, or The Little Prophet" and publish it in the *Schaubühne,* edited by Siegfried Jacobsohn, is hard to imagine. The title of the article calls to mind rather a *Völkish* anti-Semite than "Lazarus-Lessing," as his enemies were wont to refer to him.

As if all that were not enough, Lessing's polemic, which does not see eye to eye with Lublinski's literary balance sheet, begins an attack *ad hominem* on the physical and private peculiarities of that critic: stunted, press-bellied Jew, who is always hungry for a good meal. Lessing writes in the following vein: "He spoke of *Weltanschauung,* screwed up his little arms into the air and gave out his thoughts as so much oracular wisdom. Toppled false gods. Soused through the whole of German literature. In short, acted like Jehovah on the Day of Judgment: the rams to the right, the sheep to the left."

Is it any wonder then that Thomas Mann's polemic serves up similar argumentation in turn: "But I know Mr. Lessing personally (who is responsible for those he knows?!), and I will only say that whoever were to make the claim he saw a high elf in him or a primordial image of Aryan manliness would make himself guilty of certain exaggerations. . . . Humiliating experiences in his life . . . are said, as far as lack of corporeal grace is concerned, to have made him altruistic."

All this seems only the faded polemics of the era before the first great war and is yet a good deal more. Thomas Mann's animosity, whether well-deserved or not, proved fatal to Lessing, as he himself was obliged to confess in his autobiography. When in Hannover Field Marshall von Hindenburg's "character assassin"—Lessing—became the butt of public scorn and was driven out, the argument was heard that even the liberal

Thomas Mann had despised him. On August 31, 1933, in Czech exile in Marienbad, Lessing was shot to death at the same time as the Party Congress of Victory was being staged in Nuremberg. The assassins were never apprehended.

Thomas Mann looked back upon the polemics and his part in them with some misgivings. For a while he thought of treating Lessing's person and life as theme of a novella to be called *Ein Elender* (A Wretched Man). His notes for it have been preserved. Then the plan was abandoned. The author of *Death in Venice* passed on the motif to his character Gustav von Aschenbach, who has such sharp reactions to the cultural influences of "the East." Among Aschenbach's works mentioned in the story, there is one called *Ein Elender.*

What was it that provoked Theodor Lessing, a Jew, to denounce another Jewish writer as "Jew," as if that were some kind of argument? It is not the only such case in Lessing's writings. Even in his Zionist work on Jewish self-hate, Lessing, who to the end clung to the notion that he was a lyric poet of some merit, could not resist publishing verses from the year 1902. At that time he was instructor in one of the newly founded country boarding schools (*Haubinda*) after the English model, started by such pedagogs as Hermann Lietz, Gustav Wyneken, later even Paul Geheeb. Lots of children of the rich Jewish bourgeoisie were schooled there. Their teacher Lessing wrote:

Ach, meine Schüler dichten schon gemeinsam,
Und reif wie sie werd' ich mein Lebtag nicht,
Der Dichter Speier und der Dichter Cohn,
Der Dichter Meier, Frank und Mendelssohn.* [4]

The real irony of life came to be juxtaposed to the irony of Theodor Lessing insofar as his charges whom he ridicules here, Wilhelm Speyer and Bruno Frank by name, did in point of fact become better authors than their teacher.

But an author's jealousy was not at the bottom of it; Lessing apparently had no opinion whatever of such "juvenile" literature. The question is only: What was the sense of the Jewish names and genealogies amid such argumentation? Was it not just one more expression of Jewish self-hate?

Lessing seems to have expected this objection, for at that spot in his

---

*Oh yes, my pupils write poetry together / And I shall never in all my days mature as they / The poet Speier and the poet Cohn / The poet Meier, Frank and Mendelssohn.

1930 book where he comes out with his versified reminiscences, he makes every effort at distinguishing such self-abnegation from genuine anti-Semitism. But even that does not proceed without recidivism. Lessing begins to speak of the nascent anti-Semitism in the country boarding schools having as one of its results the following clause in Hermann Lietz's school charter: "Substandard children, or children of Jewish extraction, are as a general rule not to be admitted to the German country boarding schools." Whereupon the indignant Lessing resigned his position but was forced to see that the families of the Jewish bourgeoisie did not for a moment think to withdraw their children from such institutions. The bourgeois Shylock consented to anti-Semitism as long as it had to do only with others than himself.

Lessing once again saw correctly and once again argued wrongly. Instead of describing the despairing blindness of a bourgeois desire to be assimilated, which is to say, instead of diagnosing a social phenomenon, Lessing the Zionist reasoned like a racist and spoke of the "abnormality of this deracinated class." His enemy and erstwhile chum from schooldays, Klages, would not have put it any differently.

Again and again the analysis of the trauma of Jewish identity degenerates either into sentimentalism or—as so often—into a proclamation of accord with the adversary. That may have to do with the psychological peculiarities in Lessing's development, which he later—in his best book, the autobiography—came to spell out and upon which even Thomas Mann had somewhat disdainfully played. Far more important in Lessing's analytical failure is his antihistorical agnosticism following in Nietzsche's wake, which ascribes no importance to historical thinking, to say nothing of the philosophy of history. This is the reason Lessing, quite like Klages, must needs take recourse in biologism and immediately falls into the vocabulary of abnormality, rootlessness, and the German man.

"How does it happen that all people love themselves and only the Jew loves himself so little?"[5] Lessing's question is posed from a biologistic and antihistorical viewpoint, and consequently has no answer. It is the question concerning the self-love of the outsider in society. The attitude of the intellectual woman is familiar here: "I can't stand women. One can only have discussions with men." Or the homosexual's self-hatred; Gide's dictum, say: "I am not a homosexual but a pederast."

Lessing as Zionist provides an answer to his question. He caustically rejects assimilation. "You become 'one of the others' and seem extraordinarily genuine. Perhaps a bit too German to be really German."[6] The answer is once again pathetic because of insecurity, because of sublimated self-hate. "What are you? The son perhaps of the feckless Jew merchant Nathan and the worn-out Sarah? No, Judah Maccabi was your father, queen Esther your mother." In the self-contained exuberance of Zionism there is room for disdain for the feckless Nathan and the worn-out Sarah.

The six biographies that together make up the book about *Jewish Self-Hate* and are meant as demonstrations of its theses, attract one's interest and are informative in their detail but only serve as proof of the inexactness of Lessing's grasp of the phenomenon. Paul Rée, a close friend of Nietzsche's who then had a falling out with him and was his rival vis-à-vis Lou von Salomé, was, according to whatever he communicated of his philosophy, not a thinker who practiced Jewish self-hate. Neither was the poet Walter Calé who was a suicide and whom Theodor Lessing forcefully tries to make approximate Otto Weininger's conceptions of self-disgust. Neither was Maximilian Harden familiar with specific self-hate. His striving for integration was characterized unavoidably by a hypertrophy of assimilation: anti-Kaiser and pro-Bismarck, "perhaps a bit too German to be really German." His confrontation as Jewish outsider with the homosexual outsider Eulenburg provides one more repetition of the conflict between Shylock and Antonio or Heine and Platen, yet not from any sense of Jewish self-disgust.

The life of Max Steiner (1884–1910)[7] was one more that ended in suicide, like that of Weininger and Calé. Kurt Hiller edited his work on (or against) *The World of the Enlightenment,* which appeared posthumously. Steiner belonged, as did Lessing and Klages, to the phalanx of the anti-Enlightenment. Against Darwin and for Catholicism, to which he had converted. Against Georg Simmel and his philosophizing within concrete, present-day society, not a general, universal, human framework. But is that Jewish self-hate? Only if Enlightenment were to be equated with "the Jewish intellect," which then indeed Chamberlain and Klages and Theodor Lessing postulated.

Not taking into account the fifth model biography that Lessing provides, the life of a mentally ill rabid anti-Semite of Jewish birth, the case history of Arthur Trebitsch, there remains only Otto Weininger's story (next to Lessing's own) as authentic document of Jewish self-abnegation.

The book excluded any then living representatives of the Jewish conflict of identity. There is consequently no analysis of this phenomenon in Karl Kraus's life and work. One reference only is to be found, in the report on Max Steiner in Prague: "Just like his great teacher (whom he never dared approach), just like Karl Kraus, Steiner too hated the tattered Jewish literary establishment as the most dangerous carrier of mendacious ideals of power and success."[8] All this does is provide an all too simple rendering of the actual state of affairs. Karl Kraus is not anti-Enlightenment, but Enlightenment. He edited and recited the German poets of the eighteenth century, including Baron von Goeckingk, Goethe, Nestroy, and the Jew Offenbach. The metaphysics of "origins" in Kraus is not racist but melancholic conservative. The Golden Age is gone by, decline is in the offing. The press and the culture industry provide the documentation. Since they are in Kraus's world represented to a great extent by Jewish journalists and writers, Kraus takes up the struggle against them in their "Jewified" forms as well. As the avenger of the language, as he put it in his poem on epigones.

In his book on *The Decline of the World through Black Magic,* under the motto "He's still a Yid,"[9] Kraus carefully formulated without the least trace of Jewish self-hate the difference between the fundamentally neo-Darwinist racial conceptions of Weininger, Chamberlain, Klages, and Lessing, and his own struggle against the decline of the world through the black magic of the press: "I do not know whether it is a Jewish characteristic to find reading the Book of Job worthwhile, or whether it is anti-Semitism to throw a book of Schnitzler's into the corner of your room. Whether it is perceived in Jewish or German fashion to say that the writings of the Jews Else Lasker-Schüler and Peter Altenberg stand closer to God and language than anything done by German writers in the last fifty years. I am not familiar with matters of race."[10]

The theory of the self-hate of the Jews, supposedly *only* of Jews, ignores a phenomenon that had been seen and analyzed as early as Heine: the historical parallelism between the behavior of the Jews and the Germans in modern European history. Heine proposed a solution by saying that both Jews and Germans had not yet found their "liberator," something he did not mean at all symbolically but politically in quite a concrete sense. There is such a thing as Jewish self-hate, yet there is in German literature and intellectual development the phenomenon of a suffering for Germany at the hands of Germany that has no counterpart in other peoples and cultures. It is to be found in Hölderlin and Goethe, Platen and Nietzsche. "How I am sick because of my fatherland," wrote Platen the outsider. Thomas Mann quoted the verse in his journals covering the period of exile, under the heading "Leiden an Deutschland."

Nonetheless the parallelism between socially stunted German conditions and a failed Jewish assimilation is only a seeming one. A people like the Germans cannot become outsiders, because they have a language, history, and land that can act toward integration. Jewish integration in Europe proceeded from the assumption that Jewish language and history were to be sacrificed, just as Moses Mendelssohn taught; that there would be no Jewish nation. Everything was to be "adopted" from the host country and people: language, culture, region. That failed. Suffering at the hands of Germany was never anything more than the reaction of German outsiders to German rules and regularity. It was a German outsiderdom and, limited to individuals, did not become the hallmark of a general, fixed state of German affairs.

The Jewish crisis of identity in the midst of enlightened bourgeois society affects individuals as parts of a shared communalty. Their outsiderdom is not founded on an individual basis as in the case of homosexuals, but generally, by their Jewishness. It cannot be ignored; neither can it be sublimated. The supposed self-hate only proves that the Enlightenment has foundered and that one has come to recognize the fact.

The continuity of posing the question from Weininger to Theodor Lessing to Karl Kraus signifies a social discontinuity within the process of assimilation, which could be negated neither through Weininger's ethical hierarchies nor through Kraus's metaphysics of decline and fall nor through Lessing's emphatic Zionism, which remained without real consequence. The historical reality that Lessing tried to ignore by means of philosophy made answer to all problems of Jewish identification with the one alternative: Auschwitz or Israel. Nothing was changed in this if from time to time in individual cases the bourgeois Shylock was resolved to play the role of comrade Shylock.

23 Comrade Shylock

The book of memoirs, *My Life*,[1] was one of the first literary fruits of the exile imposed upon him. Beginning with his removal from the position of Soviet commissar for war and defense in January 1925, one year after Lenin's death, Leon Davidovich Trotsky saw his powers gradually withdrawn, was then expelled from the Bolshevik party and banned to Alma-Ata far off in the east in continuation of czarist policies for internal security. There on January 20, 1929, as he reports in his autobiography, he received a visit from an emissary of the G.P.U. who communicated to him that, as per resolution of the Ministry of the Interior of the Union of Soviet Socialist Republics of January 18, it had been determined that the citizen L. D. Trotsky had practiced criminal counterrevolutionary activities contrary to article 58, paragraph 10 of the criminal code, consisting in the organization of an illegal anti-Soviet party. Therefore it had been decided to deport the citizen Trotsky, Leon Davidovich, from the territory of the Soviet Union.

On January 22 began the journey out of Siberia for Trotsky, his wife, and one of his two sons. Snowstorms prevent further progress. Trotsky energetically rejects leaving the country of the October Revolution voluntarily. His request to be able to speak with his other son, who lives in Moscow, is honored. Son and daughter-in-law are brought from Moscow. Then on February 8 comes the communication that Turkey is to be the country of exile; the area around Constantinople has been agreed to in conjunction with the Turkish government as his place of residence. All attempts, Trotsky is informed, to induce the German government to grant asylum to the toppled Soviet politician have been categorically rejected. The Weimar Republic is in its final phase; Stresemann is still foreign minister, but already fatally ill; the Reich's president is one Paul von Hindenburg. Besides, German foreign affairs, not even taking Soviet contracts to German industry into account, need good relations with the Kremlin so as to be able to amortize the last war reparations to the Allies. The first signs of the deep economic crisis to come appear at the end of 1928 and beginning of 1929. Beyond all that, protests could only be expected from the growing Communist Party of Germany (KPD) against granting asylum to a deported enemy of the Soviet Union, as their official terminology would have it.

It was patently apparent that the Germans were not considering granting Trotsky asylum. That notwithstanding, there must have been a certain current in public opinion, especially in Social Democratic Party (SPD) circles, for it; the president of the Reichstag, Paul Löbe, spoke to that end in the Reichstag on February 6, the majority in agreement: "Perhaps we will even come to grant Mr. Trotsky asylum." Immediately upon his arrival in Constantinople, Trotsky, referring to this speech, himself petitioned for asylum and a visa. In a press conference with German Social Democrats he underscored his unchanged negative assessment of international Social Democratic politics.

Dr. Kurt Rosenfeld, as attorney at law and delegate to the Reichstag, tried to act in Trotsky's behalf. (He subsequently together with the left-leaning internal party opposition of the SPD founded the Socialist Workers' Party of Germany [1930] and after 1933, himself then in exile, worked together with the exiled KPD.) Trotsky provided an affidavit: "I intend to live outside of Berlin in complete isolation, under no circumstance speaking in a public forum, and keeping my literary activities within the bounds of the laws of Germany."

After peculiar divagations—Trotsky would only be allowed to stay in Germany for a limited period for medical tests and treatment—the whole of the negotiations fell apart. Löbe never answered one of Trotsky's telegrams. The government of the Grand Coalition under the Social Democratic Reich Chancellor Hermann Müller fell; Stresemann died; all attempts Stalin undertook, apparently in collaboration with German foreign policy, to oblige Trotsky to forgo any kind of political activity were doomed to failure from the start.

Trotsky tells this story not without grim pleasure in the last chapter of his autobiography under the heading "Planet without a Visa." What happened after that is well known. For four years the head of the "Trotskyites" lived on Prinkipo, a little island not far from Istanbul; once (1932) he was allowed to go to Copenhagen, having been invited by Danish socialist students. In 1933 Turkey was asked by Moscow, where a new wave of persecution against the anti-Stalinist opposition threatened to flood out of control, to deport Trotsky in turn. This time Daladier's government in Paris granted asylum. It lasted two years, then the toppled revolutionary was allowed to live in Norway, not far from Oslo, in the house of a Socialist member of parliament. Yet there had already come to be a Third Reich in Germany and an ardent propaganda in Norway in the sense of the later Quisling, financed by Berlin. At the same time the Moscow trials were taking place, which would end with the execution of Trotsky's one-time party friends and later opponents, with the deaths of Zinovïev, Kamenev, and Bukharin, and with Karl Radek being sentenced to life imprisonment. Norway was intimidated by Moscow with the specter of economic boycott.

Finally Mexico. On January 9, 1937, the Norwegian tanker with the Trotskys on board laid anchor in Tampico. The Mexican painter Diego Rivera was their first host. Demonstrations of protest by Mexican Communists ensued. On September 1, 1939, the Second World War broke out. Shortly before in the Kremlin Stalin had entered upon a pact of nonaggression with von Ribbentrop acting in behalf of his *Reichsführer*. It was a pact that would be followed with an attack upon Finland and the later invasion of Poland by the Red Army. Trotsky had already virtually prophesied all of it in the book he had finished in Norway, *The Revolution Betrayed*.

An armed attack on Trotsky's Mexican residence, transformed into a virtual fortress by the police and adherents of the now sixty-one-year-old revolutionary, failed on May 24, 1940. Yet on August 20 Leon Davidovich Trotsky was fatally wounded with an ice pick by a murderer by the name of Ramon Mercader and died the next day during surgery.

Trotsky was murdered at his writing table, while reading and making corrections in a political article his murderer had brought as so much bait. He was active writing until the very end. Yet it is not so surprising that he did not make use of the decade lying between the first appearance of his autobiography (1930) and this last phase in Coyoacan to supplement *My Life*, which had broken off with the arrival in Turkish exile (1929), with additions dealing with what had happened since. Trotsky thought of his memoirs as being principally a political documentary. Besides, his subsequent private life had long since become public. The history of the man Bronshtein/Trotsky between 1929 and 1940 had become integrated in every one of its facets into the history of the times. There was nothing private left to report unless, of course, he wanted to report the murders and court sentences and strange accidents that befell children, relatives, and friends of this antipode of Stalin's, most of them with fatal consequences. Yet that did not belong, in the view of the writer Trotsky, in a book like *My Life* but in the two volumes he wrote while still in Turkey on the two Russian revolutions of February and October 1917 or was part of the concept detailed in his volume on *The Revolution Betrayed*.

Only by sketching Leon Trotsky's later life's totality of literature, exile, and revolution does it become possible to interpret the self-representation in *My Life* beyond all documentation and beyond all literary valuation as the astonishing product of a double outsiderdom: as the work of an outsider in both literature and politics. That sounds exceedingly strange at first, for Trotsky seems scarcely qualified to be an outsider in politics, who at twenty-six was chairman of the Petersburg Soviet during the revolution of 1905, who later led an armed uprising in October 1917, who was the political and military counterpart to Ludendorff at the negotiations of Brest-Litovsk, the organizer of the Red Army, the party politician then exile who founded the Fourth International. Nonetheless Trotsky himself must have sensed discordance in the way he carried out his life. Some few—noteworthy—passages in the autobiography give one cause to think that in setting down his memoirs he did not entirely absent himself from self-questioning in this vein.

What he had undertaken was a glorious attempt, which failed in the end, to conceive an autobiography in its totality as political biography. Trotsky, filled with aversion, impatience, and dryness, wrote himself free from his own childhood, school years, and puberty. Social contradictions in the village of Yanovka in the Ukraine where young Bronshtein grew up are brought to the forefront, so that the reader will surmise: Even then! The chapter "Books and Early Conflicts" remains astonishingly vacuous since Trotsky is unwilling to name his real predilections, particularly the books that formed him by their contents and in his manner of writing. He also has little success, apart from those conditions in czarist Russia that were there for everyone, in providing any deeper motivation for the decision to lead his life as a professional revolutionary. In his life there is neither Lenin's sorrow at a brother's execution nor Stalin's hate-filled revolt against a whole form of education to which he as the child of a poor family had had to submit in a seminary.

Trotsky's family, the Bronshteins, had no difficulties with the various government offices; nor were they without influence, though they had to work hard in the village alongside everyone else. Somewhat ill at ease Trotsky reports: "The October Revolution found my father as a very wealthy man. . . . the Reds threatened him because he was rich, the Whites persecuted him because he was my father." He lost his property, directed a little mill for a people's commissariat for agriculture in the vicinity of Moscow, and died of typhus in 1922. Trotsky's mother had died in 1910.

Trotsky came from an entirely Jewish background. That his choosing revolutionary politics might have had something to do with these origins he appears to want to exclude, almost arrogantly so. There were apparently no conflicts that might have made the child into an outsider. The questionable touching up of his own childhood is especially noticeable in that the author of the memoirs projects back into his youth his later, Marxist understanding of the "nationalities question." The child Lev Davidovich Bronshtein has no anti-Semitic heckling to report in the village or in the schoolyard. Yet the fact cannot be passed over that Jews were allowed into the secondary schools as a fixed ten percent of the total student body, the reason the later Trotsky likely had to pay bribes to be accepted. His report on all this reads like a historic narrative in which the absurdities of educational and nationalities politics of the czarist government are to be demonstrated. Even here, with cutting humiliations of a gifted child, the Tacitean tone of a formal report is not relinquished for a moment. The little Lev Bronshtein lived during all of this in a Ukrainian village and later at school in Odessa in an exclusively Jewish milieu. Nonetheless he refrains from giving us any inkling whether his family, either on the paternal or maternal side, observed the biblical commandments in orthodox or relaxed or any other fashion.

What may have been planned as the negation of Jewish nationality is made so glaring and visible by the blank spots in this autobiography that all intended integration of private life by politics is held in abeyance and the tension between literature and revolution accentuated. The book *My Life,* regardless of what its author may have intended, displays in a fashion equally unusual and typical, an outsider's life among bourgeois, Communists, Jews, Gentiles, literature, and revolution.

Two significant passages in these memoirs, which belong together in sense and are found spatially close to each other, give one to sense what is here so systematically passed over in silence and ignored. They are so noteworthy because in the general scheme of the book *My Life* they suddenly covertly negate the seemingly so adamant, closed unity of public and private existence. Chapter 29 of the memoirs depicts the activities and perplexities of Trotsky and his comrades, particularly of Lenin himself, immediately after the victory of the revolution. At this juncture not only the question had to be answered: What is the task of all of us now? Hitherto the answer had been: Continue the revolution. Now, however, everyone was asking himself with some uneasiness: What should I myself do now?

Trotsky has no illusions: "The conquest of power brought up the question of my work in the government. Strangely enough, I had never even given a thought to it; in spite of the experience of 1905, there was never an occasion when I connected the question of my future with that of power. From my youth on, or to be more precise, from my childhood on, I had dreamed of being a writer. Later, I subordinated my literary work, as I did everything else, to the revolution. The question of the party's conquest of power was always before me."

The moment discovers him unprepared. That seems credible. Credible not least because one senses the inner reservations of a writer who is asked to give up the well-loved if frustrating activity of political authorship. Leon Trotsky then logically proposes to the central committee that he should be given charge of the press. This is rejected on grounds that N. I. Bukharin is equally well qualified for that. Yet Trotsky, someone who had just directed an armed uprising, continues to see his task as one of writing, that is to say for him: writing propaganda. When he is given the party mandate to take over the position of minister of foreign affairs in the new government, the Soviet of Peoples' Commissaries, he, as one of those present remembered and as he himself quotes, is supposed to have cried out: "What diplomatic work are we apt to have? I will issue a few revolutionary proclamations to the peoples of the world and then shut up shop."

Once again the hidden reservation that literature does not only have preeminence before the revolution but also within it. To that is bound in Trotsky's own report another conflict: that of the revolutionary who is a Jew. Comrade Shylock and power. Trotsky is a litterateur and a Jew. Hitherto he had been able to reconcile both with the concrete tasks of the revolutionary. A litterateur—but in the service of the revolution. Even a short while before the outbreak of the February revolution, which caught him off guard in exile in New York as his memoirs show, Trotsky was almost arrogantly rejecting any kind of position offered him in Manhattan: "But I must disappoint my American readers. My only profession in New York was that of a revolutionist."

Now the litterateur and revolutionary socialist shared the possession of power, which also meant the Jew Lev Davidovich Bronshtein. This circumstance had hitherto been shunted aside as merely a question of nationality. Besides, Zinoviev and Kamenev were also of Jewish extraction, just as were Hilferding and Rosa Luxemburg, Karl Radek and Victor Adler, Eduard Bernstein and August Thalheimer, Paul Levi and Parvus-Helphand, and also many of Trotsky's (and Lenin's) adversaries among the Mensheviks and social revolutionaries. Up to now all of this had been without significance. Without significance even after the young Bronshtein, in 1905 at the head of the Petersburg Soviet, had communicated to the czar that the revolutionary people had no intention of paying off the debts of czarism (and they did not after 1917).

Suddenly nationality becomes an important political fact. When the composition of the government is discussed at the highest Bolshevik party levels, Lenin wants Trotsky to take charge of the Ministry of the Interior, which is to say, the police and security forces, counterespionage and countersabotage. What will have had to be meant was responsibility for the repressive terror without which Lenin's party could not hope to stay in power. It meant, after a takeover that sustained no great loss of life, responsibility for a bloody civil war and combating nearly every foreign government, from Berlin and Paris to Washington. Trotsky's courage has never been doubted. This was a matter of a different sort altogether. Should it be a Jew, of all people, who is given this task after czarist anti-Semitism (the tradition of which would continue from Stalin to Khrushchev on to Brezhnev) had struck such deep root in the people? It is here that Trotsky has misgivings. Lenin becomes indignant. They have begun a great international revolution, he says, and cannot bother with such trivialities.

Nonetheless the argument is found convincing. The autobiographer, who usually provides such wealth of detail, is reticent. He notes only: "Sverdlov and other members of the Central Committee came over to my side. Lenin was in the minority. He shrugged his shoulders, sighed, and looked at me remonstratingly."

Sverdlov and other members of the Central Committee? Trotsky usually in depicting such occurrences is not miserly in naming names, especially whenever, as here, it was a matter of his attaining a majority over

Lenin and in a matter that touched upon him personally as well. It is conceivable that Stalin voted against Lenin and for Trotsky, because in truth it was a decision *against* Trotsky. Stalin's inherent anti-Semitism is conceivable as motivation, which may have brought him, in view of his own feelings, to reject the notion of having a Jew as chief of security. Sometime later, in 1952–53, a fantastic plan of Stalin's came to naught at the last moment with his death, a plan to stage show trials against Jewish doctors who—aside from the obligatory charges of conspiracy to assassinate Stalin—were to be charged with "murdering" Gorki in 1936 along with other crimes. The plan shows as much about the feelings of this Grusian Internationalist as it does about his reckoning that a trial staged as anti-Semitic spectacle would, thirty-five years after the October Revolution, only meet with widespread emotional approval.

Then Stalin would have voted with Trotsky against Lenin because he did not wish to delegate a material position of power to anyone of Jewish extraction, in view of popular sentiments naturally, not because of his own approval of such emotions. Stalin himself by the way, in this distribution of government offices immediately after the Revolution, was delegated the position of "People's Commissar for Nationalities."

A problem of nationality is exactly what Trotsky meant by his reference to his Jewish extraction. Again and again in *My Life* he reiterates that the Jewish question (he himself always speaks of the question of nationalities, and interprets Jews, Ukrainians, Soviet Armenians, and Kirghiz as parts of a whole complex of nationalities) has for him no emotional content. There is only disdain for such things. "My Marxist upbringing deepened this manner of looking at things and changed my attitudes into those of active internationalism . . . Whenever I, in 1917 and later, came to mention my Jewish background as argument against accepting some government position, then [it was] solely out of political considerations."

That is the authoritarian language of a decree. The way things are and the way they should be are made into one. Yet not completely, for there are still to be found in the world nationalists less thoroughly formed by Marxism whose emotions have got to be taken into account.

The imperious style should not lead one astray. Trotsky wrote his book in the year 1929. Both Zinoviev and Kamenev had been removed from power in the meantime. Then followed Bukharin together with Tomskii and Rykov. To be sure, there is still the Jew Kaganovich in the staff closest to Stalin, it is only that the picture of "nationalities" in the party in power, twelve years after the revolution, looks fundamentally different than at the start, as Trotsky knew. When in 1917 he rejected becoming director of the police apparatus, he knew quite clearly, even if such episodes in *My Life* are disdainfully passed over in silence, that Jewishness, at least in a sometime czarist empire, meant something else than one more nationality among many. The Georgian Stalin instead of a Russian as the director of internal security, or the Pole Derzhinskii, the one who finally took over the position: what Russian would have hated them on that account? But the Jew Bronshtein: here even Lenin had to relent.

These two episodes in the autobiography belong together. They contradict all the author's efforts at rationalizing the question of extraction by trivializing it. At the same time they provide evidence that Trotsky immediately after victory felt his participation in power as a form of self-alienation. All practice of his Marxist theory up to that point had been literary practice for him. Certainly, as literary strategy and tactic, it had a hand in the material upheaval. Now, however, the matter was tactics and strategy in war and civil war. Bronshtein/Trotsky, who was around forty at the time, was capable, despite possible and hidden feelings of frustration, of concretely realizing permanent revolution and negating the mediator's position between literature and revolution in those years between 1918 and 1923 in favor of unliterary reality. That is part of his uniqueness and distinguishes Trotsky both from significant theoreticians like Plekhanov and from the like of Gustav Landauer and Ernst Toller. Lenin was Plekhanov's pupil but was much more unliterary than his teacher, something not to be understood as indifference, as Lenin's essays on Tolstoi alone can show. Trotsky was a litterateur who had the ability to renounce himself completely, so that as organizer and strategist he did not deny enjoyment of his own role (which would have lessened his powers of persuasion in his famous addresses to the soldiers), but made all decisions from a purely objective standpoint and not from any sort of need at role playing.

That Trotsky must have felt these dangers of literary men in power as an abyss can be documented in many of his actions and writings. No one was more impatient against the mixing of literature and politics than he. Lenin and even more so Bukharin, who was extremely well educated in literary matters, both demonstrated a polite collegiality when speaking to writers who had come to Moscow to interview them. Trotsky's interviews with writers, from Fritz von Unruh to André Malraux, put one off through an arrogance that denies any communality between the man of power (or later even in exile) and literati who have no competence.

Nonetheless it is precisely Trotsky, perhaps on that very account, who again and again is found by all people who met with him to be a litterateur writing not novels and poetry but working on a gigantic drama entitled *The Permanent Revolution*. A famous anecdote stemming from 1914 was probably invented, its point being conceivable only because it had to do with Trotsky and his dual existence between literature and revolution. The Austrian foreign minister, so the anecdote goes, was warned by advisers of the danger of revolution in Austria in case of war. He supposedly answered: "I beg your pardon. Who here is going to make a revolution? Mr. Trotsky, perhaps, from the Café Central?"

Counts Berchtold and Czernin in Vienna's Ballhaus Square had been furnished the police reports. There sat literati in a café in the Herrengasse who played chess, carried on passionate conversations with no less literary representatives of Austrian Social Democracy, like Dr. Bauer, Dr. Adler, and Dr. Hilferding, differed on questions of revolutionary strategy as if over a game of chess, devoured all the newspapers, read them in all languages, and also wrote articles in all languages. What did one have to fear from them?

The point does not lie in the fact that Mr. Trotsky of the Café Central against all expectation nonetheless went on to make a revolution; also not in Lev Davidovich's suddenly in the midst of revolutionary activity changing, to use Ernst Bloch's phrase, to "recognizability" or to "unrecognizability." In the one case, that of recognizability, the revolutionary would have sojourned long and unwillingly among literati, like Hans Christian Andersen's ugly duckling until he, as a swan, could develop in the revolution. In the other case, that of unrecognizability, Trotsky was and remained a litterateur who, that notwithstanding, was able to transform himself from time to time beyond recognition: only to return at last to the original "set form." The course of Trotsky's life after his loss of power could more or less be understood like this. Most importantly, it would have to be investigated *how and why Trotsky could be toppled*. One can more closely approach this complex and singular course of events if one puts aside any hypothesis of temporary metamorphoses yet pays close attention to the real dialectic of a life between revolution, power, in a word, and literature.

The anecdote of the litterateur in the Café Central, one sees immediately, as the aura about the phrase "coffeehouse writer" at the time (around 1914) corroborates, insinuates failure, and failure in literature as well. Down and out. Writers published by no one. One would today, however, no longer dispute Trotsky's place as a great writer, one, by the way, who was materially quite successful. The official Soviet repartee that this is the mark of the renegade has little to do with the matter. The whole history of various countries' refusing or providing restricted entrance visas to Trotsky proves quite on the contrary that aside from fearing the wrath of the Kremlin, they in a very real sense feared the presence of a revolutionary communist. If Trotsky continues to be read twenty years after the death of his antagonist, it is not from a need for information that has long since been outdated but from the fascination exerted by a significant writer. One reads a book like *My Life* or the chapter on the czar and czarina in Trotsky's famous book on *Literature and Revolution* as authentic literature that has to the greatest extent had the ability to make itself independent of its author's individual existence. Precisely by the fact that Trotsky has to be accounted one of the significant writers of Jewish extraction and that he manifests peculiar characteristics of this species does the reciprocity between literature and politics, extraction and its denial, Bohemia and power, become quite clear.

There is a mean depiction of Trotsky by an adversary. The Belgian sometime Social Democrat Henri de Man seems to remember the Trotsky of the period prior to World War I as a man who spent "half the day reading and writing and half the night at the samovar or carrying on discussions in a café full of literati. He looked like a bohemian piano virtuoso and had an uncontrolled nervousness as well that belongs to a certain type of artist. When he later came to be celebrated as the organizer of the Red Army, I thought that that was a propaganda bluff."[2]

There is little to be added concerning de Man himself. The quotation is taken from a book of memoirs composed by an emigré. Henri de Man was guilty of collaboration in Belgium during the Second World War, was sentenced in absentia, and ended his days outside his home country, a onetime Social Democrat, author of a book, *Psychology of Socialism,* who dallied with the fascists. Trotsky remembers as well. In *My Life* he reports how in Finland he met Emile Vandervelde, the royal Belgian minister of state and chairman of the Second International, and de Man accompanying him. They were going to Petrograd at the behest of the International in the same train that was returning Trotsky, a few weeks after the outbreak of the February Revolution of 1917 from his American exile back to Russia. De Man asked if he did not recognize them. Whereupon Trotsky answered, "I do—although people change a lot in time of war." Looking back, Trotsky characterizes him as "an agent of his government." Henri de Man's further development would scarcely have surprised him.

The little memorial to the bohemian piano virtuoso that de Man sketched of Trotsky is the product of hate, though first published in 1953 it has suffered no attenuation, and was not softened by the knowledge of Trotsky's agonizing demise. Nonetheless, the correspondence in characterization of Trotsky between the Ballhaus Square aristocrat and the Belgian socialist politician gives cause for reflection. That the phenotype Trotsky is reckoned by them more to bohemia than to revolution is more than the simple mischaracterization of an unusual person. It corresponds astonishingly enough with certain allergies of Trotsky's to bohemia and the coffeehouse literary scene. One is reminded of an almost compulsive demarcation of self.

Chapter 16 of the autobiography provides Trotsky's own viewpoint of the Viennese coffeehouse period. The tone is unusually acrid and excitable. He is remembering and depicting his second exile after the failure of the Russian revolution of 1905. In October 1907 he settled in Vienna; Rudolf Hilferding, whom Trotsky had met, as he reports, in the summer of that year at Kautsky's house in Berlin, tried to be of service to him in Vienna and offered the Russian comrade the familiar form of you (*du*), which Trotsky accepted. "Because of this our outward relations took on the semblance of intimacy. But there was no moral or political basis to it."

Hilferding then introduced him, as Trotsky says himself, to the Café Central scene. There the emigré meets with Otto Bauer, Karl Renner, Max Adler, the representatives of so-called Austrian Marxism. They displease him intensely. Certainly Trotsky is depicting these episodes from the viewpoint of his later experiences with the Austrian Socialist Party: he projects constellations during and after the First World War back into 1907. Yet dissatisfaction and displeasure must have dominated from early on. "They were well-educated people whose knowledge of various subjects was superior to mine. I listened with intense and, one might almost say, respectful interest to their conversation in the Café Central. But very soon I grew puzzled. These people were not revolutionaries. Moreover, they represented the type that was furthest from that of the revolutionary. This expressed itself in everything—in their approach to subjects, in their political remarks and psychological appreciations, in their self-satisfaction—not self-assurance, but self-satisfaction. I even thought I sensed philistinism in the quality of their voices."

That is unusually malicious whether projected back upon the past from the future or already felt at the time. It is also unjust: five years after the writing of these memoirs, in February 1934, Bauer and Renner prove in their own turn their ability to fight the good fight, to demonstrate courage, to go into exile. At the same time too, it must be admitted, which would seem to make Trotsky right, the almost accidental, non-organic character of their revolutionary aspirations is demonstrated: the reason why the rebellion of the *Schützbundler*, politically unprepared and badly organized, could be suppressed by the Austrian Christian Socials and answered with summary courts of justice and the gallows.

Yet Trotsky has in mind something else as well. All of them, Hilferding, Bauer, and Adler are German-Austrian scholars with doctorates. He notes scornfully that they sometimes permit themselves to be addressed as "Comrade Herr Doktor." The then twenty-seven-year-old Bronshtein had nothing of the sort to show for himself. The doctorates may not have impressed him, yet he must have felt bitterness when comparing his own schooling squashed by czarism with the "self-satisfied" attitudes of these gentlemen in the coffeehouse. Perhaps on that account he mistook for subjective philistinism the seemingly frivolous tone of an Austrian bourgeoisie and aristocracy aspiring to understatement. Maxim Gorki gave a book of his depicting the hardships of his youth the melancholy title *My Universities*. Trotsky as well felt inclined in the Café Central to dispose of his frustrations by making reference to the Siberian "universities" of his apprenticeship as a revolutionary. There nonetheless remained a resentment that politically, at that time at least, was unjustifiable.

Karl Renner was charged by the Soviet Military Government after 1945 with forming an Austrian "antifascist, democratic" government. Otto Bauer died in exile. Rudolf Hilferding was captured in exile, carried off to the Third Reich, and murdered. The dissatisfaction one feels in re-reading Trotsky's depictions from 1929 has to do with this, yet there is something more. Trotsky sought to belittle Hilferding through what he thought was an especially telling anecdote. During the peace negotiations in 1918 between the imperial German and the Soviet governments, Trotsky received a letter from Rudolf Hilferding: "After the October revolution, this was the first direct voice from the socialist West. And what did I find? In his letter, Hilferding asked me to free some war prisoner, one of the inescapable varieties of Viennese 'doctor.' Of the revolution, the letter contained not a single word. And yet he addressed me in the letter as 'thou.' I knew well enough the sort of person Hilferding was. I thought I had no illusions about him. But I could not believe my own eyes."

Lenin joins in. He had known of the arrival of a letter from the author of *Finanzkapital,* the work that had grown so significant for his (and Bukharin's) own studies on imperialism. Lenin too was dismayed at the lack of mention of the Bolshevik seizure of power. He went away cursing, Trotsky informs us.

Yet what exactly might they have awaited from Hilferding and his letter? Was it so dishonorable at this juncture to recall a former friendship and try to come to the aid of a relative? Did it not seem circumspect to separate politics from the letter's immediate impetus instead of adding incidentally: By the way, hearty congratulations on your revolution! Or even: By the by, I believe your revolution to be on the wrong track.

The leading Austro-Marxists were Jews: the Adlers, Friedrich Austerlitz, Hilferding, Otto Bauer—just like Trotsky, Zinoviev, and Kamenev. Trotsky was confronted with them in two ways: as Jew and as litterateur. When he reports how he soon thereafter broke off his stay in Vienna to move on to Berlin, his depictions of August Bebel's party and of German prewar Social Democracy are suffused with a far more sober light, are on occasion almost even affectionate. In Berlin, coffeehouse intellectuals were scarcely to be found and far fewer Jews.

In his book on bohemia, *Die Boheme,* Helmut Kreuzer[3] quotes an article Trotsky wrote at the time (1910) and published in the theoretical journal of the SPD, *Die Neue Zeit.* In it Trotsky reports of experiences with bourgeois intellectuals in the Russian workers' party. His judgment is quite sharp: "By their (the radical intelligensia's) entering the workers' party, they brought all their social characteristics along with them: the spirit of sects, the cult of intellectual individualism, ideological fetishism." Through that Marxism "got torn out of shape."

This has all the appearance of denunciation and, moreover, purposely delineates the differentiation between intelligensia and revolution in an excessively sharp manner: taking no heed of those passages in *The Communist Manifesto* where the bourgeois intelligensia is welcomed to come over to the camp of the proletariat. Trotsky's theses, particularly their tone, again and again have the effect of self-denunciation. Yet this attitude, strangely, is in Trotsky's life and writings fixed to periods of inner unrest. The revolutionary Trotsky who arrogantly looks down upon literati, particularly those of Jewish extraction, shows himself once in this first prewar period in Berlin and Vienna and again in the period of his third exile forced upon him by Stalin. The victorious Trotsky of the era between 1918 and 1924 is perfectly capable of taking seriously even the bourgeois literary scene, even coffeehouse bohemia, and interpreting it according to its sociological and ideological structure (that is, according to its "ideological fetishism").

Trotsky, both as revolutionary and as litterateur, formulated his position on the complex of revolution and literature that was so decisive for his life, in a work finished in 1924, *Literature and Revolution*,[4] one of his most important and telling works. From here, something that otherwise would be inexplicable, the path leads to the surrealists around André Breton. That Trotsky who in concert with Breton drafts Surrealism's "third" manifesto is prefigured in this book on the relations between revolutionaries and literati and that Trotsky who was against pious party hopes for an autochthonous proletarian art and culture that would like to spare itself the bother of cooperation with artists, bohemia, and the bourgeois intelligensia.

Starting in the preface to *Literature and Revolution*, which is dated July 29, 1924, written six months after Lenin's death, a both acute and fair defense of artistic and literary bohemia is undertaken. *Literature and Revolution* is one of Trotsky's most astonishing works: it evidences, quite contrary to its author's intention, just how much the analyst and polemicist arguing here is passionately involved, is one with the material. This is a literary confrontation. One is forced to decide between Aleksandr Blok and Vladimir Mayakovsky, between Futurists and Formalists, the program of proletarian culture (*Proletkult*) and the poetic recipes of the so-called "Serapion Fraternity," which based itself on E. T. A. Hoffmann. Here Trotsky is one with the material. He knows his way about; he has read everything. Astonishing, this productivity of a man who at the time was entrusted the task of bringing order into the disarranged transportation system of the Soviet state, who was tied down in hazardous party struggles, yet found the time to read the works of Shklovski and Roman Jakobson, to reflect on the architectural plans of Tatlin and the sculpture of Jacob Lipschitz.

Trotsky polemicizes in two directions. The summarizing and very pointedly formulated introduction leaves no room for doubt. On the one hand is the traditional literary culture of the czarist aristocracy and the bourgeoisie that imitates it; these currents will die away. Trotsky appears to enjoy the prospect. This was once the superstructure that he as a schoolboy had to revere, that he as a revolutionary had to make war upon on account of its reactionary political tendencies. He took great care to distinguish between the exemplary writers and their epigones, between Pushkin and the neo-Romantics.

The counter current is attacked with greater insistence. It is for its sake that the book was written. The organizer of the Red Army cannot abide the noisy radicalism of the *Proletkult's* disseminations. Trotsky's literary taste is, as was Karl Marx's, deeply respectful. He dislikes the agitation of those sympathetic to the victorious revolution who now, the majority of them never having been proletarians, wish to enthrone the brand new proletarian culture in the place of toppled bourgeois culture. Trotsky's polemic against them was one of the reasons why, when Stalin commenced the struggle for succession to Lenin, those in the *Proletkult* stood against Trotsky as the protector, they claimed, of bourgeois traditionalism. Those in RAPP, the organization of proletarian-revolutionary writers, were Stalinists, quite like their German colleagues around Johannes R. Becher and Ludwig Renn. They were also hostile to tradition. The special issue of the German section in the Goethe jubilee year of 1932, the "Linkskurve," suffices to prove it. I should add that things took their course with those in RAPP exactly as they had with Stalin's other allies in the early period of battle against Trotskyism. They were eliminated when they were no longer needed. In 1934 Stalin allied himself with Maxim Gorki against them, dissolved their organizations and founded, under the literary doctrine of Socialist Realism strictly conformist to tradition, the Soviet Writers' Union that later Solzhenitsyn and Heinrich Böll would not only accuse of not protecting its members from state interference but of aiding and abetting their persecutors.

Leon Trotsky's book, appearing in 1924, could not yet register this later phase of Soviet culture: the imitation, namely, of nineteenth-century bourgeois-realistic forms of narration; canonization of the naturalistic stage production of Stanislavsky and the Moscow artists' theater; symphonic form in the following of Tchaikovsky, which understood itself in turn as being in the tradition of Beethoven; historical painting after the manner of Ilia Repin, but with workers, farmers, and red flags instead of czars. Trotsky in exile later came to interpret this turn of events as the superstructure of the "revolution betrayed."

The task of *Literature and Revolution* is to distinguish the screamers and wild theoreticians from literary talents. For Mayakovsky and against the *Proletkult*. On that account you find in the introduction: "It is fundamentally incorrect to contrast bourgeois culture and bourgeois art with proletarian culture and proletarian art. The latter will never exist, because the proletarian regime is temporary and transient. The historic significance and the moral grandeur of the proletarian revolution consist in the fact that it is laying the foundations of a culture that is above classes and that will be the first culture that is truly human."

Hereupon follow truly "human" sentences on the problem of cultural politics during such an age of transition. "Our policy in art, during a transitional period, can and must be to help the various groups and schools of art that have come over to the Revolution to grasp correctly the historic meaning of the Revolution, and to allow them complete freedom of self-determination in the field of art, after putting before them the categorical standard of being for or against the Revolution."

That was a possible alternative. The victorious Stalin rejected this form of Trotskyism as well. The politics of art was regimented, which amounted in the end, as in all the other areas of Soviet life, to police repression. In Nadezhda Mandelshtam's book[5] using the poet Osip Mandelshtam as example, the daily life of a Soviet author under Stalin's regime is soberly depicted. Murder, suicide, and silence. The suicides Yessenin and Mayakovsky; Tretyakov and Pilnyak murdered; the silenced and suppressed Formalists; the Serapion Fraternity persecuted by police like the poetess Anna Akhmatova. The ludicrousness of a Stalinist criticism that follows instructions to "unmask" in the Soviet Encyclopedia the original master of the Serapion Fraternity, the author of "Meister Floh," namely, E. T. A. Hoffmann with his anticipation of just such a police state, as an aristocratic salon reactionary.

Trotsky must have had a presentiment of much of this. His book reads like a foreboding. Chapter 8 on "Revolutionary Socialist Art" quite coolly rejects the claims of "Realism." It is, he says, not a literary category for the present, but rather a term that can be used at best to set off "mysticism." Trotsky's politics of art is inquisitive, respectful of all creative acts, open in its forms. Stalin installed a tendentious regulation, despised the powerlessness of the artists who had as many divisions at their command as the pope, ordered a normative aesthetics.

What is quite astonishing (in the fourth chapter) is Trotsky's defense of literary bohemia and Futurism. The ostensible coffeehouse litterateur from the Café Central, who had so decidedly rejected coffeehouse politics, is almost affectionately concerned with disentangling genuineness and gesture in the antibourgeois attitudes of a revolutionary bohemia. The analysis of the historical origins of Futurism in socially backward countries like Italy and Russia is prescient. A comprehensive exhibition of Russian and Italian Futurism together with their tributary movements (at the Guggenheim Museum, New York, 1973) had every appearance of being a late confirmation of Trotsky's early analyses. Trotsky speaks of the anticipation of developments by thinkers and artists in reactionary countries: in contrast to the ideology of the more advanced social orders. The comparison is as bold as it is flattering to the Futurists. "In this way, German thought of the eighteenth and nineteenth centuries reflected the economic achievements of England and the political achievements of France. In the same way, Futurism obtained its most brilliant expression, not in America and not in Germany, but in Italy and in Russia."

But what was anticipated by Futurism? In no sense an alternative to bourgeois society, despite all apparent antibourgeois content. Trotsky is on familiar terms with literary history and bohemia both. He cites the antiphilistinism of German and French Romantics, and Théophile Gautier's shocking red vest. For their part the Russian Futurists had a yellow blouse: "The Futurist yellow blouse is undoubtedly a grand-niece to this romantic vest, which inspired such horror in the papas and mammas. As is known, nothing cataclysmic followed these rebellious protests of the long hair or the red vest of romanticism, and bourgeois public opinion safely adopted these gentlemen romantics and canonized them in their school textbooks."

Bohemia is not the revolution. By the time Trotsky had written his book, Mussolini had already initiated the march on Rome and seized power. Futurists like Marinetti acclaimed him. Trotsky mentions the occurrence; it confirms his analysis. The bolshevist developments in Russia, without which the fascist counterreaction in Italy was unthinkable, nonetheless provide the Russian Futurists with artistic and social possibilities. The writer Trotsky woos Mayakovsky. It is true, bohemia is not revolutionary. One should understand correctly Mayakovsky's protest against Pushkin: a hesitancy to let epigones canonize, not as a negation of the author of *Eugene Onegin*. Trotsky formulates: "A bohemian nihilism exists in the exaggerated Futurist rejection of the past, but not a proletarian revolutionism. We Marxists live in traditions, and we have not stopped being revolutionists on account of it." And further on: "Here lies the incompatibility of psychologic type between the Communist, who is a political revolutionist, and the Futurist, who is a revolutionary innovator of form."

That reads once more like an anticipation of things to come. In a

noteworthy scene of the unsuccessful play *Trotsky in Exile,* Peter Weiss
arranges a confrontation, in the Café Voltaire in Zürich's Niederdorf,
between Lenin and Trotsky and the Dadaists around Hugo Ball and
Tristan Tzara and Emmy Hennings. Lenin is disgusted by the bohemian
goings-on; Trotsky is greatly touched and secretly drawn in. Their equality in the eyes of posterity is postulated by the drunken Dadaists. They
will be passed down in common to posterity, they say, and work in
common, the revolutionaries and the bohemians. In Trotsky's words:
"the political revolutionists" and the "revolutionary innovators of form."
The bohemian in Trotsky remained irrepressible. So it was possible for
the man in power, and later after being purged and proscribed, for the
exile to retain contact with spiritual realities. Stalin's regime systematically
established dividing lines: on this side, progress; on that, decadence.
Progressive were Stalin's painters and composers of revolutionary sym-
phonies filled with battle crescendos inspired by musical compositions
like Tchaikovsky's 1812 Overture, with the czar's hymn removed. Deca-
dent, on the other hand, were Picasso and Schönberg, Kafka and Joyce,
the Expressionists and the Surrealists.

Trotsky's nearing to Surrealism has often been discounted as an opportunistic tactic: as a search for allies wherever they may be. Attentive
reading and not simply of the book *Literature and Revolution* speaks against
this view. It is contradicted above all by the entire body of Trotsky's
writings on literature written in exile. Most editions of *Literature and
Revolution* do not include these later, often masterful analyses: so that
this work on writers and revolution is degraded to a curious historical
document. In that case, it looks as if a revolutionary with talents as a
writer, once, even if from the vantage point of cultural politics, made
some comments on the fundamental questions of a Marxist theory of
literature and never returned to them.

The actual facts are, rather, the reverse. Trotsky, passionately fascinated by writing and writers, was only really set free to write by exile.
His great historical works, his autobiography: next to them the number-
less polemics of the day and situational analyses seem to be of a lesser
order even if they all too often say what is right.

The literary analyses of the later Trotsky, on the other hand, say those
between 1930 and the year of his death, show him to be a master of
literary analysis and criticism. Reading and writing: in Prinkipo, in
France, Norway, and Mexico. The range of his reading in belles lettres
specifically causes astonishment. Immediately after the appearance of

Céline's novel, *Voyage to the End of Night,* Trotsky wrote a review of it in French.[6] The old revolutionary is deeply impressed by the plastic powers of this French novelist with the evil eye. Toward its conclusion Trotsky seems to anticipate the coming involvement of the collaborator. "In the music of this book there are remarkable dissonances. In that the artist rejects that which really exists as well as any possible replacement, he supports the existing order of things. In this sense Céline is, whether he wants it or not, an ally of Poincaré. But in unmasking the lie, he gives one to sense the necessity of a more harmonious future."[7]

For Céline, in a word, but against Malraux. That has not only to do with Malraux's occasional fidelity to Stalin but far more with the legendary picture that Malraux in *The Conquerors* paints of the, as Trotsky puts it, "strangled" Chinese revolution. The second article in particular, which responds to Malraux's replic, not only anticipates a possible critique of *Man's Fate,* which at that point had not yet appeared but also, resembling the comments on Céline in this, anticipates the subsequent ideological development of André Malraux. "As a political writer Malraux is even more removed from the proletariat and revolution than he is as an artist."[8] Malraux defends Stalin's policies toward China that led to the catastrophe of the Canton rebellion. "To protest against this form of politics in 1925 required farsightedness. But to want to go on defending it in 1931 is a sign of incurable blindness."

The most important of Trotsky's later works on art and literature is the study on "Art and the Revolution" written in the form of a letter, which Trotsky finished in Coyoacan on June 17, 1938, and submitted to the *Partisan Review.*"[9] What was developed here was the continuation, after an interval of fourteen years, of the book on literature and revolution. At that earlier time, in the young Soviet Union, the attempt had to be made to sift through and define the aesthetic concepts and currents. It meant simultaneously that a powerful politician of the Bolsheviks developed his thoughts on the politics of the party vis-à-vis art and artists. In the year 1938 Stalin administered art and literature with the help of denunciations, the secret police, and a contrived doctrine onto which had been pasted the label "Socialist Realism." Trotsky makes reply embittered and filled with scorn. That he was right in these matters, now, a generation later, scarcely requires proof. Works of art and books that came into being under such circumstances, desiring to be apologetic, speak for themselves—or against themselves.

"The style of present-day, official Soviet painting calls itself 'Socialist

Realism': the name was conferred apparently by some anonymous director of some art office. Its realism consists in copying the provincial clichés of the last quarter of the last century; the 'socialism' is contained in that which is reproduced: with the help of faked photographs and events that never took place." What is at work, he says, are writers, painters, draftsmen who possess nothing but their craft and its tools. They glorify "under the watchtowers of government officials with automatic weapons, the great and ingenious leaders who are forever removed from any spark of genius and greatness."[10]

Trotsky also believes he is acquainted with counter examples of a genuinely revolutionary art. No longer, to be sure, in Stalin's realm, but in Mexico. "Have a look at Rivera's frescoes! You want to know what revolutionary art is? Have a look at Rivera's frescoes!"

This work is dated June 17, 1938. On July 25 of that year in Mexico City the self-same artist Diego Rivera and André Breton signed a manifesto "For an independent revolutionary art." It was the third Surrealist manifesto, and yet something else as well. Fifteen years later (1953) Breton gave the public to know that the manifesto had been jointly drafted by both himself and Trotsky. Rivera's signature was used instead of Trotsky's, he said, on account of tactical considerations.

Trotskyism and Surrealism: after Aragon and Eluard broke their pact with Breton and placed themselves "at the service of the revolution" in its Stalinist manifestation, integral Surrealism and the theory of the permanent revolution found their way to each other. The manifesto is astonishing, and it expresses truth. Not merely by making the approaching certainty of war a part of its analysis; nor simply in its description of intellectuals as "those who in the twilight of blood and filth have made a profession of servility, a perverse game of spiritual self-abjuration, a habit of selling false testimony, and take a fulsome pleasure in apologizing for crime."[11]

With a decidedness such as Trotsky had never before brought forth, the absolute freedom of artistic production is decreed: "The free choice of subject matter and the absolute nondelimitation of his realm of study represent an inalienable right for the artist." The conclusion is astonishing: "If the revolution in the interests of developing material production is obliged to set up a centralized, socialist system, so must it at the same time, and from the very first, establish and assure an *anarchistic* regime of intellectual freedom."[12]

For André Breton all this is logically consistent. And for Trotsky as well? Whoever here might call tactical opportunism to mind underestimates the depth of literary substance in this writer between literature and revolution.

That is was only through exile and removal from power that the writer Trotsky "was changed to recognizability," would have been rejected by him with utmost vehemence. The writers who adapted this material never saw it any differently. And it is precisely in this manner that the so-called Trotsky novel by Joseph Roth (written around 1929, in answer to Trotsky's book *My Life,* which appeared that year) is set up: Friedrich Kargan, "who was born in Odessa in the house of his grandfather, a rich tea merchant," and the later *apparatchik* Savelli, who always remained in Russia, a bureaucrat who became powerful and despised the Kargans who are cosmopolitan and besides secretly keep a journal—that is, they are literati and without need.

Trotsky considered his Jewishness an inconsequential accident, a problem of nationality. He understood his writing to be in the service of world revolution, and to have its function there. His adversary Iosif Vissarionovich Dzugashvili from Gori in Georgia, who was not a Jew and could not write, even despised writing, was in all of this the absolute antagonist. Stalin left behind a disquieting system. Trotsky left behind disquieting books and ideas. When he, in the manifesto two years before his murder postulated the synthesis of dirigistic socialism and libertarian literary-artistic production, he had recognized for himself an existential alternative that had never been far removed from this thought, not even the day after the victory of the revolution.

Everything spoke at the end of the Second World War against the reinstitution of the dreary debates about Jews and Germans, Jewish destruction and Aryan positivism, intellect and soul, blood and soil, civilization and *Kultur,* authentic writers and mere writers: exemplified for the most part by Jewish writers who are recognized simply as literati but not as authentic *Dichter.* Such cheap antitheses, made up by anti-Semites for popular use and contrary to all historical insight, seemed, as the reports on Auschwitz, Maidanek, Lublin, and Bergen-Belsen began to appear, to have become as anachronistic as the Expressionists' patricidal tirades or the farming mythologies of Giono and Hamsun, the later Nazi collaborators.

Skeptical observers mistrusted at any event the consensus regarding the scientific unacceptability of anti-Semitic racial doctrines and the moral reprehensibility of anti-Semitism. When in October of 1944 French territory seemed liberated and the destruction of the Third Reich only a question of time, Jean-Paul Sartre noted a peculiar ambiguousness in French public opinion.[1] The Resistance had won: many Jews had participated in it; prisoners of war and deportees are spoken of who will soon be returning. The joy of fraternization of Frenchman with Frenchman. Sartre asks himself: "Are the Jews going to be mentioned? Will their return be greeted, a word spent on the dead in the gas chambers of Lublin? Not a single word. Not a line in the newspapers. For one mustn't excite the anti-Semites. France must stay unified more than ever."[2]

Such silence is useful, the response comes, even for the Jews themselves. Under no circumstance attract attention. Those involved seem to see it the exact same way. This manner of acting was all too familiar to them. Everything could be given a new start. Not even Auschwitz, where so much had been "liquidated," had resolved this conflict.

Sartre's book *Anti-Semite and Jew* originated in care and observation: it was written out in the last stages of the war while the gas chambers were at work and then published in Paris in 1946. The analysis proceeds to the conclusion, "It has got to be made clear to each and every person that the fate of the Jews is also his *own* fate. No one in France will be free as long as the Jews do not enjoy their full rights. No Frenchman will be secure as long as a Jew in France *and in the whole world* has to fear for his life."[3]

Strangely, but in fact most logically and consistently, Sartre six years later (1952) completed his book on the thief and homosexual Jean Genet with the statement that also this Genet is "our neighbor and our brother." He is, he says, a hero for our times. "He is held up to obloquy before our eyes as we are before the gaze of future centuries; the Just will not cease to cast blame on him nor will History cease to cast blame on our age: Genet is we. That is why we must read him."[4]

Nothing in all of this has been acted upon. Sartre had said in 1946, to be sure, that the full equality of the Jews, who do not wish to assimilate themselves but to make valid their human and hereditary totality, can only be attained in a socialist revolution. The young Marx understood things in the exact same fashion, yet in the measure that the liberation of the Jews means the liberation of the world from the Jew as Jew: which, despite everything, would have to mean depersonalization, an impoverishment of human substance. In the meantime however, Sartre too had seen only one possibility: to instigate the move to Jewish authenticity, in consequence to abandon sheepish cowardice and give battle to the anti-Semite in the name of a "concrete liberalism"[5]—for the anti-Semite, as the champion of a disposition toward hatred and petit bourgeois resentment against a modern pluralist society where there is a division of labor, can at the end only be headed toward the genocide of the Jews.

Sartre's palliatives were in the meantime confuted. His analysis has proved correct. The founding of the state of Israel can indeed be understood as confirmation of Sartre's thesis on the difference between the ungenuine or inauthentic Jew and the genuine, self-accepting Jew. But the result of that is only to expand the antithesis of the sometime "Jewish Question" into a geopolitical dimension. From the former isolated Jewish outsider in the midst of a non-Jewish population there comes to be a Jewish outsider state in the midst of a non-Jewish community of states. "An annihilator by function, a sadist with pure heart, the anti-Semite is at bottom of his heart a criminal. What he wishes, what he prepares, is the *death* of the Jew."[6] Naturally Sartre means the impassioned anti-Semite,[7] not the bourgeois snob. The mere fact that every political resolution having to do with the Near East has to be brought by the State of Israel's friends and allies to the point where it contains a proviso in favor of the continued existence of this state, an avowal, in other words, of nonannihilation, only confirms the continuing validity of those theses and "reflections on the Jewish question" of 1944.

Naturally Sartre had culled his examples from French reality. His anti-Semites were Frenchmen. He confronted and analyzed their specific arguments. The peasant fundament to French provincial life was a part of it and had to be brought into account. The Dreyfus affair was unforgotten. Nonetheless, the evidence and conclusions extend beyond the French experience, even if specifically French constants within anti-Semitism and later so-called anti-Zionism are unmistakable.

The considerations on anti-Semitism by Max Horkheimer and Theodor W. Adorno in their book *Dialectic of Enlightenment* came into being in the United States at approximately the same time as Sartre's French reflections. In America too, social, intellectual, and emotional substrata had to be analyzed that corresponded to the state of affairs ascertained by Sartre and that in their own turn confuted the high minded optimism according to which, after Auschwitz, the question of anti-Semitism and the hatred of Jews could be closed.[8]

In emphatic pronouncement of feeling, Adorno later, after his return to Germany, postulated that after Auschwitz poetry is no longer possible. That was an aesthetic counter to existential fact. People tried to disprove him in a no less aestheticizing manner, by referring to, say, Paul Celan's "Death Fugue." The author of that poem did not take part in the debate. On the contrary, he saw the possibility for his own poem, which was perhaps just possible itself, in that Auschwitz had remained a virtual matter of fact.

When Adorno reflected on Auschwitz and poets he should have kept in mind the analysis in the *Dialectic of Enlightenment*. There one finds "The identification tag is pasted on: everyone becomes thereby either friend or foe. The lack of regard for the subject makes it easy for the administration. Entire populations are removed to other latitudes, individuals stamped Jew are sent to the gas chambers. The indifference to the individual, which finds its expression in logic, draws its conclusions from the economic process."[9]

This is as much as to say: the phenomenon of Auschwitz has to do with hatred of Jews only in the foreground of things. It has to do, extending beyond the existence of Jews, with a global disposition of thought toward annihilation, which thinks to admit only majorities in future and is determined to equate minorities with "worthless life." Worthless are here the Jews, there the blacks, somewhere else (and everywhere) the homosexuals, women of the type of Judith and Delilah, not least the intellectuals keen on individuation and the rational exertion of that concept. "The bogeyman notion of a conspiracy of lascivious Jewish bankers," Horkheimer and Adorno write in the second thesis concerning anti-Semitism, "who are financing Bolshevism, stands as a sign of congenital powerlessness, their good life as a sign of good fortune. To this is added the image of the intellectual; he seems to think, something the others do not allow themselves, and does not expend the sweat of hard toil and the exertion of the body."[10] If the later Adorno reflecting on the antagonism between lyric poetry and the gas chamber is to respect the obviousness of this earlier analysis—likewise the beginning sentence in the seventh thesis on anti-Semitism ("But there are no more anti-Semites"), according to which the hatred of Jews of before, which had been petit bourgeois and antirational and virtually murderous, nonetheless had hidden in itself vestiges of a subjectivism that resisted total reification, while in its place more and more a global scheme of annihilation comes to the fore that has in view all minorities without distinction—then he must conclude that the lyric poet, not to speak of the poet as such, represents an excessive case of subjectivity, which in a total "scheme of things by I.D. tag" (Horkheimer and Adorno's phrase) seems predestined for annihilation. The Soviet lyric poet Joseph Brodsky, who wanted to be no more than exactly this, was brought before court as a parasite and idler. Protests were able to save him. It is not because "the pen refuses" at the thought of Auschwitz that poetry is threatened today but because the gas chambers can only mean the annihilation of all that is minority—in consequence, of the poet as well.

"They should all be gassed": the expression has crept into everyday language where it now scarcely means the Jews, but all the enemies of the moment to a growing scheme of totality that would like nothing better than to finish off the sum total of outsiders. "Frenzy discharges itself on him who is conspicuous and without protection. And just as the victims are interchangeable among themselves: vagabonds, Jews, Protestants, Catholics, each one of them can take the place of the murderers in the same blind longing for slaughter as soon as they feel themselves powerful enough to be the norm."[11]

That was written toward the end of the Second World War. The world events in the thirty years that followed helped such theses become obvious. It is noteworthy that the authors of the *Dialectic of Enlightenment* were not at all inclined to come to these conclusions from the start. As late as in Max Horkheimer's study on "The Jews and Europe,"[12] written in 1939, the persecution of the Jews was interpreted as a singular phenomenon, in which the elements of a general principle could already be demonstrated: the liquidation of liberal capitalism. "Since the failure of the market economy, humanity has been placed once for all before the choice between freedom or fascist dictatorship. As the agents of circulation the Jews have nothing left before them." And in another section: "To appeal today to the liberalist fashion of thinking of the 19th century against fascism, means to appeal to that body by means of which fascism became victorious."[13]

This is still thinking on the eve of Auschwitz. The Jewish Question is taken on the one hand as symptom of a failed bourgeois Enlightenment, on the other as indication of new state-monopolistic tendencies of capitalist economic modes, where the seemingly equal, protected Jew is economically no longer necessary. "The sphere of distribution loses its economic importance. The celebrated power of money is caught in decline."[14] That is a frame from the year 1939, frozen. Development since 1945 has disproved the assessment and conclusions. Even in the assessment, the separation of the sphere of production from the sphere of distribution had been absolutized. And in the third of the later theses on elements of anti-Semitism it is repeated: "Jews, in contradistinction to their Aryan colleagues, were to a great extent refused admission to the origination of surplus value."[15] Yet the fact is that the capital of high finance had by fusing industrial and bank capital through the economics of bank investment long since done away with this separation. The sphere of distribution, whether in the hands of Jews, Aryans, or Arabs, remained mighty. It was not here that the origin lay for Jewish powerlessness and the fury of anti-Semitism, which continued intact.

The analytical assessment in the *Dialectic of Enlightenment* is more precise. That Sartre and Horkheimer/Adorno set out approximately at the same time on the same line of consideration and for the most part came to analogous results underscores the fact that Auschwitz had been a "German" matter as far as actual practice, yet not as far as mental practice was concerned. The simultaneity is noteworthy: Sartre in Paris and Horkheimer/Adorno in California formulated their perceptions essentially in 1944, at a time, that is to say, when the defeat of the Third Reich could be brought into the analysis. Both sets of considerations proceed from the premise that there will continue to be a Jewish question after the end of the war. Both interpretations grasp the fact of a continuing, virulent anti-Semitism as the failure of bourgeois Enlightenment, though Sartre characterizes the representative of this bourgeois-humanistic construct somewhat imprecisely as the "démocrate," while the German emigrés in Los Angeles speak of bourgeois liberalism.

Common to both interpretations is a pointing out of the deep spiritual, almost erotic ensnarement of the anti-Semite with his Jewish victim. That anti-Semitism represents a fundamentally Manichean form of thought, in which again and again good is locked in battle with the satanic, the principle incarnated by the Jews, is precisely demonstrated by Sartre. In the *Dialectic of Enlightenment* as well one finds noted about the Jews: "They are branded as absolute evil by absolute evil." [16] In both analyses that is not rhetoric but the concrete interpretation of anti-Semitic texts. In the middle of the war (1940), Ludwig Klages had published the 120 pages of his introduction to the posthumously edited papers of Alfred Schuler. The introduction apparently serves as pretext for a settling of accounts with former Jewish friends, in which his boyhood friend Theodor Lessing is shunned with total silence and all his venom is disgorged upon Karl Wolfskehl, who had been driven by the hatred of Klages and those around him into antipodal New Zealand. Klages's message never wavers: "Judah itself is the golem, is the potency of Yaweh, i.e., satanism, in the mask of the human being capable, without exception, of imitating all humanity, outdoing it, and in outdoing it, annihilating it." [17]

There is an analogy of interpretation and even of perspective between Sartre and the authors of the text "Elements of Anti-Semitism—Limits of Enlightenment." Sartre hopes from a socialist demolishing of class society a definitive solution to the Jewish question; in the meantime one can only provide recommendations for deportment, for Jews and their opponents not yet fixated in hatred. Horkheimer and Adorno too differentiate the long-term from the short-term perspective. In the long term, the Jewish question could manifest itself as "a turning point of history." Namely, "in the liberation of thought from domination, in the abolition of violence, the idea could be made reality which up to now has remained unreal, that the Jew is a human being. It would be the step

away from anti-Semitic society—which drives the Jew and others to sick-
ness—to a human society."[18]

So it stood in 1944 in the sixth and last thesis on anti-Semitism. The
sentences were to be found on the last page of the analysis and seemed
with that to mark off the perspective. But when the text, which had been
completed in 1944 (the foreword is dated May 1944), appeared in book
form in 1947, the authors, in the three lines of a new foreword dated
June 1947, had the following to say: "The book contains no essential
changes in the text as it was completed during the war. The only addition
is the last thesis to the 'Elements of Anti-Semitism.'"[19]

What is the reason for this last thesis? Quite apparently the cognizance
of the events at war's end and of the mechanisms of destruction at
Auschwitz and Maidanek had made the too high minded intent of the
original text questionable. Only with the new, seventh thesis, does the
analysis of anti-Semitism and its elements properly become part of "the
dialectic of Enlightenment." At the same time it frees itself from the
specifically Jewish problematic to grasp anti-Semitism and Jews as ex-
emplifications of the phenomenon of outsiders in society. Now the other
minority possibilities are taken into account: women, blacks, intellectuals,
also Protestants in the Catholic, Catholics in the militant Protestant world.
"It has actually been shown that anti-Semitism in areas where there are
no Jews has no less of a chance than even in Hollywood."[20]

The book *Dialectic of Enlightenment* was conceived and formulated in
the midst of a war that saw the Soviet Union as the ally of the United
States, of the French Resistance, of the national majorities in the countries
occupied by the Wehrmacht. But when the book appeared and a new
last thesis on the question of anti-Semitism had to be appended, the
world of the victors was marked by a real and ideological antagonism
between West and East, imperialists and communists. That which is characterized by Horkheimer and Adorno as "the scheme of things by I.D.
tag"—the ideology of block thinking, the negation of all differentiations,
the Manichean contract between absolutely evil and absolutely good parts
of the world—divided a world whose self-identity and self-representation
knew only position and its negation. In the last thesis on anti-Semitism
one now finds a new, more skeptical and more realistic prognosis: "Freedom on the progressive ticket is, for the structures of political power to
which progressive decisions necessarily devolve, as extraneous as anti-
Semitism is to a chemical trust."[21] Put another way: monopoly capitalism
has nothing against Jews, but everything against forces in society that can

threaten positions of domination. Diversion at the expense of powerless minorities recommends itself in such cases.

On the other hand, a world power progressive from its genesis is, as world power, easily inclined to sacrifice the freedom and protection of outsiders to real interests. "It is not the anti-Semitic identification that initiates anti-Semitism, but the I.D. tag mentality as such." If one thinks this thesis through to its logical conclusion, then every I.D. mentality, which no longer represents Enlightenment but which has to calculate its abolition in a pinch, will, when the time comes, put anti-Semitism to use as much as the opposing identification.

That is the truth of our situation here and now. Whoever attacks "Zionism" but under no circumstances means to say anything against "Jews" is deceiving himself or others. The state of Israel is a Jewish state. Whoever wishes to destroy it, overtly or by means of policies that can effect nothing but such a destruction, is pursuing the hatred of Jews of former times and as it always was. How much that can be observed in the interweaving of foreign policy and domestic affairs is shown by the domestic policies of the decidedly anti-Zionist states: they understand their own Jewish citizens virtually as "Zionists" and treat them accordingly.

Jean-Paul Sartre closed his reflections of 1946 with the statement that as long as one Jew in the world has to feel himself threatened as a Jew, then no Frenchman is sure of his life either: because the global scheme of annihilation could make him as well, as Frenchman or white or whatever, into its object. When in November 1974 the congress of UNESCO decreed in Paris that the state of Israel belonged nowhere, could in consequence not become a member, Sartre protested vehemently. He saw in this a confirmation of his diagnosis thirty years after the fact.

In Horkheimer and Adorno the concluding sentence reads: "The Enlightenment, keeping itself in tow, becoming a power, was itself able to break through the limits of the Enlightenment."[22] The sentence from Marx is paraphrased here that the idea can become material power if it seizes the masses, though at this juncture of the *Dialectic of Enlightenment* there is no longer any talk of masses. Enlightenment, as it is meant to be understood in this work, poses itself against the limited, and thanks to such limitations, suffocated bourgeois Enlightenment. In whose name? In the name of impotence, not of power, of an idea without an accompanying interest.

When Shylock insisted on his document, he trusted in the law to be his protection. He commended himself into the hands of the learned and rightful judge. ("Most learned judge!—Most rightful judge!") The ghastly irony of the bond with its clause of a pound of flesh consists of Shylock's original desire to come to a reconciliation with Antonio, convinced that his debtor would be in a position to pay within the time set, and so inventing an absurd clause in order to mask the forgoing of usurious interest in case of nonpayment. At that point Jessica had not yet been abducted, Shylock's house not plundered.

The intended magnanimity bore no fruit, now the law must take its course. In a serious case, as here, the Jew receives no justice. What Portia amid the roaring laughter of the Venetians postulates as the judgment of the court, would, in reverse situation, have been unfailingly decried by the anti-Semite as Jewish Talmudism. She proceeds against Shylock in what is taken to be a Shylockian manner. The Jew is to be executed and is explicitly obliged to acknowledge his satisfaction ("I am content"). It is simply that Shylock does not always and everywhere have to be a Jew.

Open Ending

Whatever causes human suffering, the lament over reification glosses over it now rather than denouncing it. The calamity lies in the conditions that damn men to impotence and apathy and that could be changed by them, and not primarily in men and the way conditions appear to them.

Theodor W. Adorno, *Negative Dialectic*

This book proceeds from the realization that the bourgeois Enlightenment has failed. A phenomenology of intentional and existential outsiders does not seem to have brought any greater illumination than this. The world of images of women is manipulated so that the life of the feminine outsider is degraded to a pretty story, like the ones so well-loved by the Hollywood dream makers—Bonnie and Clyde or the High Couple with a weapon; the apotheosis of Marilyn Monroe; finally the synthetic superproduction starring the vamp with a weapon.

In a desperate exertion of his life's and writing's experience, Jean Genet labored at erecting a countermorality and an antiaesthetic for outsiders. The usual morality of the normal ones was not altered but instead his antiaesthetic was literarily consumed.

The anti-Semitism of the haute bourgeoisie, which aspires to the social proscription of the Jews, has remained just as much at hand as that of the petite bourgeoisie, which wants their extermination. A somewhat awkward terminology that speaks of Zionists instead of Jews, ostensibly not wishing to eliminate the Jewish outsider but the state of Israel and ostensible Jewish imperialism, has added nothing new. These are familiar theses: merely that the protagonists of this new anti-Zionism appear in something of a disguise in view of the old, well-known tradition. They are not proletarians, though anti-Semitism has remained a well-known phenomenon in working class circles. Stalin and his successors have known how to put it to use.

Open Ending

Classical French tradition demands that deductions of whatever sort proceed to a conclusion. That cannot be accomplished here, however. There is an array of solutions for outsiders like Judith and Delilah, for the men of Sodom, for a so-called Jewish question. They are familiar and can essentially be reduced to three models. In a terminology become almost repugnant through misuse, one would have to title them as liberal, fascist, and Marxist.

The liberal solution to the question of a future for existential outsiders seemingly has good news to report. There are women as elected and appointed leaders of parliaments, governments, and parties. Known homosexuals have attained to high positions in the United Nations, as foreign ministers, as ambassadors, they have been awarded the Nobel Prize, elected to the Académie Française, elevated to the rank of the nobility. Since Auschwitz, there have been Jewish mayors in Germany, a Jewish Federal Chancellor in the homeland of yesterday's *Reichsführer*, Jewish diplomats and politicians in East and West.

Yet all these are exceptions that do not refute an old and unenlightened theory and practice but denounce it anew. The excited propaganda that proclaims a Women's Year has covertly supposed that all the other years are men's. The social, economic, and political inequalities (within the framework of the principle of equality before the law) of which feminist literature constantly gives report, remain unrefuted. The liberalism of everyday American life and of the American heartland has developed with virtuosity the division of labor between the wageearning man and his wife, who spends the money and outlives him. Pascal Lainé's investigations of the image worlds of women report now as much as ever in the France of our day the established disapproval that a woman who works outside the home encounters.

A foreign minister of whom one is given the intelligence that he is not married, with which a good deal more is meant to be expressed, and of whom the praise is heard over his grave that he conducted himself discreetly, serves as a reminder that known homosexuals in all countries are treated as "security risks." They are exempt from military service by mere acknowledgment as in the day of the confidence man Felix Krull; they are hounded from their places of work and pushed aside into special fields supposedly adequate for them, like interior decorating and hair dressing. The homosexual or lesbian murderer: these are monsters sui generis and not comparable to customary evildoers.

Everywhere there is a resonant vibration of "yes, to be sure—but. . . ."

A Jewish politician who fails has failed doubly: in office and in his existence. The cases of Georges Mandel and Léon Blum were followed after the Second World War by the secret proscription of Pierre Mendès-France. The Jewish intellectuals in John F. Kennedy's train did not flourish on account of such protection.

The hindrances that embarrassed the unfolding of anti-Semitism after Auschwitz have in the meantime fallen by the wayside, if Shylock is seen as the state of Israel. In that case, the place of the sometime individual outsider is now assumed by an outsider state, which is made to feel it. The *yes, to be sure—but* that enfolds it can virtually signify the new genocide.

This is what is promulgated by the fascist variant for treating existential outsiders. The term suffers misuse, is trivialized on account of it; it is simply that there is a fascism in theory as well as in practice. As a decided counter-Enlightenment, it proclaims inequality in contrast to the postulate of equality of the bourgeois Enlightenment and its successors. Woman is not equal to man. Man is a manly man, whatever is to be understood by that: the feminine man stands out from the race and thereby becomes worthless life. Shylock must be exterminated: the only final solutions are fire and gas.

The Marxist conclusion will have to be distinguished between the thought of the classical Marxists and the realities of the Soviet Union. Equality of rights for the sexes was an inalienable postulate of the workers' movement and of Marxist doctrine. Friedrich Engels and August Bebel and many others after them had developed these theses. They could be based on the indignation of working class women whose outsiderlike special exploitation could be documented more than amply. To the same degree, I might add, that unequal treatment and pay for women workers and children could be supplanted by the unequal treatment of forced laborers and later of the so-called guest workers, disproportionalities within European capitalism came to be modified. The American economy always has had its reserve of colored workers, male and female. So too in all the emancipation movements of the working class and of suppressed nationalities the share of women protagonists has been considerable. The double outsiderdom of Rosa Luxemburg is representative.

The scanty numbers and no less scanty influential power of women at the helm of socialist states since the October Revolution of 1917 is striking. Krupskaia and Kollontai: very few otherwise, and none in the decisive committees of the Politburo. Stalin did not believe in equality of rights for the sexes. He demanded a shadow existence of his erstwhile wives, ignored a suicide, established the Politburo as a men's committee. Nothing has changed since. The ephemeral hegemony of a Rumanian woman Communist was just as soon done away with. The much cited and painted women tractor drivers only emphasize the contrast. Theoretically equality of rights reigns, yet in practice it is limited to the lower and less significant spheres. Even the woman minister was seen as an exception; the politics of the Soviet Union and of those states formed and dominated by it is men's work.

The sexual outsiders have remained such. Stalin, once he could be sure of his power, hastened to reintroduce penalities against homosexual practices and intensified them. When around 1948 Communist propaganda was unleashed against Jean-Paul Sartre, as the author of the play *Dirty Hands,* among the accents of disgust there was to be heard and read that Sartre did not shrink from scheming to introduce a thief and pederast into literature: one Jean Genet. Fidel Castro's legislation and propaganda against homosexuals as agents of American imperialism is well known.

Anti-Semitism was terminologically recircuited to anti-Socialism. At the Bolsheviks' nineteenth party congress, the last he lived to see, it was none other than I. V. Stalin who in his closing address demanded that the international proletariat take over and put into reality the postulates of the bourgeois revolution. The demand for a right to a Palestinian homeland rings hollow when the rights to homelands of so many other nationalities, not least of the Poles and Germans, is disregarded for baldly strategic reasons. Anti-Semitism, of the older or newer terminology, has since Stalin become a maxim of state administration. Jewish extraction is an integer of political suspicion; it was not starting with the trials in Prague and Budapest in the Stalin era that a Jewish surname was a negative argument.

Heinrich Mann, in Los Angeles in the last years of the war, readying his book *Ein Zeitalter wird besichtigt* (An Age Is Examined) for press, postulates in it the historical-political connection between Jacobinism and Bolshevism, between the revolutions of 1789 and 1917: "It is in fact gripping—as a human event, even if it were not a political one—this coupling, at over a century's distance, brought about by one great nation with another, with the greatest moments of the other."[1] And further on: "The fact of the matter certainly seems to be that the Soviet Union has practically disproved the old prejudice against leveling."[2] The subject at this point in the text was economic equality. No matter how economic egalitarianism is valued, as a social factum it engendered no new consciousness. The Soviet Union did not put into practice, on a socially higher level, say, the thoughts of the bourgeois rights of man. One sees that in the outsiders.

Hence all occupation with outsiders in past and present life, in art and literature, leads to the conclusion, if it is one, that all enlightened legislation which subscribes to equality must be applicable for the normal case as much as for the exception. But by that, and unavoidably so, it injures the existential particularity of the outsider. Moreover, Judith and the men of Sodom and Shylock's descendants can be named together only in their negativity. No path leads from the one to the other. There is no community of outsiders. Heine stands against Platen, Shylock against Antonio, Lulu against the Countess Geschwitz, Rosa Luxemburg against the Jewish officer among her assassins. Along with the bourgeois Enlightenment, something which Heinrich Mann was not inclined to recognize, the continuation of the Enlightenment through the states of a nonbourgeois planned economy is shattered as well.

One can only agree with Theodor W. Adorno's bitter objection: the justifiable, often repeated, often merely formally made denunciation of social reification and self-alienation remains itself an expression of reification as long as the concrete suffering of the individual human being is set aside with an allusion to a whole humanity that must be saved.[3] A species of thought that disdains every so-called personalization and recognizes only collectivities, quantitatively contrastable normed phenomena, instead of the individual case, promotes fetishized thought and with it an inhuman practice. On this account the scandals of the outsiders had to be discussed individually. It was not psychology that was attempted here but the representation of historically real constellations—either in the immediacy of historical events or in mediation through works of the spirit. In this manner phenomena and events were analyzed, without a conclusion being drawn. A sentence from Goethe's *Maxims and Reflections*,[4] which first appeared in Makaria's archive in *Wilhelm Meister's Travels,* should be taken to heart: "One does not do well to remain too long in the abstract. The esoteric only harms by its inclination to become exoteric. Life is best instructed through living beings."

Notes

Premises: Outsiders and Enlightenment

1 Ernst Bloch, *Naturrecht und menschliche Würde,* Gesamtausgabe, vol. 6 (Frankfurt: Suhrkamp, 1961), pp. 232, 237.

2 Ernst Bloch, *Das Prinzip Hoffnung,* Gesamtausgabe, vol. 5 (Frankfurt: Suhrkamp, 1959), chap. 47, p. 1103.

3 Max Horkheimer, "Montaigne und die Funktion der Skepsis," *Zeitschrift für Sozialforschung* (1938): 1ff. Reprinted in *Kritische Theorie: Eine Dokumentation,* ed. Alfred Schmidt, vol. 2 (Frankfurt: Suhrkamp, 1968), p. 201ff., here esp. pp. 217, 228ff.

4 Montaigne, *Oeuvres complètes* (Paris: Bibliothèque de la Pléiade, 1962), pp. 690–91.

5 Ibid., p. 691.

6 See Hans Mayer, "Karl Marx und die Literatur," in *Marxismus und Literatur: Eine Dokumentation in drei Bänden,* ed. Fritz J. Raddatz, vol. 3 (Reinbek: Rowohlt, 1969), pp. 330–331.

7 Euripides, "Les Troyennes," adaptation de Jean-Paul Sartre (Paris: Gallimard, 1965), pp. 7–8.

8 Walter Jens, *Der Fall Judas* (Stuttgart: Kreuz Verlag, 1975).

9 Bloch, *Das Prinzip Hoffnung,* pp. 1174ff., 1219.

10 Harry Levin, *The Overreacher: A Study of Christopher Marlowe* (Cambridge, Mass.: Harvard University Press, 1952).

11 G. W. F. Hegel, *Vorlesungen über die Ästhetik:* "Die konkrete Entwicklung der dramatischen Poesie und ihrer Arten," Theorie Werkausgabe, vol. 15 (Frankfurt: Suhrkamp, 1970), p. 560ff.

12 Leslie A. Fiedler, *The Stranger in Shakespeare* (New York: Stein and Day, 1972).

13 Ibid., p. 43.

14 W. H. Auden, *The Dyer's Hand and Other Essays* (New York: Random House, 1948), p. 231.

15 Herman Meyer, *Der Sonderling in der deutschen Dichtung* (Munich: Hanser, 1963), p. 22.

16 Wolf Lepenies, *Melancholie und Gesellschaft* (Frankfurt: Suhrkamp, 1969), pp. 94–95.

17 Rudolf and Margot Wittkower, *Born under Saturn* (New York: Random House, 1963), p. 98ff.

18 Adolph Freiherr von Knigge, *Über den Umgang mit Menschen* (Bremen: Humboldt, 1964), esp. p. 425ff.

Judith and Delilah

1
The Second Sex and Its Outsiders

1 Simone de Beauvoir, *Le Deuxième sexe*, vol. 1, *Les Faits et les Mythes* (Paris: Gallimard, 1949), p. 236 [English trans.: *The Second Sex*, trans. and ed. by H. M. Parshley (New York: Alfred A. Knopf, 1953), p. 143].

2 Goethe writes in his journals in January 1823, looking back to his work on "Pandora's Return" of 1807: "and since the mythological point where Prometheus appears had always been present to my mind and had become a vivid idée fixe, I then set to work...." Further on, writing on the connection between "Pandora" and the *Elective Affinities*, Goethe states that "'Pandora' as well as the *Elective Affinities* expresses the painful feeling of privation, and therefore they compare well indeed, the one next to the other...."

   The relationship to the disillusioned Titanism of the Prometheus period is worked out in the exact same fashion as that to the Pandora tradition as a debilitating femininity. Goethe always respected this context. In the "Marienbad Elegy" of 1823 there stand the verses: "The universe is for me, I am lost to myself / who was one the darling of the gods; / They tested me, bequeathed me Pandora, / so rich in goods, richer still in danger."

3 De Beauvoir, *Le Deuxième sexe*, pp. 16–17.

4 Fiedler, *The Stranger in Shakespeare*, p. 43ff.

5 Frank Wedekind, "Simson oder Sham und Eifersucht" [Samson or Shame and Jealousy], in *Prosa Dramen Verse*, vol. 2 (Munich and Vienna: A. Langen-G. Müller, 1964), p. 529ff.

6 Ibid., p. 595.

7 Friedrich Nietzsche, *Jenseits von Gut und Böse*, in Werke in drei Bänden, ed. Karl Schlechta (Munich: Carl Hanser, 1966), p. 703.

8 Otto Weininger, *Geschlecht und Charakter* (Vienna and Leipzig: W. Braumüller, 1903), p. 241.

9 De Beauvoir, *Le Deuxième Sexe*, p. 393.

2
The Scandal of Joan of Arc

1 George Bernard Shaw, *Saint Joan: A Chronicle Play in Six Scenes and An Epilogue* (New York: Penguin Books, 1958), Preface: Joan, a Galtonic Visualizer.

2 Johan Huizinga, *The Waning of the Middle Ages* (London: E. Arnold, 1924).

3 Shaw, *Saint Joan*, Preface: The Maid in Literature.

4 Pascal, *Pensées*, in *Oeuvres complètes*. ed Jacques Chevalier (Paris: Bibliothèque de la Pléiade, 1954).

5 Ibid., pp. 1091–92: "Dans l'esprit de finesse, les principes sont dans l'usage commun et devant les yeux de tout le monde. On n'a que faire de tourner la tête ni de se fair violence; il n'est question que d'avoir bonne vue, mais il faut l'avoir bonne...."

6 Ibid., p. 1221: "Le coeur a ses raisons, que la raison ne connaît point; on le sait de mille choses. Je dis que le coeur aime l'être universel naturellement, et soi-même naturelle-ment, selon qu'il s'y adonne; et il se durcit contre l'un ou l'autre, à son choix...." (Pensée 477). See Pensée 479 as well: "Nous connaissons la vérité, non seulement par la raison, mais encore par le coeur; c'est de cette dernière sorte que nous connaissons les premiers principes, et c'est en vain que le raisonnement, qui n'y a point de part, essaye de les combattre." In the trial this conflict is to be felt everywhere—to be sure as the contrast between subjective convictions, while Pascal is postulating here objective givens.

7 The analysis is based on materials in volume 9 of the National Edition of Schiller, ed. Benno von Wiese and Lieselotte Blumenthal (Weimar: H. Böhlaus Nachf., 1948). On the history of its development, p. 401ff. On the history of its reception, p. 438ff.

8 Shaw, *Saint Joan*, Scene IV.

9 Bertolt Brecht, Ovation für Shaw (July 25, 1926), in *Gesammelte Werke in acht Bänden*, vol. 7 (Frankfurt: Suhrkamp, 1967), p. 96ff.

10 Ibid., p. 101.

11 See the fragments and variants to *Die Heilige Johanna der Schlachthöfe* in vol. 427 of the edition Suhrkamp series (Frankfurt, 1971).

12 Brecht, *Die Heilige Johanna der Schlachthöfe*, in *Gesammelte Werke*, vol. 1, p. 785. [Verse translations are taken from *Saint Joan of the Stockyards*, trans. Frank Jones (Bloomington, Ind.: Indiana University Press, 1970).]

13 Brecht, *Die Gesichte der Simone Machard*, in *Gesammelte Werke*, vol. 2, p. 1841ff. [Verse translations are taken from *The Visions of Simone Machard*, in vol. 7 of Bertolt Brecht, *Collected Plays*, trans. Ralph Manheim and John Willet (New York: Random House, 1973).]

14 Brecht, *Der Prozess der Jeanne d'Arc zu Rouen 1431 nach dem Hörspiel von Anna Seghers*, in *Gesammelte Werke*, vol. 2, p. 2499ff.

15 The analysis is based on Friedrich Wolf's German translation and edition of *The Optimistic Tragedy* (Berlin, 1948).

16 The source here is a conversation with Vsevolod Vishnevskii at the German Writers' Congress in Berlin in October 1947.

17 Brecht, "Sozialistischer Realismus auf dem Theater," in *Gesammelte Werke*, vol. 7, p. 935.

3
Judith as Bourgeois Heroine

1 My remarks on the history of the Judith motif in German literature rely on Otto Baltzer's "Judith in der deutschen Literatur," in *Stoff- und Motivgeschichte der deutschen Literatur*, ed. Paul Merker and Gerhard Lüdtle, vol. 7 (Berlin and Leipzig, 1930). The Luther quote, ibid., p. 42.

2 Ibid., (Hans Sachs), p. 3.

3 Anton Mayer, "Quelle und Entstehung von Opitzens Judith," in *Euphorion*, 20, 1913, p. 41ff.

4 Baltzer, "Judith in der deutschen Literatur," p. 19.

5 "Great god, but that was new in his time, it was a message, an astonishing truth.... There are paradoxes that have stood on their heads so long that one has to put them on their feet to make anything even mildly daring out of them. 'He is a human being.... He is more than that'—now that is bolder, comes off better, it is even truer . . . its reverse is mere humanity." Thomas Mann, *Royal Highness*, chapter "Doctor Überbein." This passage can be taken as an anticipation of the later theses of Dr. Naphta in *The Magic Mountain*. That it corresponded in large part to the novelist's own convictions at the turn of the century can be documented in Thomas Mann's "Thoughts on the War of 1914" and in the *Reflections of a Non-Political Man*.

6 Helmut Kreuzer, "Die Jungfrau in Waffen. Hebbels 'Judith' und ihre Geschwister von Schiller bis Sartre," in *Untersuchungen zur Literatur als Geschichte: Festschrift für Benno von Wiese* (Berlin: Schmidt, 1973), p. 363. Here Kreuzer also analyzes Brecht's dramatic one-act first play, "The Bible," its author still signing his name "Berthold Eugen." Hereto Bertolt Brecht, *Gesammelte Werke*, vol. 3, p. 3029ff. Brecht sets the Judith drama in the seventeenth century. "The play takes place in the Netherlands, in a protestant town besieged by the Catholics." The grandfather who piously holds to the Bible forbids his

granddaughter surrendering herself to the Catholic commander. They all go to their ruin on account of the inaction of this presupposed Judith. The *Gymnasium* student Brecht is quite apparently confronting his school experience of Hebbel with the forms of behavior of bourgeois everyday life. Here already the neophyte playwright's mistrust of a drama of "great characters." See also Herbert Kraft, *Poesie der Idee: die tragische Dichtung Friedrich Hebbels* (Tübingen: Niemeyer, 1971) and the review by Ludwig W. Kahn dealing with Brecht's relation to Judith, in *The German Quarterly*, March 1974, p. 330.

7 See Siegfried Streller, *Das dramatische Werk Heinrich von Kleists* (Berlin: Rütten and Loening, 1966), p. 99ff.

8 Hegel, *Vorlesungen über die Ästhetik*, chap. 3. In *Werke*, vol. 15 (Frankfurt: Suhrkamp, 1970), p. 546.

9 Hebbel brought the underlying convictions of his dramaturgy most poignantly to expression in "Mein Wort über das Drama" (1843) and in the preface to "Maria Magdalena" (1844). Noteworthy is his critical rejection of *Käthchen von Heilbronn* in a melancholy-ironic review done in 1848, in *Friedrich Hebbels Sämtliche Werke*, vol. 12 (Kuh-Krumm and Leipzig: Hesse and Becker, n.d.), p. 270ff.

10 Quote taken from Ida Countess Hahn-Hahn, *Gräfin Faustine. Ein Roman aus der Biedermeierzeit*. With the life story of the authoress, newly edited by Arthur Schurig (Berlin, 1919).

11 Hans G. Helms, *Die Ideologie der anonymen Gesellschaft* (Köln: DuMont, 1966), p. 3.

12 Hahn-Hahn, *Faustine*, p. 51.

13 Ibid., p. 54.

14 Ibid., p. 339.

15 Max Horkheimer and Theodor W. Adorno, *Dialektik der Aufklärung: Philosophische Fragmente* (Frankfurt: Suhrkamp, 1969), p. 97 [English trans.: *Dialectic of Enlightenment*, trans. John Cumming (New York: Herder and Herder, 1972)].

16 Max Stirner, *Der Einzige und sein Eigentum*, 1st ed. (Leipzig, 1845), p. 490. Besides the comprehensive sociological analysis of Stirner and Stirnerism in Helms, there is the most acute attempt by Martin Kessel to make comprehensible the contradictions between Stirner's life and thought; cf. "Der Einzige und die Milchwirtschaft" in Martin Kessel, *Ehrfurcht und Gelächter. Literarische Essays* (Mainz: v. Hagen and Koehler, 1974), p. 11ff.

17 Richard Wagner, *Die Musikdramen*, afterword by Joachim Kaiser (Hamburg: Hoffman and Campe, 1971), p. 265ff.

18 Richard Wagner, *Briefwechsel mit Franz Liszt* (Leipzig, 1887). Letter of January 30, 1852.

19 George Bernard Shaw, "The Quintessence of Ibsenism" (1891); "The Perfect Wagnerite" (1898). Both essays collected in *Major Critical Essays: The Quintessence of Ibsenism, The Perfect Wagnerite, The Sanity of Art* (London: Constable, 1930).

20 Thomas Mann, "Die Kunst des Romans," Lecture at Princeton University (1939), in *Altes und Neues: Kleine Prosa aus fünf Jahrzehnten* (Frankfurt: Fischer, 1961), p. 376.

21 Georg Lukács, *Die Seele und die Formen. Essays* (Berlin, 1911). [Engl. trans.: *Soul and Form*, trans. Anna Rostock (Cambridge, Mass.: MIT Press, 1971).]

22 Georg Lukács's biographical dates compiled by Peter Ludz in *George Lukács, Goethepreis '70* (Neuwied: Luchterhand, 1970), p. 154ff.

23 Georg Lukács, "Auf der Suche nach dem Bürger" in *Deutsche Literatur in zwei Jahrhunderten*, Werke, vol. 7 (Neuwied: Luchterhand, 1964), p. 505.

24 Jean-Paul Sartre, *L'Idiot de la famille*, 3 vols. (Paris: Gallimard, 1971–72) [vol. 1 has appeared, *The Family Idiot*, trans. Carol Cosman (Chicago: Chicago University Press, 1981).]

25 Henrik Ibsen, "Hedda Gabler" in *Eleven Plays of Henrik Ibsen*, intro. by H. L. Mencken (New York: The Modern Library, n.d.). The quotations in the text are according to this edition.

26 Translation from: *Eleven Plays of Henrik Ibsen*, intro. by H. L. Mencken, The Modern Library, n.d., p. 555.

27 Ibid., p. 537.

4
The Bourgeois Way of Life as an Alternative

1 Matthew Arnold, *Culture and Anarchy*, ed. with intro. by J. Dover Wilson (Cambridge, England: The University Press, 1932).

2 Ibid., p. 107.

3 Edward Bond, *Early Morning* (London: Calder and Boyars, 1968).

4 Cited in David Thomson, *England in the Nineteenth Century* (The Pelican History of England, *8*, 1950), pp. 102–3.

5 One is reminded here of Karl Marx's desperate attempt in Victorian England to hush up the existence of an illegitimate son by his housekeeper, Helene Demuth, out of concern for negative political reactions among the working class.

6 Thomson, *England in the Nineteenth Century*, p. 107.

7 My interpretation relies on *The George Eliot Letters*, ed. by George S. Haight (New Haven, Conn.: Yale University Press, 1954–1978) and on Haight's biography *George Eliot* (New York: Oxford University Press, 1968). Of particular importance in showing George Eliot's youthful development are her letters to John Chapman, also edited by Gordon S. Haight, *George Eliot and John Chapman, with John Chapman's Diaries* (New Haven, Conn.: Yale University Press, 1940). A well-documented and illustrated version of the life story is provided by Marghanita Laski, *George Eliot and Her World* (London: Thames and Hudson, 1973). Virginia Woolf's essay on George Eliot is to be found in *The Common Reader* (New York: Harcourt, Brace, 1925). A subjective-epic representation was attempted by the lyric poet and novelist Gerald Bullett in *George Eliot: Her Life and Books* (London: Collins, 1947), which breaks off after an analysis of *Middlemarch* and only touches upon *Daniel Deronda* in brief and general fashion. The article in the *Encyclopedia Britannica* signed G. S. H., once again likely Gordon S. Haight, was also consulted.

8 Eliza Lynn Linton, in her book of reminiscences, *My Literary Life* (1899), pp. 98–99.

9 Alfred de Vigny, *Journal d'un poète*, entry of January 21, 1832.

10 The iconography of this life, which appeared in 1973, with precise comments by Georges Lubin, provides with the help of the letters and pictorial documents a good view into the processes of change that extend far beyond one individual's growing old. *Album Sand. Iconographie réunie et commentée par Georges Lubin* (Paris: Bibliothèque de la Pléiade, 1973).

11 To this belong all the representations and counterrepresentations by adherents of Chopin, Musset, and George Sand. An example from the German stage is to be found in Georg Kaiser's piece *Die Flucht nach Venedig*.

12 Andre Maurois, *Lélia, ou la vie de George Sand* (Paris: Hachette, 1952). This is no longer, as was the case with Maurois's earlier books, on Shelley, say, a *biographie romancée*, but a historically and philologically well-founded presentation, which makes use of a great amount of unedited material and tracks down sources. [English trans.: *Lelia, the Life of George Sand* (New York: Harper & Brothers, 1953).]

13 Letter of May 31, 1831 to Mme. Maurice Dupin, cited in Maurois, ibid., vol. 1, 150.

14 Samuel Edwards [Noel B. Gerson], *George Sand: A Biography of the First Modern, Liberated Woman* (New York: D. McKay, 1972).

15 Charles Baudelaire, *Mon Coeur mis à nu*. Cited in Maurois, *Lélia*, vol. 2, pp. 185-6.

16 George Sand, *Lélia*, original ed. vol. 2 (Paris, 1833), pp. 9–10.

17 Ibid., pp. 25–6.

18 Maurois, ibid., pp. 262–3.

19 Letter of June 25, 1876. Flaubert, *Correspondance*, vol. 7, p. 311.

20 Simone de Beauvoir, *Tout compte fait* [English trans. by Patrick O'Brien, *All Said and Done* (New York: Putnam, 1974).] A book like *George Sand et les hommes de 1848* by Marie-Louise Pailleron (Paris: B. Grasset, 1953) only corroborates the analysis.

21 Letter of June 19, 1848. Cited in Pailleron, ibid., p. 139.

22 Diary entry of June 1, 1871. Unpublished manuscript, cited in Maurois, *Lélia*, vol. 2, p. 245.

5
Excursus: Otto Weininger, *Sex and Character*

1 Otto Weininger, *Geschlecht und Character: Eine prinzipielle Untersuchung* (Vienna and Leipzig: Braumüller, 1926), p. iv.

2 Ibid., p. 301.

3 Oswald Spengler, *Der Untergang des Abendlandes: Umrisse einer Morphologie der Weltge - schichte*, vol. 1, Gestalt und Wirklichkeit (Munich: Beck, 1919), p. 397.

4 Weininger, *Geschlecht und Character*, p. 264.

5 Ibid., p. 276.

6 Ibid., p. 276.

7 Ibid., p. 264.

8 Ibid., p. 248.

9 Ibid., p. 266.

6
Delilah as Bourgeois Vamp

1 Paul Ernst, "Brunhild. Trauerspiel in drei Aufzügen" (Leipzig, 1909).

2 Ernst Bloch, *Das Prinzip Hoffnung* (Frankfurt: Suhrkamp, 1959), chap. 21, p. 381ff.

3 Ibid., p. 381.

4 Frank Wedekind, *Prosa Dramen Verse* (Munich: Albert Langen, Georg Müller, n.d.), p. 377ff.

5 Ibid., p. 383.

6 Martin Kessel, "Frank Wedekinds romantisches Erbteil," *Ehrfurcht und Gelächter: Literarische Essays* (Mainz: v. Hase & Koehler, 1974), p. 56ff.

7 Ibid., p. 69.

8 Karl Kraus, "Die Büchse der Pandora. Gesprochen als Einleitung zur ersten, von mir veranstalteten Aufführung am 29. Mai 1905" in Karl Kraus, *Literatur und Lüge* (Vienna and Leipzig, 1929), p. 7ff. Reprinted in Hans Mayer, *Deutsche Literaturkritik im zwanzigsten Jahrhundert* (Stuttgart: Govert, 1965), p. 135ff. Quotations are from this reprint.

9 Ibid., p. 140.

10 Ibid., p. 147.

11 Walter Benjamin, "Karl Kraus," in *Illuminationen: Ausgewählte Schriften* (Frankfurt: Suhrkamp, 1961), p. 374ff.

12 Ibid., p. 394.

13 Ibid., p. 393.

14 Karl Schönherr, *Der Weibsteufel. Drama in fünf Akten* (Munich, 1956).

15 Quoted ibid., p. 84.

16 Ibid., p. 78.

17 Friedrich Dürrenmatt, "Die Ehe des Herrn Mississippi. Eine Komödie," second version, in Dürrenmatt, *Komödien I* (Zürich: Verlag der Arche, 1957), p. 87ff.

18 Gottfried Benn, "Die Ehe des Herrn Mississippi," in *Autobiographische und vermischte Schriften* (Wiesbaden: Limes Verlag, 1961), p. 298ff.

19 Friedrich Dürrenmatt, "Bekenntnisse eines Plagiators" in *Theaterschriften und Reden* (Zürich: Verlag der Arche, 1966), p. 239ff.

20 Dürrenmatt, "21 Punkte zu den Physikern," in ibid., pp. 193–4.

21 Harold Pinter, *The Homecoming* (London: Methuen, 1965).

22 Ibid., p. 80.

23 Ibid., p. 73.

24 Martin Esslin, *Harold Pinter* (Velber bei Hannover: Friedrich, 1967), p. 86.

25 Norman Mailer, *Marilyn* (New York: Grosset, 1973).

7
Women's Liberation and Norman Mailer

1 Norman Mailer, *The Prisoner of Sex* (Boston: Little, Brown, 1971), p. 55.

2 Linda Phelps, "What Is the Difference?" a pamphlet, (3800 McGee, Kansas City, Mo., n.d., p. 4.

3 Kate Millet, *Sexual Politics* (Garden City, N.J.: Doubleday, 1970).

4 Otto Weininger, *Geschlecht und Charakter: Eine prinzipielle Untersuchung* (Vienna and Leipzig: Braumüller, 1926), p. 288.

5 Mailer, *The Prisoner of Sex*, p. 111.

6 Ibid., pp. 219–221.

7 Ibid., pp. 181–82.

8 Ibid., p. 102–3.

9 Ibid., p. 185.

10 Ti-Grace Atkinson, "The Institution of Sexual Intercourse" in *Women's Liberation: Notes from the Second Year* (1970), p. 45, quoted by Mailer, ibid., p. 65.

11 Plato's *Symposium*, Jowett translation.

12 Mailer, *The Prisoner of Sex*, p. 182.

13 Ibid., p. 229.

8
The World of Images of Women

1 Pascal Lainé, *La Femme et ses images* (Paris: Stock, 1974).

2 The descriptions of the paintings rely on the catalog of the exhibition "Richard Lindner" in the Städtische Kunsthalle Düsseldorf, June 13–July 28, 1974. The painting "The Meeting" is illustrated under catalog no. 5.

3 Richard Lindner in an interview with Wolfgang Georg Fischer, ibid., p. 6.

4 Ibid., p. 25.

5 Werner Spies, "Die Maschinerie des Unbehagens: Richard Lindners Suche nach Marcel Proust / Zu zwei Porträts des Malers" [The machinery of dissatisfaction and malaise: Richard Lindner's search for Marcel Proust / concerning two of the artist's portraits], first appeared in the *Frankfurter Allgemeine Zeitung*, January 3, 1973, reprinted in "Rich-

ard Lindner," catalogue, p. 24ff. see also Peter Gorsen's essay "Der Sexualfetisch als Ikone der Versagung" where he writes: "An artist like Lindner . . . believes himself to be an outsider and individualist, an 'unreliable character' . . . the genre of his paintings is supposed to be that of woman who surpasses man," ibid., p. 31.

6 Ibid., catalog no. 30.

7 Lainé, *La Femme et ses images,* p. 35–6.

8 Ibid., p. 37.

9 Frank Wedekind, "'Hidalla' oder Karl Hetmann, der Zwergriese. Schauspiel in fünf Akten" (1903–1904), in *Prosa Dramen Verse,* vol. 2 (Munich/Vienna: A. Langen, G. Müller, 1964), p. 177.

10 Lainé, *La Femme et ses images,* p. 253ff.

11 Ibid., p. 238.

12 Ibid., p. 243.

13 Pascal Lainé, *L'Irrévolution* (Paris: Gallimard, 1971).

14 Pascal Lainé, *La Dentellière* (Paris: Gallimard, 1974).

15 Ibid., p. 250.

16 Ibid., p. 251.

Sodom

9

A Chronicle of Murders and Scandal

1 Hans Kelsen, "Die Platonische Liebe," in *Aufsätze zur Ideologiekritik,* Soziologische Texte, vol. 16 (Neuwied: Luchterhand, 1965), p. 114ff. Most of the Greek texts quoted in the following pages are also cited in Kelsen.

2 Plato, *Nomoi* I, 8.

3 Aristotle, *Nicomachean Ethics* VII, 6. See Kelsen, *Aufsätze zur Ideologiekritik,* p. 149.

4 Ibid., p. 138.

5 Ibid., p. 142.

6 Erich Bethe, *Thebanische Heldenlieder* (Leipzig, 1891), p. 12ff.

7 The following examples are to be found in Rudolf and Margot Wittkower, *Born under Saturn* (New York: Random House, 1963), p. 169ff.

8 Ibid., p. 169.

9 Ibid., p. 170.

10 Ibid., p. 174.

11 Marcel Proust, *A la Recherche du temps perdu* (Paris: Bibliothèque de la Pléiade, 1954), vol. 3, p. 302ff.

12 Norman Douglas, *South Wind* (London: M. Secker, 1917).

13 Norman Douglas, *Looking Back: An Autobiographical Excursion* (New York: Harcourt, Brace, 1933), p. 152ff.

14 Karl Kraus, "Maximilian Harden. Eine Erledigung," in *Die chinesische Mauer, Werke,* vol. 12 (Munich/Vienna: A. Langen, G. Müller, 1964), p. 53ff., esp. pp. 56, 80.

10

Christopher Marlowe and King Edward II of England

1 Marlowe's dramas are cited according to the *Complete Plays of Christopher Marlowe,* ed. with intro. and notes by Irving Ribner (New York: Odyssey Press, 1963).

2   The biographical facts have been taken from Frederick S. Boas's comprehensive biography *Christopher Marlowe*; 1st ed. London, 1940, with many subsequent, for the most part unchanged editions.

3   *Christopher Marlowe: A Biographical and Critical Study* (Oxford, 1940).

4   Christopher Marlowe, *The Complete Poems and Translations,* ed. Stephen Orgel (Harmondsworth, England: Penguin, 1973), p. 19.

5   Boas, *Christopher Marlowe*, p. 235.

6   Jan Kott, *Shakespeare heute,* erweiterte Neuausgabe, trans. from Polish by Peter Lachmann (1970), p. 361ff. [English trans. Boleslaw Taborski as *Shakespeare Our Contemporary,* 2nd ed. rev. (London: Methuen, 1967).]

7   Bertolt Brecht, "Leben Eduards des Zweiten von England. Historie (nach Marlowe)," in *Gesammelte Werke,* 1, (Frankfurt: Suhrkamp, 1967) [Bertolt Brecht, *Collected Plays,* "Edward," trans. by William E. Smith and Ralph Manheim, vol. 1 (New York: Pantheon, 1970).].

8   Brecht, Smith and Manheim trans., p. 255.

9   Harry Levin, *The Overreacher: A Study of Christopher Marlowe* (Cambridge, Mass.: Harvard University Press, 1952).

10 Ibid., p. 156–7.

11
Winckelmann's Death and the Discovery of a Double Life

1   *Mordakte Winckelmann,* ed. C. Pagnini, German trans. and commentary by H. A. Stoll (Berlin: Akademie Verlag, 1965).

2   J. G. Herder, *Gesammelte Werke,* ed. Suphan, vol. 8 (reprint, Hildesheim: Georg Olms, 1967–68), p. 445ff.

3   *Goethes Werke,* Hamburger Ausgabe, ed. Erich Trunz, vol. 12 (Hamburg: Wegner, 1948–64), p. 12ff.

4   Letter of February 10, 1764, in J. J. Winckelmann, *Briefe,* 4 vols. (Berlin: de Gruyter, 1952–1957).

5   Gustav Bychowski, "Das Drama Winckelmanns," in *Neurose und Genialität, Psychoanalytische Biographien,* ed. with intro. by Johannes Cremerius (Frankfurt: S. Fischer, 1971), p. 215ff.

6   Ibid., p. 223.

7   See Ingrid Kreuzer, *Studien zu Winckelmanns Ästhetik: Normativität und historisches Bewusstsein* (Berlin: Akademie Verlag, 1959).

8   Richard Hamann, "Winckelmann und die kanonische Auffassung der Kunst," in *Internationale Monatsschrift für Wissenschaft, Kunst und Technik* 7 (1912–13). Cited in Kreuzer, p. 6.

9   Wolfgang Leppmann, *Winckelmann* (New York: Knopf, 1970), p. 11.

12
The Conflict between Heine and Platen

1   Heinrich Heine, *Sämtliche Schriften,* ed. Klaus Briegleb; vol. 2, ed. Günter Häntzschel (Munich: Carl Hanser Verlag, 1969), p. 830ff.

2   Thomas Mann, "August von Platen," in *Adel des Geistes: Sechzehn Versuche zum Problem der Humanität* (Frankfurt: S. Fischer, 1967), p. 434ff.

3   Ibid., p. 436.

4   *Sämtliche Schriften,* p. 443.

5   Ibid., p. 452.

6 Ibid., p. 462.

7 Karl Immermann, "Glänzendes Elend," in Karl Immermann, *Werke in fünf Bänden,* ed. Benno von Wiese, vol. 1 (Frankfurt: Athenäum, 1971), p. 645.

8 Heine, *Sämtliche Schriften,* pp. 830–31.

9 Heinrich Heine, *Sämtliche Schriften,* vol. 4, ed. Klaus Briegleb (Munich: Carl Hanser Verlag, 1971), p. 149ff.

10 Heine, *Sämtliche Schriften,* vol. 2, p. 832.

11 Immermann, *Werke,* p. 94.

12 Karl Immermann, "Der im Irrgarten der Metrik umhertaumelnde Kavalier: Eine literarische Tragödie," in Immermann, *Werke,* p. 632ff.

13 Günter Oesterle, *Integration und Konflikt: Die Prosa Heinrich Heines im Kontext oppositioneller Literatur der Restaurationsepoche* (Stuttgart: J. B. Metzler, 1972).

13
Alternatives in the Nineteenth Century

1 Andersen's letters reveal with dismaying clarity not only the vanity that was the butt of his contemporaries' wit, but also a fawning servility that takes the words of the partner of the moment into its own mouth and presses itself upon high aristocrats, as the grand duke of Sachsen-Weimar-Eisenach, quite without conviction, always eager for equal status. See *Hans Christian Andersen's Correspondence,* ed. Frederick Crawford (London, 1891).

2 Hans Christian Andersen, *The Story of My Life,* author's ed. (Boston, 1871), p. 136–7.

3 "Af en endnu Levendes Papirer udgivet mod hans Villie af Søren Kierkegaard. Om Andersen som Romandigter med stadigt hensyn til hans sidste Vörk *Kun en Spillemand,*" *Samlede Vaerker,* vol. 1 (Copenhagen: Gyldendal, 1962), p. 11ff. ["From the Papers of One Still Living. Published against his will by S. Kierkegaard. About Andersen as a novelist with special reference to his last novel *Only a Fiddler.*"] German ed. Søren Kierkegaard, *Erstlingsschriften* (Düsseldorf: E. Diederichs, 1960), p. 41ff.; notes p. 176ff. See Emanuel Hirsch, *Kierkegaard-Studien* (Gütersloh: C. Bertelsmann, 1933), p. 13ff.

4 *Andersen's Correspondence,* p. 155.

5 Signe Toksvig, *The Life of Hans Christian Andersen* (New York: Harcourt, Brace, 1934), p. 185.

6 H. C. Andersen, *In Spain and a Visit to Portugal,* author's ed. (New York: Hurd & Houghton, 1870), p. 199.

7 *The Andersen–Scudder Letters,* ed. Jean Hershold and Waldemar Westergaard (Berkeley: University of California Press, 1949), pp. 59, 74.

8 Elith Reumert, *Hans Andersen the Man,* trans. Jessie Bröchner (London: Methuen, 1927), pp. 47–8.

9 Toksvig, *Hans Christian Andersen,* p. 186.

10 See the expositions in Reumert, *Hans Andersen the Man,* p. 15ff.

11 Kierkegaard, *Erstlingsschriften,* p. 62.

12 Ibid., p. 61.

13 Ibid., p. 55.

14 Jean Giraudoux, *Les Cinq tentations de Lafontaine* (Paris: Grasset, 1938).

15 An exact analysis of the novel, in connection with Kierkegaard's first publication, is provided in Hirsch's *Kierkegaard-Studien,* p. 26ff., and in his commentary in Kierkegaard, *Erstlingsschriften,* p. 177ff.

16 Kierkegaard, ibid., pp. 77–8.

17 The interpretation of Rimbaud relies on the new and fundamentally revised edition of the Bibliothèque de la Pléiade, *Rimbaud, Oeuvres complètes,* ed. Antoine Adam (Paris: Pléiade, 1972). Therein as well the chronology of events, pp. xxxix-lii. [Translations from *A Season in Hell* and *Illuminations* are from Arthur Rimbaud, *Illuminations and Other Prose Poems,* trans. Louise Varèse (New York: New Directions, 1957).] As comparison, the Verlaine chronology in the corresponding Verlaine edition in the Bibliothèque de la Pléiade was consulted (see note 29).

18 *Lettres de la vie littéraire d'Arthur Rimbaud* (1870–1875), ed. Jean-Marie Carré (Paris: Gallimard, 1931), p. 17.

19 Ibid, p. 282.

20 Ibid., p. 296.

21 Rimbaud, *Oeuvres Complètes,* p. xxi.

22 Rimbaud, *Lettres,* p. 744.

23 Ibid., p. 816.

24 Yves Bonnefoy, *Rimbaud par lui-même* (Paris: Editions du Seuil, 1961), p. 90.

25 Rimbaud, *Oeuvres complètes,* pp. 127, 985.

26 Ibid., pp. 136–7.

27 Ibid., pp. 102–6.

28 Rimbaud, *Oeuvres complètes,* pp. 962–5.

29 The interpretation of texts by Verlaine relies on the Verlaine edition of the Bibliothèque de la Pléiade *Verlaine, Oeuvres poétiques complètes,* ed. Y.-G. Le Dantec and Jacques Borel (Paris: Pléiade, 1962). See "A Arthur Rimbaud," p. 601.

30 Ibid., pp. 522–525.

31 Ibid., pp. 510–512.

32 Paul Verlaine, "A Louis II de Bavière," ibid., pp. 426–7, 1182.

33 All Tchaikovsky studies have had to proceed from the three-volume Russian edition of Tchaikovsky's *Life and Letters* that his younger brother, Modeste Ilich, published in Moscow between 1900 and 1902. In the translation of the composer Paul Juon they appeared in Leipzig in two volumes as *Das Leben Peter Iljitsch Tschaikowsky's.* P. I. Jurgenson, the composer's Russian publisher, also published the German edition. At approximately the same time, Rosa Newmarch published in 1900 in London the book *Tchaikovsky, His Life and Works:* with excerpts from his writings and his American journal. After Modeste's extensive publication, Rosa Newmarch attempted to combine her own studies with Modeste Tchaikovsky's work and so provide an English edition. This appeared in 1905 as *The Life and Letters of Peter Ilich Tchaikovsky. By Modeste Tchaikovsky,* edited from the Russian with an Introduction by Rosa Newmarch (Reprint: New York, 1970). It was Modeste's intent, as is now certain, if only on account of his own sexual inclinations, to expunge any references to his brother's sexuality. The book by Lawrence and Elisabeth Hanson, *Tchaikovsky: The Man behind the Music* (New York: Dodd, 1966), also proceeds along this basis. The authors provide an extensive bibliography, including all the Russian literature; they make reference to the original unexpurgated passages in the letters, which do not appear in the official Russian edition of the letters, pp. ix–x. Catherine Drinker Bowen's and Barbara von Meck's work, though conceived as a *biographie romancée,* is instructive in retelling, with the help of materials from the archives of the von Meck family, the story of Nadejda von Meck [*"Beloved Friend" The Story of Tchaikowsky and Nadejda von Meck* (New York: Random House, 1937)]. The most important subsequent event in Tchaikovsky research was the edition of the journals prepared by Tchaikovsky's brother Hippolyte. Hippolyte died in 1927; after the revolution of 1917 he had directed the Tchaikovsky Museum in Klin. The Russian edition of the journals edited by Grigory Bernand was followed in 1945 by an American edition: *The*

Diaries of Tchaikovsky, trans., with notes, by Vladimir Lakond (New York, 1945). This is a sober and frank edition, which in the notes especially treats the erotic aspects without any attempt at censure.

34 Newmarch, *Tchaikovsky,* p. 721.

35 *Diaries of Tchaikovsky,* pp. 41–4.

36 Bowen and von Meck, *"Beloved Friend,"* p. 39.

37 Ibid., pp. 68–9.

38 Klaus Mann, Thomas Mann's eldest son, committed suicide in Cannes in 1949. He too, proceeding from similar impulses to those evoked by him in the figures of Tchaikovsky and Ludwig, knew an intoxication for death and expanded it in a grand essay, "Europe's Search for a New Credo," to a vision of protest through organized mass suicide. See Chapter 15 of the present book.

14
Concerning the Typology of Homosexual Literature

1 Oscar Wilde, *The Picture of Dorian Gray,* with intro. and bibliography by Jerry Allen (New York: Harper & Row, 1965).

2 André Gide, *Les Faux-Monnayeurs,* in André Gide, *Romans, Récits et Soties, Oeuvres Lyriques* (Paris: Pléiade, 1959), p. 931ff.

3 After *The Counterfeiters* appeared in 1925, Gide published a year later (1926) the *Journal of the Counterfeiters* in which he endeavored to sketch out the process of development of his first and only novel. Thomas Mann self-admittedly followed this model about twenty years later with the *Journal of Doctor Faustus.*

4 Ibid., Gide, p. 1589.

5 André Gide, *Journal 1889–1939* (Paris: Bibliothèque de la Pléiade, 1948), p. 640.

6 Ibid., p. 651.

7 Ibid., p. 754.

8 Maurice Sachs, *Le Sabbat* (Paris: Gallimard, 1960), pp. 111, 139ff., 244ff. A more extensive account of these connections will be found below in Chapter 15.

9 The analysis is based on about ten such productions that for the most part appeared on the American market in 1973 and could be freely bought in any "adult bookstore."

10 See *Der "Reigen"-Prozess* (The *Reigen* Trial), a book which appeared in Berlin in 1922. In 1920 a production of Arthur Schnitzler's play *Reigen* had been banned on grounds of immorality. The producers were prosecuted and acquitted. The trial, which was highly publicized, defined the legal boundaries between art and pornography.

11 *Perspectives on Pornography,* ed. with intro. by Douglas A. Hughes (New York: St. Martin's Press, 1970).

12 Susan Sontag, "The Pornographic Imagination," in *Perspectives,* ed. Hughes, p. 131ff.

13 Ibid., p. 135.

14 Felix Pollak, "Pornography: Around the Halfworld," in *Perspectives,* ed. Hughes, p. 170ff.

15 Ibid., p. 193.

16 The following peculiarities and techniques have been culled from the pornographic productions mentioned in note 9. They are to be met with in almost tiresome regularity over all.

15
The Alternatives of Klaus Mann and Maurice Sachs

1 Maurice Sachs's writings are cited from the following editions: *Le Sabbat* (Paris: Gallimard, 1960); *La chasse à courre* (Gallimard, 1948), which includes the continuation of *Le Sabbat*; *Derrière cinq barreaux* (Gallimard, 1952).

2 Klaus Mann, *Die Heimsuchung des europäischen Geistes. Aufsätze* (Munich: Deutscher Taschenbuchverlag, 1973): a selection from the volumes of essays *Prüfungen* (1968) and *Heute und morgen* (1969), selected by Martin Gregor-Dellin, p. 14ff.

3 Joseph Gabel, "Bedeutung des McCarthismus," in *Formen der Entfremdung. Aufsätze zum falschen Bewusstsein* (Frankfurt, 1964), p. 88ff., German ed.; original in *La Revue Socialiste,* Paris, 1954.

4 Klaus Mann, "Europe's Search for a New Credo," *Tomorrow* 8 (no. 10, June 1949): 5–11.

5 Ibid., p. 11.

6 Klaus Mann, "Der Streit um André Gide," in *Die Heimsuchung des europäischen Geistes,* p. 47.

7 André Gide, *Les Nourritures Terrestres* (Paris: Bibliothèque de la Pléiade, 1958), p. 153.

8 Sachs, *Le Sabbat,* p. 277.

9 Ibid., p. 124.

10 Sachs, *Derrière cinq barreaux,* p. 219.

11 Friedrich Sieburg, "Der Freiheit überdrüssig," in *Die Zeit,* no. 25, 1952. Also in Friedrich Sieburg, *Nur für Leser. Jahre und Bücher* (Stuttgart: Deutscher Verlags-Anstalt, 1955), p. 211ff.

12 Louis-Ferdinand Céline, *D'un Chateau l'autre* (Paris: Gallimard, 1957) [*Castle to Castle,* trans. Ralph Manheim (New York: Delacorte Press, 1968)].

13 Sieburg, "Der Freiheit überdrüssig."

16
The Turning Point of Jean Genet

1 Sartre's book on Jean Genet was printed as volume 1 of Genet's collected works, whereby it must be emphasized that Genet recognized as authentic the biographical facts contained therein. Jean-Paul Sartre, *Saint Genet. Comédien et Martyr,* Oeuvres complètes de Jean Genet, vol. 1 (Paris: Gallimard, 1952) [*Saint Genet Actor and Martyr,* trans. Bernard Frechtman (New York: Braziller, 1963)].

2 Jean Genet, *Notre-Dame-des-Fleurs,* in *Oeuvres complètes,* vol. 2 (Paris: Gallimard, 1951), p. 7ff. [*Our Lady of the Flowers,* trans. Bernard Frechtman (New York: Grove Press, 1963)].

3 Jean Genet, *Miracle de la rose,* in Oeuvres complètes, vol. 2, p. 221ff. [*Miracle of the Rose,* trans. Bernard Frechtman (New York: Grove Press, 1966)].

4 Jean Genet, *Journal du voleur* (Paris: Gallimard, 1949) [*The Thief's Journal,* trans. Bernard Frechtman (New York: Grove Press, 1964)].

5 Walter Heist, *Genet und andere. Exkurse über eine faschistische Literatur von Rang* (Hamburg: Claassen, 1965).

6 Jean Genet, *Pompes funèbres,* in *Oeuvres complètes,* vol. 3 (Paris: Gallimard, 1953) p. 7ff. [*Funeral Rites,* trans. Bernard Frechtman (New York: Grove Press, 1970)].

7 Sartre, *Saint Genet,* p. 215.

8 Ibid., p. 212.

9 Ibid., p. 537.

10 Jean-Paul Sartre, *Réflexions sur la Question Juive* (Paris: chez Paul Morihien, 1946) [*Anti-Semite and Jew,* trans. George J. Becker (New York: Schocken Books, 1948)].

11 In Chapter 27 of her book *Hope against Hope,* which deals with Bukharin, Nadezhda Mandelshtam has provided both a psychogram and a political analysis of the situation. She writes: "He [Bukharin] clearly saw that the new world he was so actively helping to build was horrifyingly unlike the original concept. . . . When the high priests are bound together by such a bond, renegades can expect no mercy. Bukharin was not a renegade, but he already felt how inevitable it was that he would be cast into the pit because of his

doubts" Nadezhda Mandelshtam, *Hope against Hope: A Memoir,* trans. Max Hayward (New York: Atheneum, 1970), p. 114.

12 *Saint Genet,* p. 543–4.

13 Ibid., p. 545.

14 Maurice Merleau-Ponty, *Humanisme et terreur: Essai sur le probleme communiste* (Paris: Gallimard, 1947) [*Humanism and Terror: An Essay on the Communist Problem,* trans. and with notes by John O'Neil (Boston: Beacon Press, 1969)].

15 In his introduction to the German translation of *The Thief's Journal,* the philosopher Max Bense analyzes this constellation: "Genet . . . undertakes the attempt of determining his own self in the ethical undetermination of the subject by placing himself in the category of an aesthetically undetermined subject which can be determined only by an already determined subject, and which then in turn negates the ethical non-determination of the original subject. One sees that in the relation of the Ethical to the Aesthetic, if one thinks processually and existentially, a never-ending reflection is unavoidable that makes every decision impossible." Bense, in Jean Genet, *Tagebuch eines Diebes* (Munich: Deutscher Taschenbuch Verlag, 1971), p. 19–20.

Shylock

17

From Ahasuerus to Shylock

1 Siegfried Kracauer, "Ahasuerus, or the Riddle of Time," in *History: The Last Things before the Last* (New York: Oxford, 1969), chap. 6, p. 139ff., esp. p. 157.

2 *Encyclopaedia Britannica,* vol. 1, p. 437.

3 H. J. Schoeps, "Ahasver," in *Die Religion in Geschichte und Gegenwart: Handbuch für Theologie und Religionswissenschaft,* ed. K. Galling, vol. 1 (Tübingen: Mohr [Siebeck], 1957), p. 191.

18

The Jew of Malta and the Jew of Venice

1 *Doktor Faustus,* Tragedy by Christopher Marlowe, trans. Wilhelm Müller, with foreword by Ludwig Achim von Arnim, edited and intro. by B. Badt (Munich, 1911). See Arnim's foreword, esp. p. 25, 33–35.

2 *The Plays of Christopher Marlowe* (London: Oxford University Press, 1966).

3 Notice of Dr. Lopez's execution in Norman T. Carrington, *Notes on Shakespeare. The Merchant of Venice* (Bath, England: n.d.).

4 W. H. Auden, "Brothers and Others," in *The Dyer's Hand and Other Essays* (New York: Random House, 1962).

5 Leslie A. Fiedler, *The Stranger in Shakespeare* (New York: Stein and Day, 1972), p. 132.

19

The Wise Nathan and the Bandit Spiegelberg

1 Hans Joachim Schoeps, *Philosemitismus im Barock. Religions– und geistesgeschichtliche Untersuchungen* (Tübingen: Mohr, 1952), p. 2.

2 G. C. Lichtenberg, *Briefe aus England,* in Lichtenberg, *Schriften und Briefe,* ed. Wolfgang Promies, vol. 3 (Munich: Hanser, 1972), p. 366.

3 Gershom Scholem in *Deutsche und Juden* (Frankfurt: Suhrkamp, 1967), p. 24.

4 Ibid., p. 25.

5 J. M. Moscherosch, *Philanders Gesichte,* vol. 2 (Leipzig: Reclam, n.d.), p. 384.

6 Curt von Faber du Faur, "Johann Michael Moscherosch, Der Geängstigte," in *Euphorion* 51 (no. 3, 1957): 233ff., esp. p. 245.

7 Theodor Lessing, *Einmal und nie wieder. Lebenserinnerungen* (Gütersloh: Bertelsmann, 1969), p. 34.

8 Gotthold Ephraim Lessing, "Die Juden," in *Gesammelte Werke in zehn Bänden,* ed. Paul Rilla, vol. 1 (Berlin: Aufbau-Verlag, 1954–), p. 531ff.

9 Lessing, "Der Freigeist," ibid., p. 573. See Cesare Cases, "Über Lessings 'Freigeist'," in *Georg Lukács. Festschrift zum 80. Geburtstag,* ed. Frank Benseler (Neuwied/Berlin: Luchterhand, 1965), p. 374.

10 Kurt Wölfel in *Lessings Werke,* vol. 1 (Frankfurt: Insel-Verlag, 1967), p. 602.

11 Lessing, *Werke,* vol. 3 (1955), p. 652ff.

12 Jochanan Bloch, *Selbstbehauptung. Zionistische Aufsätze* (Hamburg: Reich, 1972), p. 15ff.

13 Lessing, *Werke,* vol. 2 (1954), p. 319ff.

14 Günther Rohrmoser, "Lessing und die religionsphilosophische Fragestellung der Aufklärung," in *Lessing und die Zeit der Aufklärung* (Göttingen: Vandenhoeck & Ruprecht, 1968), p. 128.

15 Günther Rohrmoser, "Nathan der Weise," in *Das deutsche Drama vom Barock bis zur Gegenwart. Interpretationen,* ed. Benno von Wiese, vol. 1 (Düsseldorf: A. Bagel, 1964).

16 Herbert Marcuse, "Repressive Tolerance," in *A Critique of Pure Tolerance* (Boston: Beacon Press, 1965), p. 84ff.

17 Friedrich Schiller, in *Sämtliche Werke,* ed. Gerhard Fricke, vol. 5 (Munich: C. Hanser, 1962), "Über naive und sentimentalische Dichtung," p. 725.

18 Ibid., vol. 1 (1962) p. 481ff. The quoted passages of the "suppressed quarto," ibid., p. 917ff.

19 Gerhard Storz, *Der Dichter Friedrich Schiller* (Stuttgart: E. Klett, 1963), p. 57.

20 Schiller, *Werke,* p. 917ff.

21 Ibid., p. 919.

22 Ibid., p. 918.

23 Philipp F. Veit, "The Strange Case of Moritz Spiegelberg," in *Germanic Review* (May 1969). Expanded German version in *Jahrbuch der Deutschen Schillergesellschaft* (Stuttgart, 1973), p. 273ff.

24 See Heinrich Graetz, *Frank und die Frankisten* (Breslau, 1868).

25 *Lessings Sämtliche Schriften,* ed. Lachmann und Muncker, vol. 19 (Leipzig, 1904), p. 320.

20
The Bourgeois Shylock

1 Saul Ascher, *Germanomanie* (Leipzig, 1815).

2 Ibid., p. 68.

3 S. Ascher, "Die Wartburgs-Feier. Mit Hinsicht auf Deutschlands religiöse und politische Stimmung" (Leipzig, 1818). The author is indebted to his colleague Wolfgang Promies for the loan of the above two very rare writings by Ascher.

4 Ascher, "Wartburgs-Feier," p. 27.

5 Ibid., p. 25–6.

6 That Massmann had been arrested and persecuted on account of his political beliefs was known to Heine yet never taken into account. Massmann, like Heine, was born in 1797; he died in 1874. One of his poems, "Ich hab mich ergeben," served for a century as a popular folk song, much like the "Lorelei," though its author had been forgotten.

7 This is developed more fully in Hans Mayer, "Heine und die Deutsche Ideologie," intro. to Heinrich Heine, *Beiträge zur deutschen Ideologie* (Frankfurt/Berlin/Vienna: Ullstein, 1972), p. xiiff.

8 Ludwig Börne, *Sämtliche Schriften,* ed. Inge and Peter Rippmann, vol. 1 (Düsseldorf: J. Metzler, 1964), p. 501.

9 Heinrich Heine, "Shakespeares Mädchen und Frauen: Porzia," in: *Sämtliche Schriften,* ed. Klaus Briegleb, vol. 4 (Munich: Carl Hanser Verlag, 1971), p. 264.

10 At the beginning of the fourth book of Heine's piece against Ludwig Börne, Heine too juxtaposes the pair of *Fests,* on the Wartburg and in Hambach, yet does not come to so much of a petit bourgeois/liberal conclusion as Börne, who was wont to call up Hambach as the high point of his political activity in Germany. *Sämtliche Schriften,* vol. 4, p. 88ff.

11 See Leo Kreutzer, *Heine und der Kommunismus* (Göttingen: Vandenhoeck & Ruprecht, 1970).

12 Egon Caesar conte Corti, *Aufstieg des Hauses Rothschild* (Leipzig: Insel-Verlag, 1927).

13 Egon Caesar conte Corti, *Das Haus Rothschild in der Zeit seiner Blüte, 1836–1871* (Leipzig: Insel-Verlag, 1928), p. 230ff.

14 Nonetheless Delacroix too was a guest of the banker baron. In a recent publication on the Rothschilds not only is the painting "On the way to Smala" by Horace Vernet reproduced, which portrays James Rothschild as a fleeing Jew, but a particularly cynical story is reported as well, apparently one passed down in the family tradition. James Rothschild, according to it, stood model to Delacroix as a hungry beggar, and a painting apprentice so pitied the supposedly hungry figure he cut that he gave him a franc. On the following day, so the story continues, a servant appeared in the Rothschild livery bearing the following letter: "Dear Sir, enclosed the capital that you presented to me at the door of M. Delacroix's studio, with interest and interest on the interest. In toto the sum of 10,000 francs. You may cash the cheque at any bank you choose. James de Rothschild." [Virginia Cowles, *The Rothschilds: A Family of Fortune* (New York: Knopf, 1973) pp. 97–8]. The relations between Rothschild and Heine are discussed here as well.

15 Heine, "Ludwig Börne," p. 29.

16 Heinrich Schnee, *Rothschild: Geschichte einer Finanzdynastie* (Göttingen: Musterschmidt, 1961), p. 26.

17 Ibid., p. 29.

18 Balzac, *La Comédie Humaine,* vol. 6 (Paris: Bibliothèque de la Pléiade, 1950), p. 804ff. and 822ff.

19 Ibid., p. 822. [English translation quoted from "Scenes of Parisian Life," in vol. 8 of *The Human Comedy,* trans. Jane Minot Sedgwick (Philadelphia: George Barrie & Son, 1896).]

20 Ibid., p. 852.

21 Sartre traces Flaubert's antibourgeois bourgeoisness back to his encounter as a child with the Duchess du Berry and to his disdain for all manifestation of the "citizen king," Louis-Philippe. Sartre, *L'idiot de la famille: Gustave Flaubert de 1821 à 1857,* vol. 2 (Paris: Gallimard, 1971), p. 1337ff.

22 The biographical facts and rhetorical quotes from Disraeli have been taken from Robert Blake's biography, *Disraeli* (New York: St. Martin's Press, 1967).

23 Ibid., p. 646.

24 Shlomo Na'aman, *Lasalle* (Hannover: Verlag für Literatur und Zeitgeschehen, 1970).

25 Hermann Oncken, *Lassalle: eine politische Biographie* (Stuttgart and Berlin: Deutsche Verlagsanstalt, 1920).

26 Na'aman, *Lassalle,* p. 872.

27 Ibid., p. 707.

28 Ibid., p. 76.

29 Ibid., p. 672.

30 Ibid., p. 642.

31 Ibid., p. 664.

32 Ibid., p. 664–5.

21
Jewish Figures in the Bourgeois Novel

1 George L. Mosse, "The Image of the Jew in German Popular Culture," in *Germans and Jews* (New York: H. Fertig, 1970), p. 61ff.

2 Strangely enough, Eleonore Sterling, in her analysis of "anti-liberal liberalism" and its position vis-à-vis Jews, exempts the literary aspects. In the section on the secularization of the traditional theological concepts of the Jew this aspect is also passed over. (Sterling, *Judenhass: Die Anfänge des politischen Antisemitismus in Deutschland (1815–1850)* (Frankfurt: Europäische Verlagsanstalt, 1969), pp. 48ff. and 77ff.

3 Mosse, *Germans and Jews*, p. 71.

4 Charles Dickens, *Our Mutual Friend*, vol. 2, chap. 15.

5 Ibid., vol. 3, chap. 1.

6 This is connected with the particular social way of seeing things in Dickens's novels. Theodor Adorno called it "pre-bourgeois," indeed speaks of a "scattered baroque in the 19th century" ["Rede über den 'Raritätenladen' von Charles Dickens," in Theodor W. Adorno, *Noten zur Literatur*, vol. 4 (Frankfurt: Suhrkamp, 1974), p. 34ff.] Yet the positions taken by Dickens are thoroughly bourgeois. They hold loyally fast to eighteenth-century bourgeois Enlightenment, apply it even to the world of the bourgeois-proletarian class conflict. Thus is to be explained the fairytale/utopian character of these narrative works: as the contrast between enlightenment and class situation, which from the bourgeois standpoint tends more and more toward the recantation of such an enlightenment grown lethal. This too is why Dickens sketches his Jewish figures in a thoroughly fairytale fashion: either witchlike and evil as Fagin or angelically mild as Riah. Rothschild appears in Balzac, not in Dickens.

7 Since the author Mary Ann (or Marian) Evans, who made use of the masculine pseudonym George Eliot, herself demonstrates in the course of her life the process of an unresolved outsiderdom, as has been discussed elsewhere (Chapter 4), only the novel *Daniel Deronda* will be referred to here. The text is quoted from the edition by William L. Allison Co., New York, n.d. [1895?].

8 Illustrations in Marghanita Laski, *George Eliot and Her World* (London: Thames & Hudson, 1973), pp. 60–1.

9 Ibid., p. 103.

10 Eliot, *Daniel Deronda*, chapter 2, p. 395.

11 Marcel Proust, *A la Recherche du Temps Perdu*, vol. 3 (Paris: Bibliothèque de la Pléiade, 1954), p. 966.

12 Ibid., vol. 1, p. 90.

13 Ibid., p. 93.

14 Ibid., vol. 2, p. 288.

15 Ibid., vol. 1, pp. 97, 146.

16 Ibid., vol. 3, pp. 952–3.

17 James Joyce's *Ulysses* is quoted from the authorized edition published by Random House (New York: Random House [Vintage Books], 1961).

18 Stuart Gilbert, *James Joyce's Ulysses: A Study* (New York: Random House [Vintage Books], 1955). In particular p. 78ff. discuss Bérard's thoughts on the Phoenician origins of the *Odyssey*.

19 Joyce, *Ulysses*, p. 430ff.

20 Ibid., p. 331.

21 Ibid., p. 619.

22 Ibid., p. 682.

23 An exact analysis of the Blooms and their Jewish as well as Irish structure is provided by Morton P. Levitt, "The Family of Bloom," in *New Light on Joyce from the Dublin Symposium,* Second International James Joyce Symposium, Dublin, 1969, ed. Fritz Senn (Bloomington: Indiana University Press, 1972) p. 141ff.

22
Jewish Self-Hate

1 Theodor Lessing, *Der jüdische Selbsthass* (Berlin: Zionistischer Bücher-Bund, 1930). The book has not been reissued.

2 Alfred Schuler, *Fragmente und Vorträge aus dem Nachlass,* intro. by Ludwig Klages (Leipzig: Verlag J. A. Barth, 1940). In Klages's 120-page introduction something like the following sets the tone: "Thanks to the achievements of a long row of investigators we need no Disraeli to ascertain that the manipulators of the world war and the financial supporters of the Russian revolution were Jews. What is really involved with "humanitarianism," "cosmopolitanism," "liberalism," "Americanism," "Marxism," "internationalism," "Communism," "Bolshevism," and so forth, is nowadays not seen only by *him who does not wish to see.*" (p. 46). This was written in 1940, when Auschwitz had already begun operation. One finds in this edition of Schuler (who had died in 1923), after a poem to the swastika, the following: "The marten Juda slunk up to the heart of life. For two thousand years he extirpates the hot, pounding, overflowing, dreaming mother heart." (p. 151).

3 An exact presentation of the case is provided by Hans Wysling in "'Ein Elender'—Zu einem Novellenplan Thomas Manns," in Paul Scherrer and Hans Wysling, *Quellenkritische Studien zum Werk Thomas Manns* (Bern/Munich: Francke, 1967), p. 106ff.

4 Lessing, *Der jüdische Selbsthass,* p. 249.

5 Ibid., p. 47.

6 Ibid., p. 50.

7 Ibid., p. 132ff.

8 Ibid., p. 140.

9 Karl Kraus, "Er is doch e Jud," in *Die Fackel,* October 1913. Now in Karl Kraus, *Untergang der Welt durch schwarze Magie,* ed. Heinrich Fischer (Munich: Kösel-Verlag, 1960), p. 331ff.

10 Ibid., p. 335.

23
Comrade Shylock

1 Leo Trotzki, *Mein Leben. Versuch einer Autobiographie* (Berlin: S. Fischer, 1930). The American edition, Leon Trotsky, *My Life* (Gloucester, Mass.: Peter Smith, 1970), contains substantial material compiled in 1960 by Trotsky's widow, Natalia Sedova Trotsky, and completed for the 1970 edition by Trotsky's grandson Esteban Volkov. For this reason, particularly for the account of events in Trotsky's life after the completion of *Mein Leben,* it is the American edition that has been made use of.

2 Henri de Man, *Gegen den Strom. Memoiren eines europäischen Sozialisten* (Stuttgart: Deutsche Verlags-Anstalt, 1953), p. 130.

3 Helmut Kreuzer, *Die Boheme. Beiträge zu ihrer Beschreibung* (Stuttgart: Metzler, 1968); on p. 292 see notice of Trotsky's article, as quoted from Oskar Anweiler, *Die Rätebewegung*

in Russland 1905–1921 (Leiden, 1948), p. 33. Trotsky's article is in *Neue Zeit,* 28 (no. 2): 860.

4 Leon Trotsky, *Literature and Revolution* (New York: Russell and Russell, 1957). This edition contains the complete text of Trotsky's book only as of 1924. The German edition as well is so limited. The French edition, on the other hand, contains Trotsky's collected writings on literature and art including the last works which originated in Coyoacan. Léon Trotsky, *Littérature et révolution,* preface by Maurice Nadeau (Paris: Union Générale d'éditions, 1971). The present analysis relies above all on this edition.

5 Nadezhda Mandelshtam, *Hope against Hope: A Memoir,* trans. Max Hayward (New York: Atheneum, 1970).

6 Trotsky, "Céline et Poincaré," in *Littérature et révolution,* p. 425ff.

7 Ibid., p. 440.

8 Trotsky, "De la Révolution étranglée et des ses étrangleurs. Reponse à M. André Malraux," ibid., p. 401ff.

9 Trotsky, "L'Art et la révolution" (letter to *Partisan Review*), ibid., p. 457ff.

10 Ibid., p. 464.

11 "Pour un art révolutionnaire indépendant," ibid., p. 501ff.

12 Ibid., p. 506.

13 Joseph Roth, *Der stumme Prophet.* (Cologne/Berlin: Kiepenheuer & Witsch, 1965).

24
Hatred of Jews after Auschwitz

1 *Réflexions sur la Question Juive* first appeared in Paris in 1946 in a newly founded publishing house that later disappeared. Citations here are according to this first edition. In 1959 Gallimard republished the book in its "Collection Idées" series.

2 Ibid., p. 91.

3 Ibid., p. 198.

4 Jean-Paul Sartre, *Saint Genet. Comédien et Martyr* (Paris: Gallimard, 1952), p. 549 [*Saint Genet Actor and Martyr* (New York: Braziller, 1963), p. 599.]

5 Sartre, *Sur la Question Juive,* p. 185ff.

6 Ibid., p. 62. "Déstructeur par fonction, sadique au coeur pur, l'antisémite est, au plus profond de son coeur, un criminel. Ce qu'il souhaite, ce qu'il prépare, c'est la *mort* du Juif."

7 In his early story "L'enfance d'un chef," Sartre, using the example of a son of the haute bourgeoisie, Lucien Létillois, had treated of an "unauthentic" anti-Semite," one who had simply fallen into the role of a Jew-hater because he was able, in so doing, to acquire the semblance of individuality and specialness without any cost to himself.

8 *Dialektik der Aufklärung. Philosophische Fragmente* by Max Horkheimer and Theodor W. Adorno is cited according to the new edition (Frankfurt: Suhrkamp, 1969). [An English translation has appeared as *Dialectic of Enlightenment* (New York: Herder and Herder, 1972), yet since this translation leaves a good deal to be desired, the quotations in the text have not been taken from it. References to it are simply meant as an aid to the English-speaking reader.].

9 Horkheimer and Adorno, ibid., p. 212 [English trans., p. 202].

10 Ibid., p. 181 [p. 172].

11 Ibid., p. 180 [p. 171].

12 Max Horkheimer, "Die Juden und Europa," in *Studies in Philosophy and Social Science,* vol. 8 (New York City, 1939), p. 115ff.

13 Ibid., pp. 132–3.

14 Horkheimer and Adorno, *Dialektik der Aufklärung*, p. 182ff.

15 Ibid., p. 183.

16 Ibid., p. 177.

17 Ludwig Klages, introduction to Alfred Schuler, *Fragmente und Vorträge aus dem Nachlass* (Leipzig: Verlag J. A. Barth, 1940), p. 82.

18 Horkheimer and Adorno, *Dialektik der Aufklärung*, p. 209.

19 Ibid., p. 7.

20 Ibid., pp. 210–11.

21 Ibid., p. 217.

22 Ibid., p. 217.

25
Open Ending

1 Heinrich Mann, *Ein Zeitalter wird besichtigt* (Düsseldorf: Claassen, 1974), p. 37.

2 Ibid., p. 39.

3 Theodor W. Adorno, *Negative Dialektik*, in *Gesammelte Schriften*, vol. 6 (Frankfurt: Suhrkamp, 1973), p. 191.

4 *Goethes Werke*, Hamburger Ausgabe, ed. Erich Trunz, vol. 8 (Hamburg: Wegner, 1948–1964), p. 477.

Index

Index

Index

About the Author

Hans Mayer, one of the most eminent and prolific European literary critics of our time, was born in Cologne in 1907. In Switzerland, where he emigrated in 1933 to avoid arrest for political activities, he began his literary studies and was coeditor of the journal *Über die Grenzen*, which published such German writers in exile as Brecht, Lasker-Schüler, and Kaiser. In 1948 he settled in East Germany where, as professor at the University of Leipzig, he worked to give a new historical focus to modern German literature. By 1963 Mayer had become dissatisfied with restrictions placed on him as critic and educator and resettled in West Germany, where he taught first at Hannover and then at Tübingen. Among his books are a pioneering study of Georg Büchner and works on Thomas Mann, Schiller, Brecht, and Kleist. In addition to *Outsiders*, three of his books have been translated into English: *Steppenwolf and Everyman, Portrait of Wagner,* and *Richard Wagner in Bayreuth.*